The Judicial System in
Southern Nigeria 1854-1954

Ibadan History Series

Christian Missions in Nigeria 1841–1891
by J. F. A. Ajayi

The Zulu Aftermath
by J. D. Omer-Cooper

The Missionary Impact on Modern Nigeria 1842–1914
by E. A. Ayandele

The Sokoto Caliphate
by Murray Last

Benin and the Europeans 1485–1897
by A. F. C. Ryder

Niger Delta Rivalry
by Obaro Ikimẹ

The International Boundaries of Nigeria
by J. C. Anene

Revolution and Power Politics in Yorubaland 1840–1883
by S. A. Akintoye

Power and Diplomacy in Northern Nigeria 1804–1906
by R. A. Adelẹyẹ

The Segu Tukulor Empire
by B. O. Ọlọruntimẹhin

The Warrant Chiefs
by A. E. Afigbo

The New Ọyọ Empire
by J. A. Atanda

The Evolution of the Nigerian States
by T. N. Tamuno

The Malagasy and the Europeans
by P. M. Mutibwa

Western Yorubaland under European Rule 1889–1945
by A. I. Asiwaju

In preparation

Press and Politics in Nigeria 1880–1937
by F. I. A. Omu

For further details of the books in this series
please consult the publisher.

Ibadan History Series

General Editor J. F. A. Ajayi, PhD

The Judicial System in Southern Nigeria, 1854-1954

Law and Justice in a Dependency

Omoniyi Adewoye, PhD
Department of History, University of Ibadan

Humanities Press
Atlantic Highlands, New Jersey

First published in the United States in 1977
by Humanities Press, Inc.,
Atlantic Highlands, New Jersey 07716

© O. Adewoye 1977

Library of Congress Cataloging in Publication Data

Adewoye, O.

   The judicial system in Southern Nigeria, 1854–1954
   (Ibadan history series)
   Bibliography: p.
   Includes index.
   1. Courts – Nigeria, Southern – History. Nigeria, Southern.
      I. Title.   II. Series.
   Law   347′ . 669 ′01   77–6776

   ISBN 0–391–00735–1

Printed in Great Britain

To My Mother,
Madam Victoria Fadunkẹ,
In Memoriam

Contents

Illustrations

Abbreviations

AC	Appeal Cases, English
CO	Colonial Office, London
CSO	Chief Secretary's Office, Lagos
FO	Foreign Office, London
HCA	High Court Archives, Lagos
NAE	National Archives, Enugu
NAI	National Archives, Ibadan
NLR	Nigeria Law Report
SCA	Supreme Court Archives, Lagos
WACA	West African Court of Appeal

Acknowledgements

The publishers are grateful to the following for permission to reproduce the photographs:

West Africa (for Sir John Glover and his Hausas); Nigerian National Archives, Enugu (for Summons used at the Old Calabar Consular Court); Nigerian National Archives, Ibadan, for all the other photographs.

Preface

'The "documentation" of the law', says C. K. Allen in his classic,
Law in the Making, 'is a study for the legal historian.' This book
has been written in the firm conviction that the legal historian
should be concerned with much more than merely 'documenting'
the law or the establishment of legal institutions. That approach,
incidentally, has, so far, characterised the extant writings on the
contemporary African legal and judicial institutions. The 'recep-
tion' of European law in African countries is taken for granted; the
processes of establishing judicial tribunals are often discussed, as
it were, *in vacuo*, without any reference to the circumstances of
their establishment or the purposes which they were intended to
serve. Law is vaguely recognised in some of these writings as an
instrument of social change, but the writers stop short of proving
their contention by actual inquiries into the practical operation of
the law or of the courts of law. The province of law, like history,
covers almost the whole range of human existence. A true historical
account of the role of the law and the courts in any community
should, therefore, take cognisance of the milieu in which they were
operating.

This book, then, sets out on a new path in African legal history.
It is an attempt to examine the British-imposed judicial system in
Southern Nigeria as it operated. Particular attention is paid to the
introduction of the English legal system into the territory as an
agency of colonial control. An attempt is also made to inquire into
the motives behind the changes in the territory's judicial system,
to discuss the role of the courts in judicial administration, and to
evaluate the impact of the judicial system on the territory's social,
economic and political development. The book is not strictly a law
book, although I believe it will interest lawyers and students of law.
It will also appeal to the general reader. For from these pages the
true genesis of present-day Nigerian judicial institutions can be

learnt. Here and there aspects of substantive law are discussed, but the main concern of the book is the operation of the courts of law in Southern Nigeria.

The choice of dates for the study has not been fortuitous. In 1854 the first 'court of equity' was established at Bonny. The year 1954 marked the end of a unified judicial system in Nigeria, and the beginning of the 'regionalisation' of the judiciary.

A word about terminology. The term 'protectorate' as used in this work refers to the area of Nigeria outside the Lagos Colony. A protectorate was, in theory, supposed to be merely under the 'protection' of the British Crown without detriment to its sovereignty. It was thus legally distinguishable from a colony which was supposed to be ruled directly by the Crown. The distinction between a colony and a protectorate was, however, largely theoretical. A protectorate was as much a British possession as a colony.

The inspiration for this work derived from the PhD thesis I submitted to Columbia University, New York, in 1968 on the Legal Profession in Southern Nigeria, 1861–1943. I would like to express here my gratitude to Professor Graham W. Irwin under whom I did postgraduate studies. His liberal attitude to the study of history was, no doubt, a major factor encouraging me to embark upon what was a relatively unorthodox piece of research. I am also grateful to Professors L. G. Cowan, Alan F. Westin and Marcia Wright, all of Columbia University, who were in one way or another closely connected with my postgraduate training at the University.

Some members of the teaching and administrative staff, University of Ibadan, have been helpful with comments and criticisms. I am grateful to Professor J. F. A. Ajayi, now Vice-Chancellor of the University of Lagos, who read the thesis and suggested what possibilities it contained. I must also thank Professor Tekena N. Tamuno (now Vice-Chancellor, University of Ibadan), Professor R. J. Gavin (now of Ahmadu Bello University), Dr R. A. Adeleye, Dr J. A. Atanda and Dr J. D. Ojo, who have all made useful comments and helpful criticisms on various aspects of the work. Sometimes without their knowing it, I was testing with them some of the ideas and interpretations expressed in the book. They are, of course, in no way responsible for any errors which it may contain.

In my field-work in Nigeria and in England a number of people gave me valuable assistance. I deeply appreciate the generosity with which all those I interviewed gave me their time, some of them on a number of occasions. I had rewarding discussions with the then Attorney-General of Nigeria, later Chief Justice of the Federation (1972–5), Professor T. O. Elias, and with Professor A. N. Allott of the School of Oriental and African Studies, University of London. I must record here my appreciation for the cooperation which I enjoyed from the staff of the following institutions: University of Ibadan Library, Ibadan and Enugu branches of the Nigerian National Archives, The Institute of Commonwealth Studies, the four Inns of Court, The Public Record Office, The Institute of Historical Research, all of them in London, and Rhodes House, Oxford.

For the financial support which I enjoyed, I must thank the African-American Institute in New York who sponsored my postgraduate training in the United States. I also thank the Federal Government of Nigeria for the financial assistance which made my field-work possible, and the University of Ibadan for a research grant without which this work would have been further delayed.

I would like to thank Mr Chimezie Omerua, Departmental Secretary in the History Department, who has taken immense pains in typing the final draft of this book.

Finally, I am most grateful to my wife, Titilayọ, for her forbearance and for her encouragement.

O. Adewọye

Department of History
University of Ibadan
Ibadan
August 1976

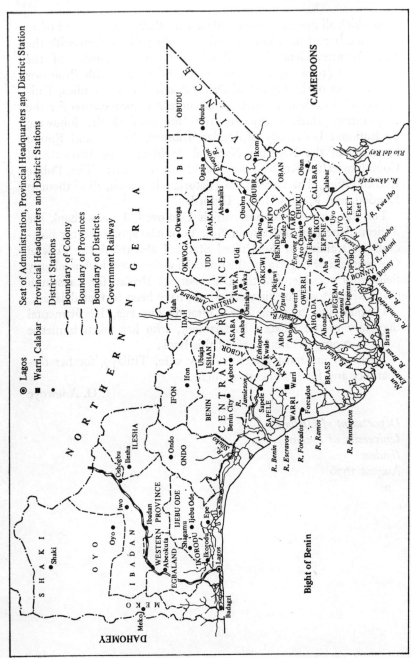

The Colony of Southern Nigeria, 1909

1 Law as an agency

> In the modern world, law has become the paramount
> agency of social control.
>
> Roscoe Pound, *Social Control Through Law*,
> New Haven, 1942, p. 20

I

In the controversy among jurists as to the end of law, there seems
to be a common ground of agreement; namely, that it is a functional element in any society.[1] The application of law may have
varied ends: the mere keeping of peace and order, the maintenance
of the social *status quo*, the furtherance of the economic interests of
the dominant class or, as this book would attempt to show, the
stabilisation of a colonial regime by one people over another. But
whatever goal is set for it by its manipulators, law is basically a
device, a technique of social ordering, 'a means of practical
action'.[2]

The primary objective of the law and its administration in the
various communities of Southern Nigeria before the advent of the
British was peace-keeping and the maintenance of the social
equilibrium.[3] A community in traditional Southern Nigeria, as in
most other pre-industrial societies, was a corporate entity, a network of kinship patterns, sometimes inter-related. The ruler and
his council of advisers took a holistic view of their society, and
often conceived of their role in terms of its welfare. In administering the law, their primary aim, in general, was to promote the
welfare of the community. They saw themselves essentially as
peace-makers, called upon to reconcile divergent interests in civil
disputes, and as preservers of the physical existence or spiritual
well-being of the whole society when this was threatened.

Was it law, in fact, that the indigenous communities administered, or customs, 'merely rules set by opinions of the governed
and sanctioned or enforced morally'? To John Austin and the later
legal positivists,[4] what is often referred to as customary law, as
it existed in Southern Nigeria, amounted to little more than

'positive morality'. Law, properly so called, in Austin's view, is a command issuing from a sovereign, and until a custom is pronounced as law by a sovereign or becomes a ground for judicial decision, it lacks the binding character of the law.[5]

Attempts have been made by writers on African law, notably by T. O. Elias, to refute the Austinian stand on customary law.[6] Generally the approach is to show the inadequacy of Austin's definition of law and emphasise the functional role of law as a body of rules governing human conduct and recognised as obligatory by members of a society.[7] But even on Austin's own ground, much of the customary law in traditional Southern Nigerian communities was law. The human sovereign was not lacking – usually in the form of chiefly authorities, as in the Yoruba and Edo kingdoms. Even in the non-chiefly Igbo societies east of the Niger, there were recognised authorities who could pronounce what was the law in given situations. The ruling authorities sometimes legislated for their subjects,[8] and were, to this extent, 'issuing command'.

Judicial decisions are of crucial importance in Austin's concept of a legal system. In traditional Southern Nigeria there were courts at varying levels pronouncing on specific cases, and thereby making the law. The proceedings in many of them might not be as formal as in European courts of law which Austin probably had in mind, although there were communities where court proceedings in the adjudication of disputes were no less ceremonious and formal.[9]

In traditional Southern Nigeria a distinction was in fact drawn between law and customs. Social pressure might make the latter more or less obligatory, but they could not be a matter for judicial hearing. Rules of law, on the other hand, were obligatory, and were divisible into what might broadly be categorises as private law and public law. Private law dealt with disputes among the members of a community, disputes which, in modern parlance, might cause a breach of the peace. Public law was concerned with various forms of anti-social behaviour, that is, offences like treason, witchcraft and religious offences in general, that were held to be 'subversive of the whole fabric of society'. It is worthy of note that attempts have been made in this century by educated Africans and by British colonial administrators to collate or restate the essence of the laws of particular communities in Southern Nigeria.[10] Law in traditional Southern Nigeria was unwritten; its principles were sometimes expressed in proverbs;[11] it might even be said to be latent in the breasts of the community's ruling elite or of the court remembrancers, and given expression only when expression was called for; but it was no less real than the written codes of continental Europe as a vital instrument for regulating the society.

II

The corporate view of the society taken by the rulers of traditional Southern Nigerian communities would explain certain features of the application of the law. Since the concern of the rulers was the welfare of the community as a whole, it seemed natural that they should draw no hard distinctions between their executive and judicial functions. In most cases, but for slight variations, the town or the village council 'was the same for both judicial and administrative purposes'.[12] Administration of justice was conterminous with peace keeping, and it was only one aspect – albeit an important aspect – of the exercise of political power.[13] This is why, in most communities, no one was made a chief at any level unless he was considered of a sound mind and knowledgeable in the laws and customs of his people.[14] Emphasis was duly placed on these mental qualities because once on the chieftaincy stool, a considerable proportion of a chief's time would be taken up in settling disputes and dealing with offenders against the public law in consultation with his council of advisers. Law and its administration were thus a vital lynchpin of the traditional society, central to the exercise of political authority.

The concern for the welfare of the community in traditional Southern Nigeria also influenced the objective of the law. A dispute between two or more individuals was, in traditional eyes, if one may employ the translated phrases of an Egba court remembrancer, 'the disjoining of the link that connects relations', the severing of 'the cord that binds humanity'.[15] The aim of the law, then, on the civil side, as it was indicated earlier, was interpersonal reconciliation. This was perhaps the most attractive and distinguishing feature of Nigerian (and African) traditional jurisprudence. In contrast to what operated in the English-style courts introduced into Southern Nigeria with the advent of the British,

3

what was sought in a dispute was not the strict legal rights of one party or the other. Parties to a suit often left the court,

> Nor puffed up nor cast down – for each a crumb
> Of right, for neither of them the whole loaf.[16]

The duty of those who administered the law in settling disputes was 'to assuage injured feelings, to restore peace, to reach a compromise acceptable to both disputants.'[17]

The peace-keeping element in the traditional approach to law and justice was much in evidence at the end of the hearing of a civil suit. It was not uncommon for the chief and his supporters to deliver end-of-trial homilies to the parties – homilies that were 'invariably as instructive as they [were] edifying'.[18] Again, the guilty party was usually expected to tender an unreserved apology to the other party in the presence of the whole court. The acceptance of the apology often 'meant forgiveness and forgetting'.[19] Since in normal circumstances it is rare in a civil dispute for a party to be wholly right or wholly wrong, members of the court would not be slow to point out the errors of commission or omission even of the party judged to be right.

The ceremonies which often closed any serious dispute further illustrate the spirit of reconciliation that underlay the traditional approach to law and justice. They were intended symbolically to bury the dispute. The disputants might be asked to share a piece of kola nut. Those present at the court vicariously took part in the reconciliation by partaking of the kola nut too. The successful party, if he was well-to-do and if the seriousness of the dispute warranted his doing so, might furnish food and drink for the whole court as a token of his appreciation for their patience and wisdom. M. M. Green in her *Igbo Village Affairs* notes how on one occasion the guilty one of two women litigants was asked to take palm wine and oil beans to the other woman 'so that they might eat together and thus make peace'.[20]

Criminal offences were often tried in most traditional communities of Southern Nigeria in a manner slightly different from that in which private disputes were resolved. Some public offences were tried in open court as ordinary civil disputes. The accused person was arraigned before the ruling authorities and given every opportunity to defend himself. If he was found guilty he could be publicly hanged. Some other public offences, usually of a religious or political nature, were tried by the secret societies, generally held

4

in great awe as the 'conservators of the public weal'.[21] The *Ogboni* society in most Yoruba communities,[22] the *Ekpo* (Leopard) and *Ekpe* (Spirit) societies in south-eastern Nigeria,[23] and the *Ndi dibia*, a professional organisation of certain spiritual leaders among the Igbo,[24] are a few of the better known secret societies in Southern Nigeria. They handled the most serious criminal offences and were usually responsible for the execution of their own judgments.[25]

It must be emphasised that even the trial of criminal offences was not altogether devoid of consideration of peace-keeping and harmonious inter-personal relations. Theft was often considered a very serious offence, but the thief was punished not so much for his theft as for the element of mistrust which he was believed to have introduced into the community by his act, making inter-personal relations rather precarious. Again, it has been said, with considerable justification, that the penalties of African law were directed 'not against specific infractions' of the law, but towards the restoration of the social equilibrium.[26] A crime was viewed as a 'disturbance of individual or communal equilibrium', and the objective of the law in imposing sanctions was 'to restore the pre-existing balance'. In most communities in Southern Nigeria, except for intentional murder and witchcraft, the penalty for each of which was death, virtually all other offences that would rank as crimes in the English-style courts could be neutralised by payment of adequate compensation to the injured party. Thus it was said of a number of villages in Onitsha Division that manslaughter and accidental death could be compensated for by the present of a woman or a cow and a piece of cloth to the family of the deceased.[27] Similarly, justifiable and accidental homicide were settled in the area of Ogwashi-Uku in present-day Bendel State, by the payment of compensation to the male next of kin of the deceased, sometimes in the form of a marriageable maiden.[28] Such was also the practice among the western Ijo in the Niger Delta area.[29] Among the Igbo clans of the Kwale division in Warri Province, as in many communities in the Owerri Province, a man who killed a slave had to replace him with one of equal value.[30] In certain areas even intentional murder could be settled by heavy compensation and the making of necessary sacrifices. Among some communities in Calabar Province, it was reported that a man convicted of a crime punishable by death 'could avoid capital punishment by paying a very large indemnity, in addition to compensation, to the injured party'.[31] A similar observation was made in respect of certain other communities in Ogoja Province.[32] At Abboh, a murderer was made to leave the town for seven years after which period he could return provided the necessary sacrifices were made.[33]

It is clear that there were deeper considerations behind the application of criminal law in traditional Southern Nigerian society than mere exaction of penalties. The welfare of the community seemed to be the primary concern of criminal sanctions. It was precisely because this was the major concern of the law that a criminal offender or a deviant – to use the more appropriate, sociological term – was easily rehabilitated into the society once the necessary compensations or ritual sacrifices were made, indicating that he had purged himself of his anti-social pattern of behaviour. Thus it is true, to a large extent, that the application of the criminal law in the traditional society often 'provided for clear-cut passage back into legitimate society with little or no stigma attached to the person who had deviated'.[34]

Yet another feature of the application of the law in Southern Nigeria before the advent of the British was its collectivist basis. A family unit took collective responsibility for the conduct of its members and this fact was evident both in civil and criminal cases. In cases of murder the murderer was usually expected by his own family to commit suicide to save the whole family from attack.[35] If the murderer failed to do this all his relatives had to flee and could only return to town if the murderer or any other member of his family paid adequate compensations or made the necessary sacrifices. A British administrative officer wrote of Ikere District in Ekiti, Ondo State: 'most violations of peace and order were not punished on the individual so much as on his family'.[36]

In civil disputes members of a family had to ensure the attendance of one of their number who had a case to answer at the village court. If he absconded from the community, members of the family, including the extended family, could be called upon to pay any fines or damages that might be incurred. Among the Igbo and some other ethnic groups, a creditor who failed to recover his money from a debtor could go to the compound of any of the debtor's relatives and capture goats or any other valuable property equivalent to or exceeding the value of the debt.[37] It is still a cardinal principle of Yoruba customary law that a debt never dies. When the debtor dies his family 'feel themselves under obligation

... to satisfy the debt'.[38] Clearly, the principle of collective responsibility not only tended to strengthen kinship solidarity, but also to prevent crimes. 'This idea of the whole family suffering for the crime of one of its members', noted a British colonial officer, 'was probably the strongest deterrent' against crimes.[39]

III

As an agency of social control and peace-keeping, law never stood alone in the traditional society of Southern Nigeria. Perhaps its major prop was religion, which seemed to pervade every aspect of traditional life. Administration of justice 'was inextricably intermingled' with religion which has been appropriately described as 'the engine of the law'.[40]

At the heart of traditional religion was a strong belief in a number of deities, including the spirits of departed ancestors. There was also the belief that the community was a continuous entity, made up of the dead, the living, and generations yet unborn. The ancestors were believed to be particularly interested in the solidarity of the community, and therefore in the whole procedure of keeping the peace and of administering justice. The law itself was believed to have the moral support of the ancestors – a potent factor 'in securing due regard for the law'. The chiefs and elders in the community who administered the law were in popular estimation the representatives of the ancestors. Until about the beginning of this century, when corruption was creeping into the traditional system of administering justice, they were likely to be impartial in their duty as peace-makers. They, like the rest of the community, believed they were under the constant watch of the ancestors.

When a dispute occurred or an offence was committed, it served no useful purpose for the parties or the accused persons to fabricate lies at the chief's court or before the elders of the community. There were the ancestors believed to be watching individual consciences. Besides there were believed to be other unseen supernatural forces capable of exacting retributive justice. The belief in the supernatural was a strong regulator of behaviour and it had its place in the administration of justice in the traditional society.

Whenever there were doubts, ordeals were used. The use of ordeals, again, stemmed from the belief in the supernatural: if

human attempts at getting at the truth failed, at least the unseen
forces would not err. The accuser, the accused or the suspect was
subjected to an ordeal, and was believed to be innocent if he
survived it.

Ordeals were of many kinds varying from one community to
another.[41] There was, for instance, the *Oyin Lele Egbele* ordeal
among the Urhobos and the Itsekiris on the Niger Delta. A fowl's
feather was besmeared with some *juju*. If the feather's quill easily
passed through the tongue of a defendant or an accused person,
that was believed to be an indication that a false charge had been
laid against the person.[42] In criminal cases among the Kalabari, as
among the Urhobos in the determination of cases of witchcraft, an
accused person could be asked to swim across a creek full of
crocodiles.[43] He was judged innocent if he came out alive. A common ordeal in a group of Igbo villages in Ogoja Province was the
use of boiling palm oil, usually in criminal offences involving
allegation of witchcraft. One hand of the accused or the suspect
was rubbed with juju and boiling palm oil was poured on it. He
was judged innocent if his hand was unscathed.[44] A usual form of
ordeal throughout Southern Nigeria was poisoning. Sasswood and
esere beans were poisonous plants in common use.

A variant of the ordeal was juju-swearing. In a serious dispute
an appeal could be made to a god or juju to rain down misfortune
on the guilty party. The Ibibio and the Efik in south-eastern
Nigeria had an *Mbiam* oath believed capable of destroying those
who swore falsely. The Long Juju (*Chuku Ibinokpabi*) in Igbo
country was the resort of many Igbo and non-Igbo litigants east of
the Niger.[45]

The use of ordeals over a long period could not fail to have some
effect on the morals of the population. Altogether it tended to
inculcate conformity with the law. Anyone who witnessed the
obvious and dramatic effects of an ordeal would be less prone to
tell lies. As Talbot pointed out, consciousness among the people
of the possibility of a dispute being resolved by an ordeal 'was
assuredly one of the greatest safeguards of justice'.[46] The possibility of trial by ordeal made perjury a rare phenomenon.[47]

There were human props of the law besides the religious and
the metaphysical. These human props in the form of certain age-
grades and secret societies facilitated the administration of the
law in two ways. They strengthened the aura of sanctity that
surrounded the community's laws and customs. Again, they were

often involved in the direct enforcement of the law. In Akure area in Ondo State, as in many other Yoruba communities, the *elegbe* were 'the soldiers and police club' of the community, keeping law and order.[48] In many Yoruba towns palace officials – the *Ilari* in Oyo, the *Odi* in Ijebu, and the *Emese* (Ife, Ijeshaland and Ekiti) – were, besides serving as other functionaries, officers of the law. They investigated criminal cases, arrested offenders and ensured their attendance at the chief's court. In Oyo and its environs it was as if the mystical awe in which the *Alaafin* (paramount ruler) was held by his subjects was also communicated to his messengers, the Ilari. For they wielded a power in the administrative and judicial system of old Oyo considerably out of proportion to their status in the ruling hierarchy. In Bonny district the head priest of the *Ikuba juju* (the 'national' cult) was said to have exerted a substantial amount of influence not only on the social life of the people but also on their system of government, including the administration of justice.[49]

In many parts of Southern Nigeria, masked dancers, purporting to represent diverse spirit cults, dealt with criminal offenders, ensured obedience to the community's laws and customs and, in some areas, even engaged in such mundane activity as recovery of debts. In relation to law and administration of justice, such, in general, were the functions and role of the *Omebe* in the Nsukka Division of Igboland, the *Nyamagbe* society in the Nnam area of Ogoja Province, the *Sekeni* society among Okrika, Kalabari, Nembe and Akassa Ijos, the *Ekpo* (Leopard) society of the Efik, the *Oro*, *Agemo*, the *Adamu-orisa* and *Gelede* cults in many parts of Yorubaland.

IV

That there was a seamy side to the application of the law in the traditional societies of Southern Nigeria, there can be no doubt. Admittedly, the legal system, heavily reinforced as it was by the force of religion, effectively 'met the needs of the time' in sustaining the societies. Again, it had the twin virtues of simplicity and cheapness. The hope of genuine reconciliation between disputants which it sought to offer has been commented on by some Western jurists.[50] But these attractive features of the law and its administration should not blind one to its defects, especially when looked at from a modern viewpoint.

It is difficult to escape the conclusion that the judicial system in traditional Southern Nigeria was rooted in fear: fear of the supernatural, fear of ordeals, fear of the ancestors and even fear of the elders, especially in the chiefly communities. Similarly, many of the religious props of the law throve on fear and ignorance on the part of the masses. It is hardly surprising that with the advent in Southern Nigeria by the beginning of this century of Christianity, Western education, the Western economic system and contact with the outside world, which all tended to emancipate the individual from such fears, the traditional machinery of justice began to lose much of its strength.[51] We must hasten to add, however, that even today, the traditional judicial system has not completely broken down. The so-called 'native' courts erected by the British administration in Southern Nigeria, and their later successors, the customary courts in independent Nigeria, have all been built around whatever remained of the indigenous approach to law and justice. Today in the towns, and even more so in the rural areas, elders and chiefs are settling private disputes in the traditional way.

It was also a major weakness of the traditional judicial system that ordeals had to be used in what were often regarded as doubtful cases. Clearly, ordeals are simply substitutes for thorough investigation. But as a means of arriving at the truth in judicial hearings, they sometimes took a heavy toll. The administration of sasswood poison ordeal in cases of alleged witchcraft could involve wholesale destruction of the compound of the alleged witch.[52] In 1905 it was reported that in the north-eastern district of Ijeshaland, in present-day Oyo State, twelve people succumbed to the *obo* poison ordeal.[53] Whatever might have been believed to the contrary, the outcome of an ordeal was no conclusive proof of guilt or innocence.

The occasional interference of status in the administration of the law under the traditional system would not meet modern egalitarian standards. Next to the pervading influence of religion, status was all-important in regulating the conduct of men and women throughout life. Each must act appropriately to his or her status. There are indications that this notion of status was carried into the realm of law and justice. Thus, for instance, in a dispute between a head of a family and a minor not belonging to that family, the latter had to be represented by someone who was of the same status as the former. A poor member of the society aggrieved by injustice suffered at the hand of a powerful chief, would best be represented by another chief who was as powerful in order to have any chance of obtaining substantial justice. It is for this reason that among the Yoruba freemen and domestic slaves often had patrons (*babaogun*: literally, father-in-battle) who represented them, informally and usually behind the scenes, in very grave matters that came before the authorities.[54]

In the chiefly communities, the concept of status interfered in an even more serious fashion. In spite of the predominance of religious influence in the administration of justice, the powerful, the wealthy and their relations were sometimes above the law. They and their relatives rarely suffered the full penalty of the law.[55] What a British administrative officer found in Calabar was true of many other communities: 'Much depended on the status, chiefly financial, of an accused and his family in judicial matters, and the power of wealth almost rendered a man immune from justice.'[56] In criminal cases, while the giving of gifts to the important section of a tribunal might not alter the judgment, it might have 'a considerable effect on the severity of the sentence'.[57] In Oyo kingdom at about the beginning of this century, the masses were considered mere objects of exploitation and the administration of justice fell short of the ideal of social harmony and reconciliation of disputants. The nefarious practice of bribe-taking and denial of justice was carried into the small towns and villages under the Oyo hegemony. In these 'outer provinces', it was said, the Alaafin's palace officials (Ilari) 'could cheat and rob to their hearts' desire'.[58]

V

If the ruling elite of the various communities in traditional Southern Nigeria made use of law, with varying degrees of success, as an instrument for peace-keeping and for maintaining the integrity of their communities, the British did not find their law wanting as an agency for the colonial control of Southern Nigeria. The story of British advent in Nigeria since about the middle of the nineteenth century has been told by many writers.[59] What has not been emphasised sufficiently is the role of the law in Britain's conquest of the country.

It is pertinent to observe at the outset that although historians of modern Africa have not paid much attention to the importance of European law in the establishment and maintenance of colonial rule on the continent, there is nothing new about the role of law in imperialist expansion. In Roman times law occupied a crucial position in the administration of the Roman Empire. As the empire expanded 'the sphere of application of Roman law grew correspondingly'.[60] Between 150 BC and AD 150 the metropolitan law of Rome expanded considerably to meet the growing needs of the empire. In the various parts the indigenous laws were never wholly replaced, but the *ius gentium*, an embodiment of Roman legal culture, stretched in all directions to embrace non-Roman peoples, thereby facilitating their incorporation within the Roman imperial orbit.[61]

William the Conqueror and his successors in the eleventh and twelfth centuries similarly used the law and the law courts to strengthen the Norman hold on England. Concerned about raising revenue as well as ensuring their supremacy, these kings of medieval England built up their royal court 'whose law was everywhere and at all times the same'.[62] As time went on, 'royal justice' 'gradually dwarfed and finally superseded all other justice' administered by the local and private courts of feudal lords in the land. In the process, the common law of England began to emerge, while the Norman regime took on the nature of a permanent conquest.

When, in more recent times, Sir Frederick Pollock spoke of 'the external conquests of the Common Law' and its predominance over the indigenous legal systems in India, the Sudan and other territories under British dominion or protection, he was indicating the extent of the role of English law in the consolidation of the British Empire.[63]

To view the role of law in its proper perspective as an agency of imperialism, the point must always be borne in mind that it never operated alone – whether in medieval England, in India or in Southern Nigeria. But while in the traditional society of Southern Nigeria the main prop of the indigenous law was largely religious and metaphysical, in the colonial context, the imported European law had behind it the ultimate sanction of force. In this connection it is instructive to note that from about 1818 the British placed along the West African coast a regular naval force which served partly to check European slavers, to protect British commerce and generally to enhance British influence among the indigenous coastal communities.[64] Off the coast of Nigeria was the island of Fernando Po, a strategic and important naval base, especially since the 1830s. Here was the seat of the British consul, first appointed in 1849, and here the base of operation of many a naval expedition against coastal and riverain townships along the Niger Delta during much of the latter half of the nineteenth century.[65] Throughout the nineteenth century in West Africa, 'the role of British gunboats in developing British control and influence continued to be a large one'.[66] The naval forces were supplemented by local corps and militias created in all the British West African settlements and by regular troops drawn from the West India regiments.

Two years after Lagos became a British colony, the settlement by 1863 had about 700 armed police. This was the Lagos constabulary which the colonial administration used against the Ijebu and Oyo kingdoms in the hinterland in 1893 and 1895 respectively, in the attempt to extend British influence in Yorubaland. The Niger Coast Protectorate, that is, the rest of Southern Nigeria east of Lagos Colony, had a regular constabulary by 1894. Four years later, the West African Frontier Force was created.[67] In May 1906 the various military units were consolidated into the Southern Nigeria Regiment of the West African Frontier Force, with 61 officers, 34 British non-commissioned officers and 1,883 privates.[68] The new force was divided into two battalions with headquarters at Calabar and Lagos respectively. It should be borne in mind that throughout the colonial era in Nigeria, the British administration had a complete command over the use of force as a means of coercion, including, on the civil side, control over the police forces.[69]

Coercion certainly played a crucial role in the conquest and control of Southern Nigeria by the British. Between 1902 and 1906, no less than twenty-three 'punitive expeditions', besides numerous small-scale patrols, were mounted against diverse indigenous communities, especially east of the Niger.[70] It was through such expeditions and patrols that much of Igboland and other areas east of the Niger became 'conquered territory'. Between 1904 and 1909 a total of some 15,912 square miles of Southern Nigeria was said to have been brought under British control by force of arms.[71] It is conceivable that in many parts of Southern Nigeria where force of arms was not directly employed, the very command of a substantial military force by the British was an important factor in the acceptance of foreign rule by the indigenous authorities.

But the limitations of the use of force in British imperialist expansion in West Africa or elsewhere must be recognised. Force might be used to weaken the will of the conquered, but it did not suffice to make colonial rule endure. It served to break down 'much of the African defences against conquest', but it was no fit instrument for consolidating colonial rule. Force might effect physical subjugation, but it did not by itself guarantee 'harmonious cooperation' between Africans and Europeans or 'an orderly and peaceful state of affairs' that would be conducive to economic and social development. 'Pacification' of colonial territories by imperialist powers in Africa was usually a long-term process and military subjugation was only one phase of it. No territory was regarded as 'pacified' until its inhabitants at least nominally accepted British authority, and perhaps, more important, until some framework of orderly administration under British supervision was established. One must therefore take cognisance of factors other than the use of force in explaining the relative stability which British colonialism enjoyed in West Africa. Some other historians have portrayed the part played by missionaries in the colonial venture as 'torch-bearers of British influence',[72] and by individual colonial administrators as human agents at crucial moments.[73] A very potent factor in consolidating and stabilising colonial rule was the imported European legal process. In the hands of British colonial administrators, law was a veritable tool, stronger in many ways than the Maxim gun. 'The basis of the operation of the English common law and equity in Nigeria', a distinguished Nigerian lawyer has written, 'derives . . . from the fact that we have by a deliberate choice adopted them.'[74] The truth is that Nigerians had no choice whether or not to adopt English law. English law and the whole paraphernalia of the English judicial process brought into Nigeria were natural servants of colonialism.

VI

The use of European law in the colonial control of Southern Nigeria began with treaty-making. It would be an arduous, if not particularly rewarding, task to enumerate all the treaties entered into between indigenous authorities in Southern Nigeria and British officials or agents of British trading companies.[75] It is perhaps no exaggeration that in the nineteenth century and early this century, 'treaties were produced by the cartload'.[76] In this spree of treaty-making, the Royal Niger Company, operating as a chartered company between 1876 and 1900 mainly along the lower Niger, played a leading role.[77] Sir Alfred Moloney, Sir Gilbert Carter, Sir Henry McCallum and Sir William MacGregor – four colonial governors whose tenures of office spanned the period 1886–1904 – were responsible for many treaties signed with the indigenous authorities in the hinterland of the Lagos Colony. In all, the treaties signed by British officials with the king and chiefs of Lagos (1852, 1861), the king and chiefs of Opobo (1884), Nana of Itsekiriland (1884), the ruling authorities of Asaba (1884), Ile-Ife (1888), Abeokuta (1893), Oyo (1888, 1893) and a series of judicial agreements in Yorubaland (1904–8) were among the most notable in the history of British conquest of Southern Nigeria.[78]

Until about 1880 most of the treaties concentrated on more or less the same themes: peace and friendship with Britain, freedom of trade, assistance to British subjects in time of difficulties, and freedom for the propagation of the Christian faith. There was a noticeable change in the tone and even the objectives of the treaties and agreements made after about 1880. By the 1880s the scramble among European powers for territories in Africa had reached a high pitch.[79] Most treaties then began to enjoin local rulers not to enter into any treaty relations with other nations 'except with the knowledge and sanction' of the British Government.[80] After 1880 Britain was demanding in her treaties with some areas exclusive rights to work their timber, minerals and other economic resources,[81] and 'full and exclusive jurisdiction, civil and criminal, over British subjects and their property' in her treaties with other areas.[82] In return for various concessions before and after 1880, African communities were usually offered British protection with or without monetary reward.

One is easily impressed by the sheer number of the treaties in Southern Nigeria and the energy shown by British officials in securing local potentates to put their marks on pre-fabricated treaty forms. In strict law, most, if not all, of the treaties were not valid. Largely because of language difficulties and of differences in political concepts, parties to the treaties were rarely *ad idem* in their intentions. As A. N. Cook has written, 'the usual method [of making treaties] was to send political agents armed with blank treaty forms to the various kings, chiefs and headmen. The provisions were then explained to the ruler by an interpreter before obtaining his signature.'[83] The interpreters for the most part were half-educated Nigerians who, because of their own limited education, could not have conveyed to the indigenous rulers the full implications of the documents they were signing. There were even instances where the interpreter did not understand the language he was supposed to interpret.[84] Sometimes the interpreter was a local Christian missionary agent all too ready to portray a treaty in the most favourable light before the ruler in his own anxiety to secure the British presence as an aid to the propagation of the Christian faith.[85]

But why was Britain preoccupied with the signing of treaties with the indigenous rulers of Southern Nigeria when no one could have raised any legal objection to her gradually consolidating her position through the use of force? The suggestion by J. C. Anene that treaties were the alternative to 'outright acquisition of territories' which might have 'precipitated vexatious wars with the innumerable African rulers' and that they were designed to prevent Europeans flying at each other's throat,[86] would not seem to go far enough. After all, Britain had enough force to deal with the 'vexatious wars', and, in any case, treaty or no treaty, she had to engage in such wars. Again, to argue that the treaties were intended to prevent conflicts among European powers is only partially true. A large number of treaties were made in Southern Nigeria and elsewhere in West Africa in the 1840s and 1850s when the emphasis in European contact with Africa was commerce rather than the acquisition of territories and the prospect of conflicts would not seem imminent.

The explanation for Britain's preoccupation with treaty-making in Southern Nigeria and elsewhere in colonial Africa would seem to be her tradition of the use of the law in the acquisition of territories overseas – a tradition going back to the seventeenth century in the colonial ventures in the West Indies, in India and on the American continent.[87] It is instructive to note that even before treaties were signed with many of the local authorities in Southern Nigeria, some legal basis had been provided for British activities in West Africa as a whole. The Foreign Jurisdiction Act, 1843, empowered the British Crown

> to establish laws and institutions and to constitute courts and officers for the peace, order, and good government of Her Majesty's subjects and others within existing and future settlements on or adjacent to the coast of Africa.[88]

British colonial expansion overseas may be said to have been characterised by a search for at least some appearance of legal certainty, and by a tradition of underwriting almost every action by the force of law. Treaty-making in Southern Nigeria in the nineteenth and early twentieth centuries was part of this tradition.

Whatever the legality or illegality of the treaties in Southern Nigeria, from the British viewpoint they served two useful functions. In the period of the scramble for territories on the African continent among European powers, they were often regarded as bases for territorial claims. For instance, it was as a result of the treaties signed by the British Consul, Edward Hyde Hewett, at Opobo and Brass in 1884 that Britain was able to exclude the French and the Germans from establishing themselves on the Niger Delta.[89] The British claim to much of Southern Nigeria and the Niger basin, recognised at the Berlin West Africa Conference, 1884–5, was based largely on the treaties signed by Britain with the various Southern Nigerian indigenous rulers up to about 1884.[90]

Treaties were also useful as a foundation for the internal organisation of British territories. In many parts of Southern Nigeria a treaty was often regarded as the basis for formal association. Once a treaty or an agreement was signed with a local community, the tendency was to construe it as conferring a legal right on Britain to order its affairs. Legal relationships were supposed to be created between Britain and the local ruler and it was irrelevant if the latter understood the treaty in a different light. The activities of John Beecroft in the period 1849–54 in extending British influence over Bonny, Opobo and some other Niger Delta states by meddling in their internal politics were based on treaties presumed to be existing between Britain and these states.[91] Relations between the British on the one hand, and the Urhobo, Itsekiri and Ijo people on the other, were predicated on the treaties of friendship and protection signed between 1884 and 1893.[92] It was on the basis of these treaties that Britain brought about 'tremendous changes' in the people's way of life.[93]

VII

If treaties and agreements represent one form of the application of law in British imperialist expansion in Southern Nigeria, the establishment of English-style machinery of justice and the introduction of English substantive law represent another. We shall examine in the following chapter the new judicial machinery set up in Southern Nigeria and how it facilitated the control of the region by the British administration. It is convenient to limit the discussion in this chapter to a consideration, in general terms, of the role of English substantive law.

The period 1862–1914 witnessed a rapid expansion of English law in much of Southern Nigeria, necessitated by administrative and economic requirements. How else could the colonial administration have dealt with the new relations that were being forged between Nigerians and the British other than by the application, albeit in a modified form, of English civil and criminal law? It was essential that an ordered administration be established in the newly conquered territory. If the colonial regime must endure, it must be able to exercise an undisputed power to settle disputes and to punish whatever it regarded as deviant patterns of behaviour. The power to punish crimes was particularly important. H. S. Freeman, the first Governor of Lagos colony, wrote: 'The exercise of the power of life and death over Lagos people is the last seal on the stability of British rule in this settlement.'[94]

If the need for the administration of criminal justice in a new colony necessitated the introduction of English criminal law, there was also the vast field of economic exploitation in which English law would also seem to be an indispensable tool. The regulation of commercial relations between Nigerians and Europeans or among Nigerians themselves, currency regulation, protection of British capital, the tapping of the territory's economic resources and the organisation of its external trade – all these and other aspects of economic development involved the application of law.

Less than two years after Lagos became a British colony, an ordinance of 1863 declared: 'the laws of England shall have the same force and be administered in this Settlement as in England, so far as such laws and such administration thereof can be rendered applicable to the circumstances of this Settlement.'[95] The Supreme Court Ordinance, No. 4, 1876, which set up a Supreme Court for the colony, spelt out the essence of the English law. Section 14 of that ordinance provided that the common law, the doctrines of equity and statutes of general application in force in England on 24 July 1874 should be in force in the colony. Common law and equity were to be administered concurrently; in cases of conflict between the rules of equity and those of common law, the rules of equity should prevail.[96] All these provisions on the position of English law in the Lagos Colony were substantially re-enacted in later legislations dealing with other parts of Southern Nigeria.

Until 1900 English law was not formally introduced into the territory east of the Lagos Colony. The area witnessed intense British activity in the nineteenth century and relations were established with African rulers (at first largely for commercial purposes) as early as the 1840s.[97] A portion of it, embracing mainly the Niger Delta, was constituted into the Oil Rivers Protectorate in 1885. The protectorate was later extended into the hinterland and renamed the Niger Coast Protectorate in 1895 under a Commissioner and Consul General, resident at Old Calabar. In 1899 the administration of the area came under the control of the Colonial Office, and on 1 January 1900 it was renamed the Southern Nigeria Protectorate.[98] Some rudimentary form of English law was administered in the area before 1900. From about 1854, various types of courts were established there, as will be shown in the following chapter, and, because the courts were dominated by British officials or British merchants, they naturally operated on the basis of some broad principles of English law.

Three related proclamations of May 1900 introduced English law and set up an English-style legal system in the newly created Southern Nigeria Protectorate. They were the Supreme Court Proclamation, the Criminal Procedure Proclamation, and the Commissioners Proclamation – all of which were intended to be taken together as one single document.[99] The Supreme Court Proclamation established a Supreme Court for the new protectorate, a superior court of record which 'shall possess and exercise, so far as circumstances admit, all the jurisdictions, powers and authorities which are vested in or capable of being exercised by Her Majesty's High Court of Justice in England'.[100] In so far as local circumstances would permit, the law to be administered by the court was to be 'the Common Law, the doctrines of Equity, and the statutes of general application which were in force in England on the 1 January 1900'.[101]

The one hundred and fifty-six clauses of the Criminal Procedure Proclamation were, in essence, an encapsulation of the principles of English criminal law and procedure. They were obviously devised for the guidance of political officers who had to administer criminal justice in the new protectorate with little or no knowledge of English criminal law. Twelve clauses dealt with the judicial

procedure in the administration of criminal law; six with inter-
rogation of accused persons; eighteen with preliminary investigation; four with the definition and meaning of 'attempt' in criminal
law; four with some general defences open to accused persons;
and seventeen other clauses with sentencing.[102]

The Commissioners' Proclamation, in the main, dealt with the
judicial powers conferred on the administrative officers who were
to be the Commissioners of the Supreme Court, thus completing
the legal and judicial machinery for the new protectorate.[103]

The introduction of English law and legal procedure into the
Yoruba states in the hinterland of the Lagos Colony at the beginning of this century was clearly prompted by the desire to protect
the economic interests of Britain and by the requirements of day-
to-day administration. Administration of some sort was being
established in parts of Yorubaland – in such important centres as
Ibadan, Ilesha, Oyo, Ijebu-Ode – towards the end of the nineteenth century. Informal councils were being established; British
officials were setting themselves up as advisers to the indigenous
ruling authorities and were adjudicating disputes.[104] As in the
territory to the east of the Niger before 1900, some 'recognised
principles of English law and equity' were inevitably being introduced into the Yoruba states.[105]

The need for some systematic administration of English law
in these states was soon felt. As many aliens (British subjects)
were penetrating into the interior of Yorubaland as missionaries,
traders, commercial agents and political officers, complex problems
of inter-personal relations were bound to arise. There was the
question of the administration of justice between the indigenous
Yoruba and the foreign elements in their midst. Which law would
apply in disputes where the parties were mixed, that is, where one
of the parties was a European or an African immigrant from, say,
Sierra Leone? The question must have loomed large in the eyes of
the colonial administration in Lagos because it had no confidence
in the indigenous system of administering justice in Yorubaland.
When Sir William MacGregor toured the hinterland in March
1903, his scathing remarks about the administration of justice at
Ibadan showed the degree of his contempt:

> The *Bale's* (ruler's) Council is also the Supreme Court of
> Justice for the town and province. There is not a single,
> enlightened man, not a man of the new school, in the Council if

there is one in Ibadan. . . . Justice, it is to be feared, is too often
sold to the highest bidder in cases that come before the native
tribunals.[106]

The Bale and members of his council were described as 'utterly
ignorant', and it was apparently no small concern of his that 'cases
of a judicial nature [which] begin to arise daily between Europeans
and Natives' were being brought before them. Indeed European
traders in Ibadan were complaining that they had to appear before
the Bale's court, resenting the very idea of Europeans 'being
judged in the purely native court'.[107]
In terms of the necessity for the establishment of English law in
Yorubaland, the requirements of the economic exploitation of the
territory were no less compelling. By 1900 Britain had considerable
economic interests in the Yoruba states. To facilitate their economic exploitation the colonial administration in Lagos had started
to construct a railway line to link them with the Lagos Colony. The
railway line, begun in March 1896, reached Abeokuta in 1899,
Ibadan in 1900 and was to reach Jebba in 1909.[108] A direct
economic consequence of the construction of the railway line was
the increased tempo of commercial activities in Yorubaland.
European (mainly British) commercial firms, based in Lagos,
were now operating in the interior with substantial capital outlay.[109]
With the European firms went their agents and individual African
traders, a large proportion of them being non-Yoruba. By 1906
there were about twenty-five principal mercantile firms in Yorubaland, established mainly at Abeokuta and Ibadan.[110]
Commercial activities in Yorubaland were being attended by
some serious difficulties. Absence of a recognised legal system, for
instance, made recovery of debts difficult, as the European firms
trading at Abeokuta found to their great inconvenience.[111] There
was the more serious problem of what must have seemed to the
Lagos administration and to the European merchants themselves
the inadequacy of the indigenous legal system. Commerce was
forging new relations in the interior, and was creating types of
offences, like fraudulent book-keeping, breach of contract, infringement of trade-mark and so on, either unknown to the Yoruba
or not given prominence in their jurisprudence.[112] In the view
of the Lagos administration, 'it was quite clear that the Chiefs [of
Egbaland and other parts of Yorubaland] could have no assistance from the traditions or usages of their country that would

enable them to deal with commercial cases of magnitude arising between their own people and European merchants'.[113] So serious was the situation considered to be that in 1902, at the instigation of Sir William MacGregor, the Egba authorities sent two young men to Lagos to be trained in the colonial courts 'in legal matters' in the hope that their acquaintance with English legal and judicial processes would be of some use in the adjudication of disputes in which British interests were involved.[114]

In Yorubaland, as in other parts of Southern Nigeria, there were also problems connected with day-to-day administration. As British officers were getting more and more involved in the internal affairs of the states, the need was urgent for the establishment of legal and judicial machinery, under British control, as basis for a firm control of the territory.

The various problems connected with the administrative organisation of Yorubaland and with commercial development in the territory compelled a formal introduction of English law and an English-style judicial system. This was effected by the signing of a series of judicial agreements with the major Yoruba ruling authorities.[115] They were signed with the *Alake* and the Egba authorities in January 1904; with Ibadan and Oyo in August 1904; Ife in September 1904; and with the *Awujale* of Ijebu in November 1908. Under these agreements, the British acquired the power to try all criminal offences, to make and administer laws protecting the persons and property of British subjects trading in Yorubaland and, generally, to adjudicate in disputes in which the interests of British subjects were involved.

To give weight to the judicial agreements, by a series of four jurisdiction ordinances enacted in 1904 and 1909, the Supreme Court of the Lagos Colony was empowered to exercise jurisdiction in virtually the whole of Yorubaland.[116] The laws of the Lagos Colony relating to criminal offences and to civil matters, that is, English common law and principles of equity, henceforth became applicable to most parts of Yorubaland in so far as local circumstances would permit.

VIII

At this stage a brief examination of the background of the English law that was being introduced into Southern Nigeria would be useful. The origin of English common law, as was indicated earlier, could be traced to the eleventh century, the time of the Norman conquest of England.[117] The royal courts set up by the Norman kings evolved common principles of law that were applied throughout England.

In time these principles became rigid and bristled with technicalities, sometimes resulting in hardship or outright injustice. It soon became the practice that those who suffered injustice through the technicalities of the common law could petition the king as the fountain of justice. At first the king himself heard such petitions in his council, but by 1450, an officer of the state, the chancellor, had assumed full jurisdiction in dealing with them. Until about 1672, the chancellor was invariably an ecclesiastic and in his judicial capacity he tended to look more to the intentions of parties and their mode of behaviour rather than the form of the law. He would not allow a claim to fail merely because the pursuant had not conformed with the technicality of the law; nor would he grant a petition if the petitioner's own behaviour in the particular case showed that he had acted unconscionably. Thus the chancellor's court or the Chancery tended to be a court of morals and its kind of law was known as equity. One of the venerated maxims developed by equity summed up its moral emphasis: 'He who comes to Equity must come with clean hands.'

At first equity had no fixed principles. But with the ascendancy of chancellors who were trained in the common law, it became systematised and acquired technicalities of its own. Equity and the common law are still two systems of law, although the Judicature Acts 1873–5 fused their administration, making it possible for an English court to decide issues involving the two systems.

Equity and common law apart, statutes or acts of parliament have also been part of English law. As has been indicated earlier, those of them that were said to be 'of general application' in England at certain dates were made applicable to Southern Nigeria. Incidentally, the meaning of that phrase – 'of general application' – in determining the extent of the applicability of English statutes in Nigeria has been a subject of judicial inquiries and legal writings.[118] In practice, in spite of the purported introduction of English statutes, comparatively few English acts have been held to be in force in Nigeria.[119]

It is not enough to know the sources of English law; one must need to understand the mentality behind it in order to appreciate its meaning in the context of Southern Nigeria. Fundamentally, the aims of English systems of laws are to secure the strict legal rights of individuals and to safeguard their lives and properties against any arbitrary acts of the state. Justice is viewed more or less in the abstract and, ideally, is devoid of any extraneous considerations – political, social or economic. Justice for the most part means justice according to the law, and legal justice is not necessarily conterminous with moral justice. The status of parties to a civil dispute is not usually an important consideration; impersonality is of the essence of English judicial administration. Parties are, in fact, almost invariably represented by professional advocates who have been called into being largely because of the law's technicalities.

Technicalities are of two kinds. There are the technicalities of the substantive law, and there are those of procedural or adjectival law. In practice they all combine to make English law 'a highly complex and esoteric matter'. Consequently, except at the lower rungs of the English judicial structure, a judge presiding over a case tends to resemble an umpire watching over the observance of the rules of a game.

Such is the mentality and the spirit of the English legal system. The contrasts which the system presents to the traditional jurisprudence of Southern Nigeria are rather obvious. While English law is individualistic, the traditional legal system of Southern Nigeria was 'collectivist' in outlook. On account of its concern for communal solidarity, traditional justice set great store by family rather than individual responsibility in civil disputes as well as in answering for offences against the public law. Justice was not an abstract concept, nor was law an impersonal agency in the search for peace and communal solidarity. The status of a litigant was, for this reason, not irrelevant; his guilt or innocence might hinge on what was expected of a person in his position in life. The law which the judges applied was neither their exclusive preserve nor that of an elite, making a study of it a life career. The law was fairly well known to all responsible adults because it was derived essentially from their common culture and traditions. Much more than English law, it was consonant with what was morally acceptable in the society. The concept of legal justice, that is to say, justice derivable by the application of some technical rules, was unknown.

The impact of English law on the development of Southern Nigeria will be examined later. All that we need to note at this stage is that by the end of the first decade of this century, a system of law and justice had been introduced into the territory, contrasting in many ways with the notions of law and justice held by the local inhabitants.

The introduction of English law, however, has not meant outright abolition of the indigenous law. The British position in many parts of Southern Nigeria at the beginning of this century was tenuous, and, quite apart from the dictates of expedience and practical politics, the colonial administration lacked the resources and the personnel to operate the English legal system on a full scale. What the administration did was to allow the operation of the indigenous legal system at least under certain conditions while adapting English law 'by judicious administration to the wants and feelings of the people'.[120] Thus the major instruments introducing English law and judicial procedure into Southern Nigeria – the Supreme Court Ordinance, 1876, the Supreme Court Proclamation, 1900 and the judicial agreements in Yorubaland, 1904–8 – all made provisions for the administration of the indigenous law in the various areas to which they applied. Section 19 of the Supreme Court Ordinance, 1876, declared:

> Nothing in this Ordinance shall deprive any person of the benefit of any law or custom existing in the said colony and Protectorate [of Lagos], such law or custom not being repugnant to natural justice, equity and good conscience nor incompatible either directly or by necessary implication with any enactment of the Colonial Legislature existing at the commencement of this Ordinance or which may afterwards come into operation. Such laws and customs shall be deemed applicable in causes and matters where the parties thereto are natives of the said Colony or Protectorate, and particularly, but without derogating from their application in other cases, causes and matters relating to marriage and to the tenure and transfer of real and personal property, and to inheritance and testamentary dispositions, and also in causes and matters between Natives and Europeans where it may appear to the court that substantial injustice would be done to either party by a strict adherence to the rules of English law.[121]

Thus, in essence, the local population would continue to employ their customary law to regulate their lives, but only under certain conditions. The law must not be 'repugnant to natural justice, equity and good conscience' – a somewhat nebulous phrase which, for all practical purposes, meant English notions of law and justice. Moreover the law should not conflict with any enactment of the colonial legislature, dominated by British officials almost throughout the colonial era. Again, by the same ordinance of 1876, once a litigant appeared to have regulated his affairs by English law, either expressly or by implication, judging from the nature of the transactions giving rise to a dispute, he was not allowed to claim the benefit of any customary law.[122] A matter of procedure, often not examined for its implication, was that a customary law to be applied in an English-style court in Southern Nigeria had to be proved, just as a foreign law does in an English court of law.

It is clear that although the customary law of Southern Nigeria continued to thrive under the new dispensation, the colonial administration ensured its subordination to the English law.

Notes

1 For a succinct account of the various schools of legal theory, see Roscoe Pound, *An Introduction to the Philosophy of Law*, New Haven, 1954, chs 1–3.
2 A. N. Allott, 'Law in the New Africa', *African Affairs*, lxvi, 262, January 1967, p. 55.
3 J. H. Driberg, 'The African Conception of Law', *Journal of the African Society*, 34, Supplement, July 1955.
4 E. Bodenheimer, *Jurisprudence*, Cambridge, Mass., 1962, pp. 89–102.
5 John Austin, *The Province of Jurisprudence Determined*, London, repr. 1954, p. 163.
6 T. O. Elias, *The Nature of African Customary Law*, Manchester, 2nd. Imp. 1962; Max Gluckman, ed., *Ideas and Procedure in African Customary Law*, London, 1969; E. Cotran and N. N. Rubins, eds., *Readings in African Law*, London, 1970, I; A. N. Allott, *New Essays in African Law*, London, 1970.
7 Elias, *The Nature of African Customary Law*, p. 55.
8 National Archives, Enugu (henceforth NAE), On Prof 1/14/243, 'Ibo Law' by C. K. Meek; Elias, pp. 187–211.
9 Compare Ladipo Solanke, 'Yoruba (or Aku) Constitutional Law and its Historical Developments', *WASU Magazine*, ii, 1.
10 A. K. Ajisafe, *The Laws and Customs of the Yoruba People*, London, 1924; C. G. Okojie, *Ishan Native Laws and Customs*, Lagos, 1960; NAE, On Prof 1/14/243, 'Ibo Law' by C. K. Meek.

11 Ladipo Solanke, 'Yoruba Constitutional Law'. See also James Boyd Christensen, 'The Role of Proverbs in Fante Culture', *Africa*, xxviii, pp. 232–42.

12 NAI, CSO 26/3, 31318; NAI, Ben Prof 7/6, VII.

13 This point was emphasised in many Intelligence Reports compiled by British administrative officers in the 1930s. Compare NAI, CSO 26/3, 30047; CSO 26/3, 31015; CSO 26/3, 31065.

14 CO 520/92, Egerton to Crewe, 11 April 1910, enclosure entitled 'Yoruba Laws and Customs'; NAE, On Prof 1/14/243, 'Ibo Law' by C. K. Meek.

15 Ladipo Solanke, 'Yoruba Constitutional Law', p. 30.

16 Quoted in Elias, *The Nature of African Customary Law*, p. 272.

17 J. N. Matson, 'The Supreme Court and the Customary Judicial Process in the Gold Coast', *The International and Comparative Law Quarterly*, II, part I, p. 48.

18 Elias, *The Nature of African Customary Law*, p. 272.

19 J. N. Matson, 'The Supreme Court and the Customary Judicial Process . . .', p. 48.

20 M. M. Green, *Igbo Village Affairs*, London, 2nd. ed., 1964, p. 113.

21 Elias, p. 197.

22 Ladipo Solanke, 'Yoruba Constitutional Law', p. 34.

23 NAI, CSO 26/3, 28242, 'Intelligence Report on Afaha Obong Clan'.

24 Elias, p. 219.

25 For various criminal offences and their corresponding penalties, see P. A. Talbot, *The Peoples of Southern Nigeria*, London, 1926, III, pp. 634–76.

26 J. H. Driberg, 'The African Conception of Law'.

27 NAI, CSO 26/4, 30752, 'Intelligence Report on the Villages of Umulokpa, Adeba and others'.

28 NAI, Ben Prof 7/6, II, 'Intelligence Report on Ogwashi-Uku District'.

29 NAI, CSO 26/3, 29182, 'Intelligence Report on the Benni Clan of the Western Ijaw'.

30 NAI, CSO/3, 26769, I, 'Intelligence Report of the Kwale Division of the Warri Province'; NAI, CSO 26/3, 28939, 'Intelligence Report on the Abam Clan and the towns of Abiriba Umuhu and others'.

31 NAI, CSO 26/3, 28242, 'Intelligence Report on Afaha Obong Clan'.

32 NAI, CSO 26/3, 29427, 'Intelligence Report on the Abanyam Clan'.

33 NAI, CSO 26/3, 29804, 'Intelligence Report on Aboh and other towns'.

34 William J. Chambliss, 'Law in Action: Inquiries of the Criminal Law Process', Mimeographed compilation at the University of Ibadan Library, p. 245.

35 NAE, On Prof 1/14/243, 'Ibo Law'.

36 NAI, CSO 26/3, 29799, 'Intelligence Report on Ikerre District, Ekiti Division'.

37 NAE, On Prof 1/14/243, 'Ibo Law'.

38 NAI, CSO 1/19, XXX, Egerton to Crewe, 6 June 1910, enclosure entitled 'The Laws and Customs of the Yoruba Country'.

39 NAI, CSO 26/3, 28360, 'Intelligence Report on Ogidi and Abacha Villages, Onitsha Province'.
40 T. N. Tamuno, 'Before British Police in Nigeria', *Nigeria Magazine*, 89, June 1966.
41 P. A. Talbot, *The Peoples of Southern Nigeria*, III, pp. 622–3.
42 NAE, Cal Prof 10/3, V.
43 Talbot, III, p. 623; NAE, CSO 1/13, XXI, Moor to Colonial Office, 22 August 1902.
44 NAE, Og Prof 2/1/511.
45 Tamuno, 'Before British Police'.
46 Talbot, III, p. 620.
47 NAI, CSO 26/3, 31216, 'Intelligence Report on Ijebu Remo District'.
48 NAI, CSO 26/3, 30014, 'Intelligence Report on Akure District'.
49 NAI, CSO 26/3, 27226, I, 'Intelligence Report on Bonny District, Owerri Province'.
50 Driberg, 'The African Conception of Law'; Matson, 'The Supreme Court and the Customary Judicial Process'; Chambliss, 'Law in Action'.
51 CO 147/160, MacGregor to Chamberlain, 11 November 1901; CO 520/92, Egerton to Crewe, 11 April 1910; NAE, On Prof 1/14/243, 'Ibo Law'.
52 N. A. Fadipe, 'The Sociology of the Yoruba', London University, PhD thesis, 1940, p. 712.
53 'Annual Report on the North Eastern District for 1905', *Nigeria Gazette*, July–November 1906, p. 756.
54 CO 520/92, Egerton to Crewe, 11 April 1910, enclosure.
55 NAI, CSO 26/3, 31217, 'Intelligence Report on the Ijebu-Ife District, Ijebu Province'.
56 NAI, CSO 26/3, 28242, 'Intelligence Report on Afaha Obong Clan'.
57 NAI, CSO 26/3, 31216, 'Intelligence Report on Ijebu Remo District'.
58 N. A. Fadipe, 'The Sociology of the Yoruba', p. 732.
59 Alan Burns, *History of Nigeria*, London, 6th ed., 1963; A. N. Cook, *British Enterprise in Nigeria*, London, 2nd impr. 1964; W. N. M. Geary, *Nigeria Under British Rule*, London, new imp. 1965; J. C. Anene, *Southern Nigeria in Transition, 1885–1906*, Cambridge, 1966.
60 W. Kunkel, *An Introduction to Roman Legal and Constitutional History*, Oxford, 1966, p. 74.
61 *Ibid.*
62 G. Radcliffe and G. Cross, *The English Legal System*, London, 4th ed., 1964, p. 24.
63 Frederick Pollock, *The Expansion of the Common Law*, London, 1924, pp. 16–17, 134–5.
64 For more on the role of the military and naval forces in the conquest of British West Africa, see P. M. Mbaeyi, 'Military and Naval Factors in British West African History, 1823–1874', unpublished DPhil. thesis, Oxford University, 1965, especially chs 2, 6, 10, 11.
65 K. O. Dike, *Trade and Politics in the Niger Delta*, Oxford, 2nd ed., 1959, pp. 128–65, 182–201.
66 P. M. Mbaeyi, 'Military and Naval Factors', p. 385.

67 T. N. Tamuno, *The Evolution of the Nigerian State: The Southern Phase, 1898–1914*, London, 1972, p. 33.
68 *Ibid.*, p. 34.
69 For more on the development of the police force, see T. N. Tamuno, *The Police in Modern Nigeria*, 1861–1965, Ibadan, 1970.
70 T. N. Tamuno, *The Evolution of the Nigerian State*, p. 35 and n. 3.
71 *Ibid.*, p. 44.
72 E. A. Ayandele, 'The Mode of British Expansion in Yorubaland in, the Second Half of the Nineteenth Century: the Oyo Episode', *Odu*, III, 1967, 2. See also J. F. A. Ajayi, *Christian Missions in Nigeria, 1841–1891*, London, 1965, pp. 53–125.
73 A. B. Aderibigbe, 'The Ijebu Expedition, 1892; An Episode in the British Penetration of Nigeria Reconsidered', *Historians in Tropical Africa*, Salisbury, Rhodesia, 1962; T. N. Tamuno, *The Evolution of the Nigerian State*, pp. 64–94.
74 B. O. Nwabueze, *The Machinery of Justice in Nigeria*, London, 1963, p. 19.
75 For treaties up to 1893, see Sir Edward Hertslet, *Map of Africa by Treaty*, London, 1894.
76 A. N. Cook, *British Enterprise in Nigeria*, p. 91.
77 Hertslet, *Map of Africa by Treaty*, pp. 450–7.
78 For the text of some of these treaties, see Alan Burns, *History of Nigeria*, pp. 316–39.
79 For more on the scramble, see R. Robinson and J. Gallagher, *Africa and the Victorians: The Climax of Imperialism in the Dark Continent*, New York, 1961.
80 Compare the treaties of peace and friendship with the Egba Authorities (January 1893); the *Alafin* of Oyo (February 1893); the *Owa* of Idanre (1894). NAI, CSO 5/1, XIX, CSO 5/1, XVIII, CSO 5/1, XXII.
81 Compare the agreements on mineral oil with the chiefs of Ondo and eleven other Yoruba towns, September 1906, NAI, CSO 5/2, XXIII.
82 Compare the treaty with Nana and other Itsekiri chiefs, 16 July 1884, which became the prototype of treaties with Urhobo towns and villages. Obaro Ikime, *Niger Delta Rivalry*, London, 1969, Appendix III.
83 A. N. Cook, *British Enterprise in Nigeria*, p. 91.
84 Obaro Ikime, *Niger Delta Rivalry*, p. 138.
85 Ayandele, 'The Mode of British Expansion in Yorubaland'.
86 J. C. Anene, *Southern Nigeria in Transition*, p. 63.
87 Sir Kenneth Roberts-Wray, *Commonwealth and Colonial Law*, London, 1966, especially chs 3, 5.
88 *Ibid.*, p. 166.
89 J. C. Anene, *Southern Nigeria in Transition*, p. 102.
90 Alan Burns, *History of Nigeria*, p. 150.
91 K. O. Dike, *Trade and Politics in the Niger Delta*, pp. 81–96.
92 Ikime, *Niger Delta Rivalry*, pp. 121–45.
93 *Ibid.*, p. 138.
94 NAI, CSO 1/1, I, Freeman to Newcastle, 4 February 1864.

95 Ordinance No. 3, 1863.
96 Section 14, Supreme Court Ordinance, No. 4, 1876.
97 Dike, *Trade and Politics*, pp. 47–127.
98 Alan Burns, *History of Nigeria*, pp. 140–56; 171–81; 210–18.
99 NAE, Cal Prof 10/2, I.
100 Supreme Court Proclamation, No. 6, 1900, sec. 9.
101 Section 11.
102 Criminal Procedure Proclamation, No. 7, 1900.
103 The Commissioners Proclamation, No. 8, 1900.
104 C. H. Elgee, *The Evolution of Ibadan*, Lagos, 1914, pp. 6–12; S. A. Akintoye, 'The Ekitiparapo and the Kiriji War', University of Ibadan, PhD thesis, 1966, pp. 331–6; J. A. Atanda, 'The New Oyo Empire: A Study of British Indirect Rule in Oyo Province, 1894–1934', University of Ibadan, PhD thesis, 1967, pp. 113–21.
105 Lagos, *Annual Reports for the Year 1899*.
106 NAI, CSO 1/3, VI, MacGregor to Colonial Office, 22 March 1903.
107 *Ibid.*
108 Alan Burns, p. 294.
109 NAI, Abe Prof 8/3; Lagos, *Annual Reports for the Year 1900–1901;* Lagos, *Annual Reports for the Year 1903*.
110 Lagos, *Annual Reports of the Colony of Southern Nigeria, 1906*, pp. 259–60.
111 NAI, Abe Prof 9/3, Punch to Acting Colonial Secretary, Lagos minute dated 10 April 1901.
112 C. H. Elgee, *The Evolution of Ibadan*, p. 16.
113 William MacGregor, 'Lagos, Abeokuta and the Alake', *African Affairs*, III, July 1904, p. 12.
114 NAI, Abe Prof 9/2, Blackwell to Acting Colonial Secretary, Lagos, minute dated 8 February 1902; Blackwell to Alake, 22 February 1902.
115 For more on the judicial agreements, see O. Adewoye, 'The Judicial Agreements in Yorubaland, 1904–1908', *Journal of African History*, xii, 4, 1971, pp. 607–27.
116 Egba Jurisdiction Ordinance, No. 14, 1904; Yoruba Jurisdiction Ordinance, No. 17, 1904; Ife Jurisdiction Ordinance, No. 20, 1904; Jebu Ode Jurisdiction Ordinance, No. 3, 1909.
117 H. G. Hanbury, *English Courts of Law*, London, 4th ed., 1967, pp. 1–61.
118 A. E. W. Park, *The Sources of Nigerian Law*, London, 1963, pp. 24–36; B. O. Nwabueze, *The Machinery of Justice in Nigeria*, pp. 17–19; A. N. Allott, *New Essays in African Law*, pp. 48–65.
119 Park, *The Sources of Nigerian Law*, p. 35.
120 NAI, CSO 1/8, VA, Glover to Kennedy, 5 August 1869.
121 Supreme Court Ordinance, No. 4, 1876, sec. 19.
122 *Ibid.*

2 The establishment of new courts of law, 1854-1908

It is on these courts that the Government mainly relies for the dispensing of justice among the natives, for the establishment of peace and good order in the territories, for the carrying out of all Administrative and Executive work . . . and for the furtherance of trade, education, agriculture etc. throughout the territories.

Ralph Moor to Colonial Office, London, 1903[1]

I

By 1908 a network of different types of courts of law had been established by the British over much of Southern Nigeria. This chapter examines these courts and the circumstances in which they were created.

Historically, English-style courts were older institutions in Southern Nigeria than English law. In almost every part of the territory, the setting up of law courts of some sort antedated the formal introduction of English substantive law in regularising relations between Nigerians and the foreign elements in their midst. The courts should not be seen as institutions designed simply 'to secure the ends of justice'.[2] It is worth emphasising that they were not established primarily for the benefit of Nigerians. English law and judicial procedure conferred undoubted benefits on Nigerians, as will be shown later, but one should be wary of the danger of *ex post facto* rationalisation of British intentions with regard to their importation. The courts might have served the ends of justice, but they served much more besides. Viewed in their larger context, they were part of Britain's armour in her conquest and control of Southern Nigeria.

From the discussion of the role of judicial power in the traditional society of Southern Nigeria, it is easy to appreciate that the establishment of new judicial institutions, whatever the quality of justice administered in them, was bound to undermine the position of the indigenous authorities. The ultimate power to redress grievances and maintain peace and order was indivisible. But by and large, the new courts were to operate outside the control of the traditional rulers, thus representing sources of justice alternative to what they could offer. In a comparable colonial situation on the Gold Coast (Ghana), Justice Marshall declared in 1878 in *Knacoe Koom v. Onsea and Kudjoe Tainee,*[3] 'The Supreme Court is not intended to supersede [the] authority of the kings and chiefs'. But in practice the new courts, in purporting to administer justice more or less independently of the traditional authorities, decisively struck at their sovereignty. Traditional authorities were to watch power slip from their hands as the new courts became fully established, and their erstwhile subjects began to realise that a 'superior' justice lay with the British administrator – superior, that is to say, in terms of effectiveness within the context of the emerging colonial structure.

There was another side to the role of the courts, especially in the period before the First World War when the colonial regime was still finding its feet in Southern Nigeria. In the course of our discussion we shall touch on the administrative functions of some of the courts, particularly the so-called 'native' courts, which, in many areas, especially in the hinterland, were the first outward and visible signs of British authority.

The establishment of colonial courts in Southern Nigeria followed the same piecemeal fashion in which the territory passed into British hands. The details of the administrative changes over Southern Nigeria in the nineteenth and twentieth centuries have been covered elsewhere;[4] for our purpose it should suffice to note that until the end of the nineteenth century, the territory was administered under three jurisdictions. Lagos Colony and much of its hinterland, including the Yoruba states which were said to be under British 'protection', fell under one administration, based in Lagos and responsible to the Colonial Office in London. A large portion of the area to the east of Lagos Colony was gradually brought under the jurisdiction of the British Foreign Office. First, the Oil Rivers Protectorate was constituted in 1885, comprising Benin, Brass, Bonny, Calabar, Degema and Opobo. This protectorate was later extended into the hinterland and renamed the Niger Coast Protectorate in 1893, under a Commissioner and Consul General, resident at Calabar. The third jurisdiction was that of the Royal Niger Company which for some thirteen years between 1886 and 1899, operated as a chartered company mainly along the lower Niger basin with its own administrative and judicial systems.[5] The company lost its charter in December 1899 and its area of jurisdiction was merged with the Niger Coast Protectorate. On 1 January 1900, the enlarged protectorate became known as Southern Nigeria Protectorate – a name which did not include the Lagos Colony and its protectorate. The Lagos Colony and Protectorate and the Southern Nigeria Protectorate were on 1 May 1906 amalgamated under one administration based in Lagos. Judicial unification lagged behind political amalgamation. It was not until 31 March 1908 that the whole of Southern Nigeria was brought under one judicial system.

In spite of variations in judicial arrangements in various parts of Southern Nigeria before 1908, the courts of law that were established did not differ much in their essential role. Anywhere in Southern Nigeria a British-established court served the dual function of forging some kind of formal relation between Nigerians and British, and of extending British influence generally. In substantiating this view, we shall, for convenience, look at the courts as they were established in the Niger Delta area, in the Lagos Colony and in Yorubaland, in that order. Throughout the discussion it should be borne in mind that the British-established courts did not entirely replace the indigenous judicial system. In matters wholly concerned with indigenes, the traditional courts continued to hold their own.

II

The earliest known English-style courts in Southern Nigeria were the so-called courts of equity set up in the Niger Delta states. The first was established in Bonny in 1854; by 1870 similar courts were found in Brass, Benin, Okrika, Opobo and Calabar.[6] Originally not a result of any grand design, the courts sprang up as a matter of necessity to administer some rough form of justice between Africans and European supercargoes trading along the Niger coast. They gained official recognition in 1872 when their jurisdiction in the Niger Delta was regularised.[7] They continued to operate until superseded about 1885 by other courts.

The origin of the name 'court of equity' for these courts is not clear. They probably took their name from the English courts of equity which, as was indicated earlier, operated side by side with the common law courts, administering rules of law different in origin and spirit from the common law. The Southern Nigeria courts of equity, like the English courts of the same name up till about the middle of the seventeenth century, grew up to administer justice without too much attention to technicalities, but with an eye to the essence of each particular case and the requirements of fairness and honesty. In the words of Thomas J. Hutchinson, Consul for the Bight of Biafra 1855–61, they were designed 'for the purpose of keeping commercial transactions between the European and Native traders on a proper basis of justice and honesty . . . [and] to hold the Natives true to the principles of fair and honest dealing'.[8] In the absence of any 'international codes of jurisprudence' to govern relations between Africans and European traders in the Niger Delta, the courts of equity were devised to serve the interest of commerce. They concerned themselves largely with trading disputes and with the regulation of matters of common interest to the European traders.

A court of equity could not be otherwise than informal. It was dominated by European traders, usually chief agents of principal trading firms, who presided in turn over the court's sessions. For obvious reasons the court administered no particular body of laws. Cases were decided on the basis of what the 'justice' of particular situations required. Often the trade customs prevailing in the court's area of jurisdiction were taken into account. Nor were the sessions of the court regular. At Calabar and some other places, the court was summoned as and when necessary. Apparently the court was actually convened only when sufficient number of its members indicated their willingness to attend.[9] Local African rulers or heads of houses (trading corporations in the Niger Delta) sat on the court, but it should be emphasised that the court remained 'an instrument of the European community'.[10] Local rulers and house heads were summoned only when the matter to be discussed required their participation. Decisions of the court were by a simple majority vote, and the usual penalty was a fine. Where the court was strong it could impose economic embargoes on those who refused to comply with its decisions.

An order in council regularising the operation of the courts in 1872 subjected them to the authority of the British consul stationed at Fernando Po. Rules of court were to be sanctioned by the consul and, in theory, all civil actions between British subjects came under his jurisdiction in the first place.[11]

In practice the consul was rarely available to provide any rigorous supervision of the courts, and no regulations for the conduct of the courts would seem to have been drawn up.[12] The courts consequently continued to operate very much on their own, calling in the assistance of the consul only when a situation was getting out of hand. Hence a court of equity was as strong or as weak as the local circumstances made it. King Jaja of Opobo, appearing for the plaintiff in *Oko Epella v. Goosey* before the Opobo court of equity on 13 May 1874, openly defied the court, indicating that he did not care for the consul or the court 'but would do what he liked'.[13] Acts of defiance were not limited to African potentates. When 'several charges of a serious nature', including fraud, were brought against one George Watts, a European trader, in October 1875 before the court of equity at Calabar, he 'entirely repudiated the court's authority'.[14] Only one member of the court indeed believed the court had any authority over him. The court was powerless to take any action. Agents of some British trading firms at Onitsha did organise a court of equity in the 1870s, 'wherein we tried to do justice and give satisfaction to any case that required attention'. But they discovered that 'every one was left to regard or disregard the decision of the body as his inclination might lead him'.[15] In contrast to these instances of weakness, in *Glassie v. Leigh*, a civil dispute involving two British subjects decided by the Supreme Court of Lagos in July 1884, the court of equity on the Brass river had earlier ordered the arrest of the plaintiff and had imprisoned him for theft.[16]

It would appear that a court of equity was powerless where vital African interests were touched upon. Alan Burns relates that the same Brass court of equity which imprisoned a European trader was in 1885 bullied by the local chiefs and forced to reverse its decisions. A member of the court, one Townsend, who complained of what he considered to be rude interruption on his beach by a 'disorderly crowd' of Brassmen, was said to have been fined by the chiefs two puncheons of palm oil 'for being proud'.[17]

As organs of judicial administration, courts of equity succeeded in achieving some degree of law and order in spite of the rudimentary nature of their organisation. They helped to discipline British traders, making them conform to local commercial rules and usages, principally through the power of economic boycott. It was a reflection of the importance attached to the courts by the

European community and of the degree of authority which they wielded that, in October 1885, when the National African Company (later the Royal Niger Company) purported to have made a contract with the chiefs and people of Aboh giving the company complete monopoly of trade in their area, the chairman of the company thought it essential to refer the contract to the court of equity at Bonny. The court refused to ratify it, handing down what amounted to a declaratory judgment in November 1885:

> Should the National African Company be allowed to make such treaties and have them duly legalized, as we believe they are expecting [us] to do, they will eventually monopolize the whole of the trade in the Oil Rivers . . .[18]

The importance of the courts transcended the judicial sphere. A court of equity performed some administrative and legislative functions, particularly with regard to the maintenance of harbours and trading 'beaches' and some minor public works in the local communities.[19] By virtue of their judicial and administrative functions, they also fostered British influence and authority in the Niger Delta. In Bonny and perhaps Opobo too, the authority of the court of equity would not seem to have been fully accepted.[20] But it is significant that in other places like Calabar and Brass the court of equity mediated in purely local disputes in which European interests were not involved. In Brass as many as fourteen chiefs could be present at a session of the court resolving an issue.[21] There is no doubt that in the courts of equity, another authority structure was building up independently of the traditional authorities. In the past, say up to the 1850s, the local ruler in most communities was the supreme authority and was so regarded by European traders who depended on him to provide the atmosphere conducive to trading. The court of equity was a tribunal not only for settling European disputes locally, but also for dealing with conflicts between Africans and European traders. Undoubtedly it marked a significant step in the establishment of British power and authority in the Niger Delta. For by the use of the court European traders and British officials were able to move away from the precincts of the African ruler and operate on the basis of an institution outside his purview. Not only did the court require no sanctions from the local ruler, in some instances it also exercised jurisdiction, formally or informally, over his subjects.

Mention should be made at this stage of the judicial powers

vested in the British Consul in the Niger Delta and of the judicial activities of the Royal Niger Company. By the 1872 Order-in-Council a set of judicial powers was prescribed for the consul independently of the jurisdiction of the courts of equity.[22] The consul's jurisdiction covered Old Calabar, Bonny, Cameroons, Degema, Brass, Opobo, Nun and Benin Rivers. He was empowered to make rules and regulations to enforce agreements, treaties or conventions entered into between the local chiefs and the British Government and also 'for the peace, order and good government of Her Majesty's subjects' in his area of jurisdiction. Apart from breaches of his regulations, he was empowered to try, with the aid of assessors, civil suits involving goods or property to the value of ₦200. He was to exercise criminal jurisdiction and could impose fines, banishment or terms of imprisonment. Arson, house-breaking, stabbing or wounding, perjury, 'engaging in or being accessory to the purchase or sale of slaves', and smuggling were specifically made criminal offences. He was given probate juris-diction over the estates of British subjects in the territory. Within his jurisdiction also fell admiralty cases involving merchant seamen, collision on the seas and the like.

The judicial powers of the consul were more formidable on paper than in reality. Up to about 1893 there was only one peri-patetic consular court: the consul himself adjudicating disputes with or without assessors wherever duty took him along the Niger Delta coast. Even today it would be an herculean task for a single officer to supervise the administration of the whole coastal stretch of Southern Nigeria. Besides the problem of communication and transport, the consul fairly frequently had to go on leave in England and could, therefore, not always be available. When in 1884 European traders on the Benin River complained that no consul had visited them for five years,[23] they were indeed pointing to a condition that was not uncommon in other parts of the Niger Delta. In fact, because of geographical and other difficulties, many areas remained inaccessible to the consul. Above all, he had no substantial force to back his orders. Naval aid was intermittent, and he had no police at his command. Not infrequently, he had to rely on such powerful local rulers as Jaja of Opobo and Nana of Itsekiri either to arbitrate in local disputes or as catspaws to advance British interests.[24]

It was fortunate from the British point of view that the men who were consuls in the Niger Delta in the nineteenth century –

in particular, John Beecroft, Hopkins, E. H. Hewett, Major C. M. MacDonald and Ralph Moor – were, generally, men of considerable energy, who, within the limitations imposed by the geography of Southern Nigeria, did entrench British influence in key areas of the Niger Delta, introducing elements of English law and judicial system in their administration.

The Royal Niger Company established courts of its own, mainly along the lower Niger basin. Since the late 1870s, the company, originally known as the United African Company, had assumed practical control of the Niger waterway and its riverain area. It was formally incorporated in July 1882 under the name National African Company. In 1886, in compensation for its treaty-making activities in the Niger basin, it was granted a royal charter and renamed the Royal Niger Company. The charter gave the company full powers of government and administration in its territories. Accordingly, it proceeded to set up its own machinery for the administration of justice.[25] The machinery remained in operation until the company's charter was revoked in December 1899.

Briefly, the district agents of the company exercised jurisdiction over all persons in their districts – Britons, foreigners and Nigerians alike – and were empowered to try certain categories of civil and criminal cases. A Supreme Court was also instituted over which sat a Chief Justice and one or more judges. The court was located at the company's headquarters at Asaba, exercising wide civil and criminal jurisdictions over all persons. It had the final say in certain matters, while the company made itself the final judicial authority in others. In the various districts under the company's administration, as in other places in Southern Nigeria coming under British influence, the local traditional courts continued to function. Indeed the company in its charter was required to respect the laws, customs and institutions of the indigenes, if only in so far as they were not 'repugnant to humanity'.

In the Niger Coast Protectorate courts of equity gave way to governing councils after 1885. With the formal declaration of a protectorate over the Niger Delta in that year, it appeared that a more systematic arrangement for the administration of justice was required. Governing councils were organised by Harry H. Johnston, then acting consul, first at Opobo and later at Brass, Bonny, Degema and Calabar. In spite of the disapproval of the Colonial Office mentioned by some writers, the councils functioned in these areas until about 1891.

A governing council met weekly to transact its business. It comprised the consul as president, a vice-president and a clerk, both Europeans, and about thirteen other members, including about five African chiefs and eight European traders. Its powers were limited to 'the carrying out of Consular orders, the preservation of peace, the maintenance of highways and means of communication, the regulation of commerce and the hearing in court of minor civil actions and criminal charges'.[26] The council's power of punishment was limited. It could not inflict a fine exceeding ten naira in value, a term of imprisonment beyond one week or corporal punishment 'to a greater extent than twelve lashes'. In a criminal case, if the accused person appeared to the majority of the council to deserve a greater measure of punishment than the council could inflict, the case should be submitted to the consul who would, if necessary, issue a written order for the infliction of the heavier punishment.

Compared with the courts of equity, governing councils gave Britain a greater grip over the areas of the Niger Delta where they operated. A governing council was much more than a mere device of merchants backed by consular authority. As the constitution of the Brass Governing Council indicates, a council was tied directly to the consular authority. It had to meet regularly, executing the consul's orders or its own orders, which were now referred to as ordinances.[27] Three members of the council could constitute a quorum – a reflection of Britain's seriousness of purpose in establishing her authority in Southern Nigeria. It is important to note, too, that the placid days when a local ruler could choose to defy the orders of a British-established court seemed to be over. A governing council had jurisdiction over cases in which Africans and African interests were involved. In trying such cases notice must be given to the 'native members' of the council 'so that an opportunity may be given them to attend'. If they absented themselves, 'they can raise no after objection to the decision or verdict of the Council which has been given in their absence'.[28] The increasing tempo of British assertion of its authority through the governing councils is obvious.

The 1890s witnessed further strengthening of the judicial machinery being evolved in the Niger Coast Protectorate. An order of 1892 empowered the judicial institutions in the protectorate to exercise jurisdiction over foreigners of nationalities other than British. Again, on the (false) assumption that the chiefs and elders of the various communities in the protectorate 'were quite willing and anxious to put themselves under a more direct Imperial administration than had hitherto existed',[29] the courts of the protectorate were reorganised in 1893. Instead of only one consular court for the whole protectorate, each Delta state was to have its own with jurisdiction similar to that of the old consular court. By 1898 there were eight consular courts in the protectorate.[30]

Besides the consular courts, there were also varieties of 'native' courts. These latter courts were the handiwork of Sir Claude MacDonald, Commissioner and Consul-General of the protectorate, 1891–5, and his successor, Sir Ralph Moor. They were built on the basic notion now being established in the protectorate of select Nigerians sharing in the administration of public order. Like the courts of equity and the governing councils, they also performed judicial as well as administrative functions. By the time MacDonald left in 1895, there were such courts at Calabar, Bonny, Degema, Buguma, Itu and a few other places.[31] Three years later, Sir Ralph Moor had increased the number to twenty-three in the protectorate, called by different names at different places.[32] Some were presided over by British administrative officers, like the High Court of the Native Council of Old Calabar, and some others, usually called 'minor courts', were presided over by local chiefs under the supervision of British administrative officers. By 1898 it had also become established that Nigerians who sat on the courts did so by virtue of the warrants issued to them by the British authorities, and they thus came to be known as warrant chiefs.[33] Few of these British-appointed chiefs had any traditional backing. The vast majority of them 'were either scoundrels or just ordinary young men of no special standing in the indigenous society'.[34] It may be mentioned in passing that the mere elevation of this new brand of chiefs as collaborators with the British administration had a disruptive influence on the socio-political structure of these areas.

At least up till the end of the First World War, the political functions of the 'native' courts would appear to be more important than their judicial functions. A Nigerian historian has expressed the view that British political penetration of the hinterland of Southern Nigeria 'was accompanied by the establishment of Native courts'.[35] One may indeed argue with considerable justification that the British political penetration of the territory was accomplished through the instrument of the courts.

The fact was that 'native' courts were very much part of the process of subjugation of Southern Nigeria by the British. Everywhere they were 'expected to give stability and permanence' to what had been achieved by force of arms.[36] In official eyes they were seen not as mere judicial institutions, 'but as instruments for bringing under effective administrative control the areas in which they were established'.[37] The organisation of 'native' courts was 'one of the most essential things for the control and welfare' of any area; for a court of some sort was usually the nucleus of an administrative machine. The local chiefs who sat on it at once became more or less servants of the colonial administration, performing administrative and judicial functions, thus relieving the European officials of 'a large amount of labour'. The higher grades of 'native' courts, up to about 1914 presided over by colonial officials, had legislative functions. They were allowed and encouraged to 'make necessary native laws affecting the tribes which they represent and over which they have control'.[38] Over and above these functions, 'native' courts and 'native' councils played an important educative role. They provided the means of instructing the chiefs 'in the proper methods of government and the administration of justice'.[39] Sir Ralph Moor was certainly not exaggerating when he wrote in 1899 that these institutions were rendering 'very material assistance' in the control and organisation of Southern Nigeria as a colonial territory.[40] It should be remembered too that by associating some Nigerians with the operation of the 'native' courts and the 'native' councils, the British were creating local interest-groups in the colonial regime that was being established.

The creation of the Southern Nigeria Protectorate in 1900 – an amalgamation of the territories of the Royal Niger Company and the Niger Coast Protectorate – brought about some judicial reorganisation in line with the new, enlarged administration. The reorganisation was contained in the three proclamations mentioned earlier: the Supreme Court Proclamation, the Commissioners Proclamation and the Native Courts Proclamation.

By the Supreme Court Proclamation, No. 6, 1900, the Supreme Court of Southern Nigeria was established with full original and appellate jurisdiction throughout the protectorate. The court was to be a superior court of record exercising, 'so far as circumstances admit', the same jurisdiction and powers as those of the High Court of justice in England. The court had full jurisdiction over all other courts in the protectorate. For the Chief Justice was empowered to transfer any case 'at any time and at any stage thereof' from any court to any other court 'with or without application from any of the parties thereto'.[41]

The Commissioners' Proclamation established commissioners' courts which were to be presided over by administrative officers as commissioners. The commissioner (also later known as the district officer) was, in his judicial activities generally subject to the directions of the Supreme Court. He was empowered to constitute himself into a divisional court of the Supreme Court, exercising the powers of a judge of the Supreme Court. The commissioner's court administered the same law as the Supreme Court: the common law, the principles of equity and the statutes of general application in force in England on 1 January 1900.[42]

The Native Courts Proclamation[43] was designed 'to systematise the practices and experiences of the years of the Niger Coast Protectorate' in the running of local judicial institutions. The 'native' courts were divided into two categories: minor courts and 'native' councils. A minor court comprised such members as were appointed by the district commissioner. The court was to elect its own president, a local traditional chief or a 'warrant' chief, who would normally officiate for a short period of three months. Under the supervision of the district commissioner, the court tried minor civil and criminal cases.

A 'native' council, located at the district headquarters, was at once a legislative and judicial body. It was presided over by the district commissioner and consisted of Nigerians holding judicial warrants from the High Commissioner (the chief officer of the protectorate) or his representative. As a judicial body, it could entertain civil suits involving goods or property not exceeding ₦400 in value. In its criminal jurisdiction, it could impose up to two years' imprisonment or levy a fine of up to ₦200. It also heard appeals from the minor courts within its area of jurisdiction. A litigant dissatisfied with its decision could, in certain categories of cases, apply to the district commissioner for leave to appeal to the Supreme Court. In its legislative capacity, a 'native' council was empowered to make rules, subject to the approval of the High Commissioner or his representative, to regulate and promote trade, to embody any native law and custom in its district, or, generally, to provide 'for the peace, good order and welfare' of the inhabitants of the district. Much hope was pinned on the councils as agents of change. They were, in official eyes, potentially, 'the most powerful and rapidly acting influence tending to elevate the natives'.[44]

In the judicial system set up over the Southern Nigeria Protectorate, the 'native' courts were the closest to the indigenous people. It is not surprising that within three years the provisions relating to them were twice amended to bring the courts more fully under the control of administrative officials. A proclamation of 1901 gave 'native' courts exclusive jurisdiction in its area of authority. A 'native' court in any district was henceforth to exercise its jurisdiction 'exclusive of all other native jurisdictions . . . and no jurisdiction shall be exercised in such district by any other native authority whatsoever'.[45] Henceforth, at least in theory, the traditional village councils and age-grades could no longer legally administer justice or execute any judgments.

An instruction issued by Ralph Moor to one of his officers in 1902 showed the extent to which the colonial regime was determined to have full control of judicial authority in the protectorate. All courts of justice, he wrote, 'must be properly constituted' as such courts were 'the only legal means of administering justice in these territories'.[46] Time was, he said, when political officers were allowed 'to assist and advise the chiefs in legislating in cases brought before them as chiefs'. But this method of administration was no longer to be tolerated; it should be done away with 'as soon as practicable and proper Native courts (were) established'.[47]

The other amendment to the provisions relating to the 'native' courts was a proclamation of 1903 which made a district commissioner a member of all the 'native' courts in his district.[48] This amendment was in line with the growing trend in the protectorate for the 'native' court to become more and more a tool in the hands of the administrative officer.

By 1903 Britain would seem to have established her influence in the Southern Nigeria Protectorate. She had succeeded to some extent through the courts in establishing her presence in this portion of Southern Nigeria. But to what extent were the indigenes employing the new judicial machinery that was being imposed on them by proclamations? There were some indications here and there that Nigerians were resorting to the new courts, but one should be sceptical about reports, official and non-official, indicating enthusiastic acceptance of the new judicial machinery. When in 1898 Harold Bindloss reported that the consular courts in the Niger Coast Protectorate were readily resorted to by Africans, sending in their criminal offenders to be tried, or bringing their trade disputes to be settled 'according to the judgment of the white soldiers',[49] one should not imagine a wholesale abandonment by the local population of their traditional courts. Those who were most prone to resort to the consular courts were not the indigenes, but the stranger elements in their midst – Nigerians from other parts of the country or other Africans from as far afield as the Gold Coast (Ghana) or Sierra Leone. This was the situation at Calabar,[50] and it was most probably true of other consular stations in the Niger Delta. The official report in 1898 that increasing consular court sessions indicated 'a growing desire for judicial adjustment of trade accounts between natives and Europeans' or that the records of the courts 'showed every year a practically widening criminal jurisdiction'[51] should be read in the same light.

The jurisdiction of the Supreme Court was practically limited to Europeans and other stranger elements. In fact it was not in a position to exercise any wider jurisdiction largely because, in the nineteenth century and early this century, it had neither the personnel nor the resources to operate effectively. 'It has always been a matter of great difficulty here to get suitable men' to man the judicial department, reported H. G. Kelly, the Chief Justice of the protectorate in 1903.[52] In the Royal Niger Company's territory before 1900, and in the Southern Nigeria Protectorate, the Supreme Court dealt mainly with cases involving foreigners and mostly with commercial disputes.[53]

As for the different varieties of 'native' courts, it took a fairly long time before the local population was reconciled to their operation. The colonial administration indeed sometimes had to resort to the use of force to compel attendance at the courts.[54] The district commissioner stationed at Warri reported in 1902 that he was experiencing 'considerable difficulty' in getting the indigenes to attend the courts even with the use of court summonses.[55] The numerous military expeditions in the Southern Nigeria Protectorate lasting until the first decade of this century, some of which were, in fact, directed against communities that had mounted attacks on British-established judicial institutions, provide ample evidence of the opposition Britain encountered in the process of forcing the people to resort to the judicial institutions she established in the territory. In the area of Afikpo in 1902, it was reported that the local population continued to employ their time-honoured judicial system of trial by ordeal – the existence of British-established 'native' courts notwithstanding.[56] Sometimes the courts were simply ignored. It was reported in Kwale District as late as 1908 that cases of theft were being tried outside the 'native' courts so that serious penalties might be imposed on the offenders, and that clubs had been formed to give effect to the heavy punishments inflicted by the traditional courts now operating more or less surreptitiously.[57]

But by and large the indigenous people of the Protectorate came to reconcile themselves to the British-established judicial institutions. This was particularly true of areas where the colonial administration had demonstrated its determination to use force. A general report on the 'native' courts in the protectorate in 1903 showed that a fair proportion of the 41 courts in the territory were becoming an integral part of the administrative system of their respective areas of jurisdiction.[58] If official reports by administrative officers are anything to go by, more and more cases were being taken to the courts.[59] This situation is not necessarily a reflection of the 'ample confidence in the administration of justice' by the 'native' courts, as administrative officers and some writers have claimed,[60] or of the extent to which the indigenes appreciated the value of the courts, but of the realisation by all and sundry that the British were becoming the predominant political force to reckon with in Southern Nigeria. In the face of the military expeditions and of the defeat suffered by all those who stood in opposition, it would not have been difficult to appreciate that the fulcrum of power in the territory was shifting gradually but surely to the British. To turn to the British-established courts was either a matter of practical wisdom, when to do so might tip the scale of justice in one's favour, or simply a matter of compulsion when the British officers would not tolerate any other kind of open court but their own.

III

As in some other parts of Southern Nigeria, the introduction of English law and English-style courts into the Lagos Colony was initially a response to the needs of commerce and the requirements of a population growing cosmopolitan in outlook. Since the beginning of the nineteenth century, European traders and agents of European mercantile houses had been actively engaged in the commercial life of Lagos and, as time went on, many took up more or less permanent residence. At the time when Lagos was formally created a British settlement in 1862, there were 22 British and European traders in Lagos.[61] The census of 1881 estimated the white population of the colony to be 117.[62] There were also 68 people classified as mulatto. The white population of Lagos continued to increase. There were 150 in 1894, and 1,648 by 1912.[63] It is obvious that the traditional legal and judicial system of the indigenous population would be inadequate to meet the needs of these foreign elements in the colony in regulating their inter-personal relations. Nor were Europeans and mulattoes the only foreign element in the population. Since the 1850s, Sierra Leonean and Brazilian immigrants – liberated ex-slaves or descendants of former slaves – had been settling in the colony. They knew of no legal system besides the Western or European one in conducting their personal affairs. An indication of the inadequacy of the traditional machinery of justice in meeting their needs is the fact that they set up their own court at Bankole Street, Olowo-gbowo.[64]

Then there were the needs of commerce. Brand, the British consul in Lagos, summed up the situation in 1860:

> Lagos at present may be said to have no Government; there is no effective protection to property, no mode of enforcing the payment of debts applicable to Europeans, and the wonder is that in such a state of things there are so few disturbances . . . [In] a large and increasing commercial community, there are questions of great importance affecting trade and property frequently arising which the Consul has not the means, even if he had the authority, of dealing with in a satisfactory manner . . .[65]

Out of sheer necessity the British consulate in Lagos had, since the 1850s, exercised 'a feeble, irregular, and irresponsible jurisdiction' over diverse matters – judicial, police, administrative – which fell outside the consul's scope of duties. This irregular jurisdiction of the consul was said to have been 'acquiesced in as a matter of necessity' by various sections of the Lagos community, but it did not particularly meet the needs of commerce. By 1857, in spite of the consul's jurisdiction, it had become 'next to impossible . . . to enforce payment of just and undisputed debts'.[66] The courts of Sierra Leonean and Brazilian immigrants used to serve some purpose, but they had proved inadequate.[67] Their limited and inadequate jurisdiction was further hamstrung in 1857 when the law officers at the Foreign Office in London ruled that the courts could not exercise jurisdiction over people other than the immigrants themselves and members of the indigenous population.[68] In the face of these difficulties relating to the enforcement of payment of debts and the conduct of commerce generally, the prospects for foreign trade in Lagos seemed bleak. At least one British merchant decided to withdraw his commercial activities from Lagos.[69] It was on account of the difficulties and in order 'to increase the legal commerce and industrial prosperity' of the colony that Consul Brand, in 1860, urged Britain to occupy it. Such a measure, he believed, would ensure 'a regular administration of justice' and protection to property.[70]

But the occupation of Lagos in 1861 meant the establishment of a formal British administration. This, in turn, hastened the establishment of formal courts of justice as an indispensable arm of government.

Although Lagos was formally declared a British colony, and although the necessity for English-style judicial machinery was plain to every colonial administrator in the colony, the establishment of courts in this part of Southern Nigeria was by no means a straightforward affair. For one thing, as will be shown presently, the colonial administration in Lagos throughout the nineteenth century suffered from a serious lack of qualified personnel – a problem which was, in fact, not limited to the judicial sphere. For another, the circumstances of Lagos did not favour large-scale judicial innovations. The majority of the people in the colony were illiterate, 'unused to the (to them) somewhat slow procedure of English law'.[71] Moreover, in the 1860s and 1870s the British hold on Lagos was as yet uncertain. As late as 1872, it was reported, 'hostilities were imminent without, and civil war within the settlement'.[72] Distrust of the colonial regime was very much in evidence. Among the indigenous population, it was said, 'the desire exists for the old state of things'.[73] In these circumstances, quite apart from the problem of personnel, it was not expedient to introduce any far-reaching innovations in the judicial sphere, or indeed in any other, that might deepen the suspicions of the indigenous population and excite ill-feeling. John Hawley Glover, the colony's Administrator, 1863–72, made it his policy to adapt English law and an English judicial system 'by judicious administration' to the requirements and circumstances of the colony.[74]

The establishment of English-style judicial institutions in Lagos up to about 1874 was characterised by improvisation. By March 1862 four courts had been 'temporarily established' by H. S. Freeman, the first Governor of the colony.[75] These were the police court, the criminal court, the slave court and the commercial court – all of them evidently designed to serve areas of pressing need in the life of the colony. The police court settled 'all petty cases', and conducted preliminary hearings in the more serious cases which were usually reserved for the criminal court. The slave court dealt with cases concerning runaway slaves, apprenticeship, emancipation and so on, while the commercial court was concerned with questions of debts, commercial contracts and the like.

This rudimentary judicial system was to undergo many alterations.[76] An ordinance of 9 April 1863 'to provide for the better administration of justice' established 'The Supreme Court of Her Majesty's Settlement of Lagos' to be presided over by a chief magistrate or his deputy. A Chief Justice was substituted for the chief magistrate as the president of the court by an ordinance of February 1864. The court was supposed to exercise the same civil and criminal jurisdiction as the High Court in England. But, in obvious consideration for the colonial environment in which it had to operate in Lagos, appeals lay from it to the Governor-in-Council, a purely political or administrative body. In July 1864 the court was renamed 'The Chief Magistrate's Court'. It now had equity jurisdiction, and for the first time, the jury system was introduced into Lagos. By Ordinance No. 5 of June 1865, the jury system was to be limited only to capital offences.

The commercial court of 1862 was renamed the Petty Debt Court by the same instrument which established the Supreme Court in 1863. Like the latter court, the Petty Debt Court also had a somewhat chequered career. In 1863 it had jurisdiction over cases 'in which the debts, claims, compensation or damages demanded or the matter in dispute' did not exceed one hundred naira. By Ordinance No. 6 of 1864, the court's jurisdiction had been scaled down to personal actions involving not more than forty naira. Again, the court had no jurisdiction over cases involving title to land, will or settlement, malicious prosecution, defamation, seduction and breach of promise of marriage. Before and after 1864 appeals lay from the court to the Supreme Court whose decision was final. The establishment of the Petty Debt Court was never confirmed by the Colonial Office – an indication of the 'highly irregular circumstances' in which some of the courts in Lagos operated.[77] The court's 'illegal' existence was brought to an end in 1870 when it was superseded by the Court of Requests, which exercised virtually the same jurisdictions.

The Slave Commission Court which had been temporarily set up in 1862 was formally established by an ordinance of 28 October 1864. The court continued to serve a useful purpose in protecting Africans liberated from slavery, apprenticing them to practitioners of various trades, and in determining the amount of compensation payable to their former owners. Regulations were now drawn up for achieving these ends.

The establishment of the Court of Civil and Criminal Justice by Ordinance No. 7 of December 1866 followed the administrative unification of all the British settlements and colonies in West Africa under one Governor-in-Chief in Sierra Leone. This new court now superseded the Supreme Court or Chief Magistrate's Court. Apparently it exercised no jurisdiction in equity or bankruptcy and would appear to have been made a less competent tribunal than the High Court in England. Its powers of punishment were also limited. Any judgment of the court in a criminal case resulting in the sentencing of the accused person to more than twelve calendar months with hard labour could not be carried out until after a full report of the proceedings in the case had been submitted to the Governor.

The West African Court of Appeal, established in 1867 for all the West African colonies, was a reflection of the strong yearning in British official circles (based largely on considerations of economy) for the administrative unification of the colonies.[78] The court was established in Sierra Leone and was intended to hear civil and criminal appeal cases from the superior courts of all the British colonies in West Africa. The court, however, was short-lived. The administrative unification of the colonies effected in 1866 came to an end in 1874 when Lagos and the Gold Coast were constituted as one colony. The new Colony of the Gold Coast (of which Lagos remained a part until 1886) had a judicial arrangement independent of that of Sierra Leone. But the idea of a West African court of appeal was not dead; it was to be revived in 1928.[79] It should also be pointed out here that since February 1867, an appeal could be made to the Privy Council in London in certain categories of civil cases.[80]

Two other courts established in Lagos before 1874 were the Vice-Admiralty Court, established to deal, among other things, with all matters relating to shipping, and the Court of Divorce and Matrimonial Causes, set up in 1872.

The creation of the Colony of the Gold Coast in 1874 to comprise Lagos and the Gold Coast proper brought about perhaps the most notable single development in the legal history of Lagos in the nineteenth century. This was the systematisation of the colony's judicial administration by the Supreme Court Ordinance, No. 4, 1876.[81] Under the ordinance, a Supreme Court, comprising a Chief Justice and four puisne judges, was set up for the enlarged Colony of Lagos and the Gold Coast. The English law to be applied in the court was spelt out in detail, and formal recognition was given to the indigenous law.[82] Detailed provisions were also made for the personnel of the court, principally the barristers and solicitors appearing before it.[83] For convenience, divisional courts of the Supreme Court were set up in each colony, and certain categories of district commissioners were empowered to exercise the powers of a judge of the Supreme Court in the outlying districts. Appeals lay from the divisional courts to the full court which was the Supreme Court with at least three judges on the Bench, including the Chief Justice. The full court was to sit at least once a year. Until 1886 when Lagos was separated from the Gold Coast, it appears that the decisions of the Lagos divisional court were also subject to appeal to the divisional court of the Gold Coast proper.

The rather impressive array of courts in Lagos between 1862 and 1876 should not give one a wrong picture of the judicial machinery in the colony. Improvisation was the keynote in this period of judicial administration, and, to some extent, the multiplicity of courts was a reflection of this fact. The establishment of many of the courts was rather irregular. By the end of 1865, for instance, only two of the courts which were said to have been established had been regularly constituted.[84] Names of courts 'were changed almost as frequently as their constitutions'. and quite a considerable number of the courts were short-lived. It is clear that not much forethought was given to the establishment of the courts. Until after 1876 no consistent effort was made to place the judicial system on a sound footing.[85] No rules of court were drawn up for the courts in Lagos until 1870.[86] As late as 1874, it was reported, 'there were no books of reference in the Chief Magistrate's office bearing upon legal questions'.[87]

Nor were the courts as well organised as one may be inclined to believe from a mere description of them. For many years the Chief Magistrate's Court (formerly, the Supreme Court), the Commercial Court, the Petty Debt Court, the Slave Commission Court and one or two others were all held 'in a mudhouse with thatch roof at the corner of Broad and Kakawa Streets' in Lagos.[88] Up to about 1906, there was never more than one legal officer with a legal professional background operating in Lagos at one time.[89] In such circumstances, it was inevitable that the same personnel sat on more than two or three courts.

Again, in practice, the courts did not function regularly. This fact is attested to by the fairly constant complaints in the press that many of the courts were dormant for considerable lengths of time.[90] It was reported in November 1872 that the Court of Civil and Criminal Justice sat for only fourteen days during the previous six months. Generally, at least up to 1872, 'it rarely, if ever, occurs that more than one court is sitting at the same time'.[91] Even after the reorganisation of 1876, the situation hardly improved. The judges of the Supreme Court of Lagos spent much of their time on the Gold Coast 'to act for ailing or absent colleagues'. For five years, between 1881 and 1886, no court of appeal was held in Lagos.[92]

One explanation for the irregularity of court sessions in Lagos was the apparently limited scope of the legal business in the colony. In July 1877, David P. Chalmers, the Chief Justice of the Supreme Court of the Gold Coast Colony, expressed the view that the business transacted at the Supreme Court of Lagos 'does not appear at present to be such as to render it indispensable that the Court should be in constant session'.[93] There appears to be some justification for the Chief Justice's view. In the period 1867–74, the highest court in Lagos, the Court of Civil and Criminal Justice, dealt with only 505 civil cases involving a total claim of ₦395,152.[95]

The fact was that in the nineteenth century and early this century, the use of the English-style courts was limited largely to the immigrant and foreign elements in Lagos, the vast majority of the indigenous population settling disputes *inter se* at the Oba's court at Idunganran, Isale Eko,[95] or at the informal courts of the community elders. They did, of course, resort to the English-style courts – to answer summonses or, as in *Banjoko v. Tiwo* (1877)[96] involving rival claims to property, to see whether the new British-established judicial machinery might secure to a litigant a claim that had been denied him by a private traditional court. Apart from the technicalities of the law and the novelty of the English judicial procedure, for the majority of the indigenous population, a deterrent factor in the use of the courts was the costly nature of the judicial proceedings there. For the man in the street, it might be impossible to employ an attorney to pursue a claim in court. Although in many cases the courts encouraged parties to a dispute to appear for themselves, the legal fee in pursuing a claim could be as high as ₦60.[97] By the 1890s there were cries against the high costs of legal actions, or what a Lagos newspaper called 'the rapacious legal exactions'.[98]

Irregularity of court sessions also stemmed partly from inadequacy of qualified personnel. The first fully qualified legal practitioner in Lagos, Christopher Alexander Sapara Williams, made his appearance in 1880, eighteen years after the first English-style courts were established.[99] Before, self-taught attorneys with more or less rudimentary knowledge of the law operated in the courts. On account of the shortage of qualified legal practitioners, they continued to serve in the courts until early this century.[100] Similarly, there were not enough qualified judges. Of the seven men who served as the chief magistrate for Lagos between 1862 and 1905, only three were qualified barristers or solicitors. Of the remaining four, two were 'writing clerks', one was a merchant and the fourth was a commander of the West India garrison at Lagos. Of the fourteen who were police magistrates in the same period, four were merchants, six were military officers, two were colonial surgeons, one was a retired naval officer, and one was a deputy collector of customs.[101] Besides the problem of lack of qualified judges, the judiciary was not immune to the difficulties created by what an educated African termed the abominable system of leave-taking by the European officers in the colonial administration which deprived Lagos of their services 'for a great part of the time'.[102]

IV

English-style judicial institutions were established relatively late in the interior of Yorubaland which is the last area of Southern Nigeria we are considering. No chartered company operated here, setting up its own courts and administrative system. Nor were there anything like the slave-trade treaties of the 1840s and 1850s in the Niger Delta which could have served as pretext for early British intervention in this part of the territory. Again, it was not until fairly late in the nineteenth century that British and other foreign traders were actively engaged in Yorubaland, creating the type of problems in their commercial dealings with the indigenous population that necessitated the setting up of courts of equity in the Niger Delta in an earlier period. The atmosphere was perhaps not particularly encouraging to foreign commercial penetration. For much of the nineteenth century Yorubaland was in the grip of recurrent civil wars which were not formally brought to an end until 1893.[103]

It is worth noting, too, that the treaties which Britain made with a number of key indigenous Yoruba authorities seem to have precluded a direct and immediate imposition of English law and an English-style judicial system. These treaties began in 1886 when the British administration in Lagos, anxious to preserve the trade links between the colony and the hinterland, sought to bring the Yoruba civil wars to a close. The Ekitiparapo confederacy joined in the general treaty for peace and friendship made in that year on the strength of the guarantee which was given for the recognition of Ekiti independence.[104] In 1888 the kingdoms of Ife and Otta were recognised as 'perfectly independent', paying tribute 'to no other power and territory'.[105] In 1893 the British Government declared that the independence of the Egba territory 'shall be fully recognized'.[106] By and large, the treaties of the nineteenth century in Yorubaland gave the British no jurisdiction in the country. The colonial government in Lagos seemed conscious of this fact. No less an official than the Governor himself, Sir William MacGregor, declared in 1903 that in the administration of Yorubaland, British hands were tied by 'the network of treaties' with the indigenous rulers, some of which recognised the independence of some of the states, and none of which could serve as a pretext for direct administration.

But the same factors which necessitated the establishment of English-style judicial institutions in Lagos or the Niger Delta were also at work in Yorubaland towards the end of the nineteenth century. Commercial contacts between the Yoruba and the foreign elements in their midst were on the increase,[107] creating the problem of adjudicating disputes. Not only would the traditional judicial machinery fail to serve the needs of the non-Yoruba; it would also not meet the complex problems arising from modern commercial dealings. Towards the end of the century, Britain was also establishing footholds in parts of Yorubaland; the need was arising for some judico-administrative machinery to underpin the jurisdiction she was *de facto* assuming. It is a reflection of the necessity for this type of machinery that British officials were exercising jurisdiction in judicial matters before they were legally empowered to do so. In 1899, the Resident for Ijebu-Ode district reported that he held a court twice a week during the year, the proceedings of the court being 'according to the Jebu custom which I did not interfere with unless probably unjust'.[108] By the same year the Resident for Ibadan and his representatives at the out-stations, the travelling commissioners, had each constituted himself into a sort of appeal court for cases heard in the traditional courts of the chiefs.[109] It had also become an established practice for the Resident to go on circuit, so to speak, to the several towns under the jurisdiction of Ibadan, deciding petty cases.[110] In the city of Ibadan itself, an (illegal) advisory court comprising the Resident, the Bale and his chiefs was set up in 1901 to determine 'all cases in which Europeans are concerned'.[111] In Oyo district, 'serious cases such as murder, arson, and revolt are referred to the resident'.[112] From Abeokuta the British Resident Commissioner reported in May 1903: 'I have been hearing civil cases and must continue to do so to prevent the country falling into a state of anarchy.'[113]

The informal judicial powers being exercised by British officials proved inadequate to meet the growing complexities of commercial and other cases arising in the interior of Yorubaland. It was still necessary, from the British point of view, to establish a more competent judicial system. Again, in view of the existing treaties recognising the independence of some of the traditional authorities, it was also necessary to regularise the judicial powers being exercised in this part of the country. These twin objectives were achieved through a series of judicial agreements made by the Governor of Lagos with the key Yoruba traditional rulers between January 1904 and November 1908. The rulers who were the signatories to the treaties have been mentioned earlier.[114]

Some technical differences apart, the essence of the judicial agreements was the same. In their respective areas of Yorubaland, the agreement purported to have given to the British:

Power and jurisdiction over all persons not being natives for the repression and punishment of all crimes and offences.

Power and jurisdiction over all persons whomsoever for the repression and punishment of the crimes of murder and manslaughter.

Power and jurisdiction for the administration and control of the property and persons of all persons not being natives.

Power and jurisdiction for the judicial hearing and determination of matters in difference where one or both of the parties is not a native.[115]

A significant provision in the agreements with Abeokuta, Ibadan and Ijebu-Ode, which has been discussed elsewhere,[116] was the clause in which the ruling authorities were said to have declared 'that it is their strong desire that barristers and solicitors shall not be allowed to practise in the courts exercising the civil jurisdiction hereinbefore acknowledged'.

Egba territory was treated differently from the other Yoruba states. In the Egba judicial agreement, provision was made for the establishment of a mixed court, an institution not duplicated elsewhere in Southern Nigeria.[117] This special treatment was, in part, a recognition of Egba independence, formally acknowledged by the British in 1893. It was also a reflection of the official belief, well-founded to a considerable extent, that in the way of European culture, the Egba were more advanced than the other Yoruba groups.[118] The mixed court was to consist of a president (an English magistrate to be appointed by the Lagos administration), and two other members to be appointed by the Egba council. The court continued to function until September 1914, its jurisdiction being limited to civil cases in which 'one or both of the parties are not natives of Egbaland'.

Further references will be made in this and subsequent chapters to the judicial agreements in Yorubaland, 1904–8. It is useful at this point to estimate their significance.

The importance of the agreements transcended their original purpose, to introduce the English legal system (albeit in a modified form) into Yorubaland as a means of safeguarding British commercial interests. Sir William MacGregor might be patting himself on the back when he declared in July 1904 that the judicial agreements were 'great changes [and] perhaps the most important ever made in the political state of the hinterland'.[119] Yet there is an element of truth in his assertion, for the judicial agreements were of crucial importance in the establishment of British authority in Yorubaland.

In this connection, the agreements differed in one vital respect from the earlier agreements made with the various Yoruba authorities in the 1880s and 1890s. These agreements aimed at establishing 'friendship' and commercial relations with the British and their terms were no more than pious declarations of Britain's wishes. They would not have been considered by the Yoruba authorities to be harmful to their interests.[120] But unlike these agreements, the judicial agreements of 1904-8 imposed a definite and substantive obligation on the Yoruba rulers. Under British leadership, they were to operate a judicial machine to deal with all indictable offences and with disputes arising between their subjects and British subjects. It is important to note that the new judicial machine – the Supreme Court of the Lagos Colony holding sessions in the interior – lay beyond their control. In view of the fact, already noted, that administration of justice was only one aspect of the exercise of political authority in most African societies, the judicial agreements struck a decisive blow against the sovereignty of the Yoruba states. The ultimate power to redress grievances, and thereby maintain peace and order is, traditionally, indivisible. The judicial agreements sought to divide that power, and consequently undermine the sovereignty of the states. It is true that under the judicial agreements, the Supreme Court of the Lagos Colony exercised its direct jurisdiction in only the five municipalities of Oyo, Ibadan, Ife, Abeokuta and Ijebu-Ode. But these were the important nerve-centres of Yorubaland and the agreements covered every town and village under their respective authorities. Certainly the agreements strengthened the hands of British officials trying civil and criminal cases in the outer districts in cooperation with local chiefs as assessors.

In terms of the colonial domination of this part of the country, three powers acquired by the Lagos administration under the judicial agreements were particularly important. There was, first, the power to try all criminal offences, which implied power to try even criminal offences committed by the subjects of the indigenous rulers. The second was power over 'the administration and control of the property . . . of all persons not being natives', which could be interpreted to mean power to devise laws to safeguard the economic interests of British nationals in the territory. The third power was implied in the stipulation that indigenous laws and customs were to apply in the adjudication of disputes only in so far as they were not 'repugnant to natural justice, equity and good conscience'. This stipulation, in effect, meant the subjection of the indigenous laws and customs to British standards of law and justice – in short, the supremacy of English law.

The agreements also marked an important beginning in the introduction of English legal ideas into the Yoruba society. To make the newly acquired jurisdiction in Yorubaland a reality, English law and English judicial processes were formally extended in to the region. By a series of four jurisdiction ordinances enacted in 1904 and 1909, the Supreme Court of Lagos Colony was empowered to exercise jurisdiction in Egbaland, and in the territories of Oyo, Ibadan, Ife and Ijebu.[121] Throughout these territories, the Supreme Court was given exclusive homicide jurisdiction, civil jurisdiction in 'mixed' cases where one of the parties was a foreigner, and general criminal jurisdiction over all foreigners. Provision was made for the observance of 'native laws and customs' where these were not repugnant to natural justice and humanity.

By the judicial agreements and the jurisdiction ordinances, the Supreme Court of Lagos Colony would, for the most part, handle two categories of cases in the interior of Yorubaland: cases between parties who were both non-Yoruba and the so-called 'mixed cases' in which one party was a Yoruba, and the other a foreigner. It is arguable that the two categories of cases carried with them the necessity of having to apply the English law. In disputes between parties who were non-Yoruba, local laws would obviously not apply. With regard to the 'mixed' cases, judges of the Supreme Court were to respect 'native laws and customs'. But it is difficult to see how they could have done so to any great extent, particularly since one of the parties was non-Yoruba. As with the first category of cases, these, too, were most likely to be decided on the principles of English law, modified as local circumstances dictated. It is a fact worth emphasising that the English judges presiding over sessions of the Supreme Court in the interior of Yorubaland (and elsewhere in Southern Nigeria) were brought up solely in the English common law tradition. In the performance of their judicial duties, they would most likely look at the indigenous laws and customs from the point of view of the English common law. Otherwise how would they judge 'repugnancy' in the indigenous laws and customs, as a clause in the judicial agreements required them to do? In Yorubaland and elsewhere in Southern Nigeria, the English judge himself, whether consciously or unconsciously, was the human agent in the introduction of English legal principles.

Until 1914 there were no more elaborate judicial institutions established in Yorubaland. The Native Courts Proclamation, 1900, applying to the Southern Nigeria Protectorate did not extend here, and hence there were no minor courts or 'native' councils as they were known in that protectorate. It should be remembered that Yorubaland and the Southern Nigeria Protectorate were administered separately until 1906. For the most part, in most areas of Yorubaland, the burden of judicial administration until 1914 fell on the traditional courts of the chiefs. [122]

In such centres of British administration as Oyo and Ibadan, the more or less formal 'native' advisory councils under the control of the political officer, continued to perform judicial functions, although they were mainly concerned with administrative and legislative matters. These councils, established towards the end of the nineteenth century, had proved 'a practical and valuable aid in all administrative purposes'.[123] An attempt was made in the Native Councils Ordinance, No. 15, 1901, to regularise their functions and to provide for their establishment in other parts of Yorubaland.[124]

The councils created by the 1901 Ordinance were designed primarily 'to enhance the prestige and authority of the chiefs for administrative efficiency'.[125] They were created at provincial, district, town and village levels, and were empowered to deal with all matters pertaining to internal administration, including the adjudication of important disputes. A local chief was normally to preside over the meetings of a council, but the British administrative officer, when present, could counsel and guide the council in its deliberations. The village and town councils were to be subordinate to the provincial or district councils.

The attempt to set up 'native' councils throughout the Yorubaland Protectorate was not successful. By 1905, however, such councils, as administrative and judicial institutions, were functioning in such important towns as Ibadan, Ijebu-Ode, Ilesha, Oyo, Ife, Illa and Epe.[126] The records show that a fair proportion of their duties was concerned with judicial matters. In its judicial capacity, each council exercised 'a complete jurisdiction without appeal or revision . . . [and] without review by the Supreme Court or any [other] judicial authority'.[127] As an interim judicial measure, the councils served some purpose in the administrative control of parts of Yorubaland.

In Yorubaland, no less than in the Southern Nigeria Protectorate, the attempt by the British to establish new judicial institutions raised some discordant notes of opposition among the indigenous population. In 1893 the Bale of Ibadan and his chiefs told Captain G. C. Denton, then Acting Governor of the Lagos Colony, that the establishment of a British Resident's court in Ibadan would undermine 'the authority and respect of the Bale and Chiefs'.[128] Four years later when the Resident attempted to draw up a set of rules for 'the better administration of justice' in the city, he had 'very up-hill work' in persuading the chiefs to accept them. The Bale and chiefs 'all fear that their power will gradually be wrested from them and in vain do I try and make them realize that their conditions will be bettered and power for good increased in proportion to the interest they take in their towns, and welfare of the people'.[129] William MacGregor, the Governor of Lagos Colony who initiated the making of the judicial agreements referred to earlier, knew that it would not be easy to create judicial tribunals outside the control of the traditional rulers in Yorubaland:

> The holding of courts is regarded in this country . . . as being an attribute of the Chief which is inseparable from his dignity and the maintenance of his position. The Chief is still in this country the 'Highgate', the 'Mikado' of justice . . .[130]

It was to forestall opposition to his scheme that he started with Abeokuta, in making the judicial agreements. The Egba of Abeokuta, he believed, were often looked up to by the other Yoruba states in dealing with Europeans, and an agreement with the Egba authorities 'would no doubt be of great use and assistance' in making similar agreements elsewhere in Yorubaland.[131]

Ironically, the stiffest opposition to the implementation of the judicial agreement in Yorubaland was encountered with the Egba authorities. The British Commissioner resident in Abeokuta reported in August 1904 that the Egba authorities 'appear disposed to dispute the jurisdiction of the Supreme Court' now exercising jurisdiction in Egba territory in accordance with the agreement.[132] This was to put the matter mildly; the Egba traditional rulers, in fact, in an extended correspondence with the Lagos government, virtually repudiated the judicial agreement and the whole process of establishing English-style courts in their territory.

The correspondence was triggered off by the announcement early in June 1904 in the Lagos *Government Gazette* that the Supreme Court of the Lagos Colony would be opened at Abeokuta on 15 June 1904, following the acquisition of judicial powers in Egbaland by the Lagos government. At once the Egba government wrote in protest.[133] The establishment of the Lagos Supreme Court in Egba territory, the *Alake* and his council noted, would be 'contrary to the spirit and letter' of the Egba judicial agreement. They insisted that all that they bargained for was an agreement whereby they and a judge of the Supreme Court, officiating 'in an extra-judicial capacity', would exercise joint jurisdiction in cases where one of the parties was a non-Egba.[134] It was never their intention to allow the Supreme Court of the Lagos Colony to adjudicate disputes independently of them. They could not have opted for an English-style Supreme Court because 'the introduction of a wholly European court with all its accessories of lawyers and technicalities and complexities of English law and its practice . . . must lead to a dislocation of the customs, institutions and, traditional usages' of the Egba people.[135] Quite understandably the opening ceremony marking the establishment of the Supreme Court jurisdiction in Egba territory was poorly attended.[136]

The Egba authorities could not have been more articulate in their opposition to the establishment of English-style judicial institutions in their territory. But like the other Yoruba traditional rulers, they bowed to the will of the British, now that the Lagos administration was becoming an effective power to reckon with, having demonstrated its ability, in the case of Ijebu in 1892 and Oyo in 1895, to crush any opposition by force of arms if necessary.[137]

V

The amalgamation, in May 1906, of the Southern Nigeria Protectorate with the Lagos Colony and Protectorate to form the Colony and Protectorate of Southern Nigeria necessitated some changes in the judicial structure to reflect the creation of one political entity over the whole of Southern Nigeria. The territory was now divided into Eastern, Central and Western Provinces. The Eastern and Central Provinces comprised, roughly, the former Southern Nigeria Protectorate, while the former Protectorate of the Lagos Colony, that is, the Yoruba hinterland, constituted the Western Province.

Over the three provinces and the Lagos Colony there was to be one Supreme Court of the Colony of Southern Nigeria, with powers similar to those vested in the Supreme Court of the Southern Nigeria Protectorate under the Supreme Court Proclamation of 1900.[138] The court was to administer throughout Southern Nigeria English common law, the doctrines of equity and the statutes of general application which were in operation in England as at 1 January 1900.

The various statutory 'native' courts were brought more closely than ever before under the direct control of the Supreme Court. Besides, some changes were also made in the 'native' courts of the Eastern and Central Provinces.[139] In these two provinces, formerly part of the Southern Nigeria Protectorate, the 'native' courts were largely manned by the so-called warrant chiefs – agents of British administration who, as chiefs, had no traditional authority in their respective communities. It was the intention of the Native Courts Proclamation, No. 7, 1906, applying to the two provinces, to bring the warrant chiefs in their judicial functions 'more directly under the Judicial Department', and thus, it was hoped, check the abuses of the 'native' court system already becoming evident to the colonial administration. Henceforth every 'native' court was to include as members the British administrative officers in its area of jurisdiction – the divisional commissioner, the travelling commissioner, the district commissioner and his assistant. In addition, the provincial commissioner was empowered to preside over the meeting of any 'native' court in his province. It was a reflection of the role which the 'native' courts were expected to play in the 'pacification' of the hitherto unsubjugated parts of the two provinces that every officer and member of a 'native' court and every chief and headman could, under the ordinance, and within his area of authority, 'arrest without warrant any native who commits in his presence or is charged by any person on oath with having committed any offence against any native or other law for the time being in force in the Protectorate'.

A noteworthy provision of the Native Courts Proclamation was that all 'native' courts in their judicial, as opposed to their administrative, functions, were to be subject to the orders of the Chief

Justice or other judge of the Supreme Court, who was empowered to transfer any case at any stage of the proceedings from a 'native' court to another 'native' court, the district commissioner's court or the Supreme Court itself. Any 'native' court could also of its own motion apply for the transfer of any cause before it to any other court, including the Supreme Court. At the end of every month, the 'native' court was to forward to the Chief Justice, or any judge appointed by him, a complete list of all criminal cases decided during the month involving a penalty of more than a fine of ₦40 or a term of imprisonment of three months. For purposes of review by the Supreme Court, the monthly returns of cases must state the offences charged together with their penalties. The Chief Justice or other judge of the Supreme Court in going over the monthly returns could 'without hearing any argument' annul or amend any judgment of a 'native' court.

It took some time before the new judicial structure for the whole of Southern Nigeria went into full operation, the courts created before 1906 continuing to function much as before. It was not until 31 March 1908 that the Supreme Court of the former Southern Nigeria Protectorate was formally abolished, bringing the whole territory under a single judicial system with one Supreme Court based in Lagos.

Although the judicial arrangement of 1906 was made to reflect the political changes taking place in Southern Nigeria, it was in a sense yet another experiment in the process of the British administration constructing a judicial machinery to meet the colonial conditions of Southern Nigeria. Earlier in this chapter, we saw in the Niger Delta the development of courts of equity, consular courts, 'native' councils and minor courts; in the Lagos Colony, the establishment of many, often temporary, English-style courts; and in the Yoruba hinterland, the creation of more or less formal 'native' advisory councils and the extension there of the jurisdiction of the supreme court in trying certain categories of cases. These courts were devised to meet changing conditions in, or the peculiar circumstances of, various parts of Southern Nigeria.

There was much that was experimental about the judicial structure erected in 1906. The Supreme Court was given a free rein in the East and Central Provinces, but continued to be restricted in the Western Province by virtue of the judicial agreements signed with the Yoruba ruling authorities. The 'native' courts in the East and Central Provinces were supposed to be subordinate to the Supreme Court, but were not completely so. They were to be under the control of administrative officers in their administrative duties and in the adjudication of civil and minor criminal cases where the parties involved were indigenes. The courts were subjected to the power of the Supreme Court only in certain categories of criminal offences. In the Western Province, where powerful traditional paramount chiefs were to be reckoned with in local administration, the relationship between the 'native' courts and the Supreme Court was not specifically defined. From the point of view of the colonial administration, grave difficulties, mainly of personnel and the relationship of judicial administration and politics, were inherent in the new judicial structure. Some of these difficulties will be examined presently when we take a close look at the actual working of the judicial system being built in Southern Nigeria.

Notes

1 NAE, CSO 1/13, XXIII, Moor to Colonial Office, 7 January 1903.
2 A tendency to see British-established courts rather too exclusively as judicial institutions is evident in the extant writings on Nigerian law. Compare T. O. Elias, *The Nigerian Legal System*, chs 3–8; B. O. Nwabueze, *The Machinery of Justice in Nigeria*, chs 3–4; E. A. Keay and S. S. Richardson, *The Native and Customary Courts of Nigeria*, London, 1966, ch. 1.
3 J. M. Sarbah, *Fanti Law Report*, London, 1904, p. 13.
4 For details of the changing jurisdictions over Southern Nigeria up to 1906, see J. C. Anene, *Southern Nigeria in Transition*, Cambridge, 1966, chs 3–6; Alan Burns, *History of Nigeria*, chs 10–14.
5 John E. Flint, *Sir George Goldie and the Making of Nigeria*, London, 1960, pp. 91–6.
6 A. E. Afigbo, 'The Warrant Chief System in Eastern Nigeria, 1900–1929', Ibadan University, PhD thesis, 1964, p. 47.
7 The jurisdiction of the courts of equity was regularised by the Order-in-Council of February 1872. See Alan Burns, *History of Nigeria*, Appendix E, pp. 321–7.
8 T. J. Hutchinson, *Impressions of Western Africa*, London, 1858, p. 108.
9 NAE, Cal Prof 3/2, 'Court of Equity, Old Calabar, 1876–1885'.
10 G. I. Jones, *The Trading States of the Oil Rivers*, London, 1963, p. 79.
11 Order-in-Council, February 1872, secs. 5, 15, 24, 26.

12 Lagos, *Reports of Certain Judgments of the Supreme Court, Vice-Admiralty Court and Full Court of Appeal, 1884–1892.*
13 NAE, Cal Prof 3/1, 'Proceedings of Court of Equity, Opobo, held May 13, 1874'.
14 NAE, Cal Prof 3/2.
15 NAE, Cal Prof 3/1, Letter to H.B.M. Consuls David Hopkins and H. C. Fait, dated 21 August 1877.
16 Lagos, *Reports of Certain Judgments of the Supreme Court. . . .*, p. 27.
17 Alan Burns, *History of Nigeria*, p. 147.
18 NAE, 'Court of Equity Proceedings, 1883–1891', bound volume.
19 G. I. Jones, *The Trading States. . . .*, pp. 78–9.
20 *Ibid.*, p. 80.
21 NAE, 'Court of Equity Proceedings, 1883–1891'.
22 Alan Burns, Appendix E, pp. 321–7.
23 *Ibid.*, p. 146.
24 O. Ikime, *Niger Delta Rivalry*, London, 1969, pp. 81–104; J. C. Anene, *Southern Nigeria in Transition*, pp. 42–86.
25 For details, see T. O. Elias, *The Nigerian Legal System*, pp. 87–93.
26 NAE, 'Court of Equity Proceedings, 1883–1891'; see the Regulations for the Constitution of a Governing Council to manage the Local Affairs of Brass.
27 *Ibid.*, see the minutes of the meeting of the Governing Council of Brass held 13 April 1888.
28 *Ibid.*, 'Regulations for the Constitution of a Governing Council to manage the local affairs of Brass'.
29 NAE, CSO 1/13, XI, 'Report on the Administration of the Niger Coast Protectorate, 1891–1894'.
30 NAE, CSO 1/13, XI, 'Annual Report on the Niger Coast Protectorate, 1898–1899'.
31 A. E. Afigbo, 'The Warrant Chief System', p. 65.
32 NAE, CSO 1/13, XI, 'Annual Report on the Niger Coast Protectorate 1898–1899'.
33 For more details on the origins of the warrant chiefs, see A. E. Afigbo, *The Warrant Chiefs*, London, 1972, pp. 37–77.
34 A. E. Afigbo, 'Revolution and Reaction in Eastern Nigeria', *Journal of the Historical Society of Nigeria*, iii, 3 December 1966, p. 541.
35 O. Ikime, *Niger Delta Rivalry*, p. 168.
36 J. C. Anene, 'Establishment and Consolidation of Imperial Government in Southern Nigeria, 1891–1904', London University, M.A. thesis, 1952, p. 273.
37 O. Ikime, *Niger Delta Rivalry*, p. 145.
38 NAE, CSO/13, XI, 'Annual Report on the Niger Coast Protectorate, 1898–1899'.
39 *Ibid.*
40 *Ibid.*
41 Supreme Court Proclamation, No. 6, 1900, sec. 19.
42 NAE, Cal Prof 10/2, I, The Commissioners Proclamation, No. 8, 1900.
43 NAE, Cal Prof 10/2, I, Native Courts Proclamation, No. 9, 1900.

44 NAE, CSO 1/13, XXVI, 'Annual Report for 1902'.
45 Native Courts Proclamation, No. 25, 1901, sec. 12, *Laws of Southern Nigeria, 1900–1901*.
46 NAE, Cal Prof 9/2, II, Moor to Divisional Commissioner, Cross River Division, Ediba.
47 *Ibid.*
48 NAE, CSO 1/13, XXIV, Native Courts Amendment Proclamation, No. 17, 1903, sec. 3.
49 Harold Bindloss, *In the Niger Country*, London, new imp., 1968, p. 147.
50 NAE, CSO 1/13, VII; NAE, Cal Prof 6/1, IV; NAE, Cal Prof 10/3, I; NAE CSO 1/13, XIII.
51 NAE, CSO 1/13, IX, 'Annual Report for the Niger Coast Protectorate, 1897–1898'.
52 NAE, CSO 1/15, IV, Kelly to Acting High Commissioner, 10 September 1903.
53 NAE, CSO 1/13, XVIII, Moor to Colonial Office, 7 January 1902, enclosure; HCA, 'Circuit Judge's Notebook, 1888–1898', 10 vols.
54 NAE, Cal Prof 9/2, II, Moor to Divisional Commissioner, Western Division, 22 May 1902; 'Annual Report on the Eastern Province for the Year 1908', in Lagos, *Annual Reports of the Colony of Southern Nigeria for the Year 1908*, pp. 65–91.
55 NAE, CSO 1/13, Moor to Colonial Office, 8 August 1902; NAE, Cal Prof 9/2, II, Moor to Divisional Commissioner, Western Division, Warri, 22 May 1902.
56 NAE, CSO 1/13, XXI, Moor to Colonial Office, 22 August 1902.
57 Lagos, *Annual Reports of the Colony of Southern Nigeria for the Year 1908*, pp. 407–13.
58 NAE, CSO 1/13, XIII, Moor to Colonial Office, 7 January 1903, enclosure.
59 NAE, CSO 1/13, IX, 'Annual Report for the Niger Coast Protectorate, 1897–1898'; NAE, CSO 1/13, XXIII, Moor to Colonial Office, 7 January 1903, enclosure entitled 'Report on the Native Courts in the Eastern, Western and Central Divisions, Southern Nigeria Protectorate'; Lagos, *Annual Reports, Southern Nigeria*, 1906, p. 314.
60 Compare 'Annual Report for the Year 1905, Western Division', in Lagos Colony, *Government Gazette*, January–June 1906; 'Annual Report on Central Province, Southern Nigeria, 1906' in Lagos, *Annual Reports, Southern Nigeria, 1906*, p. 314; E. A. Keay and S. S. Richardson, *The Native and Customary Courts*, p. 17.
61 Alan Burns, p. 131.
62 NAI, CSO 1/10, XXXIV, Griffith to Sir Samuel Rowe, 14 July 1881.
63 *Blue Book for 1894* and *Blue Book for 1912*, Lagos, 1895, 1913, p. 54 and p. 64 respectively.
64 NAI, Otonba Payne, 'A History of the Old Lagos Law Courts', unpublished MS dated 1905, p. 1.
65 NAI, *Papers Relating to the Occupation of Lagos*, 1862, p. 4.
66 FO 2/20, Campbell to Clarendon, 2 June 1857 and enclosures.

67 Jay Gordon, 'The Development of the Legal System in the Colony of Lagos, 1862–1905', unpublished PhD thesis, London University, 1967, p. 50.
68 FO 83/2203, Law Officers to Clarendon, 11 August 1857.
69 Jay Gordon, 'The Development of Legal System', p. 50.
70 NAI, *Papers Relating to the Occupation of Lagos*, 1862, p. 4.
71 NAI, CSO 1/8, VB, John Glover to Captain Kendall, 16 November 1869.
72 NAI, CSO 1/8, XIIIB, Fowler to Pope Hennessy, 8 November 1872.
73 *Ibid.*
74 NAI, CSO 1/8, VA, Glover to Kennedy, 5 August 1869.
75 NAI, CSO 1/1, I, H. S. Freeman to Newcastle, 8 March 1862.
76 For details, see T. O. Elias, *The Nigerian Legal System*, pp. 45–57.
77 Jay Gordon, 'The Development of the Legal System', p. 77.
78 For more details, see Jay Gordon, pp. 99–102.
79 Elias, p. 52.
80 *Ibid.*, p. 53.
81 Supreme Court Ordinance, No. 4, 1876, *Laws of the Colony of Southern Nigeria, 1908*, I, pp. 14–145.
82 Section 19.
83 Sections 71–4.
84 Jay Gordon, p. 91.
85 *Ibid.*, p. 109.
86 *Ibid.*, p. 113.
87 NAI, CSO 1/8, XIX, G. C. Strahan to Governor-in-Chief, Sierra Leone, 13 June 1874.
88 NAI, Otonba Payne, 'A History of the Old Lagos Law Courts', p. 1.
89 Jay Gordon, p. 112.
90 *The African Times*, 23 December 1868; 23 March 1868; *Lagos Observer*, 13 September 1883, 3 January 1884.
91 NAI, CSO 1/8, XIIIB, Fowler to Pope Hennessy, 12 November 1872.
92 Jay Gordon, p. 184.
93 NAI, CSO 1/10, XI, Lees to Freeling, 2 July 1877, enclosure containing minutes by David Chalmers.
94 *Lagos Weekly Record*, 23 January 1904.
95 Payne, 'A History of the Old Lagos Law Courts', p. 1.
96 HCA, Lagos, 'Judges' Notebook: Civil Cases, 1877–1878', pp. 93–7.
97 HCA, Lagos, 'Record Book: Civil Cases, 1878–1880', p. 396, *Foresythe v. Adam, alias Odi.*
98 *Lagos Weekly Record*, 6 May 1893.
99 For more on Sapara Williams, see O. Adewoye, 'Sapara Williams: The Lawyer and the Public Servant', *Journal of the Historical Society of Nigeria*, vi, 1, December 1971, pp. 47–65.
100 For more on the self-taught attorneys, see O. Adewoye, 'Prelude to the Legal Profession in Lagos, 1861–1880', *Journal of African Law*, xiv, 2, 1970, pp. 98–114.
101 Jay Gordon, p. 126.
102 *Lagos Observer*, 27 September 1883.

103 For more on the Yoruba wars, see J. F. A. Ajayi and R. Smith, *Yoruba Warfare in the Nineteenth Century*, Cambridge, 1964.
104 S. A. Akintoye, 'The Ekitiparapo and the Kiriji War', Ibadan University, PhD thesis, 1966, p. 330, footnote 4.
105 NAI, CSO 15/1, XV; CSO 5/2, II.
106 NAI, CSO 5/1, XVIII.
107 Lagos, *Annual Reports for the Year 1900–1901*, p. 20; Lagos, *Annual Reports for the Year 1903*, p. 21; Lagos, *Annual Reports of the Colony of Southern Nigeria, 1906*, pp. 259–60; NAI, Abe Prof 8/3.
108 Lagos, *Annual Report for the Year 1899*, p. 61.
109 *Ibid.*, p. 82.
110 NAI, Iba Prof 3/6, 'The Resident's Travelling Journal, 1897–1899'.
111 Lagos, *Annual Report for the Year 1903*, p. 23.
112 *Ibid.*
113 NAI, Abe Prof 9/3, H. W. A. Cumming to Colonial Secretary, Lagos, minute dated 19 May 1903.
114 *Infra*, p. 40.
115 NAI, CSO 5/2, XIX, XX, XXI, XXIV.
116 O. Adewoye, 'The Judicial Agreements in Yorubaland, 1904–1908', *Journal of African History*, xii, 4, 1971, pp. 607–27.
117 NAI, CSO 1/3, VII, MacGregor to Colonial Office, 15 December 1903.
118 NAI, CSO 1/3, VI, MacGregor to Colonial Office, 22 March 1903; J. F. A. Ajayi, *Christian Missions in Nigeria 1841–1891: The Making of a New Elite*, London, 1965, pp. 197–202.
119 William MacGregor, 'Lagos, Abeokuta and the Alake', *African Affairs*, III, July 1904, p. 12.
120 This argument has been amplified in O. Adewoye, 'The Judicial Agreements in Yorubaland, 1904–1908', *Journal of African History*, xii, 4, 1971, pp. 621–2.
121 Egba Jurisdiction Ordinance, No. 14, 1904; Yoruba Jurisdiction Ordinance, No. 17, 1904; Ife Jurisdiction Ordinance, No. 20, 1904; in *Laws of the Colony of Southern Nigeria, 1908*, I, pp. 254, 260, 273; Jebu Ode Jurisdiction Ordinance, No. 3, 1909.
122 Lagos, *Annual Report of the Colony and Protectorate of Southern Nigeria, 1906*, p. 21.
123 Lagos, *Annual Report for 1899*, p. 78.
124 Colony of Lagos, *Government Gazette*, 1901, p. 648.
125 J. A. Atanda, 'The New Oyo Empire: A Study of British Indirect Rule in Oyo Province, 1894–1934', Ibadan University, PhD thesis, 1967, p. 118.
126 'Annual Report for the Year 1905 on the Provinces of the Lagos Protectorate under the Supervision of the British Resident at Ibadan', 'Annual Report for 1905 on Ijebu-Ode District', 'Annual Report on the Eastern District for 1905', Colony of Lagos, *Government Gazette*, 1906.
127 F. D. Lugard, *Report on the Amalgamation of Northern and Southern Nigeria, 1912–1919*, Cmd 468, 1920, p. 21.
128 *Lagos Weekly Record*, 12 May 1906.

129 NAI, Iba Prof 3/6, 'The Resident's Travelling Journal, 1897–1899', entry for 6 September 1897.
130 NAI, CSO 1/3, VII, MacGregor to Colonial Office, 15 December 1903.
131 *Ibid.*
132 NAI, Abe Prof 9/2, Cyril Punch to Deputy Registrar, Abeokuta, 9 August 1904.
133 NAI, CSO 1/7, XXIV, Egerton to Lyttelton, 29 October 1904 and enclosures.
134 NAI, CSO 1/7, XXIV, Gbadebo Alake to Moseley, 13 September 1904.
135 NAI, CSO 1/7, XXIV, Egerton to Lyttelton, 29 October 1904, enclosure 2.
136 *Lagos Weekly Record*, 25 June 1904.
137 For their opposition to British penetration into their kingdoms, Carter marched against Ijebu in 1892, and Captain Bower bombarded Oyo in 1895.
138 Supreme Court Ordinance, No. 17, 1906.
139 Native Courts Proclamation, No. 7, 1906.

3 The courts in action, 1854-1914

> The natives are habituated by their own customs to a
> Supreme and Absolute authority . . . I therefore fear
> that the strict application of British law, which would
> certainly result from the appointment of entirely inde-
> pendent legal officers, would be the cause of much embar-
> rassment. . . .
>
> Henry S. Freeman to Colonial Office, London, 1862[1]

I

Certain features of the administration of justice in Southern
Nigeria call for comment at this stage. It was one thing for the
British, for economic and political reasons, to have introduced
English law and English-style courts into the territory; it was
quite another to maintain a standard of judicial administration
compatible with the spirit behind these institutions in their home-
land. The main burden of this chapter is that the colonial situation
and the prevailing circumstances in Southern Nigeria precluded
the importation of the same standard of justice and judicial
administration that was obtainable in England.

First, there was the problem of personnel. The courts of equity
and their immediate successors, the governing councils, had no
officers qualified in law. They administered largely their own
notions of fair play and justice. The governing councils were
indeed valued more for their quasi-legislative than for their
judicial functions.[2] In the Niger Coast Protectorate, by 1896, the
consul and twenty-one other officers, including thirteen assistant
district commissioners, comprised the executive and judicial staff,
none of them having any legal qualifications.[3] The consular courts
– there were eight by 1899 – did not differ much from the courts
of equity in the way law was supposed to be administered by officers
who had no legal qualifications. A consular court was simply the
consul or the vice-consul in his judicial capacity, acting with or
without the assistance of assessors. He dealt with such cases as
slave-dealing, firing on trade-canoes, adulteration of palm kernels,
and various types of minor civil disputes with no qualifications

other than his knowledge of the environment, 'long patience, self-command and firmness'.[4] Towards the end of the nineteenth century there was a legally qualified officer in the Niger Coast Protectorate, but he belonged to the executive branch of the colonial administration.[5] The only area of Southern Nigeria east of the Niger which before 1899 had properly qualified judicial officers was the territory under the jurisdiction of the Royal Niger Company. The company, since the appointment of Sir James Marshall as its Chief Justice in 1887, and until 1899, consistently maintained a legally qualified person as the Chief Justice of its Supreme Court.[6] Between 1891 and 1899 the Supreme Court also had a fully qualified puisne judge.[7]

At the creation of the Southern Nigeria Protectorate in 1900, the judicial department was at best a rudimentary arm of the colonial administration. The Chief Justice of the Royal Niger Company's territory, following the revocation of the company's charter, was made the Chief Justice of the new protectorate.[8] Besides the Chief Justice, Justice H. G. Kelly, there was another puisne judge, M. R. Menendez, who was to put the 'native' courts of the protectorate on a sound footing.[9] It was no easy task organising judicial machinery for the protectorate. In August 1900, there was only one judicial officer on duty in the whole protectorate, and it was noted, 'there is a very great difficulty in carrying out the work of [the Judicial] Department'.[10] It was a reflection of the grave shortage of legally qualified personnel that both the Chief Justice and the puisne judge of the Supreme Court had to draft the thirty proclamations establishing a judicial system for the protectorate between 1900 and 1901 – a singular indication of lack of differentiation between the legislative and judicial functions of government.[11] About three years after the creation of the protectorate, the Chief Justice was still regretting the unavailability of suitable men in his department:

> I have now no Chief Registrar; there is a comparatively new man who is acting in that capacity who . . . ranks only as a Chief Clerk and I have of course to be continually instructing him in his duties. The number of other clerks is insufficient to meet contingencies such as leaves of absence, illness and so on . . .[12]

The justice to be administered in the English-style courts that were being established in Southern Nigeria, in the best common law tradition, required not only legally qualified judges, but also advocates similarly well-trained in law. It is pertinent to observe that the first full-time solicitor and advocate outside the colonial administration did not appear east of the Niger until September 1908.[13] Before then the colonial attorney-general engaged in drafting agreements and simple deeds for private individuals.[14] Other lawyers came in after January 1909, and we shall have more to say about their activities in the courts.

Judicial work in the Lagos Colony and the Yoruba hinterland was also hampered by lack of adequately qualified personnel. Although various English-style courts were established in Lagos, the method of administering justice in them lacked the formality of an English court of law. There were not enough qualified judges, the Colonial Office in London being particularly reluctant to send qualified personnel to man the judiciary.[15] We saw earlier how judicial posts were held by non-professionals – soldiers, merchants, surgeons, naval and customs officers – who were usually saddled with other responsibilities in the Colonial Service.

What was true of the Bench was also true of the legal department of the colonial administration itself. Before 1874 there was no legally qualified officer in the administration. The Queen's Advocate, the forerunner of the modern Attorney-General, was appointed after the merging of the Lagos Colony with the Gold Coast Colony in 1874; but he was more often on the Gold Coast than in Lagos.[16] Between 1874 and 1906 there was never at any time more than one professionally qualified legal officer in the Lagos Colony.[17] The position of the Crown Prosecutor was on many occasions held by such men as Charles Foresythe, Arthur H. Porter, Charles D. Turton, John Augustus Otonba-Payne – amateur lawyers who were building careers in law without formal legal training.[18] Incidentally, Otonba-Payne was the registrar of the Supreme Court between 1876 and 1899, occasionally doing duty on the Gold Coast.[19]

In terms of the operation of English-style judicial machinery in Lagos, it should also be noted that until 1880, as was stated earlier, there was no professionally qualified lawyer in Lagos. The colony had the interesting experience, by no means unique in West Africa, of enrolling to practise at the Bar men who had no formal legal education, but who were judged 'fit and proper persons' to be officers of the Supreme Court.[20] These self-taught attorneys – eight of whom practised law in Lagos between 1865 and 1913 – were products of circumstances. Like the unprofessional Bench, they were a reflection of the standard of judicial administration in the Lagos Colony.

The extension of the Supreme Court jurisdiction into Yorubaland between 1904 and 1909 meant no more than that the Chief Justice of the Supreme Court of Lagos held assizes in the hinterland four times a year.[21] Judicial agreements in the Yorubaland Protectorate precluded the appearance of legal practitioners before the English-style courts in this part of Southern Nigeria and, by the same token, the establishment of any of the elaborate trappings of an English court of law. Thus the Supreme Court in Yorubaland operated informally with important local chiefs or community elders helping the sole presiding judge as assessors.

II

Lack of adequate personnel to operate the new judicial machinery in various parts of Southern Nigeria produced certain peculiarities. In Lagos, for the greater part of the nineteenth century, the method of administering justice in the English-style courts was essentially 'to discard all technicalities and by as thorough as possible an investigation of the facts to ascertain the true merits of the matters of controversy in each particular case'.[22] This observation is applicable to the courts in other areas of Southern Nigeria. Neither the courts of equity, dominated by merchants, nor the consular courts and the 'native' courts, both under political officers who were anxious, primarily, to establish British rule and influence, could afford to be concerned about the technicalities of the judicial process. They had neither the knowledge nor the inclination to do so. The Supreme Court of the Royal Niger Company between 1886 and 1899 in its area of jurisdiction similarly did not operate with the usual formalities of an English law court. Parties represented themselves, and the duty of the court was to investigate the essence of each particular case, without much attention to technical rules of procedure. Generally, rules of court were hard to come by. In Lagos, as was mentioned earlier, there were no such rules until 1870.[23] For the Southern Nigeria Protectorate, they were not drawn up until the beginning of this century.[24]

It was the rule rather than the exception that litigants pleaded their own causes. In a civil suit the parties stated their cases before the court, the illiterate speaking through an interpreter. As each party stated his or her case, the judge put relevant questions in an attempt to get at the facts. He finally decided the issue, much of the burden of adjudication resting on him. Occasionally assessors were called in, empanelled from the members of the local population – usually important men or chiefs.[25] In Lagos there was an attempt to incorporate elements of the traditional approach in the administration of justice in the English-style courts, especially under Justice James Marshall when he was Chief Magistrate. Whenever assessors were empanelled, it was the practice to call on them to express their opinions in turns, not on specific aspects of the case on hand, but on the basic question at issue, before the judge gave his verdict.[26]

In the trial of a criminal offence, it was the practice that tho accused person defended himself. The accuser was usually the Crown Prosecutor in Lagos, or the district commissioner in the other areas of Southern Nigeria. The prosecutor outlined the case against the accused person, and in trying to prove it, he might call witnesses. The prosecutor's witnesses were cross-examined by the accused person. The latter then made his defence, and in doing so, might call his own witnesses who could also be cross-examined by the prosecutor.[27] It is a reflection on the standard of justice administered in the courts in the nineteenth century that the judge presiding over a criminal case sometimes played the role of the accuser himself as in *Regina v. Ogundipe, Sadare and Ajibara*, a case of robbery and assault tried in Lagos on 6 September 1875.[28] Occasionally, in the 1870s and 1880s in Lagos a jury system was in use in the trial of criminal offences as nowhere else in Southern Nigeria.[29] After 1900 the respective Supreme Courts of both Southern Nigeria Protectorate and the Lagos Colony held criminal assizes in selected towns in the hinterland. Again, the usual practice was for the accused persons to defend themselves, the presiding judge, with the aid of assessors, deciding their guilt or innocence.[30]

In the circumstances of the nineteenth century and early this century, it is perhaps only to be expected that there would be abuses and irregularities in the judicial system. A look at the Lagos courts, relatively the best-organised in Southern Nigeria in this period, is, in this connection, particularly instructive.

Since for the greater part of the nineteenth century there were no guiding rules for the courts, court officials tended to follow their own inclinations. It was a usual practice for Benjamin Way,

Chief Magistrate 1863–71, to frame indictments for his own court and act as prosecutor and judge in the same case.[31] The court clerk under him exercised power and influence out of all proportion to his lowly status in the judicial system of Lagos. Not only was he clerk and interpreter to the court, he also acted in court as agent or attorney for European and English merchants in the colony.[32] On him lay the full responsibility for empanelling juries. There were no lists of jurors approved by the Chief Magistrate, the clerk of the Court of Civil and Criminal Justice selecting jurors entirely 'at his discretion'. Hence, as the Governor of the colony discovered in 1869, some jurors were selected who 'bear a questionable reputation in Lagos', others who understood nothing of the judicial procedure 'having to ask other jurors what [was] being said', while 'some of the most respectable citizens [were] excluded altogether'.[33] There was obviously a system of jury-packing in operation under the very nose of the Chief Magistrate. Through it the clerk of the Court of Civil and Criminal Justice could tip the balance of justice in favour of the party of his choice.

In 1869 after 'many complaints of individual dissatisfaction' with the same court, the Administrator of the Lagos Colony dismissed the clerk and the two bailiffs of the court. It had become evident to him that the clerk and the bailiffs had formed an odious triumvirate, perverting the cause of justice. All a defendant had to do to avoid being summoned to court was to bribe any of the three officers. To collect a debt, a successful plaintiff might pay up to twenty per cent of it in (unofficial) commission to the officers of the court to induce them to execute the judgment of the court.[34] It was also known that the two bailiffs abused their positions to recover debts for creditors who cared to retain them on the basis of the payment of a commission.[35]

Justice James Marshall as Chief Magistrate complained in 1875 that the registrar of the Court of Civil and Criminal Justice, Otonba-Payne, was making 'heavy charges on suitors in carrying out the orders of the court by assuming the name of Sheriff'.[36] He alleged that Otonba-Payne took 'a commission of 5% on all monies passing through his hands' as Sheriff. Specific cases were cited in support of the allegation.[37] He stated in March 1875 that he had reason to believe that Otonba-Payne 'has been enjoying no less a sum than about £2,000 [₦4,000] per annum from this source alone, viz., Sheriff's poundage, than he has had fees and salaries. He seriously frowned on Otonba-Payne's assumption of the name 'Sheriff' for which he said he could not find any 'legal origin' or any evidence of Otonba-Payne's appointment to it, and under which he was 'charging heavy fees and exercising powers over the liberty of the subject'.[38]

Corruption and indiscretion were not limited to the clerical or junior officers of the courts. It was discovered in 1871 that a police magistrate, Josiah Gerard, who had been continually accused of being partial in his rulings in favour of a European merchant, one E. Pittaluga, a widow, had actually been serving her unofficially as legal adviser on commercial matters in a way prejudicial to the interests of 'several individuals of the trading community of Lagos'.[39] The Queen's Advocate was at least until 1890 taking private cases.[40] The liberty given him to take private cases was supposed to be an economy measure. He received a meagre salary which he was expected to supplement with whatever he could secure from private legal practice. But it was only to be expected that he would use his position to foster his own legal practice. He naturally enjoyed a measure of influence with the judges which he invariably found helpful in his private practice. The notion grew by 1881 that a party to a suit who engaged the Queen's Advocate as counsel was sure of winning his case on account of the officer's intimacy with the judges.[41]

It would appear that the Queen's Advocate could even ride roughshod over the rules of the Supreme Court, for what they were worth. It was a provision of the Supreme Court Ordinance, 1876, that where either of two parties to a suit was an illiterate, no counsel was to be allowed to appear in the hearing of the suit. Thomas Woodcock, the first Queen's Advocate, allegedly appeared both on the Gold Coast and in Lagos on behalf of 'intelligent plaintiffs' against illiterate defendants – contrary to the provision of the ordinance and with the consent of the judges.[42] It was said that many of the judges did fear Woodcock and that they deliberately sought to promote his private legal interests.

The anomalies in the judicial system of Lagos are not difficult to understand. The African subordinate staff in the judicial as well as other departments of the colonial government were generally poorly paid,[43] and therefore open to temptation. As if to reinforce such temptation, the subordinate officers of the courts 'were not sufficiently looked after'.[44] But how could they have been adequately supervised when few of the judges of the courts in Lagos really understood the judicial process or were even learned in law?

We saw earlier how the courts were packed with non-professionals as judges. The few judges of the Supreme Court with legal training, until the arrival of James Marshall in 1875 as Acting Chief Magistrate, were, in fact, people of low calibre. Chief Magistrate Way was described as 'ignorant of law and wholly unfit for the important position he holds'. His successor, R. D. Mayne, was said to possess 'an indolent disposition', and was 'not a man who will ever make any mark in the world'.[45] A situation where most of the judges were more or less illiterate in law, and were, in addition, not constantly on the bench or even resident in Lagos, on account of frequent leave-taking in England, only served to encourage corruption and breed judicial and other anomalies.

Though less well documented in their general mode of operation than the courts in Lagos, the British-established courts in the remaining parts of Southern Nigeria were not much different. Until after the first decade of this century, the influence of the Supreme Court was highly limited in the interior districts of Southern Nigeria. In 1911 a colonial officer wrote of Abakaliki: 'Though in theory English law is in force in Abakaliki district, in fact, it is as yet hardly known.'[46] What was true of Abakaliki district was equally true of many other districts, especially in the Western Province where until 1914 the Supreme Court held assizes only in five towns and for only eight weeks in a year.[47]

East of the Niger there were no judicial agreements prohibiting the appearance of legal practitioners in the divisional courts of the Supreme Court. But here, perhaps because of inadequate personnel, the administration of criminal justice in particular suffered from some anomalies. If a judge of the stamp of Benjamin Way sometimes acted as judge and prosecutor in criminal cases brought before him in Lagos, the system of operation of the Supreme Court in criminal cases in the Eastern and Central Provinces of Southern Nigeria was very much loaded against the accused person. Many cases, especially murder cases, were prosecuted here by the Attorney-General or by a district commissioner with at least some rudimentary knowledge of English criminal procedure without any legal assistance given to the accused persons.[48]

Most areas of Southern Nigeria outside the Lagos Colony were covered by one variety or the other of the so-called 'native' tribunals – 'native' councils, 'native' courts or minor courts. These were all politico-judicial institutions under the control of administrative officers, performing more or less the same functions at different levels as 'the local seats of Government'. By 1907 and 1908 there were between sixty and seventy of such tribunals in each of Eastern and Central Provinces.[49]

From the beginning and almost throughout the colonial period in Southern Nigeria, a major problem with the 'native' courts was the corruption of the personnel, especially the chiefs who sat in them as judges and assessors, and the scribes to the courts. Before 1914 the courts were supposed to be subject to the supervision of the Supreme Court in at least certain aspects of their judicial functions. But the Supreme Court, staffed by no more than three or four judges at any time, proved most unequal to the task.[50] The supervision by the Supreme Court over the lesser courts was at best perfunctory, hardly touching on the actual operation of these courts. Political officers were reported in places to have devoted 'a very large share' of their time to the supervision of the courts;[51] but, in general, it would appear that the officers were too few to ensure a continuous, adequate supervision. The following table of meetings of the 'native' courts of some towns in the Eastern Province before 1915 is, in this connection, instructive:[52]

Native court	Year	No. of sittings	No. presided over by the district commissioner
Calabar	Jan–Sept 1905	78	24
Creek Town	,,	31	1
Eastern Ekoi	,,	11	1
Uwet	,,	18	—
Adiebo	,,	15	—
Owerri	June–Sept 1914	89	12
Aba	,,	56	8
Degema	,,	69	37
Ahoada	,,	34	9
Okigwi	,,	76	31

The consequence of inadequate supervision of the 'native' courts by the political officers was the increasing power assumed by the court clerks and other personnel of the courts. With increasing power went corruption and abuse of office.

Between 1900 and 1906 it was a common allegation that clerks of 'native' courts in the Eastern and Central Provinces were charging ignorant litigants excessive fees to feather their own nests.[53] In 1907 the two travelling supervisors of 'native' courts in the Eastern Province unearthed anomalies in the courts involving a sum of ₦580 and resulting in 245 queries.[54] An assistant travelling supervisor found in Owerri District in 1912 that there were many instances of fees collected by 'native' court clerks but not entered in the proper receipt books. Indeed throughout the district, no receipt books were kept either for money received or paid out.[55] We shall have more to say about the institutions of 'native' courts in Southern Nigeria in later years and the level of corruption that obtained in them.

III

Administration of justice in Southern Nigeria before 1914 was not always devoid of political and other extraneous considerations. It would appear that colonial courts, consciously or unconsciously, tended to make themselves amenable to safeguarding the interests of the colonial power. There were, no doubt, cases which were decided purely on their own merits and strictly in accordance with the law; but these were usually cases where fundamental issues of power, authority, prestige, or major economic interests of the colonial regime were not involved.

Intrusion of colour prejudice in cases where Africans and Europeans were involved, was a bane of judicial administration in Lagos as in some other British West African colonies in the nineteenth century. 'Prejudice of colour', wrote an educated African in 1869, 'exists to such an extreme on the West Coast of Africa that often times in our courts of law we sue entirely in vain for the impartial administration of justice.'[56] As far as Lagos was concerned, there is much element of truth in that allegation.

Benjamin Way as the Chief Magistrate of Lagos was notorious for 'the partiality of his decisions'.[57] Two instances would suffice. In *Regina v. Lobley* (1869), the accused, a white sea captain, was convicted for the rape of a young girl aged about seven. He was sentenced to four months' imprisonment with hard labour. But some eighteen months earlier, 'an educated Native' who had committed a similar offence had been sentenced to three years' imprisonment with hard labour by the same judge in the same Court of Civil and Criminal Justice.[58] *Regina v. Stott*, tried in the same year, also involved a white sea captain. George Stott, captain of the steamer, *The Thomas Bazley*, was charged with 'aggravated assault' on one Isaac Baker, an African. The Chief Magistrate not only acted as both prosecutor and judge in trying the case, but also committed other irregularities.[59] The jury of twelve men empanelled to try the case were divided, the two Europeans on the panel holding against the ten Africans who found Stott guilty. The Chief Magistrate discharged the jury, stating that he would empanel another the next day. But instead of empanelling another jury, he allowed the prisoner to alter his original plea of 'not guilty' to 'guilty' and fined him £10 (₦20) instead of giving him a long prison term which had met similar offences in the past. So unequal to the offence was the punishment of a fine held to be by the general public that the Lieutenant-Governor of the colony, in reaction, temporarily suspended Way and closed his court.[60]

Anyone familiar with the administration of the judicial process, particularly in the area of sentencing, would appreciate the arbitrariness of the exercise of judicial discretion in this field. It may, therefore, be argued that these two cases would not prove the allegation of partiality or colour prejudice on the part of Benjamin Way just because of the difference in the sentences imposed by him. But these were not singular cases, and the indigenous population of Lagos had sufficiently demonstrated their resentment against his racially-biased decisions. The suspension order of 1869 was, in fact, a measure to appease injured feelings.

Instances of partial administration of justice or of the intrusion of colour prejudice were not limited to Banjamin Way's Court of Civil and Criminal Justice. Captain John H. Glover, always anxious, as the Administrator of the Lagos Colony, to maintain a good public image of his administration, observed in 1869 with some uneasiness 'a steady determination [on the part of judges] to shelter the offences of the whiteman against the Natives first of all in the courts, secondly in the prisons'.[61] Josiah Gerard had to be removed from office as police magistrate and from the Colonial Service of Lagos partly on account of his contemptuous attitude towards the members of the indigenous population.[62] A petition from some two hundred Africans, which prompted his removal, indicated that 'the Native community (in particular) are tired of receiving disrespect and injustice at the hands of Gerard'.[63] At least up till 1881 instances of 'unjust and iniquitous verdicts' being delivered in cases in which Africans were involved were still being reported in Lagos.[64]

Fine points of the law or of judicial procedure could give way in matters where larger considerations of policy were involved. In the nineteenth century, the suppression of the slave trade was an important matter of policy with the colonial administration in Lagos, and the three cases of *Regina v. Bickersteth, Regina v. Palmer* and *Regina v. Ogoo*, tried in July 1880, involving alleged slave dealing on the banks of the Niger, provide an illustration of this. In examining the circumstances of the trials of the three men, it is difficult to escape the conclusion that the criminal court in Lagos was bent on convicting them.[65] Their requests for jury trials were turned down; instead they were tried by panels of assessors ranging between three and five. The prosecution witnesses brought from Accra by the Queen's Advocate were said to be persons known to be ill-disposed to the prisoners.[66] They were 'housed in the same premises in which the prosecutor and the judge had their lodgings'.[67] Even if it is not true, as it was alleged, that many of them 'were first called before the trial and privately examined and bullied into giving suitable evidence', there is something highly irregular about the circumstances in which they were placed. Some of the defence witnesses called by Bickersteth and Ogoo were turned into prosecution witnesses. The other defence witnesses were kept away from the prisoners until they actually appeared in the witness box. In the course of the proceedings, counsel for two of the accused persons fell ill. His petition for an adjournment of the trial was overruled, and the accused persons were compelled to conduct their own defence 'against a learned, able and experienced lawyer as Woodcock [the Queen's Advocate]'.

It is a well-known canon of English criminal law that a man cannot be tried twice for the same offence. Yet this principle did not seem to have had any weight with Justice Hector W. Macleod who tried the three men. The men were first arrested in the Niger Coast Protectorate by Acting Consul Easton. They were tried and sentenced to seven, ten and fourteen years' penal servitude respectively. They were then sent to Accra on the Gold Coast to serve their sentences. The Gold Coast colonial authorities, on the advice of the same Queen's Advocate now prosecuting again in July 1880, liberated the three men, having found that they were 'illegally tried and sentenced by the Acting Consul of the Bights of Benin and Biafra'.[68] They were to be provided with a passage at the government's expense, either to Lagos or to the Niger Delta. Later they were advised by the same authorities to petition the

The Supreme Court, Tinubu Square, Lagos 1889

Otonba-Payne, Registrar of the Supreme Court, Lagos, 1876-99

Sir John Glover and his Hausas

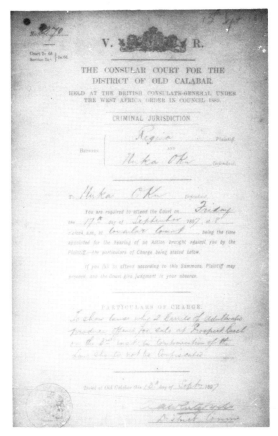

Summons used at the Consular Court, Old Calabar, 1897

Foreign Office in London for compensation for any damages they might have suffered. The passage back to the Niger Delta was duly provided, but the acting consul refused them landing at Akassa, thus compelling them to go back to Lagos. On 25 March 1880 the men were arrested in Lagos on the same charge of slave dealing for which they had supposedly been acquitted by a higher tribunal on the Gold Coast.

It is also remarkable how the verdict of 'not guilty' by the three different panels of assessors was, in each case, disregarded by the presiding judge. To overrule the opinion of a panel of assessors was contrary to section 126 of the Gold Coast Criminal Law and Procedure Ordinance of 31 March 1876, providing that the opinion of assessors should be regarded in the same light as that of a jury. In any case, in the trial of serious offences, as a group of educated Africans in Lagos observed, the finding of a panel of assessors, as a matter of practice, had always been rated 'as potent as that of a jury'.[69]

Justice Macleod in his judgment reflected the official British attitude towards what was considered the heinous crime of slave trading. He sentenced each of the three men to fourteen years' imprisonment with hard labour, regretting it lay beyond his power to pass death sentences on them. They were sent to Elmina Castle on the Gold Coast to undergo their punishment, the cries and petitions of educated Africans in Lagos notwithstanding.

The truth of the matter in the alleged slave dealing by the three prisoners seems to be that they were actually redeeming those that were being carried into slavery, temporarily retaining them as paid labourers or, in the case of the younger elements, as household servants. The evidence before the court showed that Bickersteth had redeemed a number of children and put them to school. It was also shown during the trial that since Ogoo had been arrested those whom he had redeemed had sent him a sum of three naira 'as a token of their sympathy'. At the end of his trial, one of the assessors went so far as to say that he should not only be acquitted, but also be compensated 'for his humane conduct towards those whom he had redeemed from slavery and death out of pity'.[70] But in spite of such evidence, favourable to the prisoners, the court seemed determined to make an example of them to deter others. On its part, the colonial administration could not have acceded to the petition for their release because their conviction must have been considered of great deterrent value in the eradication of a serious evil. In the desire for the extermination of the evil, the court and the administration seemed to be at one.

In the trial and conviction of Bickersteth, Palmer and Ogoo, it is possible that the interests of British commerce were being safe-guarded through the judicial process. The three men were said to be successful traders on the Niger, representatives of that class of Africans who in the nineteenth century occupied enviable middle-man positions in the trade between Europeans and Africans in the Niger Delta.[71] Tension often existed between the African middle-men and the European traders who, as the century wore on, naturally wanted to bypass them in order to maximise their profits. In the case of the three prisoners, it was alleged that a Captain McIntosh, the agent of the newly formed United Africa Company (later the Royal Niger Company) 'was anxious to get them away from the river and to command a monopoly of the trade'.[72] He was known to be a friend of the acting consul who convicted them in the first place in October 1897. In the second trial of the three men in Lagos, it is not altogether far fetched to suggest that the same commercial complex operating on the Niger was at work, fighting commercial rivalry indirectly through the judicial process.

Outside Lagos the courts were used even more brazenly to further the interests of the colonial administration in grave matters of policy. The trials at the consular courts of some prominent Nigerians who resisted British penetration in the Niger Coast Protectorate towards the end of the nineteenth century provide ample evidence for this viewpoint.

Nana Olomu was a great Itsekiri middleman trader in the Niger Delta who in the 1880s collaborated with the British, but was later at loggerheads with them when it became increasingly clear that their intention was to establish their authority and a permanent foothold on the Niger Delta rather than remain merely trading partners.[73] By the 1890s the British found him a stumbling block to their ambition to penetrate the hinterland. In 1894, the Acting Consul-General for the protectorate, Ralph Moor, acknowledged that it had 'too long been the custom of the people of Benin and Warri districts to say that they know no government but Chief Nana'.[74] In the face of the British determination to control effectively the Niger Delta and to exploit fully its wealth and resources, it was clear that a powerful chief like Nana could not survive for long. In the same correspondence in which Moor acknowledged the extent of Nana's power, he emphasised the necessity for establishing British authority in the Niger Delta to convince the people of Benin and Warri districts that Nana was not the government. An expedition was mounted against him at Ebrohimie in September 1894, and he was finally captured, after a brief escape to Lagos, in November of the same year. Then came his trial at the consular court at Old Calabar on 30 November 1894.[75]

The trial has been rightly described as 'more of a formality . . . than a conscientious effort to see justice done'.[76] It was presided over by Sir Claude Macdonald, the Consul-General and High Commissioner for the protectorate. Against Nana were preferred four charges: that he levied war against the government of the Niger Coast Protectorate; that he failed to carry out the provisions of the treaty of friendship entered into on 16 July 1884, acting in opposition to British consular officers in matters relating to the administration of justice and the development of commerce; that he committed a breach of the peace in August and September 1894 in the Benin district, and that, in doing so, he had excited others to do the same.

None of these charges was proved beyond reasonable doubt. It is true that Nana fought against British forces, but his argument that he was acting in self-defence was not contradicted with any convincing evidence. In matters of procedure there were notable irregularities in the trial. The chief prosecution witness, Ralph Moor, not only submitted to the court a number of documents as exhibits, but also summarised their contents. It has been observed that some of his summaries were 'very different' from the actual contents of the documents tendered before the court.[77] The evidence of another witness, A. F. Locke, consular agent for the Niger Coast Protectorate, amounted to hearsay. He submitted a report purported to have been written by one Heugh on a reconnoitring trip up the Ebrohimie creek to prove that it was Nana's men who first opened fire on a British boat. It would be difficult to find the grounds on which this evidence could be admitted as an exception to the hearsay rule. In respect of another witness, Jackson, Nana's clerk, hearsay evidence was similarly admitted to prove that Nana instructed his men to open fire on any approaching war boat. Yet another witness, Nana's trusted messenger, Tonwe, clearly demonstrated his unreliability. He committed perjury under Nana's cross-examination – without any reaction being shown by the court.

Thus much of the evidence on which the case for the prosecution rested could not have stood critical scrutiny, say, in an English court of law. But the trial judge evidently set no great store by the correctness of the judicial procedure. The important thing was the objective of the trial. A short while before the trial, Ralph Moor as Acting Consul-General of the Niger Coast Protectorate, had expressed the view that the deportation of Nana would be necessary for the establishment of peace, good order and commercial progress in the Niger Delta.[78] Nana's trial seemed geared towards facilitating the establishment of British presence in the Niger Coast Protectorate. The determination to achieve this political objective and the consciousness of the irregularities that might crop up during the trial would explain why Macdonald was particularly anxious to have the case tried at Old Calabar where no practising lawyer was available.

From the political point of view, the severity of the penalties imposed on Nana was also significant. He was found guilty on all counts, and sentenced to life-long exile besides forfeiting 'all the goods and chattels, real and personal property' belonging to him and his people to the government. Of the seven others tried with him on the same charges, three were acquitted, two were to be deported from Benin District for two years, and the remaining two were sentenced to penal servitude for life and forfeiture of goods.

There was nothing in the law of the protectorate to justify the severity of the sentence imposed on Nana. Article 48 of the Africa Order-in-Council, 1893, under which he was convicted for levying war against the British government, applied only to British subjects.[79] Strictly speaking, in 1894 Nana was a British-protected person rather than a British subject. One other article invoked against him was Article 102(i) of the same Order-in-Council which Macdonald interpreted as prescribing the punishment of deportation:

Where a person is convicted before a court of any crime or offence, the court may in addition to or in lieu of any other sentence order him to give security to the satisfaction of the court by recognizance, deposit or money or otherwise for future good behaviour, and in default of such security may order him to be deported forthwith or after undergoing any other sentence passed upon him.

It is obvious that Macdonald had twisted the law to suit his own purpose. The language of the law was clear: a prisoner was to be deported only if he failed to provide security for his future good behaviour – a view considered by a legal officer at the Foreign Office to be 'the better interpretation' of Article 102(i) and one likely to be upheld 'were the matter to come before the Privy Council'.[80] The paramount consideration in Nana's trial seems to have been to secure his removal from the Niger Delta; his presence was seen as a serious obstacle to the establishment of British rule. The legal niceties as to the validity of the sentence imposed on him were not important. The Foreign Office in London, in support of Macdonald, was prepared to connive at legal irregularities and 'let things slide'.[81]

The wonder is that there was a trial at all. After Nana's subjugation Britain could have simply set to the task of consolidating her position in this part of the Niger Delta without anyone raising any questions. The point was made earlier that Britain had a tradition of acting with legality or appearance of legality in the acquisition of territories overseas. A formal trial, for what it was worth, also salved the imperialist conscience that 'justice' was being done. Again, it could go some way to satisfy the relatively small, but vocal, humanitarian groups in Britain[82] that 'British justice' – a nebulous, but emotively useful concept – was not being denied to the underprivileged.

No less remarkable for their irregularities and disregard for legal niceties than Nana's trial were the Benin trials of 1897 and 1899. The trials were occasioned by the death of some European officers of the Niger Coast Protectorate in January 1897. A party of nine Europeans led by the Acting Commissioner and Consul-General, J. R. Phillips, and about two hundred and fifty African carriers, all of them probably on a spying mission, attempted to visit Benin in defiance of the authority of Oba Ovonramwen and his chiefs, without waiting for the grant of a formal permission as was customary with foreign visitors.[83] Under the apprehension that the party was a military expedition – the boxes carried by the men were believed to contain 'things that the white men will take to catch the king' – Benin soldiers, having taken up defence positions in ambush, fired on the party, killing seven of the European officials and about one hundred and twenty-four of the carriers. A massive punitive expedition followed, intended to bring to justice all those supposedly connected with the so-called massacre. Benin city was destroyed; the *Oba* and his chiefs consequently fled. About six months later, they formally surrendered to the British on 7 August 1897. Then began their formal trials. First Oba Ovonramwen and most of the Benin chiefs were tried together in September 1897. Later in June 1899 Chief Ologbose, the traditional head of the war chiefs who, with Chief Ebohon, had maintained armed resistance against the British, was eventually captured and tried.

The trial of Oba Ovonramwen and his chiefs began in the consular court at Benin on 1 September 1897, presided over by Sir Ralph Moor, Commissioner and Consul-General of the Niger Coast Protectorate, and attended by two other European officers and about seventy other chiefs of Benin city and its dependent towns.[84] Moor made it clear that he was concerned with finding out who ordered the 'massacre' of 1897. The trial was being held under native law and custom, he said, and he would, in making a judicial decision, take into consideration the views of the chiefs present regarding their native laws and customs in the matter. Quite significantly, he declared, without any regard for judicial discretion, that he already knew some of the issues involved in the case and that the chiefs were only to help fill the gaps in his knowledge.[85]

There were no formal charges, nor was any plea taken from the accused persons. The evidence of all the prosecution witnesses told virtually the same story: that for three years before the so-called massacre, there had been great expectations of war; that at the news of an approaching party of European officers and their African carriers there was a general belief that war was imminent; a public meeting was held at which all the Benin chiefs except the Ezomo and the Ero decided to send their 'boys' to Ughoton (Benin's outpost) 'to stop the white men from getting to the city'. It was clear even from the evidence of the prosecution witnesses that the decision to repel what was believed to be an attack on the city was a collective decision. Part of the evidence also revealed what Moor himself had earlier recognised in a despatch written before the trial;[86] namely, Phillips's foolhardiness and lack of discretion in not waiting at Ughoton for the return of the messenger sent to the city to apprise the Oba of the arrival of his party. Moor conveniently ignored this vital piece of evidence which would seem to indicate that the death of Phillips and his party was death by misadventure.

Perhaps the most interesting aspect of the trial of the Oba and his chiefs was how Moor propounded his own version of Benin 'native law and custom' and applied it, departing from his earlier promise to consult the chiefs present regarding their law and custom. He declared *ex cathedra* what was the Benin native law and custom relevant to the case he was trying:

> . . . If a chief kill a chief, a chief must die; if a king is killed, a king must die. There are seven white men killed, one of whom was at the time the king of the white man; therefore by native law the king of Benin city must die. The next one who was killed was the second man, therefore by native law, Chief Ero being second man to the king, must die and so on doing the same for the five others that were killed – an equal black man to be killed for each white man that was killed.[87]

He turned round to ask the chiefs by way of seeking confirmation: 'Is not that your native law?' The atmosphere was, of course, such that the chiefs could not have returned a negative answer. Had not the Oba of Benin himself once formally acknowledged the supremacy of the white man, bending his knees in public, his head thrice touching the ground, and had not the chiefs too tasted the 'demonstrably aggressive temper' of the new administration in the destruction of their city?

On the basis of the newly propounded Benin native law and custom, Moor proceeded to give judgment. Two of the chiefs standing trial, Obakhavbaye and Uso, were to be publicly executed. These two chiefs with two other chiefs, Ugiagbe and Obayuwana, had earlier been taken prisoners before the end of the trial because the evidence of three witnesses suggested they were on the Ughoton road during the 'massacre'. Their mere presence on the road was taken as evidence of their complicity. Of the four chiefs, only Obakhavbaye and Uso remained till the end of the trial, the others having committed suicide 'rather than submit to the disgrace of public hanging'. As for the others standing trial, Chief Ologbose, still at large and offering armed resistance, was condemned to death *in absentia*, while the Oba of Benin was to be deposed or, in the alternative, be made an ordinary chief if he would assist the British administration in establishing itself. The Oba attempted to escape, and, at a reconvened session of the court on 9 September, was sentenced to deportation and indefinite exile from his domain.

From the point of view of the colonial administration of the Niger Coast Protectorate, it was becoming increasingly necessary to bring Chief Ologbose and Chief Ebohon openly to justice. The two chiefs had firmly established themselves in the north-east of Benin, constituting 'a centre of resistance for all those who disapproved of the establishment of British rule in Benin'.[88] A measure of their strength was the observation by Major H. L. Gallwey, then Acting High Commissioner and Consul-General, in June 1898: 'so long as these two rebel chiefs remain at large, so long will the government's prestige hang in the balance in the Bini country'.[89] A punitive expedition against the chiefs was finally decided upon, and on 19 May 1899, Ologbose, but not Ebohon, was captured. On 27 June, his trial began at the 'full Native Court' at Benin.[90] Sir Ralph Moor presided over the court, which comprised four other European officers and eleven Benin chiefs. The charge preferred against the accused was that he led the party that committed the 'massacre' of January 1897.

The four prosecution witnesses all told virtually the same story as had been narrated two years earlier during the trial of Oba Ovonramwen and some of his chiefs, none of them giving any substantial evidence implicating the accused. The witnesses also showed glaringly the indiscretion of Phillips's party in not waiting for the Oba of Benin to signify his desire to receive the visitors, as was customary. Again, as in 1897, Moor chose not to pursue this line of judicial inquiry, considering it 'unnecessary and useless to comment on this aspect of the matter'.[91]

Ologbose's evidence in his own defence underlined the point brought out during the earlier trial of the Oba and some of his chiefs; namely, that the decision to attack Phillips's party was a collective decision of the Benin people:

> Since I was born in Benin city I had never been to the waterside. I never went as far as Jebu, but when all the people called the mass meeting at Benin city selected me to go and fight the whitemen I went. I had no palaver with the whitemen before. The day I was selected to go from Benin city to meet the whitemen all the Chiefs here present were in the meeting and now they want to put the whole thing on my shoulders.[92]

The head war chief was in 1897 responding to a call for national service. But by 1899 the nationalist spirit which had prompted the decision to repel Phillips's party seemed to have evaporated. The chiefs on the court bench, apparently cowed by the events of the previous two years, were in no mood to speak out in favour of the accused, although they did not deny his allegations. Indeed they were now anxious to please Sir Ralph Moor and to gratify his prejudice against the war chief.[93]

In giving his judgment Moor simply asked the chiefs on the court bench whether Ologbose and other war chiefs were 'sent out to fight men trying to come into your country by force of arms or [whether] they were authorized to kill any whitemen whether with or without arms' – a curious combination of questions that went very much beyond the scope of the evidence adduced before the court. The chiefs were at one in answering that Ologbose was not sent to kill any whitemen, 'and we therefore decide that according to native law his life is forfeited'. He was sentenced to be hanged the following morning.

Like the trial and deportation of Oba Ovanramwen, Chief Ologbose's trial was more of a political measure than an attempt to administer even-handed justice. Moor himself seems to have said as much after the execution of the war chief: 'The prompt trial and execution of the late Chief Ologbosheri was *as a matter of policy* essential for the firm establishment of Government and the future good order of the territories.'[94] The trial and execution were essential precisely because his presence was an obstacle to the establishment of British rule. A man of forceful personality and of undoubted military ability, for about two years he had demonstrated his determination to resist British encroachment by force of arms. In his trial political policy rather than law and the ideals of 'British justice' was the overriding consideration. It is also noteworthy that from the point of view of the establishment of British rule, the repercussions of the trial were not any less important than the actual removal of the war chief. In Moor's own words, the trial 'demonstrated with marked effect to the natives the consistent and sure execution of justice, and will be a lesson to them that crime in any form must eventually meet with its deserts'.[95]

The use of the courts for political ends in the Niger Coast Protectorate was not limited to the removal of prominent individuals who stood in the way of the establishment of British colonial rule. The judicial process could also be used at the local level directly or indirectly to aid the administration. In *Minike Eyo Asibon v. Edet Edem and two others*, the district commissioner presiding over the decision of the Supreme Court at Calabar in March 1903 found the accused persons guilty of 'disobedience to lawful orders of head of a House' and sentenced them to two weeks' imprisonment each.[96] This was at a time when the 'house' system in the Niger Delta was breaking down under the impact of Christian missionaries, contact with Europeans and the growth of individualism.[97] The 'house' system, by bringing freemen and slaves together as a trading corporation, usually under the autocratic rule of a 'house' head, served not only the needs of commerce, but also of political organisation throughout the nineteenth century.[98] Until the colonial administration established its own machinery for local government, it was only expedient for British political officers, anxious to achieve some order and stability in areas coming under British rule, to maintain the integrity of the system and uphold its authority. In the *Minike Eyo Asibon* case, all that the accused persons did was to attempt to trade on their own, independently of the 'house' to which they belonged.

Similarly in *William Brown v. Abake Brown* tried before the 'native' council of Bonny on 6 May 1904, the accused person was sentenced to three months' imprisonment with hard labour for 'disobeying orders of the Head of the House he belongs to by refusing to come and perform duties of the House when called by the Head of the House'.[99]

The case of *R. v. Okoronkwo and seven others*, tried at Owerri on 4 July 1904 by a district commissioner in his capacity as a commissioner of the Supreme Court, provides an illustration of the use of the judicial process in direct aid of colonial administration. The accused persons, local chiefs in Owerri District, were sentenced to terms of imprisonment varying from four to six months for 'refusing to attend meeting [with the district commissioner], thereby behaving in a manner likely to cause a breach of the peace'.[100] Their real offence apparently consisted in their recalcitrant attitude towards the colonial administration that was being established. As the district commissioner himself explained, 'these people in spite of being close to Owerri have never come in spite of repeated messages both by Court Messengers and friendly chiefs [which] have failed to get them to attend meetings'. The ground of their arrest was as frivolous as the charge itself: the boys of the chiefs 'came in and begged that their chiefs might be arrested in order that their town might not get into trouble with Government'.[101]

The fact was that at the beginning of this century when Britain was not fully entrenched as a colonial power in Southern Nigeria, she could hardly condone any failure to recognise her authority. The attitude of the chiefs, in official eyes, amounted to a mild form of rebellion. Consequently, the political officer was prepared to use any means at his disposal, including the judicial process, to extirpate or at least weaken it.

IV

Considerable importance was attached by the colonial administration to the exploitation of the economic resources of Southern Nigeria. It should therefore not be surprising to discover that the courts tended to promote, or were used in promoting, the economic development of the territory.

An illustration of the point is provided by the efforts made to deal with the problem of the adulteration of palm produce in the Lagos Colony and in the Niger Coast Protectorate. Adulteration of palm produce was considered a very serious problem because it was believed in commercial circles in Lagos to 'strike at the very backbone of the commerce of this Settlement'.[102] By the late 1880s its widespread practice was said to have resulted in a lowering of the price offered in European markets for palm kernels from Lagos and other parts of Southern Nigeria.[103] The crux of the problem was that some indigenous traders were offering to Europeans for sale, or in payment for goods entrusted to them, palm kernels that had been adulterated by the injection of foreign elements – iron, wood, wet bags, sand and the like – into the bags containing them, to increase their weight artificially. Palm oil was similarly adulterated with water and such local foods as *agidi* and *fufu*.[104] British and other foreign merchants in Lagos complained that such fraudulent practices were affecting them seriously. A bag of adulterated palm kernels or a tin of 'falsified' palm oil was not only turned down by buyers in Europe; it also tended to 'depreciate the value of the whole cargo'. One of the British firms in Lagos was estimated to have sustained a loss of ₦22,000 in one year 'by reason of such frauds' practised on it.[105] Loss of revenue was serious enough, but the merchants were probably more concerned about the future prosperity of Lagos as a commercial centre. Their anxiety was reflected in the repeated demands for criminal sanctions against these nefarious commercial practices.[106]

The courts were at first rather indifferent to the plight of the merchants, although some magistrates occasionally meted out 'heavy sentences' to convicted dishonest traders. The courts took so liberal a view of the whole matter that by 1875 the merchants said they were feeling 'great repugnance' in applying to the courts for the redress of their grievances. 'As the law is at present administered', they wrote, 'we rather suffer loss or some little imposition than summon any one of our traders [for fraudulent trade practices].'[107]

The attitude held by the courts before 1875 was understandable. This was a time in England itself when *laissez-faire* in economic relations was echoed in law in the maxim *caveat emptor*, the buyer of goods being expected to take every care required of a prudent person to ensure the quality and value of his goods, and their fitness for the purpose for which they were bought. The predominance of this maxim was not challenged until the passage of the Sale of Goods Act, 1893. In their reluctance to interfere on behalf of the merchants, the courts in Lagos, up to 1875, were apparently operating by that maxim. The merchants were presumed to be prudent men of business who ought to have taken reasonable care in their commercial dealings. According to W. Melton, then Acting Chief Magistrate, one reasonable measure they ought to have taken to guard themselves against bad commercial practices should have been to employ 'extra assistants and additional appliances' to examine every palm product offered for sale.[108]

The merchants, however, soon found a sympathetic judge in James Marshall who arrived in Lagos as Acting Chief Magistrate on 5 January 1875. No sooner did he arrive than the merchants poured out to him their complaints. He held extensive unofficial discussions with representatives of various mercantile houses, during which he gained intimate knowledge of the modes of business transactions in palm produce in Lagos, and of the financial plight of the European merchants.[109] The upshot was that he was prepared to throw the weight of the judiciary behind the merchants. 'If Lagos kernels continue to go to England deteriorated in quality', he wrote to the Lieutenant-Governor, 'it will of course lessen the value in general of Lagos kernels as well as of Lagos oil.'[110] What was therefore at stake was 'not merely a matter of actual loss to merchants, but the future prosperity of the Settlement'. The courts, he believed, could adequately deal with the problem without any additional legislation:

> If a man is convicted of selling or offering for sale, bartering or offering for barter, produce which he represents as pure and in good condition but which he knows to be spurious, adulterated articles or which he knows to have been wilfully and maliciously deteriorated in value, I have no hesitation in saying that *especially when viewed under the special circumstances of the Lagos trade*, such an offender can and ought to be punished in the Criminal Courts.[111]

The Chief Magistrate's proposition of law is probably unassailable, but, taking into account the merchants' private representations to him on the subject of adulteration of produce, and his own obvious interest in it, one has the impression of a learned judge very anxious to bend the law to serve a predetermined end. The trade practices complained of by the merchants amounted in English law to fraudulent misrepresentation, and one would have thought that their remedy, in individual cases, lay in *tort*, and not in the application of criminal sanctions.

It may be urged in support of the learned judge's position that in English law an act which tends to constitute a 'public mischief' may be punished as a criminal offence even when it has not been so defined by the legislature or the court. One easily recalls the dictum of Lawrence, J., in *R. v. Higgins* (1801): 'All such acts or attempts as tend to the prejudice of the community are indictable.'[112] But this dictum for a long time was considered too wide to be of any practical value. Consequently throughout the nineteenth century, in spite of the dictum in *Higgins*, *nulla poena sine lege* was held as the operative principle of criminal liability in English law. No man could be made to suffer except for a breach of the criminal law. At a time when cremation was considered offensive to many in England, Stephen, J., in *R. v. Price* (1884) refused to hold it a criminal offence to cremate a dead body instead of burying it. The courts in Lagos before Marshall's arrival in not making criminal offences of alleged fraudulent commercial practices were acting on the same *nulla poena* principle. It was not until recently that the courts in England have reasserted their claim to possess 'a residual power . . . to superintend those offences which are prejudicial to the public welfare' even where the legislature has not enjoined them to do so. The well-known cases of *R. v. Manley* (1932) and *Shaw v. D.P.P.* (1962), (The Ladies' Directory case) are indicative of this trend in English judicial thinking. But, as *R. v. Newland* (1953) would seem to indicate, the claim of the court to be the *custos morum* of its community has not been consistently made, so that perhaps it is still an open question whether judges today in England have power to create new crimes where none existed.[113]

Back in Lagos, Justice Marshall on 1 February 1875, true to his belief, tried a man for offering adulterated produce for sale and convicted him of a criminal offence. Besides punishing the offender, 'I gave public warning that others convicted of such offences would be very severely punished'. A few more cases of similar offences being met with heavy penalties were reported. The result, as one of the merchants later reported, was 'a marked change for the better in the quality of the palm kernels and other produce brought by the native traders'.[114]

Justice Marshall's view on the usefulness of the courts in dealing with commercial abuses through criminal sanctions seemed to have been vindicated. But it is perhaps significant that in February 1889 the colonial legislature formally enacted an ordinance making it a criminal offence to adulterate produce and to sell palm kernels without first taking reasonable precaution against the possibility of their being adulterated,[115] thus providing a strong legal basis for the application of criminal sanctions to eradicate the evil of dishonest trading.

The courts were also used to combat the problem of adulteration of palm produce in the Niger Coast Protectorate up to the first decade of this century. The first legislation to deal with the problem was an ordinance passed in 1897. More legislation followed between 1901 and 1905 in the form of proclamations.[116] By and large, they empowered district commissioners acting in their judicial capacity to deal severely with offenders and destroy any adulterated produce offered for sale. Besides the proclamations, many 'native' councils made local rules, enforceable by the councils, to deal with the same problem.[117]

Commenting on the enforcement of the proclamations on the subject of adulteration of produce up to the end of 1902, Ralph Moor, the High Commissioner and Consul-General, indicated that larger numbers of prosecutions had been made. He admitted that the law 'may have been carried out in a somewhat drastic manner' on account of 'the great difficulties' involved in dealing with the problem of fraudulent commercial practices.[118]

In March 1903 the Acting High Commissioner issued out a set of instructions to all district commissioners in the Protectorate on how the Adulteration of Produce Proclamation of 1902 should be enforced in the courts. It is significant that the instructions were issued in spite of a strenuous objection by the Chief Justice, claiming control over the judicial department. The Chief Justice had argued that general instructions to judicial officers as to how a law should be enforced would be out of keeping with normal judicial practice 'because the merits of each case would be different'.[119] The Chief Justice's objection was overruled. The colonial administration of the protectorate was determined to ensure that the produce exports from Southern Nigeria 'may have a good name and consequently a better price' in Europe. It would not stop short of bending the judicial process to serve this end.

The different local judicial tribunals operating in the Niger Coast Protectorate and in some parts of Yorubaland – 'native' councils, 'native' courts, minor courts – were concerned in vital aspects of their functions with the promotion of the economic development of their areas of jurisdiction. 'It is important', wrote the Acting High Commissioner and Consul-General for the Niger Coast Protectorate in 1901, 'that the Native Councils should be trained to regard themselves as being bodies for the development of trade in their districts'.[120] Up to about 1911 various tasks were assigned to them: popularisation of new currencies, as in Owerri District in 1902;[121] enforcement of new rules regarding trade tax, as in Owo, Degema and Benin River Districts;[122] the regulation of fishing activities, as in the riverain districts of Southern Nigeria in 1909;[123] promotion of cotton cultivation in several areas of Southern Nigeria;[124] the regulation of tapping of rubber and the felling of palm trees virtually throughout Southern Nigeria.[125] The administration had in mind 'the regulation and promotion of trade' when it encouraged some thirty-five 'native' councils in the Eastern Province in 1911 to make simple rules governing the acquisition of land by foreigners.[126] The local judicial tribunals were particularly valued for their role in the economic and social development of their areas. The administration relied on them not only for the establishment of peace and order, but also for the furtherance of commercial and agricultural development in the different areas of Southern Nigeria.

The emphasis on the economic development of Southern Nigeria and on the role the local tribunals could play in it was by no means purposeless in the overall design of the territory as a colonial estate. Any rapid economic development of Southern Nigeria would redound to Britain's benefit.

V

It is time to examine the relations of the executive arm of the colonial administration to the judicial system operating in Southern Nigeria up to about 1914. The important point to note is that the relations that subsisted between the executive and the judiciary in the territory was not comparable to those subsisting between the executive and the judiciary in England. By and large, the executive in Southern Nigeria exercised a degree of control over the judiciary that would have been unthinkable in England.

The reasons are not far to seek. To say that the fundamental concepts of the British approach to justice are 'diametrically opposed to the demands of colonial rule' is to overstate a case.[127] But it is true that in a colonial context the British ideals of legal justice could not always be pursued in the adjudication of disputes. A colonial administration – the imposition of foreign rule by one people over another – invariably depended on absolute control of all important organs of government. For 'one act of successful opposition on the part of the natives, even in a trifling matter, might lead to serious results'[128] – a point of view which would seem to hold good as long as a colonial regime lasted. The two chief preoccupations of every administration were the preservation of order and the orderly development of a given territory's resources. Some element of coercion might be essential in achieving either of these objectives, and an utterly independent judiciary, applying the law to the letter regardless of the colonial situation or the sensibilities of political officers, might render colonial rule unworkable. Some cooperation with the executive arm of government, some compromising of principles and not a little judicial connivance were often required of a colonial judiciary – at any rate until the colonial regime was, or felt itself to be, firmly established.

The position of the judiciary in Southern Nigeria before 1914 would support this hypothesis. No sooner were four courts established in Lagos in 1862 than H. S. Freeman, the first Governor, made it clear that he would not favour the appointment of 'entirely independent legal officers' to operate the courts.[129] He was anxious 'to have every department completely under my control' so that he would be able to 'make such arrangements and concessions' in all facets of administration as might be indispensable to the orderly organisation of the colony's affairs. In the circumstances of Lagos in the 1860s, he feared that 'the strict application of British law', resulting from the existence of an independent judiciary, might hamper the administrative control of the colony.

John H. Glover, the Administrator of the colony, 1866–72, also displayed a desire for a docile judiciary. For many years, to his great pleasure, his superintendent of police, Isaac Willoughby, wielded considerable powers in the interest of the colonial government. Some of the powers were illegally acquired and were illegally used. Early in 1871 the police magistrate, Josiah Gerard, acting in the interests of justice and apparently disregarding the cosy relations between Glover and the police superintendent, moved to curtail his powers. Later the same year when complaints were lodged against Gerard's attitude towards the members of the indigenous population, Glover seized the opportunity to demand his resignation.[130] He was replaced as police magistrate in December 1871.

Kadiri v. Kubolaku (1876) reveals another aspect of the relations between the executive and the judiciary in the Colony of Lagos: the claim sometimes made by the executive to be the ultimate 'fountain of justice' over and above the head of the judiciary, exercising, as it were, a latter-day version of equitable jurisdiction. *Kubolaku*'s case, tried by the Court of Civil and Criminal Justice, was a simple case of trespass.[131] The defendant, 'an old native woman', shared a house with the plaintiff, one Abudu Kadiri. The plaintiff claimed ₦10 as damages for his mud wall allegedly pulled down by the defendant. The latter contested the claim, but was asked by the court to pay ₦3.20, including costs. She paid the sum, but addressed a letter to the Chief Magistrate in protest. When no reply was forthcoming she petitioned the Acting Administrator of the colony, John Dumaresq, on the same issue.

Kubolaku's petition and the executive inquiries following it would tend to becloud the issues involved in the case. One thing that is clear is that the decision in the case was a result of arbitration by the acting colonial surveyor, one Campbell. The Acting

Chief Magistrate who presided over the case, James Marshall, believing that the case was 'more a question of measurement than anything else', submitted it to Campbell for arbitration, although not with the consent of both parties, as he claimed.

Whatever the merits or the demerits of Marshall's action in the case, the significant thing about it was the mode of executive intervention. The Acting Administrator of the colony, not taking a strictly legalistic view of the issues involved in the case, and apparently impressed by the additional (uncorroborated) evidence adduced in her petition and subsequent personal representation, felt 'a great injustice has been done to Kubolaku'. He then ordered that the ₦3.20 she had paid to court be refunded to her out of the year's vote for the colony's miscellaneous services. In reaching this decision, the Acting Administrator did not refer the case to the Acting Chief Magistrate, but to Campbell, a witness in the case. It would also appear that he took additional evidence of his own, allowing 'further and verbal accusations to be brought to him' against the acting chief magistrate.[132]

The acting chief magistrate claimed that *Kubolaku*'s case was not a singular instance of executive intervention. A case of eject-ment, *Joseph v. Omoleya*, had earlier been decided by him, more or less with the same results, the unsuccessful party challenging his decision and the Acting Administrator making 'private investi-gations and enquiries' of his own. 'I now find that I cannot hear or decide a cause', he wrote, 'without being liable to having accusa-tions brought against me by the unsuccessful suitor which under the name of a report I am called upon to answer.'[133]

Dumaresq, the Acting Administrator, was censured over the differences between himself and the Acting Chief Magistrate in the *Kubolaku* case.[134] But it is significant that the censure stopped short of laying down any general guiding principle on the relations that should subsist between the executive and the judiciary in Lagos. To lay down such a general guiding principle would seem to have been called for in view of Marshall's claim that *Kubolaku* was only an instance of a trend. The Acting Chief Magistrate's assertion that he would 'administer justice with the freedom and independence which is as much the right of my humble Bench, as it is of the Bench at Westminster' was certainly a misapprehension of his own position in the scheme of things in Lagos.

The administration in the Niger Coast Protectorate was no better respecter of the judiciary than in the Lagos Colony before the amalgamation of 1906. We saw earlier how the High Commissioner and Consul-General, in trying to ensure the effective enforcement of the Adulteration of Produce Proclamation of 1902, issued a set of instructions to district commissioners as officers of the Supreme Court against the objection of the protectorate's Chief Justice.

How far could the Chief Justice as head of a colonial judiciary control the disposition of staff in his department independently of the executive? That was the question the Colonial Office had to resolve in 1910 between Sir Walter Egerton as the Governor of amalgamated Southern Nigeria and A. Willoughby Osborne, the territory's Chief Justice, 1909–13. In this great controversy between the Governor and the Chief Justice the independence of the judiciary was once again called into question.

Within one year of his stay in Southern Nigeria, Willoughby Osborne had practical experience of the realities of the subordinate position of the judiciary. Two police magistrates were assigned to administrative duties without any reference to him as the Chief Justice. Others were on different occasions asked to act as solicitor-general, besides their normal judicial work, again, without any reference to him. On one occasion, he said, he received 'two apparently peremptory orders from an Assistant Secretary'.[135] In November 1909 he had to protest against an allocation of judges which the Governor was about to adopt without reference to him. Matters came to a head in April 1910 when he requested the Colonial Office to intervene 'to prevent further misunderstanding'.[136]

In the controversy between the Governor and the Chief Justice, the Governor claimed that the disposition of staff within the judiciary, as within any other department of government, was within his jurisdiction. It was the Governor 'who determines the appointment to be filled by any particular officer and the length of his tenure of that appointment'.[137] In the time before Willoughby Osborne, he said, 'the executive corresponded direct with the Magistrates and gave them such instructions and directions as seemed desirable'. In the disposition of staff within the judicial department, the Governor promised, he would always consult the Chief Justice, 'where circumstances allowed of this being done without inconvenience and undue delay'. But this was only a matter of courtesy.

Willoughby Osborne on his part believed that as Chief Justice of the Supreme Court, he was the head of the judicial department, and as such, 'the officer responsible for the general administration of justice in the Colony and Protectorate of Southern Nigeria'.[138] As Chief Justice, he claimed to be the proper officer to assign duties to officers of the judicial department and that all instructions to judicial officers should be given through him except in cases of unavoidable necessity. He should also be consulted 'before any temporary local changes in the judicial department are carried into effect, and also before any local executive officer is appointed to the judicial department'. The behaviour of the Governor in matters of disposition of staff within the judicial department, he said, would make it possible for him to pack the Bench.

The Chief Justice requested the Colonial Office for rulings on four specific questions: whether or not the Chief Justice was responsible for the general administration of justice within the jurisdiction of the court; whether or not the Chief Justice as head of the judicial department, was the proper officer to assign duties in his department; whether or not the Chief Justice had a right to be consulted before a judicial officer was given administrative duties or before an executive officer was appointed a judicial officer; and, finally, whether or not instructions from the executive authorities to officers of the judicial department should be conveyed through the Chief Justice, except in cases of unavoidable necessity.

The reaction of Lord Crewe, the Secretary of State for the Colonies, was that he could not answer any of the Chief Justice's four questions in the affirmative. The only concession he would grant was that in the disposition of staff within the judicial department, the Chief Justice should be consulted whenever it was possible to do so 'as a matter of propriety and for the better conduct of business'.[139]

One sympathises with Willoughby Osborne, who was apparently actuated by the British ideals of justice and by the desire, in his own words, 'to ensure that as far as possible, justice shall be administered without fear or favour by the Court' – a state of affairs which he believed would require that judicial officers be 'as far as possible . . . independent of direct executive control'. But the requirements of colonial rule, as Lord Crewe well knew, put limitations on the extent to which British ideals of justice could be carried into the colonies.

Willoughby Osborne was not alone in trying to maintain the independence of the judiciary within the context of colonial

Southern Nigeria. In the next chapter we shall see the stout independence of judicial outlook maintained by some other judges of the Supreme Court in deciding cases in which members of the administration were ranged against their African colonial subjects. But it is perhaps no accident that such fiercely independent-minded judges were never long in the Colonial Service of Southern Nigeria. In any case, from 1910 on, the territory's judicial system, as will be shown in the next chapter, was gradually being re-organised in such a way as to give considerable judicial powers to political officers at the expense of narrowing the scope of the operation of the Supreme Court and its judges.

Notes

1 NAI, CSO 1/1, I, Freeman to Newcastle, 8 March 1862.
2 Compare 'Governing Council, Brass: Meetings', bound volume at NAE.
3 NAE, CSO 1/13, VI.
4 Harold Bindloss, *In the Niger Country*, London, new imp., 1968, pp. 146–7.
5 NAE, CSO 1/13, XI, 'Annual Report on the Niger Coast Protec-torate, 1898–1899'.
6 NAE, CSO 1/13, XVIII, Moor to Colonial Office, 7 January 1902, enclosure. Marshall was succeeded by Samuel Moore, and then by H. G. Kelly.
7 *Ibid.*
8 NAE, CSO 1/15, IV, Kelly to acting high commissioner of Southern Nigeria Protectorate, 10 September 1903.
9 NAE, CSO 1/13, XXIII, Moor to Colonial Office, 7 January 1903.
10 NAE, CSO 1/13, XIII, Gallwey to Colonial Office, 29 August 1900.
11 NAE, CSO 1/13, XIII, Gallwey to Colonial Office, 15 September 1900, enclosure. See also NAE, CSO 1/13, XIV, Moor to Colonial Office, 22 February 1901.
12 NAE, CSO 1/15, IV, Kelly to acting high commissioner of Southern Nigeria Protectorate, 10 September 1903.
13 CO 583/44, Lugard to Bonar Law, 20 January 1916, enclosure.
14 NAE, CSO 1/13, XXII, Moor to secretary of state for the colonies, 2 December 1902.
15 Jay Gordon, 'The Development of the Legal System . . .', p. 109.
16 NAI, CSO 1/10, XI, Lees to Freeling, 2 July 1877.
17 Jay Gordon, p. 112.

18 NAI, CSO 1/1, VII, Griffith to Ussher, Accra, 30 August 1880;
   NAI, CSO 1/10, XXXVII, Griffith to Rowe, 28 October 1881;
   HCA, Lagos, 'Chief Magistrate's Minute Book, May 1872–August
   1876', 'Criminal Record Book, 1871–1875', 'Judge's Notebook:
   Criminal Cases, 1881–1885'.
19 NAI, CSO 1/11, I, Beech to Lees, 8 February 1879.
20 *Infra*, pp. 95–6.
21 NAE, CSO 1/15, IX, Egerton to Elgin, 15 May 1906, enclosure.
22 CO 96/114, D. P. Chalmers to Colonial Office, 3 June 1873.
23 Jay Gordon, p. 112.
24 NAE, CSO 1/13, XIV, Moor to Colonial Office, 22 February 1901.
25 HCA, Lagos, 'Chief Magistrate's Minute Book, 1872–1876',
   'Judge's Notebook in Civil Cases, 1877, I,' 'Chief Justice's Civil
   Cases Record Book, March 1898–November 1898'.
26 Compare *Banjoko v. Tiwo* (1877) and *Saidu v. Oduntan and Oku*
   (1877), in HCA, Lagos, 'Judge's Notebook in Civil Cases, 1877, I'.
27 HCA, Lagos, 'Chief Magistrate's Criminal Record Book, 1866–
   1868', 'Criminal Record Book, 1871–1875'.
28 HCA, Lagos, 'Chief Magistrate's Minute Book, May 1872–August
   1876', pp. 193–9. The trial was essentially an inquisition, the judge
   cross-examining the defendants from the beginning to the end.
29 Compare *Regina v. Moses Williams* and *Regina v. Adebayo*, both tried
   in 1872, HCA, Lagos, 'Chief Magistrate's Minute Book, May 1872–
   August 1876'. See also NAI, CSO 1/10, XXXVIII, Griffith to Rowe,
   30 November 1881.
30 HCA, Lagos, 'Circuit Criminal Record Book, 1907'.
31 Jay Gordon, p. 116.
32 NAI, CSO 1/8, VIA, Glover to administrator-in-chief, Sierra Leone,
   11 February 1870, enclosure.
33 *Ibid.*
34 *Ibid.*
35 CO 147/17, Kennedy to Granville, 14 March 1870.
36 NAI, CSO 1/10, II, Marshall to Lees, 8 February 1875.
37 *Ibid.* See also NAI, CSO 1/10, II, Marshall to Lees, 12 March 1875,
   enclosure.
38 NAI, CSO 1/10, II, Marshall to Lees, 15 March 1875.
39 NAI, CSO 1/8, XI, Glover to Gerrard, 8 September 1871.
40 HCA, Lagos, 'Record Book of Civil Cases, September 1878–
   September 1880'; 'Civil Record Book: Chief Justice's Notebook,
   February 1887–August 1890'.
41 *African Times*, 2 May 1881.
42 *African Times*, 1 August 1881.
43 Compare the salary scales of Otonba-Payne and Charles Foresythe,
   two overworked officers of the colonial service. Neither earned up to
   ₦400 per annum. NAI, CSO 1/8, VIIIA, Glover to Kennedy, 25
   February 1871, NAI, CSO 1/10, II, Payne to Lees, 3 March 1875.
44 NAI, CSO 1/8, VB, Glover to administrator-in-chief, Sierra Leone,
   16 November 1869.
45 CO 147/17, Kennedy to Granville, 14 March 1870.

46 NAI, CSO 1/19, XXXVI, Egerton to Colonial Office, 20 January 1911, enclosure.
47 NAE, CSO 1/15, IX, Egerton to Elgin, 15 May 1906, enclosure.
48 Compare *R. v. Udo Ekong Asano and others*, *R. v. Eze and others*, and *R. v. Egon and others*, all tried at Calabar in 1904. NAE, CSO 1/13, XXXI.
49 Lagos, *Annual Report for the Colony and Protectorate of Southern Nigeria, 1907*, p. 19; Lagos, *Annual Report for the Colony and Protectorate of Southern Nigeria, 1908*, p. 407.
50 J. C. Anene, *Southern Nigeria in Transition*, p. 266.
51 'Annual Report on the Eastern Province for the Year 1907', in Lagos, *Annual Reports of the Colony of Southern Nigeria, 1907*, p. 36.
52 A. E. Afigbo, *The Warrant Chiefs*, London, 1972, p. 108.
53 NAE, Cal Prof 10/1.
54 'Annual Report on the Eastern Province for the Year 1907', in Lagos, *Annual Reports of the Colony of Southern Nigeria, 1907*, p. 36.
55 Afigbo, 'The Warrant Chief System in Eastern Nigeria . . .', p. 139.
56 *African Times*, 23 August 1869, Letter to the editor by 'An Observer'.
57 NAI, CSO 1/8, VIB, Glover to Kennedy, 30 April 1870.
58 NAI, CSO 1/8, VB, Glover to administrator-in-chief, Sierra Leone, 16 November 1869.
59 NAI, CSO 1/8, VIA, C. A. Montagu to Kennedy, 17 January 1870.
60 NAI, CSO 1/8, VIB, Glover to Administrator-in-Chief, 16 November 1869. See also *African Times*, 24 January 1870.
61 NAI, CSO 1/8, VIB, Glover to administrator-in-chief, 16 November 1869.
62 NAI, CSO 1/8, XI, Ali Balogun and 208 others to Glover, 31 August 1871. Extracts from the minutes of council held over the petition on 11 September 1871.
63 NAI, CSO 1/8, XI, Ali Balogun and others to Glover, 31 August 1871.
64 NAI, CSO 1/10, XXXVIII, Griffiths to Rowe, 30 November 1881; *Lagos Times*, 23 November 1881.
65 The transcripts of the cases are found in NAI, CSO 1/10, XXVII, Griffiths to Ussher, 8 November 1880, enclosures.
66 NAI, CSO 1/10, XXVIII, Moloney to Griffiths, 24 December 1880, enclosed petition by J. B. Benjamin and 55 others.
67 *Ibid.* See also NAI, CSO 1/10, XXVII, Griffiths to Ussher, 8 November 1880, enclosed petition by C. A. S. Williams.
68 NAI, CSO 1/10, XXVII, Griffiths to Ussher, enclosure A.
69 NAI, CSO 1/10, XXVIII, Moloney to Griffiths, 24 December 1880, enclosure.
70 NAI, CSO 1/10, XXVII, Griffiths to Ussher, enclosure N.
71 K. O. Dike, *Trade and Politics in the Niger Delta, 1830–1885*, Oxford, 1956, pp. 97–127, 206, 215–16.
72 NAI, CSO 1/10, XXVII, Griffiths to Ussher, 8 November 1880, enclosed petition by C. A. S. Williams.
73 For a biographical study of Nana, see O. Ikime, *Merchant Prince of the Niger Delta*, London, 1968.

74 FO 2/63, Moor to Foreign Office, 8 August 1894.
75 The full transcript of the trial, *Regina v. Nana Alluma*, 1894, is contained in NAI, CSO 1/13, IV.
76 O. Ikime, *Merchant Prince of the Niger Delta*, p. 160.
77 *Ibid.*
78 FO 2/64, telegram from Moor to Foreign Office, 13 September 1894, and Moor to Foreign Office, 15 September 1894.
79 The Africa Order-in-Council 1889 (and 1893) is contained in Appendix I of F. E. Hodges, *Consular Jurisdiction in Her Majesty's Protectorate of the Niger Coast*, London, 1895.
80 FO 2/64, Macdonald to Foreign Office, 13 December 1894, Minutes on the despatch by 'WEW' dated 18 June 1895.
81 FO 2/64, Macdonald to Foreign Office, 13 December 1894, Minutes on the despatch dated 18 June 1895 and 19 June 1895.
82 For more on the humanitarian groups and their role in shaping British policy in West Africa, see K. D. Nworah, 'Humanitarian Pressure Groups and British Attitudes to West Africa, 1895–1915', unpublished PhD thesis, London University, 1966.
83 An account of the trials is given by P. A. Igbafe, 'The Benin Trials of 1897 and 1899', *Odu* n.s., No. 5, April 1971.
84 The transcript of the trial is contained in NAI, CSO 1/13, VII, Moor to Foreign Office, 18 October 1897.
85 NAI, CSO 1/13, VII, Moor to Foreign Office, 18 October 1897.
86 NAI, CSO 1/13, XI, Moor to Colonial Office, 2 July 1897.
87 NAI, CSO 1/13, VII, Moor to Salisbury, 18 October 1897.
88 P. A. Igbafe, 'The Benin Trials of 1897 and 1899', p. 83.
89 NAI, CSO 1/13, VIII, Gallwey to Foreign Office, 24 June 1898.
90 For the full transcript of the trial, see NAI, CSO 1/13, XI, Moor to Colonial Office, 2 July 1899, enclosure.
91 NAI, CSO 1/13, XI, Moor to Colonial Office, 2 July 1899.
92 *Ibid* , enclosure.
93 Igbafe, 'The Benin Trials . . .', p. 88.
94 NAI, CSO 1/13, XI, Moor to Colonial Office, 2 July 1899. Italics supplied.
95 *Ibid.*
96 NAE, Cal Prof 10/4.
97 K. O. Dike, *Trade and Politics in the Niger Delta*, pp. 153–65. See also 'Annual Report on the Eastern Province for the Year 1910', in Lagos, *Annual Reports of the Colony of Southern Nigeria for the Year 1910*.
98 Dike, pp. 34–7.
99 NAE, CSO 1/13, XXXII, Egerton to Colonial Office, 7 December 1904, enclosure.
100 *Ibid.*
101 *Ibid.*
102 NAI, CSO 1/10, II, Hutchinson to Lees, 20 January 1875.
103 CO 147/69, Moloney to Knutsford, 27 February 1889, enclosure.
104 NAI, CSO 1/10, I, Lees to Strahan, 5 October 1874, enclosed petition from the mercantile community in Lagos.

105 NAI, CSO 1/10, II, Marshall to Lees, 3 February 1875.
106 NAI, CSO 1/10, I, Lees to Strahan, 5 October 1874, enclosure; NAI, CSO 1/10, II, Petition of foreign merchants in Lagos, dated 23 January 1875.
107 NAI, CSO 1/10, II, Petition of foreign merchants in Lagos, dated 23 January 1875.
108 NAI, CSO 1/10, II, Melton to Administrator, 17 December 1874.
109 The content of his memorandum on the subject of adulterated produce indicated the extent of his knowledge NAI, CSO 1/10, II, James Marshall to Lees, 3 February 1875.
110 *Ibid.*
111 *Ibid.* Italics supplied.
112 This case and the other English cases cited in this section are discussed in D. W. Elliot and J. C. Wood, *A Casebook on Criminal Law*, London, 1963, pp. 7–31.
113 I. G. Carvell and E. S. Green, *Criminal Law and Procedure*, London, 1970, p. 8.
114 NAI, CSO 1/10, II, Hutchinson to administrator, 5 February 1875.
115 CO 148/2, Ordinance I, 14 February 1889.
116 Adulteration of Produce Proclamation, No. 24, 1901; No. 3, 1902; No. 9, 1905.
117 Compare rules relating to adulteration of produce made by native council of Benin River, March 1904, and similar rules made for Sapele and Warri, December 1903. NAI, CSO 1/13, XXVII, Fosberry to Colonial Office, 30 December 1903; NAI, CSO 1/13, XXIX, Fosberry to Colonial Office, 21 March 1904.
118 NAE, Cal Prof 9/2, IV, Moor to Secretary, African Association Ltd., 6 November 1902.
119 NAI, CSO 1/13, XXIV, Probyn to Colonial Office, 9 May 1903 and enclosures.
120 NAI, CSO 1/13, XV, Leslie Probyn to Colonial Office, 10 August 1901.
121 NAE, Cal Prof 9/2, II, Moor to divisional commissioner, Owerri, 22 May 1902.
122 NAI, CSO 1/13, XXII, Moor to Colonial Office, 12 November 1902; NAI, CSO 1/13, XXV, Probyn to Colonial Office, 2 June 1903, Fosberry to Colonial Office, 2 April 1904.
123 *Southern Nigeria Gazette*, 9 February 1910, pp. 202–3.
124 NAI, CSO 1/13, XXVIII, Fosberry to Colonial Office, 8 March 1904.
125 *Southern Nigeria Gazette Extraordinary*, 21 March 1911, pp. 544–615; *Southern Nigeria Gazette*, 1911, pp. 460–516.
126 *Southern Nigeria Gazette*, 1911, pp. 1049–51.
127 Jay Gordon, 'The Development of the Legal System . . .', p. 189.
128 NAI, CSO 1/1, I, Freeman to Newcastle, 8 March 1862.
129 *Ibid.*
130 CO 147/21, Kennedy to Kimberley, 27 November 1871 and enclosures.
131 NAI, CSO 1/10, VIII, Dumaresq to Lees, 11 August 1876 and enclosure.

132 NAI, CSO 1/10, VIII, Marshall to Lees, 11 August 1876.
133 *Ibid.*
134 NAI, CSO 1/10, VIII, Lees to Dumaresq, 11 November 1876.
135 NAI, CSO 1/19, XXVIII, Egerton to Earl of Crewe, 12 April 1910.
136 *Ibid.*
137 NAI, CSO 1/10, VIII, Lees to Dumaresq, 11 November 1876, enclosure F 13.
138 *Ibid.*, enclosure I.
139 NAI, CSO 1/20, XXXIII, Crewe to Officer Administering the government of Southern Nigeria, 28 June 1910.

4 Lawyers and the administration, 1865-1914

> These coloured lawyers travel about with their clerks seeking out, reviving and fomenting suits for their own pecuniary advantage; they deride and endeavour to undermine for the same purpose the authority of the district staff upon which West African administration depends.
>
> Memorandum by A. J. Harding, Colonial Office[1]

I

Lawyers are strictly not part of a judicial system, though very essential to it. For sound administration of justice and the development of the law itself, in the best common law tradition, require a well qualified Bench, and an adequately trained, vigilant Bar. Ordinarily, some discussion on lawyers would not be inappropriate in a work on a judicial system. But in the circumstances of Southern Nigeria, the position of the lawyer, particularly the African lawyer, merits a special discussion. By virtue of his training and profession, the African lawyer occupied a crucial position in a colonial situation, standing in an ambiguous region between the administration on the one hand, and the masses of his people on the other; regarded with a considerable amount of suspicion by the former, and for a long time accredited with exaggerated powers by the latter. As will be seen presently, the lawyer's position touched on sensitive aspects of colonial administration, and his role cannot be understood solely within the narrow confines of judicial administration. In particular, an understanding of his role in the wider context of the colonial society of Southern Nigeria is necessary to appreciate much of what motivated the policies governing judicial organisation for a long time after 1914.

II

The development of a modern legal profession in Southern Nigeria had a rather shaky beginning. The first professional 'lawyers' operating in the courts of Lagos, as was pointed out earlier, were not people formally trained in the law, but those who had practical experience of the law or of the operation of an English-style judicial system. Creatures of circumstance, they were variously referred to as 'local-made solicitors', 'self-taught attorneys', 'colonial solicitors' or simply 'attorneys'. They were called into existence because in spite of the predilection of the colonial establishment for a non-technical approach to the administration of justice, the courts could not do without advocates of some sort. The complexities of commerce in Lagos; the problem of communication between the Bench on the one hand, and the parties to disputes on the other; and the very presence in Lagos of Sierra Leonean and Brazilian immigrants, Englishmen and other Europeans who knew no other legal system than the English or the European – all these were compelling factors. By the 1870s cases were being conducted 'more in the character of litigiosity than had previously been the case',[2] and hence the self-taught attorneys' smattering of the law served some useful purpose.

It is of interest to note that in resorting to the employment of self-taught attorneys, the Lagos administration was simply borrowing from the experience of the other British West African colonies. The practice of enrolling people not professionally qualified as officers of English-style courts actually started in Sierra Leone in 1821 when William Henry Savage went to London and had himself appointed a notary public for Sierra Leone.[3] Other attorneys were locally appointed to practise law in the 1820s and 1830s. The last self-taught attorney, Daniel Carrol, was appointed in 1860.[4]

Following the establishment of the Supreme Court on the Gold Coast (Ghana) in 1853, some educated Africans began to present cases in the court as attorneys. By 1864 there were about six of them, but they do not appear to have enjoyed the confidence of the Court.[5] For alleged professional malpractices, they were disbarred one after another. By 1896 the admission of self-taught attorneys to the bar on the Gold Coast had stopped.[6]

In Southern Nigeria nine attorneys were enrolled between 1865 and 1916 to practise law in the courts. Of the nine, eight practised in Lagos; the remaining one, and the last to be enrolled, practised at Calabar between 1908 and 1916. Their position and mode of admission were regularised by the Supreme Court Ordinance, 1876, and by subsequent orders made under that ordinance.[7]

Essentially part-time professionals, the local attorneys did play a useful role in the operation of the courts in Lagos. Charles Foresythe, the first local attorney, 'materially assisted to organize the courts in Lagos', and it was he who introduced most of the legal forms used in them.[8] It is not far-fetched to argue that the attorneys helped in the economic development of Lagos. For a long time before the arrival of properly qualified barristers and solicitors, the attorneys' smattering of the law was useful in the city's commercial life. If Foresythe said he confined himself to conveyancing between 1871 and 1874,[9] it is not inconceivable that he and others like him drew up simple contracts, facilitating commercial transactions.[10] In the 1860s and 1870s some of the local attorneys like Charles Foresythe and Charles D. Turton were retained by a number of European trading firms.

The attorneys were also useful to the colonial administration. Up to the end of the 1870s Foresythe and Turton prosecuted for the Crown in criminal cases. Although John Augustus Otonba-Payne was not formally enrolled as an attorney until 1900, he had also, as the registrar of the Lagos Supreme Court, 1877–99, prosecuted for the Crown on several occasions.[11] In his capacity as registrar of the court, he acted as the sheriff, the bailiff, the interpreter and 'was, in fact, a living embodiment of almost the whole machinery of jurisprudence' in Lagos.[12] It was he who 'shepherded the life of the Supreme Court' in its formative years. Two other attorneys, Turton and James Neville Porter, both Europeans, held important posts in the judicial service of the colonial administration. Porter acted as Chief Magistrate in 1876;[13] Turton was appointed acting stipendiary magistrate in 1877 and in the following two years, acted as a puisne judge of the Supreme Court.[14]

In familiarising the Lagos population with aspects of the English legal and judicial process, the attorneys also played their part. To cite their most obvious contribution in this regard, they made the people familiar with the adversary system inherent in the English approach to justice. Although he hailed 'with pleasure' the appearance of the first two qualified barristers in Lagos in 1880,[15] it is significant that Otonba-Payne, a meticulous chronicler of events, later did not reckon their appearance among 'principal events in Yoruba history'.[16] That he did not do so reflects credit on the pioneering efforts of the attorneys. For by 1880 English-style judicial and legal institutions were already functioning in

Lagos when the qualified legal practitioners arrived, and it was right of Payne to trust 'to their usefulness at the Bar and on the Bench' now that the foundations of these institutions had been laid.

The arrival of fully qualified legal practitioners on the legal scene in Lagos from 1880 on, did not seem to have any immediate impact on the 'professional' activities of the attorneys. The Supreme Court not only allowed them to continue to practise, but also recruited more of their kind. For one thing, the needs of the courts still outstripped the supply of fully qualified lawyers. Up to 1900, Otonba-Payne as the registrar of the Supreme Court was prosecuting for the Crown in criminal cases. For another, except in two or three cases, the properly legal practitioners were not always resident in Lagos. Christopher Sapara Williams, the first Nigerian barrister to enrol at the Lagos Supreme Court in 1880, practised extensively on the Gold Coast which he would appear to have made his base in his early years of legal practice.[17] Most of the other African qualified barristers shuttled between Lagos and the Gold Coast. Up to about 1900, English or European qualified legal practitioners occasionally appeared in Lagos.[18] But there is no indication that they stayed for any considerable length of time. Sir William Neville Geary, the best known, was enrolled at the Supreme Court in July 1898, but returned to England the following year. The next professional trip he made to Lagos was in 1909.

In these circumstances there was still room for the type of services offered by the attorneys. They continued to operate in the courts until pressure from the fully qualified lawyers arriving in Southern Nigeria forced the Chief Justice to rule in 1913 that no more of their kind would be recruited.[19] In that year there were about twenty-five qualified legal practitioners, concentrated mainly in Lagos and Calabar.[20] The legal profession, properly so-called, could be said to be coming of age.

The fully qualified legal practitioners were products of the English Inns of Court; that is, Lincoln's Inn, the Inner Temple, the Middle Temple and Gray's Inn. Until 1962 these were the only institutions for training Nigerian lawyers, just as they were also responsible for training lawyers from other British African possessions during the colonial era. Between 1879 and 1914 about 56 per cent of the Nigerian lawyers were trained at the Middle Temple; about 24 per cent at the Inner Temple and about 20 per cent at Lincoln's Inn. Gray's Inn received its first Nigerian students only as recently as 1921. It is curious that the proportion of students trained at the various Inns of Court up to 1954 remained substantially the same, with Gray's Inn having only about two per cent of the total.[21]

The popularity of the Middle Temple among Nigerian law students is obvious from the figures above, and yet is not easy to explain. According to lawyers and judges, ex-students of the Inns, interviewed by the present writer, there are no fundamental differences between one Inn or another; only differences in traditions. It might be that the Middle Temple was easier on admissions than the others. The explanation could simply be force of attraction. As more and more of the early Nigerian law students went to the Middle Temple, others, in some instances, relatives, followed their footsteps in to the same institution. We may note in this connection that almost all the lawyers of Egba origin in the period of this study were students of the Middle Temple.

The three-year training in law given the Nigerian lawyers at the English Inns of Court was not really geared to Nigeria's needs; it was designed for students intending to practise law in the United Kingdom. In Nigeria as well as in the rest of Commonwealth West Africa, the legal profession has always been fused – a direct result of the problem of finding qualified men to serve in the English-style courts in the early years. Thus there is not the professional demarcation that exists in Britain between solicitors and barristers. But whereas Nigerian lawyers were expected to practise both as barristers and as solicitors, they received no training at all in the solicitor's side of their profession, often a most important part of a lawyer's work.[22] Over the years one result of the one-sided training the lawyers received has been too great a preponderance of advocates in Southern Nigeria.

Objections could also be raised, on psychological grounds, against the system of training the lawyers in England. At the Inns of Court they received no instruction at all in African law or the Nigerian legal system. Having received his training in an English environment and exclusively in English law and English legal institutions, the African lawyer might return to his country less sympathetic to African law and judicial institutions than he had been before he left. From this point of view, the training of African lawyers in England was not unlike a conditioning process. After his training, the African lawyer, consciously or unconsciously, might tend to regard the English legal system as the model from which there should be no departure.[23] It was an African lawyer on the Gold Coast who once wrote that previous to the enactment of the Supreme Court Ordinance, 1876, there was nothing like 'native law', 'for there was neither a Native tribunal of recognized authority nor a native legislature'.[24] This view smacks of the legal theory of John Austin, the great English jurist of the nineteenth century. But the lack of sympathy for African legal systems is all too evident. Almost in the same vein, one of Nigeria's foremost early lawyers once contended that before the advent of the British there was no law or order among the peoples of Southern Nigeria. It was the British, according to him, who, by introducing English-style courts, 'started them on lines of justice and honour'.[25]

When all the deficiences in the training of Nigerian lawyers in England are noted, it is well to remember that the deficiencies were relative, not absolute. The deficiencies were not much in evidence until fairly recently when the demands of the new nation that is Nigeria require that lawyers concern themselves with more than mere litigation. The early generation of lawyers, say up to about 1914, must be viewed against the background of the era of self-taught attorneys. At least they had a greater grasp of the law and more reasons for confidence than the attorneys. It should not be forgotten, too, that the law the Nigerian lawyers had to practise in Nigeria was to a large extent the common law of England, so that they did not really return to Nigeria 'entirely ignorant of Nigerian law'.[26] The additions to the common law of England were local statutes and the Nigerian indigenous customary laws. The former could not have been too difficult to pick up in the course of legal practice, and when the latter were involved, they were no more than matters of fact to be established under legal rules of evidence. Significantly, some European, West Indian and other foreign barristers successfully practised law in Southern Nigeria, appearing as counsel in a considerable number of what they usually referred to as 'native cases'.[27]

III

Since the 1860s the attitude of the colonial administration to professional advocates of any sort could be depicted as ambivalent at best. On two or three occasions in 1863, the privilege of having a professional advocate plead in the court was said to have been

Three early Nigerian lawyers: C. A. Sapara Williams, J. Egerton Shyngle, Kitoyi Ajasa

Sir Ralph Moor

Sir Donald Cameron

'most emphatically denied'.[28] When the Supreme Court Ordinance was enacted in 1876, an order made under it enjoined that where the parties to a suit were illiterate. 'the employment of Barristers or Solicitors shall not be allowed' except in some special circumstances.[29] In the judicial agreements negotiated with prominent Yoruba rulers between 1904 and 1908, the colonial administration of Lagos, in an identical clause in the agreements, ensured that legal practitioners would be precluded from appearing before the English-style courts that were to operate in much of Yorubaland. In their respective judicial agreements, as we noted earlier, the Yoruba authorities were said to have expressed their strong aversion to barristers and solicitors appearing in the British-established courts in Yorubaland.[30] The extent to which this was the genuine feeling of the Yoruba ruling authorities will perhaps never be known. But it is significant that at the time they were supposed to have declared their antipathy to lawyers, no lawyer had ever practised law in Yorubaland; hence the indigenous rulers could not be said to have been conversant with the role of barristers and solicitors in the English approach to the administration of justice. It is significant, too, that the exclusion clause was couched in identical words in the various judicial agreements, occupying the same relative position in the text of the agreements. Nor was any reason given for the exclusion of lawyers from the courts. It is an interesting commentary that some of the same Yoruba ruling authorities who were said to have declared their opposition to the appearance of legal practitioners in the courts had their own legal advisers.[31]

As will be shown later, even more drastic measures than the exclusion clause in the Yoruba judicial agreements were taken by the colonial administration in later years to curtail the professional activities of lawyers in Southern Nigeria. It is useful at this stage to examine some of the bases of the official attitude towards professional lawyers in general.

At least in the early years of colonial rule, one possible consideration against the employment of professional legal practitioners in the courts could have been the desire not to depart too radically from the indigenous modes of administering justice. The administration, aware that the employment of professional advocates in the adjudication of disputes was alien to the African way of life,[32] might have thought it politic – at a time when the colonial regime was far from being secure – to keep as close as possible to the traditional approach to justice 'without infringing [upon] the integrity of British law'.

The desire to adapt English law and the English judicial system 'to the wants and feelings of the people', if it ever weighed heavily with the colonial administration, was certainly not the only explanation for the official reservation about lawyers. Historically, the reservation also stemmed in part from the general bad reputation enjoyed by the self-taught attorneys, not only in Lagos, but throughout West Africa. In the period 1874–86 when Lagos was administered as part of the Gold Coast Colony, British officials had considerable difficulties with the attorneys operating in the southern part of the Gold Coast proper. Apart from the allegation that the attorneys were, for understandable reasons, not competent in the discharge of their duties, they were also said to be fleecing their clients, and fomenting litigation. They were said to be exciting much discontent in the local communities, making the work of administration difficult.[33] One can see the direct repercussions of the Gold Coast experience on Lagos in the clauses in the Supreme Court Ordinance, 1876, restricting the categories of cases open to advocates of any sort, and in the measures of Order VIII of the Supreme Court dealing in some detail with the fees of the attorneys and generally purporting to regulate the scope of their professional activities.[34]

In Lagos itself the reputation of the attorneys was not particularly high. Two of them, Allan MacIver and George Ernest Moss, both Europeans, were struck off the roll of solicitors of the Supreme Court in 1879 and 1881 respectively for employing a notorious ex-convict to tout for business and for engaging in other professional irregularities.[35] Charles Foresythe, the attorney who practised longest at the Lagos Bar, also had a record of malpractices, including misapplication of clients' funds, withholding clients' money and outright extortion.[36] He was disbarred in October 1880, but reinstated by the Supreme Court by July 1881, no doubt on account of the acute dearth of legal talents in the Lagos community.[37]

The corruption of the attorneys must be understood against the background of the general anomalies and irregularities discussed earlier, as being characteristic of the judicial system in Lagos as a whole for much of the nineteenth century.[38] But the instances of corruption on the part of the attorneys certainly did not give them a good image in official circles. In 1880, Justice Hector W. Macleod declared that he did not have any 'exalted opinion' of them, and would be reluctant to recommend the abrogation of the rule of the Supreme Court which prevented illiterate persons having the assistance of counsel.[39] But for the dearth of qualified men, he said, he was inclined to recommend that no one be allowed to practise in the courts 'unless he had been duly admitted to the Bar as we understand that [in England]'.

Corruption and malpractices of the attorneys might engender official distrust, but perhaps the most fundamental explanation for the official attitude towards professional advocates was their very position in the colonial situation. 'The actual injury done' by the Gold Coast attorneys, wrote Chief Justice D. P. Chalmers in 1873, 'consists mainly, first, in exacting excessive remuneration, and second, in stirring up unnecessary litigation [which could] aggravate class feelings and animosities'.[40] The Chief Justice in the second part of his observation was pinpointing a source of anxiety to the colonial administration and, therefore, a major cause of distrust for professional advocates. Unless they were strictly controlled, professional advocates might constitute a 'harmful' element, threatening the political stability of a colonial order. Their professional activities might endanger peaceful administration in a colony, and, indirectly, threaten British hold on it. It is not far-fetched to argue that such fears underlay the restrictions placed on professional advocates by the Supreme Court Ordinance, 1876.

The clauses in the Yorubaland judicial agreements 1904–1908, excluding lawyers from the courts in the territory, must be understood in the same light. Sir William MacGregor who initiated the agreements had a great interest in the Yoruba traditional authorities, regarding them as valuable agents through whom Yorubaland could be administered at a future date with minimum cost to the British. It was indicative of his interest in them that he once analysed the causes of their decline.[41] In 1901 he created semi-autonomous 'native' councils to shore up their authority. By 1904 African lawyers were already appearing in the English-style courts in Lagos. The Governor must have seen them as a serious threat to the authority of the traditional Yoruba rulers, knowing full well that lawyers could be disturbing elements in the new local administrative structure he was trying to build up.

The other aspect of the position of the professional advocate which made him an 'incongruous' element in colonial society was the considerable amount of influence he was capable of wielding independently of the colonial authorities and sometimes to their detriment. This was particularly true of the fully qualified African legal practitioners who began to arrive on the legal scene in Southern Nigeria from 1880 on. At a time when the higher posts in the civil service were closed to Africans, the legal profession, for those who could afford the high expenses of training in England, offered a relatively sure way of making a comfortable living in Southern Nigeria. By the turn of this century, the notion grew – and it was, to some extent, well-founded – that a capable legal practitioner could amass a fortune at the Bar. In a situation where the colonial administration was the largest single employer of labour and controlled all avenues of power, it was a fact pregnant with serious implications for the colonial authorities that the African lawyer, alone of the educated elite, not only could live in relatively grand style, but also did so independently of the administration. Again, the lawyer, by virtue of his position, enjoyed a measure of personal freedom denied to most other professionals. It was for this, among other reasons, that the legal profession was about the only one 'where an educated African could feel himself on a par with his expatriate rulers'.[42]

Along with the personal freedom which the lawyer enjoyed, was the high social prestige that tended to accrue from the nature of his profession in a colonial context. As will be shown later, in certain parts of Southern Nigeria, lawyers were credited with almost unbelievable powers. A serious charge by the colonial administration against an African invariably seemed like political persecution, and an African defence counsel, at least in the eyes of the non-literate masses, often assumed the posture of a fighting hero even at a time when the nationalist spirit was not really in vogue.[43] That counsel defended the accused person for money hardly mattered. Part of the prestige of the lawyer also derived from the fact that by virtue of his profession, and if the circumstances of a particular case warranted his doing so, he could put the seemingly all-powerful political officer in the dock and cross-examine him. Anything he said in the course of doing so would be privileged. What was more, he could even challenge the administrative acts of the political officer in open court.

The African lawyer in the colonial situation occupied a crucial position indeed, and was potentially a serious threat to the smooth running of affairs. For its stability, a colonial regime depended not

only on absolute or near-absolute control, but also on the regard
with which its officials were held by the indigenous population.
The African lawyer threatened both. In his professional activities
he was, consciously or unconsciously, a veritable agent in making
individuals among the indigenous population aware of their
personal rights, and, for that reason, could make administrative
control more difficult that it would otherwise have been. R. J. B.
Ross, an administrative officer and *quondam* judicial officer in the
Eastern Province, remarked in 1913 that the town of Degema
'was at one time so much in the hands of the lawyers that it was
almost impossible to ask the way of a native without being told,
"I must consult my lawyer first" '.[44]

With the lawyer around, the prestige of the political officer was
also at stake. There was the possibility of cross-examination of a
white officer by a black barrister. Even more ominous: a district
commissioner with no more than a smattering of legal knowledge,
administering justice in the rural areas as an officer of the Supreme
Court, could be made to appear an object of ridicule by a better-
trained African lawyer defending a client before him. The lawyer
might raise technical points of law which would only embarrass
the political officer or show up his weakness, thereby undermining
his position and effectiveness as an administrator in his area of
jurisdiction.

The above is an account of some of the considerations which
made the lawyer in the colonial context of Southern Nigeria an
object of distrust in official circles. The rest of this chapter is an
attempt to substantiate it by examining the activities of lawyers in
parts of Southern Nigeria up to about 1914.

IV

Between January 1909 and February 1914 there were about
fourteen practising lawyers in the Eastern and Central Provinces
of Southern Nigeria.[45] They were based in the three principal
towns of Calabar, Onitsha and Warri. There were a few from
Lagos, but most of them came from outside Nigeria: Silas Dove,
Sierra Leone; C. W. Clinton, Gold Coast (Ghana); Samuel
Nduisi Lewis, Sierra Leone; F. A. Davies, Sierra Leone; L. E. V.
McCarthy, Sierra Leone; Jacob Galba Bright, Sierra Leone; J. W.
Maxwell, Sierra Leone; A. E. Gibson, Sierra Leone; and Clarence

Maxwell Abbensetts, British Guiana (Guyana).[46] It is no wonder that the lawyers in these two provinces were once branded 'strange barristers from Sierra Leone and Gold Coast'.

In the two provinces the legal profession had a free rein. Here, unlike the Western Province where the judicial agreements with the Yoruba authorities had hedged round the Supreme Court and its operation, the Supreme Court had an almost unlimited scope of operation. There were no judicial agreements to hamper the operation of the Supreme Court or curb the professional activities of lawyers.

Again in these two provinces, the Supreme Court was by far the most popular of all the judicial institutions established by the British, speaking of course, in relative terms. It should not be imagined that members of the indigenous population all eagerly sought the intervention of the court in the adjudication of their disputes. Cases, especially criminal cases, were still being heard and determined in the traditional way even though under the pain of heavy penalty meted out by the British authorities. But the fact remained that if a litigant had to make a choice between the supreme court and any other British-established judicial institution, he would prefer the Supreme Court if the court was accessible to him. The 'native' courts in the two provinces did not operate to fulfil the expectations of the colonial administration. The traditional administrative and judicial framework within which the courts might have functioned was not as well-developed in the greater part of the two provinces as in the chiefly society of the Western Province. The 'native' courts set up in the two provinces were in the nature of foreign institutions, manned, as we noted earlier, by appointed 'warrant chiefs' who enjoyed no traditional authority. The appointed chiefs might be influential because they were props of the colonial administration, but they did not command the respect accorded traditional chiefs, say, in the Western Province. This lack of the backing of tradition naturally reflected on the effectiveness of the 'native' courts. The courts were rarely looked upon by the indigenous population as the final place for the resolution of their conflicts.

It is true that the Supreme Court was as foreign as the 'native' courts. But it was different from them in several important respects. For one thing, it was better organised than the 'native' courts. For another, the divisional courts of the Supreme Court were presided over by district commissioners who were apt to be considered impartial in their judicial duties principally because they were foreigners. The district commissioner as an officer of the Supreme Court was also regarded as better trained in law than the 'warrant chief' whose 'native' court, in fact, became more and more a parody of the Supreme Court in its approach to the administration of justice. Whatever the deficiency of the district commissioner in the stock of his legal knowledge, the law which he was supposed to administer was a more articulate and a more certain system of law than the hotch-potch 'native law and custom' concocted *ad hoc* by the 'warrant chief' as occasion suited him.

These factors explain the relative popularity of the Supreme Court in the Eastern and Central Provinces of Southern Nigeria and why lawyers found the Eastern Province in particular a richer pasture than any other part of Southern Nigeria.

Land matters formed and for a long time continued to form the main staple of legal practice in the two provinces – an unfortunate development from the point of view of the colonial administration because they were also 'the most fruitful source of litigation'.[47] There were very few commercial cases, Calabar's commercial position as a port being nothing to compare with that of Lagos. George Graham Paul, a Scottish solicitor who arrived at Calabar in April 1914, was soon to gather within his legal practice the retainers of the few commercial firms there.

From about 1910, the fear was growing within the colonial administration that the involvement of lawyers in land matters in the Eastern and Central Provinces was having harmful effects. It was feared that the non-literate indigenous people were being exploited by the 'alien legal practitioners'. Even members of the judiciary lent weight to the expression of the fear. 'The sole object' of these alien lawyers, Chief Justice A. W. Osborne noted in 1913, 'is to make as much money as possible and return to their own homes.'[48] He also testified that communal land disputes provided lawyers with 'fat fees'. Two years earlier, he expressed the view that fees 'have been charged out of all proportion to the value of the services rendered or the subject matter of the dispute' in many instances of litigation.[49] Significantly, in April of that year he had to step in and regulate lawyers' professional charges in the two provinces. After 1911, legal practitioners there were required to deposit with the provincial registrar of the Supreme Court a certified copy of every agreement made with clients regarding any remuneration in excess of one hundred naira.[50]

The same social and economic conditions which tended to produce litigations in land matters in the two provinces must have rendered ineffectual any attempt to regulate lawyers' fees in the way the chief justice did. On the economic side, there was the fact that land was of the utmost importance to the indigenous population. In parts of the Eastern Province, it was reported in 1911, 'the population . . . is too great for the amount of land available'[51] – a serious problem indeed in a peasant agricultural economy. It was a reflection of the high economic value of land that communities in the two provinces were competing for the best lawyers to handle their land disputes – a state of affairs that was typical of probably the whole colonial era in Southern Nigeria.[52] One should also note that communal land boundaries laid down by British administrative officers in their attempt at resolving land disputes were largely arbitrary and a source of seemingly interminable litigations.

Social conditions, too, encouraged exploitation by lawyers. As the Chief Justice noted, 'a very large proportion of the litigating natives' were illiterates. A by-product of illiteracy was the exaggerated degree of influence and power ascribed to lawyers. In the words of an administrative officer: 'The Native lawyer is looked upon as a species of God by the Native Chiefs.'[53] It was from such notions that the lawyer's power and influence derived. In some parts of Southern Nigeria, an administrative officer once wrote, the African lawyer had 'more power with the people than the District Commissioner himself'.[54]

The political implications of lawyers' involvement in land litigation were no less disturbing to the colonial administration. It was discovered that the political influence of the district commissioner was being eroded. The administrative practice in settling a land dispute before the arrival of lawyers had been arbitration by the district commissioner who rarely took a strictly legalistic view of the matter in dispute to find a solution more or less agreeable to all parties. But as time went on, parties to a land dispute were no longer amenable to political arbitration by the district commissioner once a lawyer was employed who, they were convinced, would 'give them back [their] land'.[55] This was one of the ways by which government 'was hampered by the influence of the lawyers'.[56] Again, from the point of view of the administration, interminable land disputes were in themselves a factor in political instability.

It would also appear that lawyers were interfering directly in the domestic affairs of towns and communities in the two provinces, thus retarding the 'pacification' or the political organisation of these areas.[57] From what has been said earlier about the position of lawyers among the non-literate masses, it is easy to appreciate that this development was inevitable. It was certain that the lawyer would be drawn into the internal politics of the area in which he practised his profession. If a chieftaincy title fell vacant and became a matter for contest between two or more parties, one party or the other called in the lawyer's assistance. With the establishment of the colonial regime, political power and authority was shifting from the traditional chiefs to the administrative officers.[58] A new hierarchy of power had been created, dominated by the colonial masters. The English-style courts turned out to be suitable forums for contesting positions in the lower echelons of the hierarchy of power now reserved for traditional or appointed chiefs under the so-called 'Indirect Rule' system of administration. The lawyer, believed to be capable of taking a political matter like chieftaincy dispute into the English-style courts and eventually of tipping the balance in favour of the party that hired him, naturally came into the show.

In the minds of many, there was a corollary to this view of the usefulness of both the court and the lawyer in matters political. A desperate man with a doubtful claim to a chieftaincy title and without much scruple about traditions could make his claim good if only he could employ a capable lawyer to press it.

An illustration of this point and, generally, of the degree of power and influence ascribed to lawyers in parts of Southern Nigeria, is provided by the Ogwashi-Uku incident in 1910 in the Asaba Division of the Central Province.[59] Obi Nzekwe was the ruler of Ogwashi-Uku. He had been rightly installed as ruler, for he received the blessing of Chief Oberago of Agidiese Quarter, as required by tradition. What was even more important in the colonial context, he was recognised as the ruler by the administration through the district commissioner at Asaba. He was reputed to be 'a man of very great power in the district', and altogether an efficient ruler.

Nzekwe had a rival in the person of one Okonjo. Having unsuccessfully tried on many occasions to destool Nzekwe and establish his title to the Ogwashi-Uku chieftaincy, Okonjo took his supporters' advice in January 1909 'to put my case in the hands of the lawyers'.[60] He consulted two lawyers: a man named Boston and Silas Palmerston Dove, both based at Onitsha. The former he paid £47 (₦94.00) through his clerk, and the latter, at various times, sums totalling £80 (₦160.00). Boston did nothing, but Dove promised to make Okonjo the head-chief of Ogwashi-Uku.

Okonjo proceeded to play upon the fact that he was employing lawyers. It was illustrative of the power and influence ascribed to lawyers that the events that followed were dominated by fear on the part of Nzekwe and his supporters that lawyers were surely going to put Okonjo on the Ogwashi-Uku throne. When the district commissioner summoned Nzekwe to another village in an attempt to reconcile the two rivals, he was afraid to go. If he went, he reasoned, the government and the lawyers to whom Okonjo had paid so much money would seize him, deport him and make Okonjo the ruler.[61] He firmly believed the rumour spread by his rival's supporters that lawyers would bring troops into Ogwashi-Uku to put Okonjo on the throne.

Troops did arrive at Ogwashi-Uku by April 1910. But they were the troops sent by the administration to quell what had erupted into large-scale fighting between the supporters of the two rivals. The arrival of the troops, however, seemed like a confirmation of the rumour that had gained ground that Okonjo's lawyers were sending troops. Nzekwe, with the large majority of the population supporting him, thought that they were fighting the troops sent by Okonjo's lawyers. 'We could not fight', Nzekwe later said, 'because the lawyer sent too many soldiers.'[62] The civil war was soon at an end. Nzekwe realised his mistake about the troops and came out of hiding. By June 1910 he was restored to his former position.

The idea that lawyers could command troops was by no means restricted to Ogwashi-Uku. At about the same time as the Ogwashi-Uku incident, events in the Calabar Division of the Eastern Province showed that the idea held sway there too. One Amuqua Tobi, said to be an agent or employee of Harold H. S. Davies, a lawyer based at Calabar, promoted the belief in connection with a political struggle between Igbo and Itam, two small towns in the division. If the Igbo people paid him one hundred pounds (₦200.00), Amuqua Tobi was reported to have promised, 'his master Davies will bring troops and destroy the neighbouring town of Itam'. Should they fail to provide the money, he was said to have threatened, the lawyer would bring in troops to destroy Igbo itself. He successfully employed this threat to force the Igbo community to build him a house and supply him with yams and fowls for two months 'without further consideration or payment'.[63]

Silas Dove, the lawyer in the Ogwashi-Uku incident, was mentioned in connection with other activities somewhat political in nature, all adding up to the image of the lawyer in the first decade of this century as an obstacle in the way of smooth colonial administration. The towns of Abagana, Nemo and Ukpu, all within a radius of four miles from Onitsha, were reported in May 1910 to be 'disaffected'. Other towns were 'in sympathy' with them: Aba, Enugu, Umaleri and Ukpu Efile. Dove was said to have gone round the towns 'making all sorts of promises to the people through certain chiefs, interpreters and persons who have been acting as his touts'.[64] The principal agent of the lawyer was said to be one Nwa Obele whom he allegedly promised to make the paramount chief of the 'disaffected' towns. With Dove's backing, it was said, people in these towns were refusing 'native' court summonses and were no longer willing to supply labour to the officers of the administration for public works. Whether it was true or not that Dove received sums of money totalling about £340 (₦680.00) excluding gifts, as the district commissioner alleged,[65] the fact remained that in Dove the people of the 'disaffected' towns saw a champion of their oppositionist stand against the administration.

The 'rebellious' attitude of the towns around Onitsha was similar to that of Chief Eva of Igbo town in the Calabar Division of the Eastern Province. Chief Eva was reported to have refused to take orders from the district commissioner stationed at Afikpo, or to answer any warrants summoning him to a 'native' court to reply to a charge of looting a canoe. Behind Chief Eva was Amuqua Tobi who allegedly advised the chief to refer any matter to Harold Davies, the lawyer at Calabar. Behind the confidence of Chief Eva was, in short, the lawyer.

The point that is being made here is that by 1910 the administration was finding the position of lawyers in the Eastern and Central Provinces politically inconvenient. As if to compound the administration's difficulty in 'pacifying' the area, lawyers were directly challenging the actions of political officers in open court as never before. It is, of course, part of a lawyer's duty to defend his client against any arbitrary actions by the government, if need be; but in a colonial context, and especially at a time when colonial rule was, in fact, not completely established, such action, from the point of view of the colonial regime, carried serious implications. An action in a court of law which challenged the decisions of a political officer struck at the very foundation of colonial governmental authority. At least, that was the interpretation given to the incidents now to be related in which lawyers took administrative officers to court.

In December 1909 a clash broke out between two towns in the Eastern Province, Abini and Akunakuna, reputed to be traditional enemies. The district commissioner in charge of the area, one Duncan, imposed a fine of £500 (₦1,000) on one of the towns, Akunakuna, 'for their rebellious conduct in taking up arms against Abini'.[66] The town could not or did not pay the fine; its headman, Chief Nyang Nyang, was removed to Afikpo where he was detained as a political prisoner pending the payment of the fine.

On 4 February 1910, Sigismund Macaulay, solicitor to Chief Nyang Nyang, appeared before Justices Stoker and Webber at the divisional court of the Supreme Court at Calabar to apply for a writ of *habeas corpus* on behalf of his client. Macaulay contended that Chief Nyang Nyang was unlawfully detained – a submission which the court upheld in its decision of 25 February 1910. The court directed that the chief be released from prison, ordering Duncan, the District Commissioner, to pay twelve guineas (₦25.20) costs.

In the *Nyang Nyang* case it was not only the authority of the district commissioner that was at stake, but the Governor's too. It was Sir Walter Egerton as Governor and Commander-in-Chief who on 25 December 1909, had ordered action against Akunakuna – a fact which, as A. R. Pennington, the administration's Attorney-General, claimed, the court conveniently ignored. The Attorney-General suggested that the court's decision was, in fact, aimed at the governor and that 'the court seems to have been only too ready to assume everything and anything against the Executive authorities'.[67] 'In any case, especially in a country like the Eastern Province', he warned, 'the court should not belittle the Executive officers except for very good cause.'

If such a warning was ever passed to the court at Calabar, it was certainly not heeded. Some time in April of the same year, 1910, Francis Rising, an assistant district commissioner in the Eastern Province, locked up one of the lawyers, Harold Davies, for some hours on the ground that Davies 'refused to remove his hat in his presence'.[68] Davies took the political officer to court for assault. He was awarded £20 (₦40.00) as damages, and the officer was ordered to pay fifteen guineas (₦31.50) costs besides.

From the point of view of the administration, the *obiter dictum* of Justice William H. Stoker in *Davies v. Rising* was no less significant than the judgment passed on the political officer. The judge's remarks, in the view of the provincial commissioner for the Eastern Province, amounted to a disparagement of the administrative branch of the colonial government.[69] Justice Stoker was reported to have said that there was no such thing as a political officer's privilege, and that there were a lot of 'honourables' around who had no right to the title. (The title 'honourable' in government circles was a mark of official courtesy used to address officers of the rank of provincial commissioner and above, other than the governor who was referred to as 'His Excellency'.) Stoker was also reported to have said that government officials 'must be treated in the same way as ordinary members of the public'. The provincial commissioner for the Eastern Province struck the nail on the head when he remarked that such views, expressed in open court, were 'bound to prejudice the position and impair the authority of the Provincial Authorities generally'.[70] The independence of mind which Justice Stoker seems to have shown in the performance of his judicial duties was held to be out of place in a colonial situation.

The touts whom the African lawyers were said to be employing in the Eastern and Central Provinces deserve mention as another thorn in the flesh of political officers. The general belief in official circles was that the lawyers in the two provinces were employing touts to further their professional interests. The provincial commissioner for the Eastern Province reported in February 1910 that members of the local bar were obtaining most of their cases in the interior districts 'through their travelling agents whom they disown if they get into trouble'.[71]

The conditions under which lawyers operated in the two provinces necessitated their employing agents of some sort. Since the lawyer in those provinces was invariably a stranger, at least until the 1920s, he had to depend on local people to keep in touch with litigants. Such 'contact men' were semi-educated, but at least familiar with the rudiments of the English language and able to act as interpreters or intermediaries between the lawyer and his clients. One point that is often missed, however, is that not all the touting was due to the prompting of the lawyer. Generally, in

Southern Nigeria touting grew up as a quasi-independent profession, if it may be so called, feeding on the needs of the legal
profession. There were men who, of their own accord, raked up
old disputes or 'trumped up cases', piloting one of the parties to a
lawyer with a view to receiving a commission.

The problem of the lawyer's tout was two-fold. In the first
place, the intermediary position of the tout tended to add to the
cost of litigation. As in the case of Amuqua Tobi, referred to
earlier, the tout not infrequently used his position to exploit the
non-literate litigants. Secondly, the activities of the tout were
usually productive of litigation which was not in the interests of
good order and political stability which the administration was
anxious to maintain in the interior districts.

V

As compared with what obtained in the Eastern and Central
Provinces, the professional activities of lawyers in the Western
Province presented little or no difficulties to the colonial administration. In this province the practice of the legal profession was
very much localised in Lagos. This fact may be explained partly by
the judicial agreements with the Yoruba authorities excluding the
appearance of legal practitioners in the English-style courts of
Yorubaland. But the more important explanation is that Lagos
seems to have been the only place where lawyers' services were truly
essential. Lagos was (and still is) Nigeria's commercial centre *par
excellence*, with a great diversity of commercial and other activities
requiring the services of legally trained men. Lawyers did operate
in the interior of Yorubaland to defend accused persons in
criminal cases at the assizes of the supreme court or to give legal
advice to the Yoruba authorities. But, generally, until the late
1940s, they thought very little of the Yoruba states as field for their
professional activities.[72] Partly on account of the relative strength
of the traditional institutions, including judicial institutions, in
these states, the Supreme Court did not enjoy the same degree of
initial popularity as it enjoyed in the Eastern and Central Provinces.

In Lagos the professional activities of lawyers gave the Supreme
Court Bench no cause for alarm. The legal adviser for the Southern
Provinces in 1914 strongly criticised the professional practices of

lawyers in Southern Nigeria, but he made an exception of those in Lagos. 'My experience with them', he wrote, 'has always been of the pleasantest, both sitting as a Judge, and when I have had to appear for the Crown at Assizes and in other actions.'[73] Chief Justice A. W. Osborne apparently had no cause to complain about their professional conduct. When in April 1911 it was decided to regulate the remuneration of legal practitioners in the Eastern and Central Provinces, he informed the Governor of Southern Nigeria that the new provision 'is not in our judgment required in Lagos and the Western Province'.[74] Other measures before 1914 purporting to regulate the practice of the legal profession, as we shall see presently, similarly did not apply to Lagos or to the Western Province.

The difference between the reputation of the lawyers in the Eastern and Central Provinces on the one hand, and of those in Lagos (including the Western Province) on the other, requires explanation. First, there were certain factors in Lagos, lacking in the Eastern and Central Provinces, which tended to restrain lawyers in the practice of their profession. As far as charges went, there was in Lagos a relatively keen competition which, as the Chief Justice observed, 'keeps charges within reasonable limits'.[75] Again, the public in Lagos were relatively more enlightened than in the two provinces. The longer contact which Lagos had had with western civilisation, and the cosmopolitan nature of the city's population – including immigrant educated Africans and European merchants – could account for this development. In particular, the Lagos public were long used to the Supreme Court and the lawyers.

In Lagos, too, there was a flourishing press which helped to educate the public. By 1914 it could be said that the climate of public opinion there, again, relatively speaking, was becoming critical. At a time when lawyers were believed capable of commanding troops in the Eastern and Central Provinces, the Lagos press was exposing what it regarded as the drawbacks of the Supreme Court system of administering justice. Two Lagos newspapers, the *Lagos Weekly Record* and the *Lagos Standard*, were particularly critical of the English approach to justice as imported in to Southern Nigeria. On several occasions the newspapers pointed out the increasing cost of litigation, the effect of English laws on the indigenous social fabric, and even the indirect effect of litigation on commerce.[76] It is a fair claim that such a relatively critical attitude on the part of the press and the public provided a safe-guard against abuses. One looks in vain for such a climate of opinion in either the Eastern or the Central Province during the period under discussion. The first local newspaper east of the Niger was not established until the 1930s.[77]

As another explanation for the difference between the standard of the practice of the legal profession in Lagos and in the two Provinces, it should be noted that it was in Lagos that the senior members of the Bar and the senior judges of the Supreme Court resided. The lawyers in Lagos were more in the limelight than their counterparts east of the Niger. The presence of the Supreme Court judges and of the senior members of the Bar tended to have a salutary effect on the younger members of the profession.

It is perhaps important, too, that the legal practitioners in Lagos were largely people who, either for reason of birth or for some other reason, had identified themselves with their environment. One should be wary of crediting the Lagos practitioners with a patriotism or sense of professional dedication which probably they did not possess; but the awareness that they were working among their own people could well have been a restraining factor in the practice of their profession. The charge that the legal practitioners in the Eastern and Central Provinces were 'men who had no interest in the country'[78] may not be altogether unfounded. Of the African lawyers in the two provinces before 1914, only C. W. Clinton, originally from Axim, Gold Coast (Ghana), stayed long enough to suggest that he might have identified himself with Nigeria. Most of the rest were short-term residents. Not long after 1914, when the scope of their legal practice was seriously curtailed, they disappeared from the scene one after another. Money-making was their primary objective. They scuttled out as soon as this objective had been achieved or the avenue for realising it became closed.

From the point of view of the colonial administration, the practice of the legal profession in Lagos did not lack disturbing features. The prominent lawyers in Lagos invariably had strong links with the Yoruba states, serving more or less as legal advisers to such paramount rulers as the *Awujale* of Ijebu, the *Owa* of Ijeshaland or the *Alake* of Egbaland in their dealings with the Lagos colonial administration.[79] The position of the lawyers as advisers to some of the traditional rulers in Yorubaland occasioned not a little anxiety in official circles.

There was an incident in 1902 which illustrates the anxiety entertained by the administration about the lawyers' presence in the interior of the Western Province. Christopher Sapara Williams, partly because of his Ijesha ancestry, wielded considerable influence in Ilesha, particularly with the *Owa*. Some time between December 1901 and January 1902, on one of his occasional visits to Ijesha, Williams allegedly 'acted in some pseudo-judicial capacity' in a dispute among some important chiefs. He was said to have imposed a fine of one hundred and fifty pounds (₦300.00) on one of the chiefs. This was at a time when a 'native' council had just been formed in Ilesha District as elsewhere in Yorubaland – the council was expected to decide all administrative and judicial matters under the supervision of the resident British officer, and without any interference from the outside. Captain W. G. Ambrose, the travelling commissioner for Ilesha District, frowned on the action of Sapara Williams. 'I think at this stage it would be wrong', he wrote to the colonial secretary in Lagos, 'to allow the possibility of parties ousting the jurisdiction of the newly formed Council by resorting to arbitration.' He added, quite significantly: 'As a political officer, I see very good reasons for keeping people of the class in question [that is, lawyers] out of up country tribunals altogether.'[80]

True to his conviction, Captain Ambrose summoned a meeting of the Ilesha 'native' council. At this meeting he himself proposed a resolution barring legal practitioners from practising in any court in Ilesha District and forbidding them from arbitrating in any matter or dispute within the jurisdiction of the Ilesha council. The resolution was said to have been carried unanimously and copies of it were sent to the attorney-general in Lagos and to Sapara Williams himself. There is, one suspects, a correlation between the whole incident and the clause in the judicial agreements in Yorubaland, 1904–1908, excluding legal practitioners from the English-style courts in the territory.

VI

The activities of lawyers in the Eastern and Central Provinces did provoke reaction on the part of the colonial administration. In the absence of anything like the judicial agreements of the Yoruba states, direct measures were taken to restrict the scope of the practice of the legal profession in the two provinces.

The decision to curtail the jurisdiction of the Supreme Court and thereby restrict the activities of lawyers in the two provinces grew out of the desire to 'strengthen the power of the Executive in the less settled Districts of the Eastern and Central Provinces'.[81] It was believed, moreover, that the Supreme Court, exercising its jurisdiction 'immediately on the heels of the troops' was fundamentally not a suitable machinery of justice in the 'less settled areas', especially as regards land disputes. 'To anyone who knows the inhabitants of these interior districts', wrote Sir Walter Egerton, 'it is nothing less than ludicrous that the boundaries between town and town and tribe and tribe should be a matter for enquiry and a decision by a Judge of the Supreme Court with a barrister before him bringing such witnesses as he chooses to put in the witness-box.'[82] The Supreme Court and the lawyers, Sir Walter reasoned, were apt to see only the strict legal rights of one party or the other without taking into consideration 'the expansion and practical necessities of the communities', or 'the equitable rights and the political requirements and consequences'. Land cases were therefore essentially 'political cases . . . which must be tried on the spot', the political officer and the parties concerned collaborating to reach a solution acceptable to all parties. It was for this reason that the administration considered it necessary to protect the political officer in the performance of his duties from what seemed like harassment from the lawyers acting under the cover of the Supreme Court.

Early in February 1910 a 'Peace Preservation Ordinance' was proposed to 'make further and better provisions for the preservation of the public peace' in the Eastern and Central Provinces. [83] The ordinance was to empower the Governor to declare any area of the two provinces an 'unsettled district'. Within an 'unsettled district', the district commissioner exercised almost unlimited powers. He could detain any person without search warrant and could impose a fine of up to ₦1,000 on anyone involved in a civil disturbance. Three provisions of the ordinance were aimed at the Supreme Court and the lawyers. Section 14 of the ordinance affirmed that the district commissioner or a military officer 'shall be protected with regard to any suit brought against them for anything done by them in the execution of their duty under this Ordinance'. According to the following section, a district commissioner or a military officer could detain anyone for one year with or without hard labour, 'anything in the Supreme Court

Ordinance to the contrary notwithstanding'. Section 17 sought to put a brake on the extension of the jurisdiction of the Supreme Court: any district hitherto not under its jurisdiction was to be deemed an 'unsettled district'. The tone of these stringent provisions showing the temper of the executive branch of the colonial government, was somewhat modified in the final form of Ordinance No. 14 of 1912. But the spirit of the draft provisions remained.

Other measures in the same vein as the 'Peace Preservation Ordinance' were enacted. The 'Unsettled Districts Ordinance', No. 32 of 1911, re-enacted as No. 15 of 1912, was primarily aimed at getting rid of 'objectionable persons trading in the unsettled districts of the interior'.[84] On the instruction of the Colonial Office, section 2 of the ordinance defining 'alien' or 'non-native', was modified to give it 'a wider scope'. It was considered desirable that the government should 'have power to exclude the black lawyer and the Lagos agitator' from the 'unsettled districts'.[85]

By an order made under the Supreme Court Ordinance of 21 April 1911, the jurisdiction of the court in land matters was directly limited to 'the more settled and developed portions of the Protectorate in the Eastern and Central Provinces'. The order was considered a necessary measure 'to prevent the Court dealing with any more disputes as to the limits and boundaries of tribal lands'.[86] The jurisdiction of the court in land matters was limited to small areas in Calabar District, certain parts of Opobo and Degema Districts, Brass, Forcados, Warri and Sapele Districts. In the following towns the court's jurisdiction was limited to the area lying within a radius of two miles from the district commissioner's office: Onitsha, Asaba, Idah, Aba and Itu.[87] The effectiveness of the order is, however, open to question.

A number of further measures against lawyers were proposed, but were not enacted into law. Some of these are noteworthy because they demonstrate further the attitude of the colonial administration towards the Supreme Court and the lawyers in the Eastern and Central Provinces. Others are important because they foreshadowed the measures that were to come during the administration of Sir Frederick Lugard, dealing with lawyers on a wider basis than that of Southern Nigeria alone.

Two proposals of 1910 were not directly related to the legal profession or the Supreme Court, but it cannot be doubted that they were aimed at the two. One was a suggestion by J. Winkfield, then acting chief justice, made in June 1910, to establish a special land board to deal with matters relating to land.[88] The land board was to be empowered to demarcate boundaries of land and to compel transfer of land from one community to another, where such a transfer was considered necessary. As far as possible, a surveyor should be a member of the board. The idea of such a land tribunal continued to be an attractive proposition until the 1930s. No such tribunal was ever constituted, but obviously the objective was to take away land disputes from the purview of the Supreme Court and the lawyers.

The other proposal was the 'Limitation of Suits Ordinance' made also in June 1910. Ostensibly, the ordinance was proposed in the interest of commerce: a suit to collect a debt would be unenforceable after a certain specified period. The proposal had to be dropped in the teeth of very strong opposition in Lagos. But it is clear the intention was, in part, to limit the scope of the legal profession. 'I believe such a law would diminish the number of unjust claims and considerably lessen litigation', Egerton informed the Colonial Office in London.[89]

The Central and Eastern Provinces Administration Ordinance, also proposed in 1910, was a bold attempt to reorganise the courts in the two provinces so as to eliminate or minimise the inconvenience caused by lawyers to political officers.[90] The ordinance was to establish a provincial court in each province to replace the divisional court of the Supreme Court. The provincial court was to be presided over by the provincial commissioner, a high-ranking administrative officer. In each district would be established a district court of the provincial court, to be called the District Commissioner's Court of Civil Jurisdiction. Appeal from the provincial court to the Supreme Court would be at the discretion of the Governor, and only if the value of the matter in dispute was over £100 (₦200.00). Legal practitioners were to be barred from the provincial court. Nor were the decisions of the political officers administering justice in this court or the district commissioner's court to be open to challenge in the Supreme Court. These provisions were welcomed at the Colonial Office as 'heroic measures' and the Earl of Crewe, the Secretary of State for the Colonies, found himself 'in entire agreement' with Southern Nigeria's Governor, Sir Walter Egerton.[91] For some political considerations, however, the proposed provincial courts ordinance was shelved, but, as will be apparent in the next chapter, not forgotten.

Similarly shelved was the Southern Nigeria Native Courts Ordinance, proposed in June 1911. A central provision of this measure was that no legal practitioner was to be allowed in the 'native' courts even though the procedure in the courts 'shall be the same as the procedure in the Supreme Court'.[92] Again, decisions of political officers acting in their judicial capacities as presidents of the courts were not to be open to challenge in the Supreme Court.

The administration did not cease to be preoccupied with judicial reorganisations or with the problem presented by the presence of lawyers in the interior districts of Southern Nigeria. The fact was that African lawyers were seen as an ever-present threat to political stability. Sir Frederick Lugard, who succeeded Egerton as Governor in 1912, took up the whole question where his predecessors had left it. He soon devised far-reaching measures of his own to meet what had become, in the official mind, an intractable problem.

Notes

1 CO 583/12, A. J. Harding, 'Memorandum on the Judicial System in Nigeria'.
2 CO 96/114, D. P. Chalmers to Administrator-in-Chief, Sierra Leone, 3 June 1873.
3 Christopher Fyfe, *A History of Sierra Leone*, London, 1962, pp. 147–8.
4 *Ibid.*
5 David Kimble, *A Political History of Ghana, 1850–1928*, Oxford, 1963, pp. 68–70.
6 *Lagos Weekly Record*, 22 March 1913.
7 Supreme Court Ordinance, No 4. 1876.
8 NAI, CSO 1/8, XV, Berkeley to Administrator-in-Chief, 17 April 1873, enclosure.
9 *Ibid.*
10 NAI, CSO 1/10, XXVII, Griffith to Ussher, 8 November 1880, enclosed petition of D. C. Taiwo and other African traders.
11 HCA, Lagos, 'Judge's Notebook, Criminal Cases, November 1881– January 1885'.
12 *African Times*, 6 October 1899.

13 J. A. Otonba-Payne, *Payne's Lagos and West African Almanac and Diary for 1894*, London, 1893, p. 37.
14 *Ibid.*
15 *Ibid.*; Preface to the 8th edn, p. 12.
16 Payne, *Table of Principal Events in Yoruba History*, London, 1893.
17 For more on the professional activities of Sapara Williams, see O. Adewoye, 'Sapara Williams: The Lawyer and the Public Servant', *Journal of the Historical Scoiety of Nigeria*, vi, I, December 1971.
18 SCA, Lagos, 'Roll of Barristers', I.
19 *Lagos Weekly Record*, 3 May 1913.
20 SCA, Lagos, 'Roll of Barristers', I.
21 The percentage figures in this paragraph have been worked out from the 'Records of Admissions' of the four Inns of Court.
22 Colonial Office, London, *Report on Legal Education for African Students*, Cmd. 1255, 1961, p. 11.
23 L. C. B. Gower, *Independent Africa: The Challenge to the Legal Profession*, Cambridge, Mass., 1967, p. 91.
24 'Native Law', *The Gold Coast Assize*, November 1883.
25 C. W. Clinton, 'Anomalies of the Native Court System', *Nigerian Law Journal*, iv, 44, p. 73.
26 B. O. Nwabueze, *The Machinery of Justice in Nigeria*, London, 1963, p. 280.
27 See Memorandum submitted by R. F. Irving and Graham Paul in *Petition Against the Provincial and Native Courts Ordinances by the Nigerian Reform Association*, Lagos, 1917.
28 *The Anglo-African*, 10 October 1863, editorial.
29 Supreme Court Ordinance, No. 4, 1876, Order VIII, sec. 5.
30 NAI, CSO 5/2, XIX, XX, XXIV, Clause 6 in the agreements with the authorities of Egba territory, Ibadan and Ijebu.
31 Until 1914, Adebesin Folarin was the paid legal officer of the Egba United Board of Management, while Sapara Williams was the legal adviser to the *Owa* of Ijeshaland and the *Awujale* of Ijebu-Ode.
32 CO 96/118, Strahan to Carnarvon, 31 March 1876.
33 CO 96/68, Conran to Cardwell, 7 October 1865.
34 CO 96/114, Secretary of State for the Colonies to Officer Administering the Government, Gold Coast, 17 July 1874.
35 HCA, Lagos, 'Letter Book, April 1877–August 1881', Payne to MacIver, 18 February 1879; Payne to MacIver, 11 March 1879; *African Times*, 1 August 1881 and 1 October 1881.
36 HCA, Lagos, 'Letter Book, April 1877–August 1881', Payne to Foresythe, 13 July 1877; Payne to Foresythe, 28 April 1879; HCA, Lagos, 'Judge's Notebook, March 1879–October 1880', *Dada v. Foresythe*, tried 15 June 1880.
37 HCA, Lagos, 'Letter Book', Payne to Foresythe, 27 July 1881.
38 *Supra*, pp. 134–8.
39 HCA, Lagos, 'Letter Book', Macleod to James Marshall, 11 May 1880.
40 CO 96/114, Chalmers to Administrator-in-Chief, Sierra Leone, 3 June 1873.
41 CO 147/160, MacGregor to Chamberlain, 11 November 1901.

42 Justice J. I. C. Taylor, present (1973) Chief Justice of Lagos State, Interview, 28 January 1967.
43 *Lagos Weekly Record*, 2 February, 1907 editorial.
44 NAI, CSO 1/21, XXII, Lugard to Harcourt, 21 May 1913, enclosure containing memorandum by R. J. B. Ross.
45 HCA, Lagos, 'Roll of Barristers', I
46 *Ibid.*, pp. 98–119.
47 CO 520/12, Lugard to Harcourt, 25 May 1914, enclosure.
48 NAI, CSO 1/21, XII, Lugard to Harcourt, 21 May 1913, enclosure.
49 CO 583/103, Egerton to Harcourt, 17 May 1911, enclosure.
50 *Ibid.* Also Rule No. 6, 1911, made under the Supreme Court Ordinance, 1876.
51 'Annual Report on the Eastern Province for the Year ended 31st December 1911', in Lagos, *Annual Reports of the Colony of Southern Nigeria for the Year 1911*, Lagos, 1913, pp. 121–4.
52 F. O. Lucas, former magistrate in the Eastern Provinces of Nigeria. Interview, Lagos, 7 March 1967.
53 NAI, CSO 1/21, Lugard to Harcourt, 21 May 1913, enclosed memorandum by R. J. B. Ross.
54 *Ibid.*
55 NAI, CSO 1/21, Lugard to Harcourt, 21 May 1913.
56 NAI, CSO 26/19701, II, 'Intelligence Report, Ogoja Province'.
57 CO 520/93, Egerton to Crewe, 7 May 1910, confidential.
58 See Obaro Ikime, 'Reconsidering Indirect Rule: The Nigerian Example', *Journal of the Historical Society of Nigeria*, iv, 3, December 1968.
59 NAI, CSO 1/21, VI, J. J. Thornburn to Crewe, 16 June 1910 and enclosures.
60 *Ibid.*, enclosed 'Sworn Evidence of Okonjo'.
61 *Ibid.*, enclosed 'Sworn Evidence of Iwedike of Agidiese Compound, Ogwashi-Uku'.
62 *Ibid.*, enclosed 'Sworn Evidence of Obi Nzekwe'.
63 CO 520/92, Egerton to Crewe, 5 April 1910 and enclosed copy of telegram to solicitor, Calabar, dated 8 February 1910.
64 CO 520/93, Egerton to Crewe, 21 May 1910, confidential, 'Further Report on the towns of Abagana, Nemo and Ukpu'.
65 *Ibid.*
66 CO 520/92, Egerton to Crewe, 5 April 1910, enclosure 6.
67 *Ibid.*
68 *Ibid.*, enclosed memorandum on *Davies, v. Rising.*
69 *Ibid.*, enclosure 9 by W. Fosbery, commenting on *Davies v. Rising.*
70 *Ibid.*
71 *Ibid.*
72 Chief Obafemi Awolowo, Interview at Ibadan, 16 March 1967. Chief Awolowo was among the first to set up legal practice in the interior of Yorubaland in 1947.
73 CO 583/12, Lugard to Harcourt, 25 March 1914, enclosure 2.
74 CO 520/103, Egerton to Harcourt, 17 May 1911, enclosure.
75 *Ibid.*

76 'Our Law and What It Costs Us', *Lagos Weekly Record*, 6 May 1893. For articles written in the same vein as this, see the issues of 8 October 1904 and 14 October 1905. See also *Lagos Standard*, 5 July 1905.

77 Fred. I. A. Omu, 'The Nigerian Newspaper Press, 1859–1937: A Study in Origins, Growth and Influence', unpublished PhD thesis, University of Ibadan, 1965, p. 109.

78 NAI, CSO 14/5, A2808/1913, 'Memorandum on the extension of the Jurisdiction of the Supreme Court' by A. R. Pennington.

79 NAI, CSO 12/21, 288/1902; *Lagos Standard*, 28 August 1912; *Nigerian Pioneer*, 26 June 1914.

80 NAI, CSO 12/21, 288/1902, 'Resolution passed by the Ilesha Council on 13 January 1902'.

81 CO 520/93, Egerton to Crewe, 21 May 1910, confidential.

82 CO 520/92, Egerton to Crewe, 5 April 1910, confidential.

83 *Ibid.*, enclosure 8.

84 For this and other ordinances mentioned in this section, see CO 583/3, 'Acts: Southern Nigeria, 1908–1911'.

85 CO 520/103, Egerton to Harcourt, 17 May 1911, minute by J. A. Anderson, 10 July 1911. Also, Harcourt to officer administering the government of Southern Nigeria, 18 July 1911.

86 CO 520/103, Egerton to Harcourt, 3 May 1911, confidential.

87 Order No. 12, 1911, *Southern Nigeria Government Gazette*, 1911, pp. 992–3.

88 CO 520/94, Egerton to Crewe, 6 June 1910, enclosure.

89 *Ibid.*

90 CO 520/92, Egerton to Crewe, 5 April 1910 and enclosure.

91 CO 520/92, Crewe to Egerton, 26 July 1910.

92 NAI, CSO 1/21, VI, A. G. Boyle to Colonial Office, 21 June 1911.

5 Judicial reorganisation, 1914

This country needs justice and not law, and the justice must be administered on the spot and as promptly as possible.

S. M. Grier[1]

I

It was in the same year, 1914, that the Northern and Southern Provinces of Nigeria were amalgamated that a vast reorganisation of the country's judicial system was undertaken by the colonial administration. The philosophy behind the reorganisation, best summed up in the statement by a top-ranking administrative official quoted above, operated in Nigeria until almost the end of the colonial era.

Some aspects of the judicial reorganisation were the result of the political amalgamation: the unification of the laws of the hitherto separate administrations, and the appointment of one Chief Justice and one Attorney-General for the whole country. But the more substantial aspect of it – the establishment or rather the reconstitution of three types of courts, a Supreme Court, provincial courts and 'native' courts – grew essentially out of the exigencies of the colonial situation in Nigeria. It was the result, not of a mere desire to amalgamate or streamline the judicial systems of Northern and Southern Nigeria, but of the difficulties which the colonial administration was experiencing in operating the Supreme Court system in the Southern Provinces. The aim of the 1914 judicial arrangement, it was officially and privately admitted, was to combat 'the influx of a swarm of native legal practitioners who employ touts to prompt ignorant people to litigation'.[2]

The judicial reorganisation was thus in the nature of a response to what was considered a serious political or administrative problem: how to curtail the influence of the African lawyer. Our discussion so far regarding the position of the lawyer in the colonial situation of Southern Nigeria leads to this conclusion. It will be apparent from what follows that the provisions of the ordinances of 1914 reconstituting the courts in Nigeria were intended to achieve the same objective. To stress only the mere relations of the three courts constituting the judicial system after 1914, as it is common with the extant works on the Nigerian legal system,[3] is indeed to miss the motive force behind the judicial policy operating in much of Nigeria up to the 1930s. The result of misunderstanding the motive behind the judicial reorganisation has been a tendency to overestimate the contribution of such a central figure as Lugard (who fathered the scheme) in the overall development of the Nigerian legal system.[4]

The important point about the Supreme Court, as reorganised by the Supreme Court Ordinance, No. 6 of 1914, was that its jurisdiction was drastically curtailed. The jurisdiction of the court was limited to the Lagos Colony and a few small enclaves along the coast. In 1914 these enclaves were limited to thirteen towns in Southern Nigeria.[5] Provision was made for an extension of the jurisdiction of the court as the economic and social development of the country should warrant. By 1928 it was exercising jurisdiction in only eighteen towns in the Southern Provinces: Aba, Onitsha, Sapele, Warri, Forcados, Bonny, Opobo, Port Harcourt, Oyo, Ibadan, Abeokuta, Ondo, Benin, Burutu, Calabar and others.[6]

The main reason for having these 'pockets' of Supreme Court jurisdiction in the interior was that the towns put under Supreme Court jurisdiction were commercial centres, containing foreign elements in their population – European traders, missionaries and immigrant Africans from outside Nigeria – who could not be properly subjected to the jurisdiction of any other court than the supreme court.[7] In such towns, too, the Supreme Court could relieve political officers of considerable judicial burdens in matters not directly related to administration. It would appear, however, that the Supreme Court was not intended to have jurisdiction over the indigenous population of these selected towns.[8]

Over the whole country the Supreme Court, from 1914 on, exercised its jurisdiction in two divisions or circuits, western and eastern, the River Niger being regarded as the demarcation line.

In the rest of the Protectorate of Nigeria were set up provincial courts and 'native' courts. Between them these courts exercised jurisdiction over more than 95 per cent of the population of Nigeria. Their powers and those of the Supreme Court have been discussed elsewhere;[9] it is sufficient for our purpose to sketch only their salient features.

The provincial court system was first established in 1900 in Northern Nigeria where it was said to have 'proved itself an unqualified success'.[10] The 'success' of these courts consisted in their usefulness as a vital aid to administrative control. Political officers who wrote feelingly about the courts would seem to have been most impressed, not by the quality of justice administered in them, but the speed with which they disposed of cases, especially criminal cases, without too much attention to technicalities of law or of procedure. Again, a provincial court was insulated from the Supreme Court, its judge usually being a political officer with, at best, a nodding acquaintance with the law or the legal process. The officer was 'not hampered by legal technicalities', and could thus bring to bear on any question 'a strong "common-sense" point of view',[11] including, if necessary, a consideration of what was politically expedient. Thus the court's jurisdiction complemented the powers of the political officer. Frederick Lugard, who as High Commissioner in Northern Nigeria (1900–1906) devised the provincial court system, employed the courts to strengthen his administrative control of the territory.[12] It was, undoubtedly, this 'success' of the courts which prompted their extension into Southern Nigeria at amalgamation.

In each of the nine provinces into which Southern Nigeria was now divided was established a provincial court presided over by the Resident or the Commissioner in charge of the province.[13] The law to be administered in the court was 'the Common Law, the doctrines of Equity and the statutes of general application which were in force in England on the 1st January, 1900'.[14] 'Native law' was to be administered, too, side by side with English law, as in the Supreme Court, provided such law was not 'repugnant to natural justice, equity and good conscience'. Significantly, from the point of view of this study, no legal practitioners were allowed to appear before a provincial court, the provision for the administration of English law notwithstanding. With the consent of the Governor, an appeal could lie from the provincial court to the Supreme Court in a civil suit involving property valued at over one hundred naira. If such an appeal was allowed, again, no legal practitioner could appear at the hearing without the previous consent of the chief justice. The chief justice on his part was to give his consent only 'where the appeal involves a question of law in the determination whereof the court . . . would be assisted by legal argument'.[15] There was no right of appeal in criminal cases.

Below the provincial courts were the 'native' courts – four grades of them ranked A, B, C and D in accordance with varying powers and jurisdictions. An important change in the constitution of the 'native' court after 1914 was that it was no longer to be presided over by the British political officer. The president of any grade of 'native' court was to be a local chief, with the political officer playing a supervisory role. The latter also constituted a sort of avenue for appeals in causes determined by the court. In a few selected centres like Benin, Oyo, Ibadan, Ijebu-Ode were created judicial councils which were at once deliberative assemblies and appeal courts for the 'native' courts within their areas of authority. It is important to note that both judicial councils and 'native' courts were designated 'native authorities' in their respective areas of jurisdiction. As native authorities they were empowered to make and enforce rules which could be additions to or modifications of the indigenous laws and customs.

The requirement to keep records of the 'native' court in the English language and to maintain some procedure and order in the court necessitated the establishment of the offices of the native court clerk and the court messenger. The former became the pivot of the 'native' court system; he was not only the scribe and the interpreter of the court, he was also the vital link between the court and the political officer. The latter served summonses on litigants, ensured the attendance of witnesses at court and helped to maintain order and discipline when the court was in session.

No legal practitioner *qua* legal practitioner was allowed to appear before a 'native' court, although provision was made for the representation of a litigant by a duly authorised relative.[16] In terms of the actual operation of the 'native' court system in Southern Nigeria, this provision was vital, as will be shown later. The law to be administered in the 'native' court was essentially the local law and custom 'not opposed to natural morality and humanity'.

II

Sir Frederick Lugard, now Governor-General of Nigeria (1914–1919), gave what appeared to be the reasons for the reconstitution

of the courts when he addressed the Nigerian Council on 12 March
1914. Having assured the council that he was acting in the best
interests of the country and of good government, he proceeded to
discuss what he called the defects of the judicial system hitherto
in force. The Supreme Court, he declared, 'has not been found to
be a success'. For one thing, the jurisdiction of the court had led
to much 'useless litigation without good results'. For another, 'the
procedure of the Supreme Court is too elaborate, the rules by
which it is bound are too rigid, for adaptation to a society such as
exists among [the] primitive tribes' of the interior of Nigeria.[17]
The operation of the court, in Lugard's view, had also occasioned
grave difficulties. There was, for instance, the difficulty of transporting witnesses over long distances to a Supreme Court town.
The procedure in the court had also produced delays, often leading
to a heightening of tension in civil disputes and to the escape of
criminals in criminal cases. There was, in sum, the need for a
'more summary procedure' in adjudicating disputes and investi-
gating crimes in the interior – such a procedure as the provincial
court, hopefully, would provide.

The reasons Lugard gave for the exclusion of legal practitioners
from both the provincial courts and the 'native' courts were a
mixture of popular prejudice and official fear. As a rule, he said,
barristers were often willing to accept a brief from either party in a
dispute even though only one of the parties could be in the right.
The barrister for one of the parties, he implied, must be something
of a professional liar. On that ground alone he would not approve
of the activities of lawyers in the interior. One other ground was
that 'the presence of counsel in civil suits has been productive of
many evils'.[18]

The last point is about the only disclosure made by Lugard
regarding the real motive force behind the judicial reorganisation
of 1914. There were, admittedly, difficulties in operating the
Supreme Court system before 1914 – particularly problems of
staffing and facilities and of inadequate transport and communication systems. But from what we saw in the last chapter regarding
the administration's experience with the Supreme Court and the
lawyers, especially in the Eastern and Central Provinces, it is easy
to appreciate that the practical difficulties in operating the Supreme
Court system were not the main considerations in the judicial
reorganisation of 1914. The fact was that perhaps from the time
of Sir William MacGregor as Governor of Southern Nigeria

(1899–1904), and until about the end of the colonial era, those who administered the government in Nigeria seemed motivated by two basic desires. There was the desire to set up efficient administrative and judicial machinery 'along native lines'. There was also the desire to 'protect' the non-literate masses of the population from exploitation by their relatively more advanced fellow-countrymen. The two desires are tied up in the concept of the 'Dual Mandate' which Sir Frederick Lugard elaborated upon in a book written after he left Nigeria.[19] Even before Lugard wrote this book in 1922, the idea had gained ground that people under colonial rule should be guarded in their growth and development.

Lawyers and the Supreme Court system, in the official, paternalistic view of Nigeria's development, were not wholesome influences. The alleged exploitation of the masses by lawyers apart, the very presence of lawyers in the interior districts did not seem compatible with the 'good government' which Lugard as well as those before him were anxious to build. At the basis of the 'good government' was the concept of 'Indirect Rule', assigning only a supervisory role to British political officers, while it was the task of colonial peoples to administer their own affairs through their own rulers. Theory, of course, differed widely from practice. In practice the lynchpin of the 'Indirect Rule' was the political officer who gathered in his hands a mammoth variety of political and administrative duties.[20] In the official view, if the political officer was to be effective in guiding the development of his area of authority, he would have to operate in an atmosphere in which his official actions would not be called into question. A situation in which lawyers could challenge the activities of political officers in the open court could easily undermine the authority of the officer and thereby hamper his effectiveness.

The provincial and the 'native' courts were seemingly geared to the concept of Indirect Rule. In the 'native' court the indigenous population would adjudicate their own disputes in their own way. Behind the scenes was the district commissioner, or the district officer as he was called after 1914, occasionally using the paternal hand of correction to guide, warn and advise. Sir Frederick Lugard himself spelled out fully the role the district officer was expected to play in the operation of the 'native' court system.[21]

The provincial court, administering English law and yet without the technicalities and the trappings of the Supreme Court, could well be a model for the 'native' court. In September 1912

Lugard had considered the establishment of a kind of model court in the protectorate as 'a more hopeful means' of educating the people than simply allowing the 'native' courts to continue as they were in Southern Nigeria.[22] The 'absolute impartiality' supposedly demonstrated at the provincial courts – the quoted phrase is Lugard's – would be beneficial to the 'native' courts in upgrading the quality of justice administered by them. As the general population became more enlightened, the 'native' courts might begin to copy the methods of administering justice employed by the provincial courts. There would come a time, Lugard hoped, when the 'native' courts would enforce or administer not only 'native law and custom', but also the ordinances of the protectorate. It was his desire, as he impressed it on his political officers, that 'the closest cooperation' should be maintained between the English-style courts like the provincial courts and the 'native' courts.[23] The 'native' court and the provincial court might, in time, evolve between them a method of administering justice *sui generis* and well adapted to the requirements of native administration in its 'simplicity, cheapness and rapidity'.

Not least important was the expectation that the operation of the provincial and 'native' courts would eliminate the influence of lawyers. Illiterate litigants would be spared the lawyers' 'excessive fees'. Administrative officers could proceed with their duty of building the structure of native administration in the protectorate without much fear of interference or opposition from lawyers.

Thus the judicial reorganisation of 1914 was essentially a political measure, and few perceptive, educated Africans of the time were unaware of this fact. The provisions of the Provincial Courts Ordinance, declared a Lagos newspaper, 'are part of a concerted and deeply laid plan designed for the purpose of preventing any interference with and all opposition against the Government'.[24] Those are strong words, but they contain a kernel of truth about the judicial reorganisation of 1914. In theory, the newly devised judicial arrangement seemed to offer adequate answers to the problems of administering justice under the Indirect Rule system. We shall defer to the next chapter an examination of the extent to which the political hopes pinned on the provincial and 'native' courts were realised.

One point that must be made here is that the problem of litigation in Southern Nigeria which loomed large in the official mind in the reorganisation of the judicial system, had deeper roots than was realised. It was an inadequate view held by administrative officers for the most part – and by some modern writers[25] – that all litigations, particularly those over land, were the handiwork of lawyers and their touts who fomented them. If political officers had realised the complexity of the problem of litigation, they might have adopted a more liberal attitude towards the Supreme Court and the lawyers.

It was not realised, for instance, that litigation over land stemmed partly from the enhanced value of land in many parts of Southern Nigeria. The 1890s witnessed the beginning of commercial agriculture. The rubber industry had started up,[26] and was to be followed by the still more spectacular development of the cocoa industry. The colonial administration itself was a big dealer in land transactions. For building and construction projects it acquired land and paid compensation to anyone who could establish his or her title to the land acquired. Private African merchants and European trading houses were similarly purchasing land for commercial use in the interior.[27] The desire to purchase land was also manifested by missionary agencies, the British Cotton Growing Association (in Ibadan Province), and by all those, prompted by opportunities opening up under the colonial regime, who migrated from one part of the country to another. As time went on, increased population in Southern Nigeria put another pressure on the use of land.

In the face of the demands for land, the sanctity of communal land ownership was being rudely shaken. 'The old law', as Sir Edwin Speed reported in his investigation of land tenure in Ibadan in 1916, 'was persistently disregarded by everyone who had the desire and the opportunity to profit by breaches thereof, and, *inter alios*, by those who, by virtue of their position were specially responsible for its enforcement'.[28] With the increasing demands for land, the concept of individual land ownership was creeping into the economic thought of the people. It was a concept apt to be sharpened as economic development proceeded apace and as the pressure of population increased.

The concept of individual land ownership and the increased value of land were together a direct invitation to the burgeoning of land disputes. Individuals as well as communities were anxious to lay claim to as much land as they possibly could. There were no survey plans fixing territorial holdings and proper deeds of conveyance were rare commodities especially in the rural areas. In the absence of survey plans or deeds of conveyance, the plea of *res judicata*, when a matter in dispute seems to have been settled, quite often, was no bar to protracted litigation over land. In *Oboli v. Gbosa* (1917), tried at the Onitsha Assizes, plaintiff sued the defendant for trespass on his family land, claiming £100 (₦200) damages. In a previous action, *Ogbolu v. Ejiofor*, the same issue, involving the same families as in the present case, appeared to have been decided in favour of the plaintiff's family who had been awarded £5 (₦10) damages. Counsel for the defendant now raised the plea of *res judicata*. Justice Webber, acting in what appeared to him to be the interests of justice, refused the plea: 'It is not quite clear from the [previous] judgment . . . as to what is the boundary between these people. . . . The Court in that case had not the benefit of a plan. The boundary not having been determined, I am unable to hold that the plea . . . is a good one, and the case must be proceeded with.'[29]

It was a fact worth noting that under the new colonial structure with its courts, a well-pitched legal battle in a land dispute could yield good results. Land boundaries were therefore not only disputable; they would also continue to remain so as long as there was the money or the will to contest the decision reached by a court of law. It was a common practice to redress an old, settled land dispute and bring it to court at every change in the office of the district officer or the Resident.[30] What the administration failed to realise was that litigants would continue to seek access to the Supreme Court as the highest court in Nigeria, the limitations of the 1914 judicial reorganisation notwithstanding, precisely because of the sociological and economic factors at work.

Another root of litigation lay in the inter-communal hostilities which had existed in some places before the establishment of colonial rule and which colonial rule did little to remove. The reports of administrative officers in certain areas up to the 1920s and 1930s contain accounts of continuing inter-communal hostilities.[31] The presence of colonial officials did not mean an abrupt end to such hostilities; the superimposition of colonial rule merely drove them underground. While the stationing of soldiers in the interior by the administration checked outbreaks of open hostilities, it did not bring about positive peace in some localities.[32] In a number of places inter-communal hostilities continued, but found expression in the English-style courts that came with colonial rule. Hence litigation over land between one community and another, while it might have been motivated in part by the new economic demands, could also be a continuation of an old traditional feud. As Chief Justice Edwin Speed discovered in Calabar Province, land disputes were 'nothing more or less than tribal disputes brought before the Court on the suit of some chief who alleged that he sued on behalf of himself and his people'.[33] The eagerness with which communities contributed money to be handed to lawyers to 'fight' on their behalf in a land dispute was not unlike the zeal for war. The eagerness was at once a demonstration of a feeling of hostility and of a determination to win. In such a situation lawyers were but the old 'war boys' in wig and gown.

It has been suggested that litigation in the British-established courts had a considerable emotional value as a source of excitement.[34] A big dispute provided the opportunity for a whole village to organise collection of money to pay lawyers, as sometimes happened, and to make frantic efforts to prepare for the hearing of the dispute in a court of law. Behind the feverish activities, it has been suggested, was 'not a burning desire for justice, but an intense will to win and enjoyment of the struggle'.[35]

There may be something to be said for this psychological analysis of litigation in Southern Nigeria under colonial rule. The experience of some lawyers who were in practice in the 1920s would seem to support such an analysis.[36] There was an occasion, one of them informed the writer, when the amount of money collected to finance a land dispute in which he was to appear in Warri was far greater than the value of the land in dispute. There might be a strong traditional or emotional attachment to a piece of land, but this, he said, was not apparent. The struggle and the excitement seemed to be the important thing. The suggestion he said he made to his clients to spend the money in purchasing another plot of land was quietly ignored.[37] As if in support of the lawyer, the British Resident for Warri Province in 1925, F. B. Adams, sounded the same note on the type of excitement people seemed to derive from litigation. 'In many cases', he wrote, 'justice is the last thing sought by those who initiate the proceedings, and when they get it, they complain violently.'[38] The achievement of victory in a dispute seemed like an anticlimax.

In considering the roots of litigation in Southern Nigeria one should not fail to mention the growth of individualism. The factors that contributed to this development are connected with the imposition of colonial rule itself: the opening up of the country to the outside world, western education, missionary influence, the new money-oriented economy, foreign travel and the like. These various factors imbued the people with new values, sometimes out of tune with the traditional mores.[39] Among the educated Africans in particular, there was a heightened consciousness of the individual's worth and, by the same token, a decreasing emphasis, in varying degrees, on kinship ties and obligations. With individualism went feelings of independence and personal freedom. The individual resorted to the court if he felt his rights were being encroached upon – thanks to the over-arching British colonial umbrella under which such rights could be enforced. This was the sociological environment in which the British-established courts had been operating in Southern Nigeria before 1914. Surely, one cannot ignore it in judging the wisdom or otherwise of the direction of the judicial reforms of 1914.

III

In the colonial history of Nigeria perhaps no other measure aroused so much opposition and protest as the judicial reorganisation of 1914. The protest movement which was in some respects international in scope lasted until 1933 when the provincial court system was abrogated.

Lawyers, both indigenous and expatriate, were, of course, prominent in the protest. Apart from the protest activities of the two branches of the Nigeria Bar Association at Lagos and Calabar, individual lawyers formed themselves into reform clubs in the 1920s for the purpose of fighting the judicial reorganisation of 1914.[40] Of the expatriate lawyers who subscribed to the protest, Sir William N. M. Geary was the most active. His theatre of operation was the British press through which, more than any other single individual, he informed the British public about the conditions under which justice was being administered in Nigeria.[41] Lugard's administration was not a little disturbed by the weight lent to the protest movement by William H. Stoker, the independent-minded puisne judge we met earlier on, who in January 1915 wrote a scathing criticism of the judicial system operating in Nigeria.[42]

Contrary to the official view and the view of some modern writers, the protest movement was not an affair of lawyers alone.

In Lagos in particular the judicial reorganisation was the subject of many petitions and public meetings which were in most cases convened by such men as Dr O. Obasa and Dr John Randle, medical practitioners, S. H. Pearse, a notable merchant, and J. Osho Davies and Patriarch J. G. Campbell, popular writers and commentators.[43] A committee headed by Dr Obasa submitted a memorandum on the administration of justice in Nigeria to Hon. W. G. A. Ormsby-Gore, the British Under-Secretary of State for the Colonies, during his visit to the country in 1926.[44] So did the Nigerian National Democratic Party (NNDP), Nigeria's first political party, founded by Herbert Macaulay. The need for continuous struggle against the judicial system was, in fact, written into the party's constitution.[45] After 1923 educated Africans found in the colonial legislative council in Lagos an important venue for fighting the provisions of the 1914 judicial reorganisation.[46]

The role of the press in the protest movement has been discussed elsewhere.[47] All that need be said here is that the newspapers in Lagos fought strenuously against the judicial system of 1914.

Educated Africans in the other British West African colonies were at one with their Nigerian counterparts in denouncing the Nigerian judicial system. A common front was easy to maintain against the judicial system because, in the sphere of administration of justice, all the British West African colonies had more or less the same grievances. In all of them the executive and the judiciary were intertwined in their respective interior districts. On the Gold Coast (Ghana), lawyers were not allowed to practise in Ashanti or the Northern Provinces until 1933.[48] On account of their common grievances over administration of justice, the National Congress of British West Africa held at Accra in March 1920,[49] adopted a fourteen-point programme on judicial reforms. The Congress called for the abolition of the Provincial Courts Ordinance in Nigeria, and demanded that legal practitioners be allowed to appear in all cases involving life or liberty, and that a right of appeal should lie from the 'native' courts to the Supreme Court.[50] A delegation of the Congress went to England in October 1920 to meet King George V himself over these and other demands.

Finally the protest movement reached as far as the House of Commons in London. The Commons, including a large number of lawyers, seemed an ideal place in which to launch an attack on the judicial system in Nigeria. Between 1914 and 1932 about fifty-two questions were raised on the floor of the House of Commons by individual members of parliament in connection with the operation of the provincial and 'native' courts in Nigeria[51] – all aimed at bringing pressure to bear on the Colonial Office to effect changes in the judicial system of Nigeria.

The question may be raised here as to how far the local opposition to the judicial system was genuine. The belief gained ground in official circles in Lagos and at the Colonial Office in London that the opposition to the judicial system was being engineered mainly by lawyers, their touts and their relatives. It must have seemed significant to the administration that the opposition to the judicial system was strongest in such places as Lagos and Calabar, where the jurisdiction of the supreme court was not curtailed and lawyers could practise their profession. Outside these two cities, except for a few letters from the interior to some newspapers in Lagos, there was no articulate public opinion expressed against the provincial court system. Under these circumstances, it was easy to conclude that the cry against the judicial system was motivated by the desire of lawyers and all interested parties to have a freer scope for the practice of the legal profession in the less sophisticated areas of the country, which might offer richer pastures in the form of land cases. In 1919, five years of opposition to the new judicial system left the administration with no other conclusion than that 'the continued hostility' to it was being 'promoted solely by local [legal] practitioners and their friends who resent the loss of profits which their exclusion from the Provincial and "Native" courts involves'.[52] The same conclusion is implicit in Margery Perham's recent analysis of the opposition to the judicial system: 'The majority of the leading citizens and politicians who had been educated in Britain were lawyers, and their exclusion from the new Native courts in the Southern Provinces hit their pride and their pockets very severely.'[53]

There is no reason to doubt that the opposition met with by the judicial system of 1914 was genuine. It was the product of a widespread fear that the increased powers now given to political officers in judicial matters under the new judicial arrangement would be wielded to the detriment of Africans, literate and non-literate alike. There were sufficient indications even before 1914 that the rule of administrative officers could be irksome. In particular, Lugard's own method of administration in the Northern

Provinces (1900–1907, 1912–14) did not inspire confidence among educated Africans. The idea was widespread that he was highly dictatorial and intolerant of criticism.[54]

Without the increased judicial powers, administrative officers before 1914 had been known to wield virtually absolute powers in their domains. Captain W. A. Ross was reportedly ruling Oyo with an iron hand, exacting hard labour, arbitrarily imprisoning alleged offenders and enforcing prostration by chiefs and commoners alike.[55] We saw earlier that the issue involved in *Davies v. Rising* (1910) was that Davies refused to remove his hat before the defendant, a district commissioner in the former Eastern Province. There were reported cases of public floggings by administrative officers. In 1907 one Captain Hughes ordered eleven Itsekiri men in Warri to be flogged for alleged unwillingness to work.[56] Other instances of public flogging in Warri were reported.[57] Silas Dove, the lawyer in the Ogwashi-Uku incident, 1910, was reported to have been publicly whipped at Onitsha in 1914 at the instance of an administrative officer.[58]

In explaining the fear of the educated Africans, it should also be noted that the provincial court system had operated in the Northern Provinces for about thirteen years before it was introduced into the south. Largely through reports reaching the south from the north about the operation of the provincial courts, the notion was widespread among educated Africans that the system inevitably led to abuse of power by administrative officers.[59]

Whether the allegations of official high-handedness and miscarriages of justice were true or false is not pertinent to our argument; the significant thing is that the allegations were made at all. They disclosed the reason for the widespread apprehension regarding the consequences of greater judicial powers being accorded to administrative officers under the provincial court system. It was in relation to the abuses of power by administrative officers that the Supreme Court was looked upon as the only possible check, in judicial matters, against their autocratic powers. The exclusion of lawyers from the courts in the protectorate and the curtailment of the Supreme Court's jurisdiction were therefore bound to cause much uneasiness and arouse fears about the fate of Africans under the new judicial system. Those who would really suffer under the system, said the editor of a Lagos newspaper, were not the legal practitioners, but the non-literate masses and educated Africans in the protectorate who were now placed more firmly under the control of political officers.[60]

Two expatriate lawyers, Robert F. Irving and George Graham Paul, testified to the sincerity of the fears expressed by the indigenous communities about the new judicial system. The two lawyers could not be said to be interested parties since their legal practices, in Lagos and Calabar respectively, were based largely on retainers from European firms. They were therefore not affected by the enactments forbidding lawyers to practise in the protectorate. Graham Paul, in fact, made it clear that his legal practice was 'mainly European and to that extent absolutely unaffected by the Provincial Courts Ordinance'. Robert Irving said he came into contact with 'representatives of every class of native opinion' in Lagos and he could testify that there was 'a genuine, sincere and universal dread and dislike of the enactments in question'. He denied meeting 'a single native' who favoured the enactments, and he had been struck by 'the absolute faith which all classes of natives have in the Supreme Court of Nigeria'.[61] Graham Paul wrote from Calabar in the same vein. In his experience with Africans, he said in 1917, everyone was hostile to the new judicial system after three years' experience of it.[62]

As to why educated Africans in the coastal towns were most anxious about the operation of the provincial courts in the protectorate, the explanation is not far to seek. A large percentage of the educated Africans in the coastal towns, especially in Lagos, had their roots in the protectorate. There was therefore a natural feeling of affinity on their part with their people in the interior. A petition against the Provincial Court Bill sent to Lugard in February 1914 declared that the petitioners felt 'intimately connected with the Protectorate'. The petition was therefore sent 'on behalf of themselves and their brethren of the Protectorate'.[63] A Lagos newspaper struck the same note of identity: 'We say emphatically that the interest of the Protectorate is our interest for we represent here not only the Colony.'[64]

In the anxiety shown by educated Africans in the coastal towns over the operation of the provincial court system, there was also a strong element of self-interest. An educated African in Lagos or any other coastal town could have occasion to go into the protectorate. As a 'native', he would be subjected to the jurisdiction of the provincial court or the 'native' court if he committed any offence there. To people who were enjoying the full benefit of

Supreme Court jurisdiction in Lagos or Calabar, the prospect of being arraigned before a provincial court in the protectorate without the assistance of counsel could not have been altogether a pleasant one.

IV

The theoretical arguments raised in the course of the protest movement against the judicial reorganisation of 1914 are worth considering. They provide a useful insight into the nature of the judicial system in a dependency, such as Southern Nigeria was.

First, against the judicial reorganisation, it was contended that the new judicial system was segregationist and racialist. 'Non-natives', for all practical purposes meaning Europeans, were not subject to the jurisdiction of the provincial court in civil as well as in criminal cases, even though the court, like the Supreme Court, also administered English law. The implication of the new judicial arrangement was that the provincial court was not good enough for the European, and all were obviously not equal before the law. There was thus a strong element of colour prejudice inherent in the new system of administering justice.[65]

Although the provincial court was supposed to administer English law, the political officer presiding over it was not trained in the law. The assumption seemed to be that a plain, honest man, without any knowledge of law, could always bring common sense to bear on a given set of facts and come to a reasonable judgment. Even if the assumption had been true, the system left the law uncertain. Judgments would vary as the conscience or intelligence of the individual officer dictated. Again, it was doubtful whether political officers had sufficient time for their judicial duties since their administrative functions were 'sufficiently arduous and engrossing'.[66] In most cases, the administrative officer was the only white man in a district or a combination of districts, and he was in charge of all departments of the local administration: prison, police, public works, taxation, accounts, posts and telegraphs, and so on.

Even if the administrative officer could combine judicial and administrative duties, it was argued, it was open to question whether such a combination promoted the cause of justice. Judicial and executive functions could, on occasions, clash; the administrative officer might then give way to expediency, ignoring the dictates of justice.[67] What, in fact, prevented the district officer, remote from the glare of public observation, from using his judicial powers to aid the political? Could an educated African, considered 'dangerous' by the administration, expect to obtain justice in a 'native' court, supervised by the political officer, or in a provincial court directly under his control? There was also the possibility that a political officer could use his judicial powers to enforce any rule prescribed by him, however unreasonable. One such rule in the protectorate, never officially promulgated, but nonetheless real, was that Africans, however highly educated, must doff their hats before Europeans. There were instances when political officers used their judicial powers to enforce that rule.[68] Prostration before Captain W. A. Ross was an 'accepted' code of behaviour in Oyo Province which, if broken, could lead to a term of imprisonment. In any polity, except perhaps in Plato's *Republic*, the dangers of combining judicial and executive functions in a single authority are real indeed.

The members of the Bar at Calabar pointed out that the working of the 'native' and provincial courts was open to miscarriages of justice in some instances even if political officers were credited with the best of intentions. In their own words, the courts left 'an open door for a great deal of injustice'.[69] There were some features of the working of the two categories of courts which lent strength to this assertion. In the higher grades of the 'native' court and in the provincial court the English language was the medium of expression, and the use of English always raised the problem of interpretation. Since a lot depended on whatever facts were conveyed to the presiding judge through the interpreter, so the argument ran, the interpreter might, conceivably, be influential in determining the outcome of an issue before the court. Nor were the possibilities of miscarriage of justice obviated by the 'power of review' vested in the political officer. It was pointed out that review could not be other than perfunctory, and that it could never take account of such seemingly intangible, but by no means unimportant aspect of judicial administration as, for instance, the demeanour of witnesses in court.[70] Much the same thing could be said about the power of review vested in the Resident and the Chief Justice of the Supreme Court over cases tried at the provincial courts. There was yet another fundamental objection to 'review' as a judicial process. A political officer wishing to save his face over a case that had been badly tried for political reasons could always write his report of the case to fit his judgment.

The grant of an appeal, as of right, from the 'native' or the provincial court to the Supreme Court could have served some purpose in minimising occurrences of injustice. But under the 'native' and the provincial court systems, the opponents of the courts pointed out, appeals were made to depend heavily on the favour of political officers.

From the point of view of the opponents of the new judicial system, underscoring all the other defects of the provincial courts was the exclusion from them of legal practitioners. This was considered particularly serious in criminal cases, because the English approach to justice was still a novelty among the non-literate masses of the protectorate. In the English-style courts, as an administrative officer admitted, 'everything is against the unsophisticated native'.[71] The 'unsophisticated native' brought before a provincial court administering English law stood at a very grave disadvantage when deprived the assistance of counsel who understood the law and who could speak for him. It was for this reason, among others, that the Provincial Courts Ordinance 'imperilled the liberty of His Majesty's subjects within the areas reached by it'.[72] The *African Times and Orient Review* drew a more serious inference: 'If the right of legal self-defence is taken away from the Native subject who is left neither his natural defenders, the barristers, to safeguard his interests, nor properly constituted courts presided over by efficient judges to investigate his claims, it will not be a very difficult matter to totally enslave him.'[73] Sir William Geary wondered: 'What security is there in a criminal trial by an untrained judge and the accused not defended by counsel, that the true facts will be elicited?'[74]

With remarkable insight into the problem of socio-cultural change in Southern Nigeria under Western or European impact, A. E. M. Gibson, a practising lawyer based at Calabar, argued that, contrary to official belief, the exclusion of legal practitioners from the courts in the protectorate, would not prevent non-literate litigants from being 'bled to death' in expensive litigations.[75] To exclude lawyers from the process of administering justice, he said, was to encourage interference by men far less trained than the lawyers and not necessarily any more scrupulous. Anyone with a smattering of education and in the position of some authority in the new judicial system could prey upon the ignorance of an illiterate litigant and exact fees perhaps more exorbitant than a lawyer would dare to demand. Transactions between this class of persons and the litigants who happened to fall their way would be impossible to detect. The arrangements would be 'sealed with charms, native oaths and ceremonies'.

Up to 1933 the judicial reorganisation of 1914 did not lack its defenders. In 1914 Sir Edwin Speed, the Chief Justice and the brain behind the judicial reorganisation, asserted in a memorable phrase that the provincial court system 'brings English justice practically to the door of everyone'.[76] Through the provincial court system, it was argued, Nigerians in the protectorate enjoyed the benefit of English law administered in a simple manner and at minimum cost. In the words of a puisne judge of the Supreme Court in the 1920s, the provincial courts made justice 'cheap and freely accessible to the ordinary people'.[77] In these courts, it was said, the ordinary people had their cases tried by political officers 'whom they know and trust rather than by "red Judges" and lawyers whom they do not know and therefore fear'.[78]

The provincial courts also fitted the stage of development of the vast majority of the population of Nigeria who were non-literate.[79] The courts stood midway between the highly developed and highly technical Supreme Court and the customary approach to the administration of justice. The administration of English law in the courts without the technicalities of the Supreme Court was but a gradual and necessary step towards the full introduction of the Supreme Court system throughout the country. In this connection they provided 'a simple and easy method' of extending the Supreme Court's jurisdiction as the needs and the development of the country would dictate. In particular the courts were well suited to the trial of land disputes which were said to require special handling. Land disputes, at least in the official view, usually involved political questions which were by their nature 'generally beyond the purview of the Supreme Court'.[80] A judge of a provincial court would have no difficulty visiting a given piece of land in dispute and appreciating the political or social implications of the case before him. The objective to be aimed at in settling land disputes in the circumstances of the Protectorate of Nigeria 'must frequently be in the nature of a compromise' – an objective that would be achieved more easily at the provincial court than at the Supreme Court.[81]

There were also financial considerations in the establishment of the judicial system of 1914. It was contended that the full operation of the supreme court throughout the country would necessitate the augmentation of the judicial staff, and this the administration could not afford or would not undertake.

Although administrative officers might not be trained lawyers, the proponents of the new judicial system maintained, they were qualified in other ways to make them well fitted to administer justice in the Protectorate of Nigeria. Their knowledge of the locality and their understanding of the customs and sometimes the language of the people among whom they were working helped to compensate for their lack of legal training.[82] The law administered in the provincial courts, it was pointed out, was simple, consisting largely of native law and custom 'best known to political officers'. C. L. Temple, one of Lugard's lieutenants in the Northern Provinces, even doubted the sufficiency or the efficacy of legal knowledge in administering 'native' justice. In his *Native Races and their Rulers*, published in 1918, he contended that far and above legal knowledge, what was essential in the administration of justice in the less developed areas of a colonial territory was 'experience and knowledge of native men and affairs'.[83] Without the 'experience of native character', he argued, 'no extensive knowledge of the law' would produce any good results. To understand the 'native character', a judge must 'be in touch with the natives'. The officials in the best position to do so were not the Supreme Court judges, but administrative officers who spent a good deal of their time with the 'natives'. It was for this reason that Temple considered the provincial court system not only as justifiable but in fact as 'the only sound system' in the circumstances of colonial Nigeria.

There was no want of arguments to defend the exclusion of lawyers from the trial of criminal cases in the provincial courts over the charge that the courts were wantonly taking lives in the protectorate. It was argued that criminal cases tried in the courts were not conducted by trained lawyers for the Crown; it would therefore be unfair to have lawyers for the defence. In criminal as well as in civil cases, since the judge of the provincial court was himself not a lawyer, lawyers, if they were to appear before him, would tend to assume a bullying attitude on technical points of the law – a situation which would impair the efficiency of the judge and destroy public confidence in his decisions.[84] The provincial court Bench, for lack of legal training, would be unable to 'prevent quibbles being given the appearance of principles and vice versa'. Hence lawyers appearing before judges not trained in law would be able to adduce technicalities to free known criminals, thereby 'bringing British justice into disrepute and prompting the natives to take the law into their own hands'.[85]

In the late 1920s, administrative officers of various ranks in Nigeria stoutly defended the provincial court system and the limitations placed on the Supreme Court's jurisdiction on the basis of policy considerations. Their views deserve a close examination not only because they themselves devoted much time and energy over a period of some five years to a consideration of the relations of the judiciary to colonial policy in Nigeria,[86] but also because these views are particularly relevant to an understanding of the rationale behind the judicial system operating in Nigeria up to 1933.

By the 1920s the notion seemed to have emerged more clearly than ever that the objective of a colonial administration, if not the justification for its existence, was the development of the indigenous communities along lines that were not necessarily European.[87] The view generally held by administrative officers was that the Supreme Court was inimical to the social and political development of the indigenous communities in Nigeria. The court, with its use of English law and English legal and judicial procedure, by its very nature, 'must be disruptive of native political and social organisation'.[88] In land and other matters in Southern Nigeria, it was contended, customary law was being steadily replaced by English law and English legal notions. Where customary law was too strong to be ousted completely, elements of confusion had accompanied the introduction of English law. The result was that 'in place of solidarity and security which should be associated with a reign of law, we find native society filled with uncertainty, suspicion and fraud'.[89] Moreover 'the misunderstood individualism of English law' seemed to be accelerating the effects of economic and other factors along the road to the 'social disintegration of the indigenous communities'. Thus the influence of a foreign judicial system like the Supreme Court, if not curbed, would destroy much that was valuable in the indigenous society, and 'the native communities will lose their life and soul'.[90]

It was also pointed out that the task of building up viable native administrations in the protectorate for the purpose of governing the vast majority of the Nigerian population was hampered by the

Supreme Court in subtle ways. As the Lieutenant-Governor for Southern Nigeria argued, 'it is extremely difficult, if not impossible, for a Native Administration to function properly within a Supreme Court area'.[91] The court was being regarded by the people as 'the most powerful organ of Government'. Such a notion about the court, it was said, even if it was not accurate, was bound to have serious repercussions on the development of native administrations as institutions with considerable autonomy in internal affairs. The people's eyes would be directed to Lagos and to the Supreme Court as the ultimate source of power and authority. In these circumstances, said another administrative officer, it would be impossible for the people to 'think Provincially'.[92] The psychological effect on the administrative staff might be to depress initiative in general and dampen their zest for 'guiding the development of the native communities'.[93]

It was also a serious matter to administrative officers that administrative or political decisions were sometimes overruled by the Supreme Court. Yet, in the opinion of E. M. Falk, a Resident east of the Niger, to frequently overrule the decisions of an administrative body, whether it was a native ruler, a native council or a body of British political officers, was to undermine the prestige of that body in the eyes of the ordinary people. Deprived of its prestige, its influence was bound to wane and it would be impossible to carry out policies laid down by the central government. Even under the existing system of limited jurisdiction granted to the Supreme Court in the protectorate of Nigeria, the Resident wrote, 'the policy of the Government is being stultified . . . and the Administration is being weakened rapidly'.[94]

What made the Supreme Court system inimical to the development of native administrations, wrote H. L. Ward-Price, a one-time Resident for Abeokuta Province, and himself a lawyer, was not so much the rules of procedure in the court as its personnel.[95] The judges of the Supreme Court were usually 'strangers to the local natives'. As strangers to their environment, they could not be in a position to weigh and assess accurately the evidence presented before them in court. To arrive at the 'true meaning' of such evidence often required 'local knowledge and an insight into the local atmosphere'. Furthermore because the judges of the court were generally 'ignorant' of local customs and traditions, they were not fit to guide the 'natural development' of the indigenous laws and customs.

Then there were the lawyers. The African barrister, after his experience at the English Inns of Court, came back to his country ignorant of the laws and customs of his own people, but 'thoroughly imbued with English manners and beliefs'.[96] Far from being upholders of African ways of life, African barristers stood out clearly as 'opponents of things African'. What was more, their professional role in the protectorate was only to direct the eyes of the masses deliberately away from the Resident and the chiefs and towards the Supreme Court as 'the only seat of authority'. Every case taken out of the hands of the chiefs and away from the provincial court 'is another step upwards in their progress towards attaining political power', because of the importance attached in popular estimation to the exercise of judicial powers.[97] It was the chief secretary to the government, H. M. M. Moore, who clinched the argument by saying that unbridled exercise of jurisdiction by the Supreme Court in the protectorate 'can only end in the political supremacy of the lawyer over these communities'.[98]

The political power the African lawyer would wield in the interior districts would be 'inimical to our native policy', opined another administrative officer.[99] The African lawyer returned to his country imbued with political notions about representative government, the party system, rule of law and the like – notions that were 'hopelessly inapplicable to the circumstances of the West African Protectorates'.[100] The lawyer was thus not only out of sympathy with African indigenous institutions, but also was very apt to stand in direct opposition to the administrative officer, 'who has made it his business to forget English politics and the party system of government in order to study the customs and thought of the people for whose welfare he is responsible'.

It is impossible to determine, purely on a theoretical basis, the merits or the demerits of the case for or against the judicial reorganisation of 1914. A mere examination of the arguments on both sides of the judicial reorganisation does not help us to know, for instance, how successful it was in achieving the objectives set for it: how to keep out lawyers from the protectorate and minimise the cost of litigation. It is necessary, therefore, to see how the provincial and the 'native' courts worked in practice. A true assessment of their relation to the development of Nigeria can then be made.

But even here, one may point out that some of the arguments offered in the defence of the provincial court or the curtailment of the jurisdiction of the Supreme Court were certainly not such that could silence opposition. To defend the provincial court system on financial grounds, for instance, seemed to many ridiculous. It was easy to point out that the administration of justice in Nigeria was more than paying its way. The revenue returns showed annually a profit on the administration of justice in the years before the judicial reorganisation.[101]

Unduly heavy emphasis has also been placed on the ignorance of lawyers and judges of the Supreme Court about Nigerian 'native law and custom'. An attempt was made earlier to show that in the legal system of Southern Nigeria, in which customary law was subordinated to English law, there was no particular difficulty in administering customary law. Any rule of customary law was no more than a matter of fact to be proved by evidence.

Again, the argument about the importance of 'experience of native character' on the part of administrative officers in administering justice in the protectorate will not stand close analysis. Experience is necessarily relative. What degree of experience would be adequate is a question that none of the defenders of the provincial court system answered. Significantly, C. L. Temple, one of those who employed this argument, admitted that the experience was not easy to acquire and that the process of acquiring it could be long and tedious. There was also a basic assumption in the minds of those who employed the argument which was not always well founded: that administrative officers were permanent in their stations and had the time to acquire experience of the 'native' character of their respective areas. As a matter of fact few of them enjoyed such permanence. Captain W. A. Ross, who spent about a quarter of a century in Oyo Province as a political officer, was a singular exception.[102]

The iconoclastic picture of the Supreme Court that was painted by the defenders of the provincial court system was overdrawn. It is not true that the Supreme Court administered nothing but English law to the detriment of indigenous customary laws or indigenous institutions. Indeed, as will be shown in a later chapter, the history of the Supreme Court in Nigeria is notable for the conscious efforts made by the court to adapt English common law to the Nigerian soil.[103]

Whatever the weakness of some of the theoretical arguments against the judicial reorganisation of 1914, it is remarkable that among who who favoured the reorganisation were judges and some administrative officers who were lawyers by training. Sir Edwin Speed, Chief Justice 1914–19, was the brain behind it. In 1925 the successor to Speed, Sir Ralph Combe, asserted that the introduction of the provincial courts in the Southern Provinces of Nigeria 'has been fully justified'.[104] Frederick van der Meulen, puisne judge of the Supreme Court 1919–26, after retiring from the judicial service of Nigeria, vigorously defended the provincial courts in the pages of *The Times* of London in 1932.[105] One lawyer among the administrative officers who has not been mentioned is S. M. Grier, Resident for Oyo and Ibadan between 1913 and 1920, and afterwards holder of diverse high-ranking offices in the Colonial Service. In his view, expressed in 1928, the curtailment of the jurisdiction of the Supreme Court in the Protectorate of Nigeria amounted to a moral obligation on the part of Britain, a measure of self-restraint in the process of developing Nigeria along lines that were not necessarily European.[106] The support given to the judicial reorganisation with all its restrictions by these men, conversant with the English legal system and the requirements of judicial administration under it is, I think, a reflection of the general feeling now prevailing both in administrative as well as in judicial circles that some ideals of British approach to justice should necessarily be sacrificed in the interest of upholding a British administration overseas.

V

The criticisms levelled at the judicial reorganisation of 1914 did not fail altogether to influence the administration in effecting some modifications to the judicial system in Nigeria.

One way of meeting the constant flow of criticisms was to extend the jurisdiction of the Supreme Court. The court's jurisdiction was progressively extended in 1915, 1922, 1927 and 1928. By the latter date, as was mentioned earlier, the court was exercising jurisdiction in about eighteen towns in Southern Nigeria.

Some other amendments were designed as an answer to the criticism that alleged criminals were being tried for their lives in the provincial courts without the aid of counsel. In an attempt to minimise the 'political' dominance over the courts, an amendment of 1918 to the Provincial Courts Ordinance made the Chief Justice, and no longer the Governor, the authority to decide in which cases appeals were to be allowed from the provincial courts to the Supreme Court.[107] By the Supreme Court (Amendment) Ordinance, No. 28 of 1918, the Chief Justice was empowered to transfer 'any cause or matter at any stage thereof' from the provincial court to the supreme court 'on the application of any party thereto to a Lieutenant-Governor or a Resident'.[108] Significantly, the Chief Justice, 'if it appears to him to be expedient to do so', could order the transfer of a case by telegram which would 'have the same validity and effect as if it were the said order'.[109] Again, from 1922 on, a litigant at a provincial court could apply for the transfer of his case to the Supreme Court.[110]

The absolute power which the Resident had over a provincial court was, at least in theory, also modified in 1922. By the provincial Courts (Amendment) Ordinance, No. 13 of that year, a provincial Resident or any other commissioner of a provincial court having the judicial powers of a Resident, 'may, in his discretion, . . . sit with assessors at the trial of any case'.[111]

As if in response to the charge of executive dominance over the 'native' courts, these courts were somewhat linked to the Supreme Court in 1920 in areas where the latter exercised jurisdiction. By the Native Courts (Amendment) Ordinance of that year, 'every Commissioner of the Supreme Court may at any time direct that the records of a native tribunal relating to any cause or matter arising within the local limits of his jurisdiction shall be transmitted to him and such record shall be transmitted accordingly. . . .'[112] The commissioner in reviewing any such cause or matter might confirm or modify the decision of the 'native' court or order a new trial.

It should be emphasised that these amendments were not intended to bring about any significant change in the judicial policy inaugurated in 1914, either as regards the executive control over the provincial and the 'native' courts or the exclusion of lawyers *qua* lawyers from these courts. The territorial extension of the jurisdiction of the Supreme Court, for instance, did not amount to much. The court's jurisdiction in the towns in the protectorate to which it was extended was limited to 'pocket handkerchief enclaves' within these towns. In fact in such towns as Buguma and Bakana, east of the Niger, and Akure in the west, the Supreme Court rarely exercised its jurisdiction for lack of legal business within the very narrowly defined areas of the towns supposedly subject to the court's jurisdiction.[113] The links between the provincial and the 'native' courts on the one hand, and the Supreme Court on the other, were tenuous, and were not intended to derogate from the judicial powers of the political officers in the protectorate, or in any way undermine their prestige. In the circumstances of colonial Nigeria in which the political officer wielded near-absolute powers in his area of jurisdiction, it is rather obvious that the empanelling of assessors at the provincial courts after 1922 was, in every respect, an innocuous exercise.

In practice, however, the amendments to the judicial system of 1914 were of considerable importance in the actual operation of the judicial system, especially after 1918. The amendments, as will be shown in the next chapter, made the operation of the judicial system less burdensome than it would otherwise have been. The amendments, moreover, constituted the thin edge of the wedge by which lawyers were opening their way to the Supreme Court, making nonsense of the policy of restricting their professional activities.

One proposed modification in the judicial structure, though not implemented, deserves close attention. In their search for a judicial system in the protectorate that would be immune to sharp criticisms and at the same time capable of meeting the requirements of native administration, administrative officers, after some three years of lengthy discussions, came up with a proposal for an additional court in the protectorate, to be called the Protectorate Court. A meeting was held at Government House, Lagos, on 3 February 1931 between the Chief Justice on the one hand and the Lieutenant-Governors for the Northern and Southern Provinces on the other. It was there that what appeared to be the final form of the protectorate court was drawn up.

The court was designed as a sort of appeal court for the whole protectorate.[114] The jurisdiction of the Supreme Court was to be limited to the colony. The limited areas in which the court exercised its jurisdiction in the protectorate, it was hoped, would gradually diminish as the proposed Protectorate Court, supplemented by the 'native' courts in its operation, came to establish its influence. The provincial courts would continue to function; but it was hoped that they too would eventually cease to exist as time went on. If the Protectorate Court was established, there would be no more transfer of cases from the provincial courts to the Supreme Court. Nor would there be any need for the latter court to extend its jurisdiction. There were to be two divisions of the protectorate court, one for the Northern Provinces and the other for the Southern.

The Protectorate Court was clearly to be under executive authority. Each of the two Lieutenant-Governors would supervise the operation of the court, determine which cases were to be tried before it, the places of trial of such cases and even the itineraries of its judges. The judges themselves were to be appointed from the rank of administrative officers with legal qualifications. Such judges should preferably have 'extensive experience of and knowledge of administrative conditions in Nigeria and the working of the Provincial courts'. They would also be subject to the Lieutenant-Governor's control 'in all matters touching their personal position and condition of service'. W. Buchanan-Smith, the Lieutenant-Governor for the Southern Provinces, considered it desirable, quite significantly, that the Lieutenant-Governors should be in constant touch with the Protectorate Court to 'ensure that there is adequate appreciation of native customs and local conditions which have a bearing on the circumstances of cases and the character of the sentences to be imposed'.[115]

Although lawyers would be allowed to appear before the proposed Protectorate Court, this concession did not amount to much. For one thing, the original jurisdiction of the court and even more so its appellate jurisdiction, were to be strictly limited. The court would handle only cases involving non-natives. For another, the power vested in the executive over the court would be a serious obstacle to the appearance of lawyers before the court. In fact, the two Lieutenant-Governors made it clear that they intended to use their power over the court to limit the appearance of lawyers before it.[116] It is also important to note that land cases, believed to be the real prizes lawyers hankered after in the protectorate, were to be entirely outside the jurisdiction of the Protectorate Court.

It is difficult to escape the conclusion that the Protectorate Court was the provincial court writ large. Indeed the Protectorate Court would appear to be more independent of the Supreme Court than the provincial court and no less under executive control. In other respects the court was to resemble the provincial court as much as possible. As the Lieutenant-Governor for the Northern Provinces suggested, the judge's red robe and the lawyer's wig and gown 'which to the Protectorate native are meaningless and confusing' should be avoided in the court as they were in the provincial court. The Protectorate Court would also, as the provincial court was supposedly doing, administer justice 'based upon common sense and knowledge of the country and its people, rather than upon niceties of technical points'.

The proposal for a Protectorate Court as outlined above is a major evidence that in spite of modifications in the 1914 judicial structure, the official thinking regarding judicial policy in Nigeria, until 1933, remained basically unchanged. At the bottom was the notion, almost amounting to an obsession, that the Supreme Court, with its technicalities and English rules and procedure, was incompatible with the administrative requirements for establishing local units of government in the vast Protectorate of Nigeria under the guidance of British political officers.

Notes

1 NAI, CSO 26/3, 21496, I, S. M. Grier, Director of Education, Southern Provinces, 'Memorandum on the Supreme Court'.
2 NAI, CSO 14/5, A2808/1913, 'Nigerian Courts'.
3 Compare T. O. Elias, *The Nigerian Legal System*, pp. 125–39; B. O. Nwabueze, *The Machinery of Justice in Nigeria*, pp. 59–64.
4 Compare B. O. Nwabueze, *The Machinery of Justice*, p. 24; T. O. Elias, *Makers of Nigerian Law*, London, 1957, pp. 18–25.
5 'Memorandum as to Judicial Reorganization of Nigeria on Amalgamation', *Nigerian Pioneer*, 10 July 1914.
6 Elias, *The Nigerian Legal System*, p. 126, n. 1.
7 F. D. Lugard, *Memorandum No. 3: Judicial and Legal*, Lagos, 1918, p. 5.
8 *Nigerian Pioneer*, 10 July 1914.
9 B. O. Nwabueze, *The Machinery of Justice;* pp. 59–64; Elias, *The Nigerian Legal System*, pp. 116–19.
10 NAI, CSO 14/5, A2808/1913, 'Nigerian Courts'.
11 Margery Perham, *Lugard: The Years of Authority, 1898–1945*, London, 1960, p. 162.
12 *Ibid.*, pp. 160–2.
13 The provinces were Abeokuta, Ibadan, Ijebu-Ode, Benin, Warri, Onitsha, Owerri, Ogoja and Calabar, *Nigeria Government Gazette*, 24 December 1914, p. 20667.
14 Provincial Courts Ordinance, No. 7, 1914, sec. 9.
15 Provincial Courts Ordinance, sec. 32(2).
16 Native Courts Ordinance, No. 3, 1914, sec. 21.

17 'Supreme Court Bill, March 12, 1914: Speech by the Governor-General', *Various Papers, Nigeria* (binder's title), University of Ibadan Library.
18 *Ibid.*
19 F. D. Lugard, *The Dual Mandate in British Tropical Africa*, London, 1922.
20 Alan Burns, *History of Nigeria*, 6th ed., pp. 233–4; G. I. Jones, *Life and Duties of an Administrative Officer in Nigeria*, London, West African Pamphlet, No. 211.
21 F. D. Lugard, *Native Courts in the Southern Provinces: Memorandum to Political Officers*, Lagos, 1914.
22 NAI, CSO 1/21, XII, Lugard to Harcourt, 21 May 1913, Minute of 24 September 1912 in enclosure.
23 Lugard, *Native Courts in the Southern Provinces*, p. 2.
24 *Times of Nigeria*, 5 May 1914.
25 Compare Alan Burns, *History of Nigeria*, p. 281; T. N. Tamuno, 'The Development of British Administrative Control of Southern Nigeria, 1900–1912', PhD thesis, University of London, 1962, p. 308; Margery Perham, *Lugard: The Years of Authority, 1898–1945*, p. 426; *Report of the Native Courts (Western Provinces) Commission of Inquiry*, Lagos, 1952, p. 8.
26 *Lagos Weekly Record*, 14 November 1896.
27 E. A. Speed, *Report of Commission of Enquiry into Land Tenure in Ibadan*, Lagos, 1916, p. 5.
28 *Ibid.*, p. 4.
29 HCA, Lagos, 'Circuit Judge's Notebook, 1911–1918', entry for 3 April 1917.
30 NAI, CSO 21/169, 485, 'Annual Report, Ogoja Province, 1920–1921'.
31 NAI, CSO 26/2, 11930, 'Owerri Province Annual Report, 1923'; CSO 26/2, 11857, 'Warri Province, Annual Report 1927'; CSO 26/2, 11874, VIII, 'Ondo Province, Annual Reports, 1929–1930'.
32 A. H. St. John Wood, 'Nigeria: Fifty Years of Political Development Among the Ibos', in Raymond Apthorpe, ed., *From Tribal Rule to Modern Government*, Lusaka, 1959, p. 129.
33 Oxford, Rhodes House, Lugard Papers, 47, Speed to Lugard, 14 April 1919.
34 A. H. St. John Wood, 'Nigeria: Fifty Years of Political Development . . .', pp. 129–30.
35 *Ibid.*
36 Interviews with Chiefs A. Desalu, Ayodele Williams, A. Shoetan, T. A. Doherty and Messrs C. H. Obafemi, F. O. Lucas, E. A. Franklin and P. W. Holm between September 1966 and March 1967 in Lagos.
37 E. A. Franklin, Interview, 9 February 1967, Lagos.
38 NAI, CSO 26/2, 11930, III, 'Annual Report for 1925, Owerri Province'.
39 CO 520/92, Egerton to Crewe, 11 April 1910, enclosure entitled 'Yoruba Laws and Customs'.

40 *Petition Against the Provincial and Native Courts Ordinances by the Nigerian Reform Association*, Lagos, 1917; CO 583/171, Memorandum of C. W. Clinton to Halden Club, June 1932.

41 Between 1914 and 1933 articles by Geary on the Nigerian judicial system appeared in such English papers as *The Times*, the *Daily News and Leader*, the *Morning Post*, the *Pall Mall Magazine*, *West Africa* and *West African Review*.

42 *Anti-Slavery Reporter and Aborigines' Friend*, London, January 1915.

43 *Nigerian Chronicle*, 20 February 1914; *Times of Nigeria*, 27 March 1914; 5 July and 12 July 1920; *Nigerian Advocate*, 14 May 1924.

44 *Report by the Hon. W. G. A. Ormsby-Gore on his Visit to West Africa during the Year 1926*, Cmd 2744.

45 Article VIII of the Party's Constitution, Macaulay Papers, IV, No. 15, University of Ibadan Library.

46 *Legislative Council Debates, 1923–33*, Lagos, 1923–33.

47 F. I. A. Omu, 'The Nigerian Newspaper Press, 1859–1937: A Study in Origins, Growth and Influence', Unpublished PhD thesis, University of Ibadan, 1965, pp. 259–67.

48 *Nigerian Pioneer*, 24 February 1914; *West Africa*, 4 March 1933.

49 Organised by J. E. Casely Hayford, a Gold Coast lawyer, in 1920, the National Congress comprised educated Africans from the four British colonies on the West Coast. It was little more than a forum for ventilating common grievances, although even as such, it served a useful purpose in West Africa's political development. It died with its founder in the early 1930s.

50 *Various Papers: Nigeria*, University of Ibadan Library.

51 Compiled from *Official Report (Fifth Series): Parliamentary Debates (Commons)*, 1914–32.

52 *Report by Sir F. D. Lugard on the Amalgamation of Northern and Southern Nigeria and Administration, 1912–1919*, London, 1919, p. 25.

53 Margery Perham, *Lugard: The Years of Authority, 1898–1945*, p. 589.

54 F. I. A. Omu, 'The Nigerian Newspaper Press', pp. 255–6.

55 *Times of Nigeria*, 12 May 1914, 30 June 1914; J. A. Atanda, 'The New Oyo Empire: A Study of British Indirect Rule in Oyo Province, 1894–1934', PhD thesis, University of Ibadan, 1967, pp. 187–9.

56 *Lagos Weekly Record*, 2 February 1907.

57 *Times of Nigeria*, 23 June 1914.

58 *Times of Nigeria*, 9 March 1914.

59 *Nigerian Chronicle*, 10 April 1914; *Times of Nigeria*, 27 March 1914.

60 *Nigerian Chronicle*, 27 March 1914.

61 *Petition Against Provincial and Native Courts Ordinances by the Nigerian Reform Association*, p. 20.

62 *Ibid.*, Memorandum by Graham Paul, p. 26.

63 *Nigerian Chronicle*, 20 February 1914.

64 *Nigerian Chronicle*, 27 March 1914, editorial.

65 W. N. M. Geary, 'Memorandum as to Judicial Reorganization of Nigeria on the Amalgamation', *Nigerian Pioneer*, 10 July 1914.

66 W. H. Stoker, 'The Judicial System in Nigeria', *Times of Nigeria*, 20 April 1915.
67 A. E. M. Gibson, 'Constitutional Method in Nigeria', *Times of Nigeria*, 7 April 1914.
68 *Ibid.*
69 CO 583/10, Lugard to Harcourt, 12 February 1914, enclosed petition of the members of the Nigeria Bar, Calabar.
70 O. Alakija, 'Notes on the Provincial Courts Ordinance', *African Messenger*, 14 September 1922.
71 C. L. Temple, *Native Races and their Rulers*, Cape Town, 1918, p. 194.
72 CO 583/11, Lugard to Harcourt, 18 March 1914, enclosure entitled 'Resolution unanimously adopted at a mass meeting at Onitsha'.
73 *African Times and Orient Review*, London, 9 June 1914.
74 Geary, 'Memorandum as to Judicial Reorganization', *Nigerian Pioneer*, 10 July 1914.
75 A. E. M. Gibson, 'The Provisional Courts Ordinance', *Times of Nigeria*, 17 February 1914.
76 E. A. Speed, 'Memorandum on the Supreme Court', *Nigeria Gazette*, 1914, pp. 555–6.
77 'Justice in Nigeria: The Provincial Courts', Letter to the editor, *The Times*, London, 9 September 1922.
78 *Ibid.*
79 *Nigerian Pioneer*, 24 April 1922.
80 CO 583/118, Clifford to Duke of Devonshire, 27 March 1923.
81 *Ibid.*
82 Lugard, *The Dual Mandate*, p. 544.
83 C. L. Temple, *Native Races and Their Rulers*, pp. 185–91.
84 E. A. Speed, 'Memorandum on the Supreme Court'.
85 Lugard, 'The British in Nigeria: Administration of Justice', Letter to the editor, *The Times*, London, 6 January 1925.
86 NAI, CSO 26/3, 26359, I, 'The Supreme Court and its Relation to Native Policy'. See also NAI, CSO 26/3, 21496, I, II.
87 NAI, CSO 26/3, 21496, I, Memorandum on the Supreme Court by E. J. Arnett.
88 *Ibid.*, Memorandum by Gordon J. Lethem.
89 *Ibid.*, Memorandum by E. J. Arnett.
90 *Ibid.*, Minute by Gordon J. Lethem dated 10 July 1928 to the chief secretary to the government.
91 NAI, CSO 26/3, 21496, II, Memorandum on the Supreme Court by W. Buchanan-Smith.
92 NAI, CSO 26/3, 21496, I, Memorandum by H. L. Ward-Price.
93 *Ibid.*, Memorandum by E. J. Arnett.
94 *Ibid.*, Memorandum by E. M. Falk.
95 *Ibid.*, Memorandum by H. L. Ward-Price.
96 *Ibid.*, Memorandum by E. J. Arnett.
97 *Ibid.*, Memorandum by H. L. Ward-Price.
98 *Ibid.*, Memorandum by H. M. M. Moore.
99 *Ibid.*, Memorandum by F. B. Adams.

100 *Ibid.*, Memorandum by E. J. Arnett.
101 Geary, 'Memorandum as to Judicial Reorganization of Nigeria'.
102 J. A. Atanda, 'The New Oyo Empire . . .', p. 131.
103 Ch. 8, *infra*.
104 NAI, CSO 26/1, 09876, Combe to Thomson, 15 January 1925.
105 'Justice in Nigeria: The Provincial Courts', Letter to the editor, *The Times*, 9 September 1932.
106 NAI, CSO 26/3, 21496, I, Memorandum by S. M. Grier.
107 CO 656/4, Provincial Courts (Amendment) Ordinance, No. 21, 1918.
108 CO 656/4, Supreme Court (Amendment) Ordinance, No. 28, 1918, sec. 34(i).
109 Sec. 34(ii).
110 CO 657/9, 'Report on the Supreme Court of Nigeria, 1923–1924'.
111 CO 656/5, Provincial Courts (Amendment) Ordinance, No. 13, 1922.
112 CO 656/4, Native Courts (Amendment) Ordinance, No. 16, 1920.
113 CO 657/20, 'Annual Report on the Southern Provinces for 1927'.
114 NAI, CSO 26/3, 76359, I, 'Proposals for the establishment of a Protectorate Court', G. H. Findley to chief secretary, Lagos, 23 February 1931.
115 NAI, CSO 26/3, 26359, I, Secretary, Southern Provinces, to chief secretary, Lagos, 23 March 1931, enclosure.
116 *Ibid.*, Secretary, Southern Provinces, to chief secretary, Lagos, 23 March 1931, enclosure; Gordon J. Lethem to chief secretary, Lagos, 23 May 1931, enclosure.

6 The provincial and the 'native' courts, 1914-33

There is a practice prevailing . . . under which litigants approach the [Native] courts through men who they think may be influential in getting the ear of the court.

Captain W. A. Ross[1]

How could the Resident expect an illiterate person, *viva voce*, to argue points to convince the Resident except through a literate person by writing?

Edema Arubi[2]

I

In this chapter it is proposed to examine the provincial and the 'native' courts as judicial institutions in Southern Nigeria. The aim is two-fold: to see how the courts functioned in practice so as to determine the degree of their success in fulfilling the objectives set them in 1914, and to evaluate their impact on the territory's development.

There was little doubt among most administrative officers that the provincial courts were adequate judicial institutions. A conference of Residents held on 29 November 1929 not only reaffirmed their faith in the suitability of the provincial court system, but also sought to extend its jurisdiction.[3] Administrative records are replete with reports by Provincial Residents indicating their satisfaction with the provincial courts and their supposed acceptance by the people. 'The Provincial Court', wrote the senior Resident for Oyo Province, Captain W. A. Ross, in 1923, 'appears to answer the purpose for which it was established and the people are perfectly content to appear in it.'[4]

More significantly, some important judicial officers held more or less the same views on the courts as the administrators. About a year after the inauguration of the provincial court system, Sir Edwin Speed, then Chief Justice of Nigeria, said he was convinced that the judicial system was working well 'beyond our most sanguine anticipation'.[5] One immediate result of the working of the provincial courts, he noted, was to curtail 'or rather extinguish' the fomenting of land disputes in the up-country districts. The provincial and the 'native' courts were said to be taking an enormous share of the judicial work that used to burden the Supreme Court. The judges of the latter court, in consequence, were able to keep abreast of the criminal cases coming before them, while they had sufficient time to deal with a large number of cases transferred from the provincial courts. The provincial court, he concluded, was 'a vast improvement' upon the judicial system in operation before 1914.

In 1925, the successor to Speed, Sir Ralph Combe, as was mentioned earlier, justified the introduction of the provincial courts into Southern Nigeria. He said he was impressed by the way in which judges of the provincial courts, many of them without legal qualifications, tried their cases. There had been mistakes, he conceded, but, in general, cases were carefully tried by officers who were 'obviously . . . anxious to do justice'.[6]

Yet another judge of the Supreme Court, Frederick Alan van der Meulen, said he was 'deeply impressed' by the functioning of the provincial courts and by 'the ability and great fairness with which the political officers have discharged their judicial duties'.[7]

It is not very clear what criteria Sir Edwin Speed and the other judges of the Supreme Court used in justifying the provincial court system in Southern Nigeria. For the provincial and the 'native' courts can be judged from many different points of view. Since the expedition of court procedure in criminal cases was one of the objectives the administration had in view in establishing these courts, they can be examined from the point of view of how far they contributed to the 'speeding up' of justice. The administration also intended that the courts should bring justice 'cheaply' to the people, saving them from being 'bled to death' in exorbitant legal fees by lawyers. Another criterion for judging the adequacy of the courts, again considering the objectives of the administration in setting them up, is how far they succeeded in keeping out lawyers from land disputes in the interior districts of Southern Nigeria. There is, finally, the question of justice itself and the extent to which the courts even-handedly dispensed it.

The only incontestable claim that can be made for the provincial courts is Sir Edwin Speed's claim that they took a lot of judicial burden off the Supreme Court and thus helped to 'speed up' the administration of justice at the highest level. A close look at the working of the provincial courts in some other respects does not wholly justify the high opinions held about them.

It was perhaps only to be expected that political officers purporting to administer English law without legal qualifications would not maintain a particularly high standard of judicial performance. The justice they administered in the courts has been described as 'executive justice [which] enclosed the lives of Africans with a strong iron ring'.[8] The generality of Nigerians might not have suffered to the extent that this description suggests, but it is certainly true that the standard of justice at the provincial courts was not remarkably high. Lacking formal legal education, most of them naturally possessed a judicial outlook out of keeping with the quest for justice under English law. It was the Resident for Warri Province who wrote in 1926:

> In the Provincial Court a case is tried as soon as possible after the event, on or near the scene of action, and *every possible piece of evidence is brought forward.* The case can be adjourned day after day *until the judge is satisfied that all available proof of the real conditions of affairs is produced, while his local knowledge will enable him to ask for the best evidence* and to appreciate the value of that brought before him.[9]

The Resident was extolling what he considered a great virtue of the provincial court system, but anyone familiar with the English law of evidence will appreciate at once the dangers inherent in this statement (particularly those portions italicised by the present writer) as a working principle of criminal judicial administration. The statement, taken as a whole, in fact, puts the burden of proving the guilt of an accused person squarely on the judge rather than the prosecutor.

The vast majority of cases handled by the provincial courts were criminal cases; most civil cases were settled either at the 'native' courts or at the Supreme Court in areas where the latter court exercised jurisdiction in the protectorate. It is significant that in respect of civil cases, a Provincial Resident, after about four years' experience of the provincial court system, confessed to the difficulty of trying civil actions without assistance from counsel.[10] The civil law in the form of the English common law which the courts were supposed to administer had its 'mysteries'. In his view, 'some accurate knowledge of the law and its practice is essential, not merely advisable'.[11]

Two related features of the administration of criminal law at the provincial courts are observable: emphasis on deterrence as the goal of criminal justice, and indifference to (or ignorance of) technical rules of the law or of procedure. The emphasis on deterrence is evident in the heavy sentences usually imposed by the courts which were sometimes reduced or quashed by the Supreme Court.[12] It is also sometimes evident in judicial pronouncements.

In a court that emphasised deterrence as the objective of criminal sanctions, or perhaps because the Resident presiding over it was not conversant with the law he was supposed to administer, cognisance was rarely taken of such defences in criminal law as provocation, mistake, absence of *mens rea*. In *R. v. Umo Eden Oduk* (1918), tried at the Ikot-Ekpene Provincial Court, the defence of provocation ought to have been raised in favour of the accused at least to reduce a charge of murder to one of manslaughter.[13] The accused had been living in concubinage with a woman, one Adiaha Ekpo, whom he allegedly murdered. The woman's husband had died, and her eldest son 'would not look after her'. Other relatives had also refused help. Eventually she ran to the accused, asking him to marry her. Together the accused and the deceased woman moved to her father's house, where the accused fulfilled the role of husband for all practical purposes. He took care of her mother when she fell ill, and on her death, he buried her, supplying 'three fathom clothes, seven manillas and goats' in performing the usual burial rituals. He also paid off Adiaha Ekpo's debt which was said to have run up to five hundred manillas. After some time they moved to Ikot Ebek, the town of the accused. There he planted 'three pieces of farm' for her. Events took a dramatic turn when the woman changed her mind and sought to run to another man. At the pleading of the accused, the deceased woman allegedly told him: 'Don't you see I have run from Akpan Ukpong [a former concubine] as soon as I had 'eaten' all his property. Akpan Ukpong is running about, and you will do the same. When I've eaten all your things I will run.' Would a reasonable man of Ikot Ebek in the circumstances of the accused have reacted in the same way as he did in losing his temper and killing the deceased? Perhaps one requires more evidence than was contained in the records of the proceedings to see whether the defence of provocation would be sustained; but the question was not even raised. The only point in favour of the accused, noted the divisional officer trying the case, was that the murder was not premeditated. The empanelled assessors were unanimous in their verdict of guilty, and the divisional officer agreed with them.

The murder case of *R. v. Nda Udo Uyo* (1915), tried at the provincial court, Calabar, raised the question of legal insanity which, again, the court failed to consider. The murder allegedly committed by the accused was described by the assistant district officer who tried it as 'a particularly brutal and cold-blooded one'.[14] The 'extreme callousness' of the case prompted him to order a medical examination. 'Beyond his being somewhat dull and stupid', the medical officer reported, he found him mentally fit. Hence the medical report, according to the trial officer, 'does not support the defence of insanity'. Yet in criminal law, insanity is a term of art, and is not the same thing as medical insanity. In view of the officer's own observation that the demeanour of the accused during his trial 'was such as to lead the Court to suppose that he did not appreciate the grave position in which he stood', a defence of insanity could perhaps have been made successfully under the McNaugton rules.[15] This case, like the preceding one, did not reach the Supreme Court. In both cases, the accused persons were convicted and hanged.

There might be difficulties in the provincial courts, because of unqualified officers presiding over them, in handling the technical terms of the law. In *R. v. Obona* (1920) tried at Aba, a boy apparently told lies to induce a woman *sell* some goods to him, and was convicted of 'intent to defraud'. He was whipped, and thus, in the view of the Chief Justice, 'made a felon for a purely imaginary offence'.[16] From the Ilorin provincial court in the north came *R. v. Ansah* (1921) in which the accused was charged with being accessory before the fact to a burglary. He was convicted and sentenced to eighteen months' imprisonment on what was described as 'amazingly negligible evidence'. The conviction was later quashed by the Chief Justice, though only after the accused had served one month in jail.[17]

It would not appear the courts were particularly strong on matters of procedure. In *R. v. Lawrence B. Offiong* (1924) the accused was charged with forgery for which he was convicted. The Chief Justice's comment on the case is illuminating: 'The accused pleaded not guilty and at the close of the case for the prosecution, there was no evidence against him and he should not have been called upon to make his defence.'[18] The conviction was quashed, six months after the accused had begun to serve his terms in jail.

In *R. v. Isong Uyo and six others* (1925) the Chief Justice repri-
manded the trial judge, an officer of many years' experience in
Southern Nigeria, for conducting a trial 'in a manner which
offends not only against every rule of procedure on the trial of a
criminal case, but also against the most elementary of the principles
of fair play on which these rules of procedure are based'.[19] The
accused persons were charged with 'conspiracy to bring false
accusation of murder against three accused persons' in another
case. There was nothing to indicate that the accused persons had a
common felonious intent, nor did the prosecutor (the judge himself) submit any case for them to answer. The record of proceedings was nothing but a record of cross-examination of the accused
persons by the court, with one of the accused persons set against
the rest. This was a case substantiating the allegation made by a
Nigerian criminal lawyer in 1922, that at the provincial courts the
onus was usually on the accused person in a criminal charge 'to
establish his innocence beyond all reasonable doubt against an
almost irrefutable presumption of guilt . . . formed immediately
on arrest'.[20]

It may be objected on methodological grounds that merely to
cite instances of mistrials or errors of law committed by the
provincial courts does not prove conclusively that the courts were
inadequate institutions of justice in the contemporary circumstances of the Protectorate of Southern Nigeria. Instances of
mistrial or error of fact or of law could similarly be cited even for
the Supreme Court, much venerated among the educated Nigerians
as an independent and impartial tribunal. There is, however,
additional telling evidence against the provincial courts as courts
of justice, supplied, unwittingly, by Donald Kingdon, Chief
Justice of Nigeria, 1928–45. He drew up a catalogue of criminal
cases tried at the provincial courts between 1929 and 1933 which
were transmitted to the Supreme Court for review.[21] It is significant
that less than 25 per cent of the cases brought up for review during
this period received the Chief Justice's commendation. In some of
the cases the procedure at the trial was held to be unsatisfactory,
even though the sentences imposed by the provincial courts were
confirmed. In other cases, new trials were ordered. In yet others
the convictions were simply annulled. By 1929 the provincial
courts surely should have attained a higher degree of performance
than the Chief Justice's notebook indicated. The Chief Justice
probably knew he should not expect too much from the political

officers presiding over the courts. Contrary to the view once expressed by a senior administrative officer,[22] criminal work in the courts, in the best common law tradition, requires much more than mere common sense. It requires a sound knowledge of the elements of criminal law and, no less important, a mastery of the rather technical rules of evidence and procedure.

There were grounds to justify the fears of those who held that administrative officers used their judicial powers under the provincial court system for political ends. Quite a sizable proportion of the alleged criminal offences tried before the provincial courts involved infringements of local ordinances and bye-laws intended to enhance local administration or, ultimately, to safeguard the economic interests of the colonial power.[23] The power of the court was sometimes invoked to secure labour for the service of the colonial administration. In *R. v. Bira of Bewa* (1925), the accused, a head chief in Opobo District, was convicted of 'conduct likely to cause a breach of the peace by failing to repair the Government Rest House at Bewa after due notice'.[24] There was always a political undertone in the prosecution of village headmen at the provincial courts for alleged evasion of taxes. Failure to pay taxes or delay in paying them 'may amount to a form of passive resistance'; prosecutions in the courts 'were necessary to convince the people' of the strong position and determination of the colonial government.[25]

Yet another aspect of the political use of the provincial court was to invoke its power to supress elements in the indigenous population, usually 'recalcitrant' chiefs and educated Africans whose activities were considered inimical to the interests of the administration. When Oyebajo was destooled as the *Akarigbo* of Ijebu-Igbo in 1920 his presence in his former domain was found to be politically inconvenient for the administration. It was not difficult for the provincial court at Shagamu to convict him of 'making preparations to carry on warlike undertakings against a Native Chief', that is, his successor supported by the administration.[26] The conviction would have been difficult to sustain under a true judicial inquiry. The alleged offence, if established, constituted an attempt in law, and the onus was on the prosecution to demonstrate that his activities were unequivocally referrable to the one single intention of levelling war against his successor. But such fine points of the law were not considered in the provincial courts. Oyebajo and two other chiefs were deported to Calabar on 27 April 1921.

Professional letter-writers, whom we shall discuss presently, were particular targets for political repression by provincial courts. Yehorogba was a letter-writer in Bonny who, on the instructions of a number of village elders or perhaps at his own instigation, wrote to the district officer that all royalties payable in respect of timber felled in their area were to be paid to the head chief of the village. The district officer caused the letter-writer to be arrested, convicted of a trumped-up charge, and sentenced to eighteen months' imprisonment – a conviction which was later set aside by the Supreme Court.[27]

Herbert Aladeshulu, a letter-writer at Owo in Ondo Province, was described as 'an anti-Government journalist and letter-writer' who suffered 'a good deal of persecution' at the hands of the political officers, including the punishment of banishment in 1921. Another instance of such persecution which attracted the attention of the central administration in Lagos, in 1932, was the severe punishment meted out to him for what was described as a mild infringement of the law governing the operation of professional letter-writing.[28]

In *R. v. A. O. Coker* (1932) the accused was convicted by the provincial court at Ife for various alleged offences against the same law governing letter-writing. He was sentenced to two years' imprisonment with hard labour. In the words of the Lieutenant-Governor, reviewing the case, 'the long series of charges read as if the District Officer had been determined to justify a severe sentence, and, to my mind, the character of the sentence inflicted was quite unjustified by the evidence'.[29]

There were various ways by which the colonial administration attempted to rectify the inadequacies of the provincial court system. Administrative officers were encouraged to take examinations in law with emphasis on criminal law and procedure. By 1923 a local examination for administrative officers in law, general orders and colonial regulations had been instituted.[30] The subjects in the law aspect of the examination comprised criminal law and procedure, principles of English law, and law of evidence[31] – the essence, so to speak, of the intellectual equipment of a judge trying mostly criminal cases in the provincial courts.

Over the years the flow of instructions from the Supreme Court and the secretariat of the government in Lagos to political officers on various aspects of the working of the provincial court system was enormous. The instructions dealt mainly with the trial of criminal cases, covering such matters as preliminary investigations, hearsay evidence, sentencing, reports on cases tried, and so on.[32] The circular letter issued from the secretariat of the Southern Provinces to all Residents in April 1927 was typical, both in spirit and intention, of many such circulars designed as additional safeguards in the operation of the provincial court system:

> The report [on every criminal case being forwarded to the supreme court for purposes of review] should summarize the evidence and should briefly describe the demeanour and credibility of the various witnesses. It should indicate the state of culture of the accused (more particularly when that state is low). If the accused belong to a District which is not under close administration, the fact should be stated. If the murder was due either wholly or partly to belief in witchcraft, jujus or the like, the report should show to what extent in the opinion of the officer who tried the case, such superstitions ought to be regarded as extenuating circumstances. Finally the officer should invariably state whether or not he makes any recommendation for mercy.[33]

As part of the effort at rectifying the inadequacies of the provincial court system, we saw in the last chapter how amendments were made from time to time in the instrument establishing the courts. In December 1915 a circular letter was issued by the Lieutenant-Governor of Southern Nigeria correcting 'some misapprehension' then current among political officers regarding the appearance of legal practitioners before the provincial courts. Political officers were then instructed that section 32(i) of the Provincial Courts Ordinance dealing with the appearance of legal practitioners was not intended to be interpreted too narrowly. A litigant before a provincial court was free to consult any person outside the court 'whether a legal practitioner or not'.[34] This view was reiterated by Ralph M. Combe, Chief Justice, in *R. v. Nwa Essien and seven others* (1925), a criminal case from Calabar Provincial court reviewed by the Supreme Court.[35] By 1918 the Chief Justice could transfer any case at any stage to the Supreme Court from the provincial court at the instance of either party to the case, a Resident or the Lieutenant-Governor. The jurisdiction of the Supreme Court was also progressively extended. After 1922 a litigant at a provincial court could apply for the transfer of his case to the Supreme Court.

The impact of these various measures designed to enhance the working of the provincial court system must have been minimal. There was no way of ensuring that political officers in their domains paid attention to the specific instructions on the administration of justice in the provincial courts. Again, the facility supposedly provided for the transfer of cases from the provincial courts to the Supreme Court was largely theoretical. Except through the influence of a lawyer, few accused persons charged before the provincial court had the courage to ask for the transfer of their cases to the Supreme Court, if they ever knew they could do so. There were, no doubt, instances of injustice corrected in the process of review or appeal to the Supreme Court. Yet, as late as 1929, as we saw, the provincial courts still showed a record of a high incidence of maladministration of justice.

II

The 'native' courts as institutions for administering justice were, in general, worse than the provincial courts. Exceptions could be found here and there,[36] but in most cases the courts left much to be desired. That they seemed incapable of efficiently administering justice was a fact that many administrative officers accepted with philosophic resignation. 'Impartiality and purity of justice', wrote J. Watt, the Senior Resident for Owerri Province in 1922, 'are high ideals which can be obtained among these people only after the passing of many generations.'[37] The same note was struck in the official report on the courts in 1924: 'It is not possible to create a class of people possessing judicial minds in a few years.'[38]

Corruption was rife in the courts:

> In spite of the fact that strenuous efforts have been made to raise the standard of justice, the courts are . . . far too prone to sell justice to the highest bidder or to favourites. Too many cases are adjourned for decisions after the evidence has been recorded and too many persons are seen privately in the houses of court members and clerks before, during and after the hearing, but before judgment is delivered.[39]

Such was the picture of the native courts in Ijebu Province in 1933. It was typically true of the vast majority of the courts in Southern Nigeria throughout the colonial era. They were once characterised as 'hot beds of intrigue, corruption and injustice'[40] – a view of the courts which a number of other writers have confirmed in their studies of various parts of Southern Nigeria under colonial rule.[41]

The root cause of corruption lay in the very structure of the courts. The 'native' court clerk, the only official who sat permanently in the court, was the vital link between the court and the administrative officer. The latter, supposedly exercising a supervisory power over the court, was not always around because of his other multifarious administrative duties. Inevitably the clerk assumed an importance and wielded a power out of all proportion to his low educational standard or his position in the theory of the 'native' court system. He was almost invariably the master of the court, and was, indeed, addressed as such in parts of Eastern and Southeastern Nigeria.[42]

> He issues every summons without any reference to any Chief, gives orders for arrests, controls the court messengers, takes charge of prisoners and conveys to the . . . Chiefs instructions sent from the Divisional Officer.[43]

On account of the illiteracy of the chiefs sitting as judges in the courts, the clerk was in many places the arbiter of law and procedure.[44] Depending on the strength of character of the chiefs in particular areas, the court clerk could force the chiefs to reconsider a decision which went against his interests by threatening punishment by the political officer 'for so flagrantly going contrary to government law in their decisions'.[45] In all, the court clerk held 'a position of extreme importance in the eyes of the populace'.[46]

It was common knowledge even among colonial administrative officers that the clerk abused his 'unchallenged position in the Native court' to feather his own nest and amass private fortunes. Litigants sought his favour with monetary and material gifts since the outcome of a case could depend on whatever he recorded in the court books and on his 'interpretation' of the 'law' the court was supposed to administer. In South-eastern Nigeria the government-appointed 'warrant' chiefs, too, similarly sought his favour to select them to sit on the court Bench.[47] He sometimes colluded with the chiefs on the court Bench to settle cases privately. Throughout Southern Nigeria it was a common practice for 'native' court clerks to lend money to litigants before the court at usurious rates of interest. Virtual lords of their communities, they had command of free labour for use on their private estates through their manipulation of the judicial machinery.

The period 1914–30 has been referred to with justification as the 'golden age' of 'native' court clerks.[48] In spite of their meagre salaries,[49] they were among the few in the society who could afford to put up fine, well-ventilated buildings, send children overseas for higher education and acquire such symbols of modern living as bicycles and even motor-cars. In 1928, six of the 'native' court clerks in Onitsha Province were said to have had their own motor-cars.[50] It would be tedious to relate instances of corruption by the court clerks; it is sufficient to note that their perfidious role in the 'native' court system was in the 1920s considered 'the greatest administrative problem' facing the colonial regime in Southern Nigeria.[51] Attempts at reforms were made in 1927–8 to ensure that the clerks did not 'run' the courts.[52] But the fact was that until the 'native' court chiefs were literate and the masses of litigants were conscious of their rights before the courts, no amount of official regulations could effectively check the powers of the court clerks.

Corruption in the 'native' court system was not limited to the court clerks. Every other officer associated with a 'native' court and hence in a position to exert some influence or authority, exploited the ignorance of the non-literate masses. The court messengers who served summonses on litigants and helped to maintain law and order in the court premises, and the court interpreter (where there was one) all paraded themselves as agents of the government, exacting unauthorised fees and taking bribes.[53] Believed to be acting on the orders of the government, the officers of the courts sometimes conducted themselves above the law. It was not unusual for the officers of a 'native' court to purchase articles in the open market at prices fixed by themselves.[54]

No less corrupt than the officers were the chiefs who sat in the courts as judges and assessors. In many areas of Southern Nigeria, especially where chiefly institutions were created by the British, most of the chiefs on the 'native' court Bench 'regard[ed] their position as a means of enriching themselves at the expense of their people'.[55] It is, again, the structure of the 'native' court system that provided an avenue for the corruption of the chiefs. As a rule they received no regular salaries, and usually they had to sit in rotation. They were paid for each sitting of the court in which they took part. They were not slow to realise that their remuneration varied directly with the number of sittings they had. It was evidently in their interest to protract litigation, pay unnecessary visits to disputed real property so as to exact 'visiting' fees from both parties,[56] take bribes from both parties to a dispute, and even directly foment litigation.[57] A divisional officer in Warri Province reported in 1923 that the chiefs of the 'native' courts were encouraging 'dowry' cases 'in order that they may get fees'.[58] As the chiefs saw the situation, the logic seemed to be that they should squeeze as much as they could from litigants while their names remained on the court roster. On account of the readiness with which chiefs took bribes and advanced their own financial interests generally, judgments of a 'native' court in particular cases might be at variance with both the spirit and the requirements of the customary law that it was supposed to administer.[59]

A safeguard against corruption in the courts was said to be provided in the review process undertaken by the administrative officers. A review, theoretically, 'is a method whereby a check may be kept on a court's proceedings in order to prevent a serious miscarriage of justice caused through acts or omissions on the part of the court'.[60] But the effect of reviews on corruption in the 'native' court system was very negligible. For one thing, the political officers had very little time to devote to a detailed examination of the cases brought before them for review. No less an officer than the Governor, Sir Hugh Clifford, observed in 1921 that the supervision exercised over the 'native' courts was 'very inadequate'.[61] For another, there was a tendency, born of political expediency, on the part of the officers to be wary of upsetting the decisions of the courts except where glaring injustices compelled them to do so. It was the general belief that to reverse the decisions of the 'native' court chiefs too often was to undermine their prestige and authority.[62] A political officer reviewing cases was more ready to connive at acts of 'minor' injustice than reverse the decision of a 'native' court. Not infrequently appeals from the courts through the review process were met with the simple fiat: 'Let the judgment of the chiefs stand.'[63]

Political considerations apart, certain procedural difficulties stood in the way of review process as an effective remedial measure. All that the political officer had to go on when reviewing a case were the notes of evidence written by the 'native' court clerk. But the records of proceedings were usually so crudely kept that very little reliance could be placed on them. In 1937 a political officer estimated that in his division, the proportion of cases in which the evidence given was correctly recorded was no more than fifteen per cent of the cases heard.[64] Where the 'native' court clerk's personal interest was involved, the so-called record of evidence might not necessarily represent the petitioner's case.[65] Again, the review process presupposed a fair trial in the first place; that is to say, that evidence had not been wrongly admitted, that the appropriate burden of proof had been discharged by the parties, that the demeanour of every witness appearing before the court was taken into account in weighing his or her evidence, and, above all, that the law administered in the court was certain or at least ascertainable.

The 'native' courts were certainly not strong in matters of procedure and evidence. Judgments were sometimes 'based on probability rather than on direct evidence'.[66] A curious development in many parts of Southern Nigeria was the use of juju or oath-swearing, not to ensure that a witness before the court was telling the truth, but to decide the very issue the court was being called upon to adjudicate. This was until the late 1930s a prominent feature of administration of justice in the 'native' courts of Warri, Calabar, Ogoja, Onitsha and Benin Provinces.[67] In *Nwaefi v. Esedo and others*, a case of an alleged theft of ivory reviewed by the Resident of Onitsha Province in 1935, the judgment of the 'native' court 'was that the plaintiff should swear an oath produced by the defendant that her ivory was taken by their father and that the cost was £10 (₦20.00)'.[68] The plaintiff in *P. N. Oba v. Chinye* (1936), (both of Asaba in Benin Province), was claiming the return of the 'dowry' he allegedly paid on his wife who had deserted him. The court's decision was that the defendant was to produce juju for the plaintiff to swear upon within three weeks to the effect that he paid the 'dowry' he alleged to have paid.[69] It is instructive that failure on the part of the plaintiff to produce juju for the defendant to swear upon, as in *Lucy Mazeli v. Menkiti and another* (1933),[70] *Okosun v. Ekpu and Ugua* (1936),[71] *Okeleke Igboji v. Okoafor Onagbo* (1938),[72] was taken as an admission of guilt resulting in judgment for the defendant.

The interesting thing about this procedure of judgment by oath-taking was that administrative officers encouraged and even defended it. 'An oath', wrote the Resident for Onitsha Province in 1939, 'is to the people the very best evidence available.'[73] On reviewing cases from the 'native' courts, the same officer confessed, 'the reviewing officer, confronted by a mass of conflicting and often irrelevant evidence, has frequently no alternative but to support native oath taken by one side or the other'. Thus in *Lucy Mazeli v. Menkiti and another* (1933), a case of recovery of debt, the assistant divisional officer, on review, decided:

> All are now agreed that Menkiti shall produce an oath for Lucy Mazeli and Ndulue [a key witness for the plaintiff] to swear. If the oath is produced and sworn, or if the petitioner fails to produce it, then, the plaintiff is to win her case. If either plaintiff or Ndulue refuses to swear, then, defendant is not liable for payment.[74]

Again, in *Mgbeke v. Okolie* (1937), a case of alleged wilful damage to property tried at Asaba 'native' court, the divisional officer decided on review:

> Parties agree to swear *juju*. Defendant says he will produce *juju* for plaintiff to swear as to her ownership of the plantains [allegedly destroyed]. She agrees to this and I enter an order accordingly. Members of court to supervise swearing.[75]

The court records are replete with instances of administrative officers on reviewing cases affirming decisions of 'native' courts arrived at by oath and even of officers suspending judgments until an oath was taken by litigants deciding the question in issue one way or the other.[76] In places there were even attempts at regularising the procedure of judicial decision-making by oath, with appropriate fees for particular types of juju.[77]

The practice of deciding cases by oath, as some administrative officers argued in its defence, might well be in line with the traditional judicial practice in Southern Nigeria of invoking the 'supernatural' to resolve difficult issues. But, in the final analysis, it amounts to an admission by the court (and the administrative officers) that they could not make up their minds on the merits of the case before them. The practice might be good religion in the past, and, to some extent effective as a measure in judicial proceedings in days before Christianity and Western education eroded many of the props of the traditional society. But it was evidently bad law. As a technique of judicial decision-making, it could be open to abuse. 'The readiness with which all and sundry express their willingness to swear their most potent *juju* for the merest trifles', wrote the divisional officer, Abakaliki Division of Ogoja

Province in 1937, 'convinces me that the performance is nearly always a farce.'[78]

A series of disturbances that convulsed Southern Nigeria between 1914 and 1930 testified most pungently to the unsatisfactory operation of the 'native' courts, although, one must add, the courts were not the sole factor in the disturbances. There was the Ijemo episode in Abeokuta in 1914;[79] the Okeho-Iseyin rising in October 1916 in Oyo Province;[80] the Tax Agitation Movement in 1924 in Ogbomosho;[81] the Anti-Taxation Movement in 1927 in Warri Province; [82] the series of disturbances between 1925 and 1929 in Ogoja Province;[83] and the famous Calabar-Owerri disturbances in December 1929.[84] The last outbreak was serious enough to warrant a full-scale investigation by the colonial administration.[85] In each of these incidents the 'native' court was either a source of complaint or, in some instances, a target of physical attack. In the Okeho-Iseyin rising two court messengers were murdered and two 'native' court buildings were destroyed.[86] During the Calabar-Owerri disturbances about fifteen court buildings were destroyed or partially destroyed.[87]

III

The operation of the provincial and 'native' courts in Southern Nigeria brought into existence a class of quasi-professionals in the protectorate. They were the champions-at-law and the public letter-writers. Their role in the judicial system merits a full discussion.

Champions-at-law operated mainly in the 'native' courts, and were called by various names in different parts of Southern Nigeria. Among the Yoruba they were the babaogun we met in an earlier chapter. Champions-at-law were not brought into existence by the establishment of the 'native' courts. As was pointed out in the first chapter, a form of representation in the settlement of disputes was known in pre-colonial Southern Nigerian society. But now the traditional 'pleaders' found a new role – thanks to the provisions of the Native Courts Ordinance, 1914. That ordinance provided for the representation of litigants at the 'native' courts by their relatives or friends.[88] The practice grew by which litigants employed people who could be 'influential in getting the ear of the court' to 'plead' their cases in the 'native' courts.

The methods of championing causes in the courts varied since different types of people could play the role. A champion-at-law pretending to be the relative of a litigant could go before the court openly and 'plead' his client's case. In the Eastern Provinces the champions-at-law, usually semi-educated Africans, operated largely in this way, gaining a reputation in colonial official circles of helping to confuse and distort 'native law and custom' by their 'specious pleading'.[89] A champion-at-law could also be an intermediary between litigants and a chief sitting on the 'native' court Bench. Since the chief was himself not averse to championing causes,[90] it was easy and rewarding for any of his followers to pilot prospective litigants to him. It was a common practice in the Eastern Provinces for chiefs to attract litigants to themselves through their followers.[91] Captain W. A. Ross, the Resident for Oyo Province in 1924, reported that the men in the entourage of the 'more important Chiefs' in Ibadan were seeking litigants in the 'native' courts.[92]

In the case of the intermediary champion-at-law, it was the chief himself who fought the legal battle at court. As a member of the court, he could not plead openly for his client. What he normally did was to use his influence behind the scenes. A chief declaring his interest in a dispute usually had his way among his peers, unless there was a powerful chief protecting the interests of the other party. When there were two chiefs thus opposing each other in a dispute involving their clients, what would determine the outcome of the dispute would be the relative strength of the chiefs or perhaps the merit of each party's case.

Champions-at-law were a potent force to reckon with under the 'native' court system, although, because of the very nature of their operation, the extent of their influence is not easy to document. In *Aminu v. Sinatu Ode* (1937), the plaintiff was appealing to the Resident of Oyo Province over a judgment delivered at an Ibadan 'native' court.[93] At the 'native' court he had claimed ₦24.00 as the bride-price which he said he had paid on the defendant, Sinatu Ode, his former wife. The court had awarded him only half of his claim. 'The reason or reasons why the court would not give actual judgment', petitioned Aminu, 'was that [the defendant] was having a *babaogun* who had influence over the justice.' He decided to petition the Resident over the case rather than appeal to a higher 'native' court, the judicial council at Ibadan, because 'the influence of the *babaogun* will follow us to the [higher "native"] court'.[94] There must have been some substance in the plaintiff's allegation because the Resident ordered a retrial of the case.

A fair degree of the corruption in the 'native' courts could be attributed to the influence wielded by people having direct or indirect connections with the courts who championed others' causes for remuneration. The divisional officer for Ishan Division of Benin Province reported of Ewohimi District 'native' court in 1938: 'There are a lot of unsatisfied judgments in this court, many of which might be enforced if the debtors were not friends of the court members and are therefore given unlimited time to pay.'[95] Ewohimi District court was by no means an isolated example of a 'native' court unwilling to enforce its own judgments. The 'friends of the court members' were invariably champions-at-law. The corruption of the champions-at-law stemmed from their somewhat parasitic role in the 'native' court system. They often had no other visible means of income, practically living by their wits. They were in the courts 'to get money by any possible means',[96] and were once likened to vultures living on the ill fortune of others.[97]

Their role in the judicial system could be obstructive and tend to confusion. They paraded the courts 'like a public market where people are selling and buying', egging on hesitant litigants, and fomenting cases, especially divorce cases. Around the court premises they could be a menace to litigants. In 1952, there were estimated to be about 78 babaoguns operating in two 'native' courts at Ibadan.[98] It was a serious problem to drive them off the court premises periodically. Again, because of their connection or influence with known chiefs, champions-at-law could at the very least hold up the functioning of the 'native' court machinery. It was said of the babaoguns of the Ibadan 'native' courts:

> They have influence [because] they are relatives to some chiefs in the town and they did not care for courts' orders whether from the chiefs or officials.[99]

The cost of the 'services' of champions-at-law to litigants could be high. The chief's follower, who stood as an intermediary between a litigant and the chief, besides making his own separate demand, often overstated that of the chief so that he could have his share of whatever a litigant gave. It was also a common practice for the champions-at-law, particularly the powerful chiefs in the community, to retain for their own use money awarded by the courts to their clients.[100] Many ordinary men who piloted cases as babaogun in the Ibadan area in the 1930s, the writer was told, lived in relative affluence, putting up impressive modern buildings.[101] As late as 1940 being a babaogun was considered 'a lucrative business'.[102]

Of greater importance than the champions-at-law in the 'native' court system were the public letter-writers. Letter-writing as a profession originated in the Lagos Colony. It gained official recognition, so to speak, in 1896 when an ordinance was passed to regulate its operation.[103] The primary function of letter-writers was to address petitions to the English-style courts on behalf of non-literate litigants. An extension of their function was the writing of petitions to government authorities on political or administrative issues. By 1900 letter-writing had become an officially recognised trade, governed by an ordinance, the Illiterates' Protection Ordinance, which was amended periodically as time went on.[104]

Until now the ordinance, with its amendments, has constituted the only important measure governing public letter-writing. It was promulgated not so much to regularise letter-writing as to protect non-literate litigants from exploitation, as the title of the ordinance itself suggests. The most important provision of the ordinance in this regard was the rate of remuneration prescribed for letter-writers' services. In 1910, for instance, the ordinance stipulated that for every hundred words of every letter or document, the charge was to be ten kobo.[105]

The colonial administration at first took steps to exercise control over letter-writers. The Illiterates' Protection Ordinances, 1905, 1910, required them to take out annual licences. A licence, obtainable for a fee of one naira, was not transferable. The holder was required to produce it on demand at the request of any political officer, member of the police force, or any member or officer of a 'native' court.[106] The intention of the administration was clearly to check irregularities and perhaps to set up a standard of admission to the profession.

The system of issuing out licences to letter-writers soon led to serious abuses. The licences gave to letter-writers an official recognition which they readily took advantage of. Brandishing their licences before the public, they represented themselves as qualified solicitors. They did not confine themselves to writing petitions; they carried out practically all forms of legal transactions.[107] There were also indications that they charged excessive fees.

In 1915, partly in deference to the feelings of qualified legal practitioners, the administration abolished the system of issuing licences to letter-writers. Though considered necessary at the time, this measure was a step in the wrong direction. The issuing of licences to letter-writers did provide a means of exercising some control over them. The licences were issued annually, and the renewal of a licence could be made to depend on good behaviour on the part of the licensee. Moreover it would not have been too difficult to use the system to set some educational requirements for prospective letter-writers. It may be urged that the system of issuing licences had not worked well for five years and that there was no reason to expect that matters would improve. The fact remains that a little control, even if imperfect, was better than no control at all. Henceforth, after 1915, anyone with any claim to a modicum of education could be a letter-writer. All that was required of him was familiarity with the current Illiterates' Protection Ordinance.[108] Some letter-writers were 'trained' by their more senior co-professionals in typing and in 'drafting' documents. But no such training was officially required, and a prospective letter-writer undertook it only if he felt himself in any way inadequate for the profession. The administration's policy towards letter-writers amounted to complete abandonment and it put in their hands enormous powers.

From Lagos, Abeokuta, Calabar and other towns, letter-writers began to find their way into the farther interior districts after 1914. A number of them had been clerks in lawyers' offices, mercantile houses or in the government service. A few of them came from the Gold Coast (Ghana) and Sierra Leone.[109] The number of letter-writers increased over the years; by the 1930s every important administrative centre could boast of them. In the 1930s and early 1940s, for instance, about twenty-five operated in Ibadan administrative Division.[110] By 1936 there were thirty-eight in Ijebu Province, twenty-three of them in Ijebu-Ode alone.[111] At least twenty-five operated in Aba township in Onitsha Province between 1931 and 1939.[112] In the period 1934–41 no less than eighteen erected their offices at Onitsha for varying lengths of time.[113] At least ten were actively engaged in Warri in the 1940s.[114] These figures represent only those who seem to have made a profession of letter-writing. The records of administrative officers indicate that there were literally hundreds of others who engaged in it more or less as a hobby. This latter category of letter-writers lacked what the 'professionals' seem to have possessed as basic requirements: a typewriter (usually bought at second-hand), typing papers with printed letter-heads, other stationery, and a well-situated 'documentary office' for the purpose of receiving clients. The better type of letter-writers also possessed copies of important colonial statutes, like the Criminal Code, and books on principles of English law.[115]

In view of the ban placed on lawyers' appearance in the provincial and 'native' courts, letter-writers found a ready role to play in the judicial system operating in much of Southern Nigeria up to 1933. It must be said at once that they fulfilled a need.

Short of personally appearing in the courts, they functioned in all respects as barristers and solicitors. Nor was their function limited to litigation, as we shall see presently. They were called 'Wigless lawyers',[116] and indeed thought of themselves as lawyers or advocates. In this connection, the names they gave to their business premises are revealing. At Ibadan in the 1930s there was Windorff's Defenders' Office.[117] There were the following at Ijebu-Ode by 1933: Ajetunmobi Champion Public Office and Olurombi Advocating Secretariat.[118] The United Public Letter-Writers' Bureau at the same place was, as its letter-head indicated, 'for the illiterate and unsophisticated Mass'.[119] Edema Arubi, a letter-writer at Warri, set up his 'Civic Illiterates' Defence Service' for the Itsekiri, Sobo (Urhobo) and Ijo people. By 1936 his letter-head was carrying a Burkian, suggestive declaration: 'Government is a contrivance of human wisdom to provide for human wants.'[120]

The most important function performed by letter-writers was the writing of petitions. From the financial point of view, the writing of petitions was also 'the soul of the business'.[121] With the grave imperfections of the 'native' courts, litigants before these courts had much to petition about in connection with alleged miscarriages of justice. Within the 'native' court system the notion also grew, to the obvious advantage of letter-writers, that a letter addressed to an administrative officer could reverse an unfavourable decision of a 'native' court even if there had been no miscarriage of justice. In the writing of petitions the letter-writer was not simply a hired hand setting down in writing whatever his client dictated. His skill, or what may be called the technique of his profession, lay in the writing. He was expected to use every artifice or any degree of polished language that could achieve his client's objective. Contrary to the expectations of administrative officers,[122] letter-writers operated essentially as advocates in presenting petitions.

The method of writing petitions varied. There were letter-writers who literally pleaded the causes of their clients before the administrative officers in most flattering terms. A letter-writer of this type could plead with 'Your Benign Honour' (the administrative officer) 'with deepest reverence . . . as your honour listens with compassion to all complaints from all sorts of people, poor or rich', appealing to 'British justice and fair play' and to the British Government which 'is a sacred institution ordained by God'.[123] The petitions of some of the letter-writers in this category were hardly intelligible; in most cases their 'absurd jumbling of words'[124] could not have served any useful purpose.

At the other end of the spectrum were those who argued their cases effectively, using materials supplied by their clients and their own knowledge of customary law. From the petitions written by the latter category of letter-writers, it is clear that they were at least sometimes, if not always, present in court at the initial trial of the case over which they were petitioning. It is equally plain that they were also familiar with at least the rudiments of English law and legal procedure.[125] J. D. Adepoju, a letter-writer at Ibadan, once petitioned on behalf of the defendant in *Chief Ogundoyin v. Shitta* against the judgment given by the Ibadan Judicial Council.[126] It was a case of an alleged assault for which the defendant was said to have been found liable. The judgment in the case was invalid, he wrote to the Resident, because evidence had been improperly taken during the retrial of the case. He contended that Chief Ogundoyin brought people to the court as witnesses who were not present when the alleged assault took place. He noted that the witnesses sat closely to each other in the court and that Chief Ogundoyin 'was so conveniently placed that he answered questions for his witnesses'. In addition to improper procedure, the letter-writer argued, the judgment of banishment given in the case was much at variance with the tort of assault. It was a well-known fact, he said, that no British subject could be banished from his place of residence 'unless for very special reasons'. The petition was allowed, and the judgment of the Ibadan court reversed by the Resident.

Edema Arubi in Warri Province handled the largest proportion of the petitions addressed to administrative officers, and was undoubtedly the most popular letter-writer in the province.[127] After about twenty years in the colonial government service he took to letter-writing in the late 1920s. It may be too dashing to describe him as possessing a 'legal' mind, but he was certainly above the ordinary run of letter-writers. Noted for his courage and tenacity of purpose, he would not stop short of petitioning the Colonial Office in London if he found it necessary to do so.[128] Judging from the records of his professional activities, it was not an empty boast that he held the colonial Governor 'not in any higher esteem than the most junior British political officers in Nigeria'.[129] Arubi would not simply state his client's case, he would go to great lengths to argue the facts, citing similar cases decided elsewhere on the same issue and even sometimes quoting principles of English law to buttress his points.[130] Indeed, so lawyer-like was his approach to letter-writing that the Resident once refused to entertain the petitions he wrote on behalf of his clients because they were considered to be written arguments, not petitions.[131]

Letter-writers performed other functions besides writing petitions. The introduction into Southern Nigeria of a money-oriented economy and of new economic institutions, the enhanced value of land resulting from the development of new economic crops, the growth of individualism and the general replacement of status by contract in interpersonal relations in the society – all these factors created a need in the economic sphere which letter-writers readily filled. They drew up simple contracts (or, to use their language, agreements) between parties covering a wide variety of activities: the letting of shops, purchase or lease of farm-lands, pawning of cocoa or palm tree farms, raising of loans, sale of goods, terms of trade-apprenticeship and the like.[132] Two samples of agreements drawn up by letter-writers are contained in the Appendix below.

Debt-collecting was an important related activity performed by letter-writers. In this sphere of their activities they were like solicitors. They notified the debtors of their creditor-clients that payment was due, adding that 'legal steps' would be taken if no payment was made within a specified period. Such was the confidence letter-writers displayed and such was the power they believed themselves capable of wielding that a group of them had a form printed for use in summoning debtors to their office.[133] There was no provision in the Illiterates' Protection Ordinance allowing letter-writers to collect debts. But this activity, like the preparation of simple contracts, was a response to a need. For collecting debts and rents, letter-writers were apparently paid by results. They were supposed to be given a certain percentage – about ten per cent – of whatever was collected.[134]

Considered strictly within the context of the administration of justice in Southern Nigeria, letter-writers, on the whole, performed an essential function. In some places by the 1940s, when the 'native' courts could be said to have acquired some sophistication, they were, in fact, indispensable to the 'native' court system. The Resident for Ijebu Province wrote in his draft annual report for 1946:

> Public letter-writers are playing a more prominent part than ever in the work of the courts. It is not uncommon for statements of claim prepared by the gentlemen of the local 'bar' to be attached to summonses. The Ijebu Remo Appeal Court insists on appellants filing grounds of appeal and often on the respondent filing a rejoinder. Three quarters of the complaints heard by administrative officers are in connection with Native court cases and about 80% of these complaints being long documents prepared by letter-writers.[135]

It cannot be denied that many decisions of the 'native' courts were reversed or modified by administrative officers largely on the strength of petitions written by letter-writers. It was as a result of a letter-writer's intervention that the plaintiff in *Ayisa tu v. Niwo* (1933) was released from detention after she had been unlawfully detained by the 'native' court at Ijebu-Ode in Ijebu Province.[136] The accused in *Odumodu Umunya v. Ibegbuna* (1936) was, as a result of petitioning by a letter-writer, acquitted of the charge of theft of yams, having been previously sentenced to six months' imprisonment by the Awkuzu 'native' court in Onitsha Province.[137] In *In Re Mogboruko Olomuro* (1945), Edema Arubi, through persistent writing of petitions, successfully defended the right of a woman-contractor in Warri to her private property against official high-handedness, securing for her the best market value for her article of trade.[138] The instances of letter-writers tilting the scale of justice in favour of their clients could be multiplied. It is fair to say that they probably made the 'native' court system less intolerable than it might have been without them.

Letter-writers also played an educative role. Anyone who reads through the petitions addressed to the administrative officers cannot but be impressed by the way the better sort of letter-writers expounded aspects of Nigerian customary law as these touched on their particular cases.[139] There is no indication that any administrative officer acknowledged how much he learnt from letter-writers; on the contrary, letter-writers were usually the object of invective and even political persecution. But it is fair to suggest that one important source of administrative officers' education in Nigerian customary law lay in the petitions written by letter-writers. They did not, of course, set out to educate administrative officers in Nigerian customary law. It could, indeed, be argued that their petitions, being partisan, were of doubtful educative value. But the fact remains that they wrote about customary law as no other group of professionals in the protectorate did. The extent to which an administrative officer learnt from the petitions of letter-writers would obviously depend on the officer's native intelligence or his willingness to learn.

The educative role of letter-writers is also discernible in other ways. The 'bush lawyers', as they were sometimes called, helped to popularise some English legal concepts serving modern needs. Their activities in the sphere of contractual relations come to mind. It is worth noting that the better sort of letter-writers gave themselves some form of legal education. The writer was told (and the records of petitions seem to confirm) that a number of letter-writers spent substantial sums of money on law books for their private legal education.[140] Again, current editions of local ordinances were often among the tools of their trade. A number of them had also been lawyers' clerks.

The relationship of letter-writer to client was very close, and it is conceivable that in the course of his 'professional' activities the letter-writer educated his clients in the legal process, even if such education might, on occasion, have been in the nature of the blind leading the blind. In any case the 'bush lawyer' was invariably the 'bush legal adviser'. Except in the remotest parts of Nigeria, few people today, even when they are not literate, would undertake any serious obligation of an economic nature, like leasing farmland, without entering into some written 'agreement'. To a considerable extent the consciousness of the need for contract-making as a legal concept has been a result of the influence of letter-writers.

Obafemi Awolowo has argued that letter-writers, by sometimes appealing over the heads of junior political officers, contributed to the breakdown of what he called 'the myth about the omniscience and omnipotence of the Administrative Officer'.[141] Whatever contribution letter-writers made in this regard could be considered as a factor in the political awakening of the people of Southern Nigeria. The point, however, must not be exaggerated. The letter-writers who played the role Awolowo has ascribed to them were few in number.

That there was a seamy side to the activities of letter-writers there can be no doubt. The situation in which they found themselves in the protectorate was such that they could not but abuse their positions and it is barely necessary to say that they exploited their clients. In the eyes of the non-literate litigants the letter-writer was an important figure. Few of them, if any, knew of the provisions of the Illiterates' Protection Ordinance that stipulated letter-writers' fees. It is true that few letter-writers in the period covered by this study were charged with violating the provisions of the ordinance. But letter-writers were operating in circumstances that made detection of malpractices difficult in the vast majority of cases. Until the 1940s, letter-writers had no recognisable bodies that could exercise any discipline on their members. As was pointed out earlier, the administration lost its one measure of control over them in 1915. Thus their 'professional' activities did not come directly under the eyes of the authorities. Not infrequently, their dealings with their clients were bound up with secret oaths – a fact which made any reporting of their malpractices difficult, if not impossible. Again, it was almost impossible to obtain a conviction under the Illiterates' Protection Ordinance, for the letter-writers often took care to ensure that there were no witnesses to the transactions between them and their clients.[142] In any case the clients themselves usually had no previous experience with letter-writers or persons performing similar functions; they probably did not realise the extent to which they were being exploited.

The petition sent to the administrative officer might indicate that the letter-writer's fee was in accordance with the rate of remuneration prescribed by the Illiterates' Protection Ordinance or even that the letter-writer provided his services free of charge. But behind the scenes, in most cases, a private arrangement must have been worked out by which he took substantial sums of money in fees. In 1915, Sir Frederick Lugard himself, the author of the new judicial system, suggested that the fee in such circumstances could run up to eighty or a hundred naira.[143]

In Abeokuta Province it was said that the activities of letter-writers were causing 'oppressions on their clients'.[144] Here as elsewhere in Southern Nigeria they sometimes resorted to the use of force in collecting debts, and it was not uncommon for them to retain for their own use the money they collected from debtors. The chiefs of Igbo-Ora in Ibadan Division had occasion to report a public letter-writer, one Enebeli, whose thugs were molesting people in Igbo-Ora and the neighbouring towns, taking them to their master's office and forcing them to put their thumbs on 'agreement papers'.[145] In Ijebu Province the malpractices of letter-writers reached such a height in the late 1920s that the local authorities were induced to pass very stringent regulations to curb their activities.[146]

In the Eastern Provinces letter-writing was said to be 'undoubtedly a lucrative occupation'. This was because the illiterate litigant was 'exploited and bled to an enormous extent', as an administrative officer reported.[147] The Resident for Calabar Province complained in 1922 of the 'enormous sums of money' that letter-writers were making out of the non-literate litigants.[148] In the same year the Secretary for Native Affairs reported that letter-writers were 'a very real evil' in the Eastern Provinces.[149] At the Residents' conference held at Enugu in November 1929, the officers discussed proposals for a closer control of letter-writers' activities on account of 'the excessive fees' paid to them by their clients.[150]

From the point of view of the colonial administration, the activities of letter-writers and other quasi-advocates produced two undesirable results. One was that letter-writers were, in places, as sharp thorns in the flesh of administrative officers as lawyers were considered to be before 1914. The outstanding example was Edema Arubi of Warri. He earned the reputation of being 'a considerable nuisance' among administrative officers of Warri Province; but he left no doubt in their minds that he regarded himself as 'the protector of natives . . . against the oppressive acts of local administrators'.[151] Behind some of the political disturbances mentioned in connection with the 'native' courts were letter-writers.[152] That such men were active in local politics was to be expected. From writing petitions to administrative officers on behalf of private litigants, it was only a short step to airing political grievances in petitions to these same officers.

The other result of the activities of letter-writers and other quasi-advocates was what the administration had feared about lawyers: touting. Under the 'native' court system, letter-writers, champions-at-law and even money-lenders, eager to give money to litigants at biting rates of interest – all, in varying degrees, touted for business. It was the practice to waylay unsuccessful parties at the 'native' courts and, if the matter in issue seemed to deserve the effort, to urge further pursuance of their causes until the Supreme Court was reached. As a result of these touting activities, it became increasingly difficult to keep the courts in the protectorate completely detached from the supreme court as administrative officers would have wished, and, as it was indeed intended in 1914. The Resident for Benin Province reported in 1922 that the provisions of the provincial courts ordinance notwithstanding, his first reaction when trying a land case was to transfer it to the Supreme Court. Provided there was money, he wrote, 'touts and letter-writers will ultimately get it there'.[153] It was a common experience of administrative officers that they had difficulty keeping land cases strictly within the confines of the provincial or the 'native' courts.

IV

It is time to assess the effectiveness of the provincial and the 'native' courts from the point of view of the objectives which were set for them in 1914. The reader will recall that the two categories of courts in their combination were intended to restrict the professional activities of legal practitioners in the Protectorate of Nigeria, to keep the cost of litigation low, thereby saving the people from being 'bled to death' in legal fees, and to take land cases, supposedly the 'juice' of legal practice, away from the ambit of the supreme court. The establishment of the provincial and the 'native' courts, as was pointed out earlier, was not so much a judicial, as a politico-administrative measure, and it is from this standpoint that the effectiveness of the courts must be judged.

Considered against the objectives they were intended to achieve, the judicial system devised in 1914 was, at best, only a partial success. It was successful only in so far as the system worked at all for almost two decades. To start with the issue of cost of litigation and financial exploitation of the masses, whether letter-writers and the other quasi-advocates who operated in the protectorate were less extortionate than the lawyers and therefore the lesser of two evils is a question which, for obvious reasons, cannot be answered with any finality. One thing, however, is certain:

their activities did not make litigation cheap. If administrative officers' reports are to be believed, it is difficult to imagine how legal practitioners, even if they had been allowed free rein in the practice of their profession, could have been more oppressive than the letter-writers in the way they extorted money from their clients in some places. There was the case reported in 1921 of a letter-writer at Calabar, one John S. Wellington, who duped a local chief to the tune of two hundred naira under the colour of an agreement supposedly enforceable by the courts.[154] From all indications letter-writers and champions-at-law kept the cost of litigation high in the protectorate despite the good intention of the administration to bring justice cheaply to the people.

We may note here that champions-at-law and letter-writers were not alone in making litigation ruinously expensive. Money-lenders also traded on the plight of litigants. They advanced money to litigants at exorbitant rates of interest to pursue, at the instigation of the money-lenders themselves, what were sometimes hopeless causes. The Nkwerre people from Orlu in Owerri Province were particularly notorious for this type of money-lending business. Their money-lending brought ruin to many individuals and even to whole communities.[155]

The corruption of the 'native' courts in Southern Nigeria was proverbial. The provincial courts, too, presided over by the administrative officer, were not free from the same vice. At the provincial court the court interpreter wielded a power fairly comparable with that of the court clerk at the 'native' court. The interpreter's position was crucial in judicial proceedings. He sometimes succumbed to the temptation to receive bribes from litigants 'to make their palaver good with the big boss'.[156]

It is significant that litigants continued to avail themselves of the services of lawyers in spite of the difficulties imposed by the judicial system of 1914. Mention was made earlier of the amendments in the structure of the provincial courts intended as a relief to litigants: facility for transfer of cases from the provincial courts to the Supreme Court and progressive extension of the jurisdiction of the latter court. Although these amendments were not intended to make much difference in the operation of the judicial system, they were a boon to lawyers making professional inroads into the forbidden ground of the protectorate.

Land cases, among others, were being transferred to the supreme court from the provincial courts, especially those in the

Eastern Provinces. It is true that applications for the transfer of land cases from the provincial courts to the Supreme Court were not always granted.[157] But the rate at which such transfers were effected was considered alarming enough. One factor in favour of practising lawyers and, by the same token, a sore disappointment to administrative officers, was the tendency on the part of the judges of the Supreme Court were put a liberal construction on the supervision they were supposed to exercise over the provincial courts. This liberal attitude, from the point of view of administrative officers, amounted to 'defeating the plain meaning of the law'.[158] In considering appeals from the provincial courts the Supreme Court judges were supposed to allow the appearance of legal practitioners only where points of law were involved. But it would appear that the judges were wont to be generous in allowing lawyers' appearances or that the lawyers were not slow in locating the required 'points of law' in the appeals from the provincial courts.

Sir Hugh Clifford as Governor of Nigeria noted in 1923 that leave to appeal from the decisions of the provincial courts was so frequently given by the judges of the Supreme Court east of the Niger that the Residents sitting at the provincial courts there regarded the time spent by them in hearing land cases as time wasted. They were, in fact, often tempted to arrange for the trial of land cases at the Supreme Court in the first instance. The Supreme Court would be reached ultimately, Clifford complained, 'no matter how painstaking the hearing in the Provincial court may be, and no matter how sound the decision that may be recorded as the result of that hearing'.[159] A legal practitioner was reported to have told an administrative officer that it was a matter of course for lawyers to appeal against the decisions of the provincial courts in land cases.[160] Much the same thing could be said about litigants making applications through their lawyers for the transfer of land cases, especially east of the Niger.

It is a sad reflection on the futility of the government's restrictive measure in judicial matters that even the 'native' courts were not successfully insulated from the influence of legal practitioners. One runs across instances in the administrative records in the Eastern Provinces of lawyers presenting reasoned arguments to divisional officers or Residents on specific cases that were to come before them for review.[161] The aim might be to alert the officer about recent legal development relevant to the case in hand, or, as in *Uche Haran of Umuikan Nekede v. Onorobo of Umuohia Daogu* (1932), simply 'to place this case properly before you'.[162]

Ironically, it was the litigants who were made to suffer more than the lawyers the consequences of the policy of restriction. One only has to bear in mind the restrictions placed on the practice of the legal profession to realise that lawyers would make the most of whatever legal business came their way. Once the lawyer was involved in a case, whether by writing a petition on it or by making an application for its transfer to the Supreme Court, he normally took his fees. The outcome of his efforts was irrelevant.

Interference by lawyers in land cases meant that the provincial court system failed to achieve one of the 'political' objectives dearest to the administrative officer's heart: the exclusion of lawyers from the protectorate in order to make 'administrative' settlement of land cases possible. 'There is almost always appeal to the Supreme Court', noted the resident for Ogoja Province in 1929.[163] Ogoja Province was by no means exceptional in that regard. In general, administrative officers found it an exasperating experience to sit on land cases at the provincial courts. At the trial of a land case or after it, one of two things happened: either an application was entered for the transfer of the case to the Supreme Court or an appeal was made to the same court against the provincial court's decision. Whatever the Supreme Court subsequently did in such cases served little to discourage future applications and appeals by others – as long as the channels to the Supreme Court remained open.

V

Although the judicial system of 1914 failed in its objectives, there can be no doubt about the impact of the provincial and the 'native' courts as judicial institutions in other directions. In considering the impact of the courts, especially the 'native' courts, it is necessary to go beyond 1933, the terminal point of discussion for this chapter.

First, from the point of view of the colonial regime itself, the courts facilitated administration, and to this extent, strengthened the regime. Mention was made earlier of the 'political' uses of the provincial courts. Even more directly involved in local administration, from their inception, were the 'native' courts. Indeed, as was shown earlier, and as some other writers have demonstrated,[164] these courts were political, no less than they were judicial, institutions. They were conceived of, initially, as a means of consolidating British rule, and throughout the colonial period, they remained central to local administration. 'A native court', wrote Donald Cameron, Governor of Nigeria in 1931, 'is merely one of the exemplifications of the authority of a Native Authority.'[165] Not only were the courts the 'eyes' of the colonial regime in the provinces, they also provided the wherewithal by which day-to-day administration was sustained. There is copious evidence on the success of the courts as revenue-making institutions.[166] In each province they provided a sizable proportion of the finances for building or maintaining local amenities like roads, schools, health facilities and the like and for paying the salaries of chiefs and the staffs of the various local government units.[167]

We saw in Chapter 3 what role 'native' courts played in the 'pacification' of Southern Nigeria and how they were used to promote the economic interests of the colonial power through the enforcement of local ordinances safeguarding economic crops or stamping out such bad commercial practices as adulteration of produce. After 1914, both the provincial and the 'native' courts continued to play an important role in the economic development of the region. Heavy sanctions against such 'uneconomic' activities as indiscriminate tapping of rubber or destruction of timber and other economic trees continued to be imposed by the courts.[168] New regulations for the economic development of the territory were promulgated and enforced by the courts.[169]

Since 1918, when Lugard approved a set of 'Land Rules' for Ibadan,[170] the 'native' courts had been instrumental in easing the burden of customary land law and, to this extent, had promoted economic development. By customary law, land was, in most places, communally owned, although individual rights to land use were recognised. Within a community or family land was, therefore, not easily alienable. The Ibadan Land Rules which were adopted in some other communities in the Western Provinces, permitted some degree of alienation of land in the form of a lease provided the 'native' court gave its consent to any agreement purporting to grant the lease. In a relatively more remote area like Ilaro Division of Abeokuta Province, it was the divisional 'native' court itself rather than the local government council which in July 1929 promulgated similar 'Land Rules' and enforced them.[171] The effectiveness of local rules enforceable by the 'native' courts should not be doubted. It was officially acknowledged that the mere passing of an order by a native administration or a 'native' court and the certainty that the court would enforce it often achieved the intended objective.[172]

Even where there were no formal rules encouraging alienation of land, the judicial activities of the courts tended to promote it or at least to popularise the notion that land could be sold and alienated. There are numerous instances in the Yoruba Provinces, for instance, where a 'native' court, sometimes under the guidance of the administrative officer, ordered the sale of land to settle a debt, upheld an agreement to sell land, or compelled an outright sale of land where a tenant had been in 'undisturbed possession for many years' and the grantor had acquiesced in his performing acts inconsistent with the nature of his grant.[173]

Perhaps the most enduring aspect of the impact of the provincial and the 'native' courts as judicial institutions lies in the socio-cultural sphere, where they constituted an important factor of change. Socio-cultural change may be defined as a significant alteration in the patterns of social interaction and customary modes of behaviour.[174] In the context of Southern Nigeria which has undergone the colonial experience, the phenomenon of socio-cultural change has been a result not of one factor but of a wide variety of factors. The missionary influence, Western education, the new cash-oriented economy, the influence of foreign travel, the process of colonial rule and the law and the courts brought in its train – all these, in varying degrees, have contributed to the phenomenon of socio-cultural change.

When one realises that the legal system imposed on Nigeria was imbued with its own set of (English) values, that it had elements of 'command' in the Austinian sense,[175] or that it was made to predominate over the indigenous legal rules and customs in certain matters, one begins to appreciate how law and the courts, giving it expression, could have contributed to social change. One cannot draw a rigid line between the role of the law and that of the courts, for the latter are the outward and visible embodiment of the former, and they give it expression.

The law which the provincial court was supposed to administer in the protectorate was 'the English common law, the doctrines of Equity and the statutes of general application which were in force in England on 1 January 1900', subject, of course, to any necessary modifications that might be made. Allowance was also made for the observance of indigenous laws and customs, but only in so far as they were not 'repugnant to justice, equity and good conscience'. This proviso, as it was pointed out earlier, was the famous 'Repugnancy doctrine', the application of which we shall examine presently.

The 'native' courts dealing with the bulk of the Nigerian population who were largely illiterate, were supposed to keep as closely as possible to the indigenous laws and customs. But it is noteworthy that the 'Repugnancy doctrine' operated when the courts administered customary law. The rules of customary law applicable in the courts were those 'not opposed to natural morality and humanity'.[176] Again, the courts were also empowered to enforce special rules made by the colonial administration from time to time – rules which might import 'modifications of existing laws or customs'.[177] The combined effect of these two provisions and the supervisory role of administrative officers over the courts tended to make the courts something of a foreign institution, both in their mode of operation and, to some extent, the type of law they administered. It was a common experience among administrative officers that 'native' courts tended to ape the judicial procedure of the Supreme Court and, under the influence of the court clerks, to administer a corpus of law, 'neither British nor Native', that was believed to meet the standard of justice of the supervising administrative officer.[178] G. I. Jones, a government anthropologist in the Eastern Provinces in the 1930s, saw a 'complete divergence both in theory and in practice between Native law and custom and the law actually administered in the Native court'.[179] It may not be true, as an administrative officer remarked, that the law administered in the courts 'is entirely contrary to their original ideas'.[180] But there can be no doubt that as institutions, 'native' courts, through their officials and through the supervising administrative officers, imported into the society and did enforce notions of law and personal relations that were not quite in keeping with the traditional ideas of Southern Nigerian peoples.

Against the background of 'native' courts as more or less foreign institutions in Southern Nigeria, it is easy to appreciate their potential as a factor in socio-cultural change. Even as mere institutions they are known to have made an impact on their respective localities in terms of social change. They tended to play the same role for which mission houses were known in the early days of

British colonial establishment: as beacons of European culture and civilisation.[181] A court-compound was, in the words of an administrative officer, 'a little oasis of quasi-civilization'.[182] Together with the 'rest-house' usually adjoining it, it served as 'a model and a reminder of the new way of life which the British brought with them'.

It should be mentioned, too, that in the Eastern Provinces the very existence of the 'native' courts tended to be disruptive of the social order. In the absence of easily recognisable chiefly institutions in most of these areas, 'warrant chiefs', created by the British, were, among other things, responsible for manning the courts. As was mentioned in the second chapter, the vast majority of the 'warrant chiefs' lacked any traditional authority. With the courts as the main prop of their authority, they literally usurped the powers and functions of the traditional village heads and village assemblies, setting themselves up as a new power elite.[183]

Outside the Eastern Provinces the disruptive influence of the 'native' courts as new institutions was more subtle, but no less real. If it is true, as it has been suggested, that the British administration, even more than the missionaries, contributed to 'the lowering of the prestige of the chiefs in the eyes of the masses',[184] the courts established in the protectorate were certainly among the important factors that eroded the chiefs' power and prestige. The courts, quite unlike the traditional politico-judicial system in which status was always a paramount consideration, were by and large no respecter of persons.[185] A chief could now be punished in them like any other person for the infringement of any rules or regulations laid down by the administration, or, as in *R. v. Oyebajo, ex-Akarigbo and others* (1921),[186] for the perpetration of any offence considered by the court to be against the spirit of English law. Again, as was mentioned in the opening chapter, the new courts inevitably undermined the traditional basis of power in the society. The chiefs, no less than the masses, were progressively aware that real power lay not with the traditional authorities but with the British administrative officers. This fact was reflected in the relative ineffectiveness of the chiefs in finalising disputes at the 'native' courts and in the innumerable volumes of petitions over 'native' court cases addressed to the officers.

Apart from these considerations about the position of the provincial and 'native' courts in relation to the traditional socio-political structure of Southern Nigeria, the impact of the courts in socio-cultural change has been felt in three main areas: the growth of individualism, the elevation of the status of women in society, and changes in customary practices.

In discussing the growth of individualism in Southern Nigeria, one must give pre-eminence to economic and social factors operating outside the courts. They are the same factors just mentioned, all of which have tended to sharpen in the individual a sense of his personal worth and have, by the same token, served to weaken the traditional modes of social control.

But the courts have contributed to this process. The basis of the law they administered, even at the level of the 'native' court, was individual responsibility in contrast with the traditional emphasis on family, or even sometimes communal, responsibility in the adjudication of disputes. In place of the 'collective responsibility of the extended family and to some degree of the kindred for the conduct of its members',[187] the British-established law courts were concerned only with the individual in so far as his acts or omissions were called in question in particular cases. It is for this reason that the loosening of family ties among the Yoruba has been attributed with some justification to 'the enforcement of English social laws [and] the individuality of English life' as reflected in the laws enforced by the courts.[188]

A corollary of the fact that the courts were no respecter of status was that the courts constituted an important lever by which ordinary men in the society, aided by the power of wealth or education, among other factors, asserted themselves.[189] It was no accident that by the 1940s people were becoming 'more legal minded' in their inter-personal relations, especially in the urban areas.[190]

The attitude of the courts to matters of marital relations reflected the greater scope being accorded by them to the personal status of women in society. In the words of an administrative officer, the law and the courts tended to 'liberate them from the old position of servitude to which they were doomed'.[191] In particular the courts were wont to put a liberal construction on requests for divorce – in defiance, so to speak, of the traditional code of behaviour by which marital separation was rare. 'Women who wanted to renounce their husbands', N. A. Fadipe has found, 'simply went up the "hill" to the office or the court of the [British] Resident Commissioner to sue for divorce.'[192] Similarly, young girls 'availed themselves of the opportunity' offered by the law and the courts to defy tradition by rejecting unwanted marriage proposals imposed by their parents.[193] The result of these developments was what was often regarded by administrative officers as a serious social problem threatening the solidarity of the diverse communities. This is not to say that every petition for divorce was granted; but the rate at which such petitions were granted by the 'native' courts in particular was sufficiently alarming even to the administrative officers themselves. In this connection it is significant that over the years marital cases predominated among the civil cases heard in the courts. From a study of the court records it would appear to be the rule rather than the exception that divorce was granted. In one court, out of a total of 125 petitions for divorce in 1924, divorce was granted in 123.[194]

It is easy to explain the attitude of the courts. In addition to a propensity on their part, referred to earlier, to ape the procedure and the 'law' of the Supreme Court, the administrative officers themselves supervising the courts often imported a large measure of liberalism into the judicial activities of the courts. A circular letter issued by the Resident for Calabar Province in 1929 to his divisional officers stated, quite unequivocally, that in marital cases they 'must have a free hand to make any equitable order when they are appealed to . . . and grant divorce under such conditions as appear to be equitable'.[195] In marital matters it was to be expected that administrative officers with their English background placing heavy emphasis on the rights of the individual, would tend 'to grant divorce to women much more easily than was the case under the traditional judicial system'.[196] Their attitude apparently became contagious as far the chiefs were concerned. Captain W. A. Ross reported in 1920 that the chiefs who sat in the 'native' courts as judges in Oyo Province 'seemed to assume that the granting of divorce on application was the ideal aimed at'.[197] Captain Ross's observation was certainly true of other areas of Southern Nigeria.[198]

By the combined application of criminal sanctions and the 'Repugnancy' doctrine, the provincial and the 'native' courts have left their imprint on the essential culture of Southern Nigeria. They have been instrumental in eliminating from it, with varying degrees of success, elements that would now seem offensive to modern civilised opinion. There is now some justification for the prognosis of the 'native' courts made in 1902, that they would be 'the most widespread, powerful and rapidly acting influence tending to elevate the natives'.[199]

Trial by ordeal was one element of culture that did not meet with the approval of the courts. Although trial by ordeal had its uses in the traditional judicial system, the colonial administration, impressed more by its ruinous effects than by its merits, invoked the powers of the courts to suppress it. Direct action was sometimes taken to break up shrines and other juju places connected with the administration of ordeals.[200] But the law courts were assigned a large role in the attempt to stamp out the practice. It was believed that through the courts, especially the 'native' courts, closely supervised by the administrative officers, the sentiments and social behaviour of a given community could be 'moulded and controlled'.[201] From about the beginning of this century courts of law were involved in the suppression of ordeals, although one should admit that whatever degree of success they achieved in this regard was aided by other enlightening factors. The Ordeal, Witchcraft and Juju Ordinance was promulgated in 1903, spelling out the categories of prohibited ordeals and prescribing penalties.[202] There were evidential problems in prosecuting cases of promotion of ordeals, but prosecutions were nonetheless made and sometimes extreme penalties were exacted.[203]

The courts were relatively more successfully used against slave-dealing and the maintenance of the status of slavery in certain communities. The role of the courts in this connection dated almost from the beginning of the establishment of the first quasi-judicial tribunals in the form of judicial councils at the end of the last century.[204] Within the ambit of the courts came the enforcement of the Slavery Ordinance, 1916, abolishing the legal status of slavery throughout the Protectorate of Nigeria. The records indicate that the provincial and the 'native' courts dealt with many cases of slave-dealing and a related offence, child-stealing.[205] It was at once a reflection of the role of the courts in certain areas of Nigeria and of the intractable nature of the problem that they had to deal with that as late as 1930 the Resident for Ogoja Province reported that 'far too many cases of child stealing and slave dealing' were coming before the provincial court.[206]

The 'Repugnancy' doctrine has played into the hands of administrative officers presiding over the provincial courts or supervising the 'native' courts to mould the traditional culture of Southern Nigeria. It will be recalled that the doctrine was enshrined in the early legislation establishing English judicial process and English law in Nigeria, and it was to the effect that a customary law to be applied and enforced in the British-established courts (including the 'native' courts) must be such that it was not 'repugnant to justice, equity and good conscience' or, in the phraseology of the Native Courts Ordinance, 1914, 'opposed to natural morality and humanity'. The application of the doctrine has been described as the idealistic approach to judicial administration.[207] Simply because in the colonial days all the judges of the provincial courts and all the administrative officers supervising the working of the 'native' courts were Englishmen born and bred in a different cultural milieu, this judicial approach has been the one most often applied by administrative officers consciously or unconsciously.[208] In being called upon to pronounce on the equity or otherwise of indigenous customary law and practices, they inevitably brought their English background into play. For, if one may echo Sir Frederick Pollock,[209] the only justice and equity they knew was English justice and equity.

It would be tedious to enumerate the instances when the 'native' courts applied the 'Repugnancy' doctrine to particular cases, some of them reaching up to the Supreme Court. The provincial courts were no less conscious of the doctrine. Thus the provincial court at Calabar once considered it 'contrary to British equity' to force a husband to put his wife into the fattening house or to force a woman against her wish to be compulsorily fattened.[210] It was similarly held in *Ekpenyong Edet v. Nyon Essien* (1932) to be repugnant to natural justice and equity to allow a man lay claim to the child of another merely because his 'dowry' paid on the woman bearing the child for the other man had not been repaid.[211] This judicial view, reforming customary marital practice in South-eastern Nigeria, was upheld by the divisional court of the Supreme Court at Calabar, and, interestingly, formed the subject matter of a circular letter to all senior administrative officers in Southern Nigeria. It was intended that the court's view on the case should guide them 'when dealing with cases of this kind'.[212]

The 'Repugnancy' doctrine was not consistently applied or rather the courts did not view with iconoclastic eyes all that was indigenous or customary. The traditional practice of levirate, for instance, was upheld in a number of cases up to the level of the Supreme Court.[213] But in spite of the inconsistencies in the application of the doctrine, on the whole, it was a convenient tool in the hands of judges and administrators 'for the refashioning of certain outdated rules of customary law', and, generally, the results were 'salutary and enlightening'.[214]

A noteworthy variant of the application of the doctrine notice-able especially in the records of the 'native' courts and administra-tive reports was the propensity among administrative officers reviewing cases from the 'native' courts to grant petitions for divorce based upon absence of true consent to marriage contract. While the consent of the parents of both parties to a marriage was essential to a valid marriage, in the traditional society the consent of the parties themselves was not a legal essential.[215] A girl could, in fact, be forcibly conveyed to her prospective husband's house. Again, with the necessary consent between two families a child might be 'betrothed' to a man and be subsequently married to him on her reaching marriageable age. In some communities a child might be given in marriage, the husband taking care of the child-wife under his roof until she was old enough to perform her marital obligations.[216]

Under the supervision of British administrative officers the 'native' courts tended to upset these customary practices, and in particular frown upon child marriage.[217] Occasional circular letters from provincial headquarters on the subject of customary marriage practices were apt to reinforce this development.[218]

One still comes across instances of child marriage and of marriage without the consent of one of the parties, but there is no doubt that the attitude of the courts has brought about a modifica-tion of traditional marriage practices. A recent investigation of the Ibo customary law indicates that in principle at present there can be no valid customary law marriage without the consent of the prospective spouses.[219] Among the Yoruba, the courts and society take the view that a woman is free to repudiate a contract of marriage where her true consent has not been obtained. In *Alice Folashade v. Ibitayo*, (1962), tried at the Grade B Customary court, Ilesha,[220] the plaintiff was promised to the son of the defendant when she was young. She now sought the aid of the court to free herself from the contract of marriage which her father had sup-posedly entered into on her behalf. She indicated her objection to her would-be husband, and the court found no difficulty in nullifying a contract which 'she has not ratified . . . now that she has some sense'. Part of the *ratio* in that decision was that it was 'contrary to custom for the parents to give consent [to marriage] on behalf of the daughter'. That reasoning is, indeed, a serious departure from the true traditional practice. It is a measure of the modification which society is accepting in its indigenous laws and marriage customs.

It would be extremely difficult (and, in the view of the present writer, historically false) to attempt to quantify or determine the exact role of the courts in socio-cultural change in Southern Nigeria. Socio-cultural change, as it was mentioned earlier, has been a product of many concurring and interacting factors. Reference was made to the main agencies of the phenomenon, some of which, like Western education or Christian missionary influence, would appear to have been more pervasive than the law and the courts in their impact on Southern Nigeria. But the fact of the interaction of the various factors of change is not in doubt, and it would be unrealistic to attempt to delimit the extent of each. In the growth of individualism, for instance, where does one draw the line between the influence, say, of Western education, foreign travel, Christian missionaries, and of the law and the courts which provide the atmosphere in which the individual could assert himself and have his rights safeguarded? It is clear that there can be no mathematical formula covering all cases; the impact of each of these and other factors would vary from one person to another.

One point shat should be emphasised about law and the courts is that they have one quality which some other factors of change do not seem to have possessed. They bear the stamp of authority and were an embodiment of some powers of sanction acquired by the colonial rulers. In whatever areas of life the courts seem to have imported a modification of the socio-cultural pattern of behaviour, either by their decisions in civil disputes, by the application of criminal sanctions, or by the enforcement of colonial regulations, they were, by their fiat, underlining the fact of change. This is so even when such a change was prompted or considerably influenced by factors operating outside the courts. In this mode of operation of the combined forces of the law and the courts lies perhaps their unique contribution to socio-cultural change in Southern Nigeria. It is not inconsistent with this view of their role that they have, on occasions, operated against change. By their fiat, the courts in their conservative vein have tended 'to reinforce some of the traditional rules making for the stability of the indigenous social structure under the impact of new forces of change'.[221] It is a significant reflection of the recognition of the place of law and the courts in social change that in the 1920s when the need for change in marital practices was felt in many communities (no doubt as a result of the impact of factors operating outside the court rooms), the colonial administration was besought to empower the 'native' courts to pass and enforce new rules. This was the report given by Sir H. Moorhouse as Lieutenant-Governor of Southern Nigeria after a tour of the various provinces early in 1925.[222] Altogether it is fair to say that the courts, in both their 'progressive' and conservative veins, have influenced the direction of social change.

Finally, it would appear that the 'native' courts have contributed more to socio-cultural change in Southern Nigeria than the provincial courts. For one thing, they were far more numerous. By 1947 there were 1,255 of them in the territory.[223] In an area like Ogoja Province there was one court per 4,284 of the population, reaching down to the sub-clan level.[224] For another, because the 'native' courts exercised jurisdiction over the bulk of the population, they touched on the lives of the ordinary citizens more directly than the other categories of courts.

Mention should also be made of the rule-making proclivity of the 'native' courts as judicial institutions – a fact which distinguished them from the provincial courts and the Supreme Court. It was a peculiarity of the 'native' courts which tended to enhance their power to influence socio-cultural change that they were regarded not merely as judicial institutions, but also as 'civilizing agents'. Under the supervision of British administrative officers, they made rules – usually backed by criminal sanctions – on matters touching on various aspects of the life of their areas of jurisdiction, ranging from birth and death registration to the cleaning of towns, maintenance of markets and slaughter houses, and the regulation of marriage practices.[225] It may not be easy to generalise about the effectiveness of such rules, but they were known to have been vigorously enforced at least in some places,[226] with varying degrees of success in the achievement of their objectives.

Notes

1 NAI, CSO 26/2, 12723, II, 'Oyo Province, Annual Report, 1924'.
2 NAI, CSO 26/3, 23610/S.514, 'Edema Arubi: Complaint by Against the Resident, Warri Province'.

3 NAI, CSO 26/3, 21496, II, 'Comments and Decisions of Residents on the Jurisdiction of the Supreme Court'.
4 NAI, CSO 26/2, 12723, I, 'Oyo Province: Annual Report, 1923'.
5 NAI, CSO 20/2/NC 54/14, Speed to Lugard, 1 April 1915.
6 NAI, CSO 26/1, 09876, Combe to Thomson, 15 January 1925.
7 F. A. Van der Meulen, 'Justice in Nigeria: The Provincial Courts', *The Times*, London, 9 September 1932.
8 E. U. Udoma, 'Law and British Administration in South-Eastern Nigeria: An Analytical Study', Unpublished PhD thesis, Trinity College, Dublin, 1944, chs 5, 18.
9 NAI, CSO 26/2, 11857, IV, 'Warri Province: Annual Report 1926'.
10 NAE, Cal Prof 4/6/9.
11 *Ibid.*
12 HCA, Lagos, 'Record Book: Appeals from Provincial Courts'.
13 NAE, Cal Prof 5/8/474.
14 NAE, Cal Prof 5/5/511.
15 McNaughton rules are the summary of the advice given by the judges to the House of Lords in the *McNaughton's Case* (1843). One Daniel McNaughton (also spelled McNaghten or M'Naghten) murdered the private secretary of Sir Robert Peel, but was acquitted on the ground of insanity. The acquittal sparked off a serious controversy in the House of Lords, and hence the opinion of the judges was sought. The judges' answers have generally been regarded as the rules of the common law on the subject of insanity. They are as follows:

    (i) Everyone is presumed to be sane until the contrary is proved.
    (ii) It is a defence to a criminal prosecution for the accused to show that he was labouring under such a defect of reason, due to disease of the mind, that either he did not know the nature and quality of his act, or, if he did know this, that he did not know that he was doing wrong.
    (iii) Where a man commits a criminal act under an insane delusion, he is under the same degree of responsibility as he would have been on the facts as he imagined them to be.

16 NAE, Aba Dist 1/12/20.
17 Olayimika Alakija, 'Notes on the Provincial Courts Ordinance', *The African Messenger*, 14 September 1922.
18 NAE, Cal Prof 5/14/13.
19 NAE, Cal Prof 5/15/11.
20 O. Alakija, *The African Messenger*, 14 September 1922.
21 HCA, Lagos, 'Record Book: Appeals from Provincial Courts'.
22 NAE, Cal Prof 4/6/9.
23 NAE, Ben Dist 13/5, 'Annual Report: Benin Division, Benin Province, 1917'; NAI, Ben Prof 7/2/9, 'Benin Province, Annual Report, 1923'; 'Fugar Native Council Rules', No. 1, 1908, *Southern Nigeria Gazette*, August 1908; NAE, Kwale Dist 1/812/1; NAI, Abe Prof 1, ABP 445.
24 NAE, Cal Prof 5/15/12.

25 NAE, Oki Dist 3/4/2.
26 NAE, Cal Prof 4/10/16.
27 O. Alakija, *The African Messenger*, 14 September 1922.
28 NAI, CSO 26/3, 26359, Secretary, Southern Provinces to colonial secretary, Lagos, 12 May 1932, enclosed petition by Herbert Aladeshulu.
29 NAI, CSO 1/32, 114, Cameron to Sir Philip Cunliffe-Lister, 9 July 1932, enclosure.
30 NAE, Cal Prof 5/12/761.
31 NAE, Og Prof 2/1/2640.
32 NAI, J136/1927; NAI, CSO 26/2, 11857, XI; NAE, Cal Prof 5/18/115.
33 NAE, Cal Prof 5/18/115.
34 NAE, Cal Prof 4/4/39.
35 NAE, Cal Prof 5/15/11.
36 Compare NAI, CSO 26/2, 11875, 'Abeokuta Province, Annual Report, 1923–1931'; NAI, CSO 26/2, 12723, VII, 'Annual Report, Oyo Province, 1929'.
37 NAI, CSO 26/2, 09501, 'Annual Report, Owerri Province, 1922'.
38 CO 657/13, 'Report on the Working of the Native courts in the Southern Provinces', Sessional paper, No. 31, 1924.
39 NAI, Ije Prof 4, J 490, 'Annual Report, Ijebu Province, 1933'.
40 NAI, CSO 26/2, 06003, 'Annual Report, Ogoja Province, 1921'.
41 J. C. Anene, *Southern Nigeria in Transition*, Cambridge, 1966; O. Ikime, *Niger Delta Rivalry*, London, 1969; A. E. Afigbo, *The Warrant Chiefs*, London, 1972; J. A. Atanda, *The New Oyo Empire*, London, 1973; P. A. Igbafe, 'Benin Under British Administration, 1897–1938', Unpublished PhD thesis, University of Ibadan, 1967.
42 Afigbo, *The Warrant Chiefs*, p. 181.
43 C. T. Lawrence, *Memorandum as to the Origin and Causes of the Recent Disturbances in the Owerri and Calabar Provinces*, Lagos, 1930, p. 21.
44 A. E. Afigbo, 'The Warrant Chief System in Eastern Nigeria, 1900–1929', PhD thesis, University of Ibadan, 1964, pp. 231–4.
45 Afigbo, *The Warrant Chiefs*, p. 316.
46 NAI, CSO 26/2 11679, IV, 'Onitsha Province, Annual Report 1926'.
47 Afigbo, *The Warrant Chiefs*, p. 186.
48 *Ibid.*, p. 180.
49 CO 657/13, 'Report on the Working of the Native courts in the Southern Provinces', Sessional paper, No. 31, 1924, pp. 3–7; NAI, Ben Dist 13/5, 'Annual Report, Benin Division, Benin Province, 1917'; NAI, CSO 26/2, 11857: 'Annual Report, Warri Province, 1929'; NAE, Aba Dist 1/28/12.
50 Afigbo, *The Warrant Chiefs*, p. 189.
51 NAI, CSO 26/2, 11679 IV, 'Onitsha Province, Annual Report, 1926'.
52 NAE, Aba Dist 1/28/12.
53 NAI, CSO 21/169, 485, 'Annual Report, Ogoja Province, 1920–1921'; NAI, Ijaw (W) 1, C2/1; NAI, CSO 26/2, 09488, 'Calabar

Province, Annual Report, 1922'. Afigbo, 'Revolution and Reaction in Eastern Nigeria', *Journal of the Historical Society of Nigeria*, iii, 3 December 1966, p. 544.

54 *Report of the Commission of Inquiry Appointed to Inquire into the Disturbances in the Calabar and Owerri Provinces, December 1929*, Lagos, 1930, para. 322.

55 NAI, CSO 26/2, 11679, VIII, 'Onitsha Province: Annual Report, 1930'.

56 NAI, CSO 26/2, 11857, IV, 'Warri Province, Annual Report, 1926'.

57 NAI, CSO 26/2, 11930, XVI, 'Annual Report, 1943: Owerri Province'.

58 NAI, CSO 26/2, 11857, I, 'Warri Provincial Annual Report for 1923'.

59 NAI, CSO 26/2, 09488, 'Calabar Provincial Annual Report, 1922'.

60 NAI, Ughel Dist, 1126/4, Divisional Officer, Urhobo Division, to native court clerk, Isoko federal court, Ughelli, 2 September 1952.

61 NAI, CSO 21/3464, Comments on the native courts by Sir Hugh Clifford.

62 Lugard, *Native Courts in the Southern Provinces: Memorandum to Political Officers*, Lagos, 1918, pp. 1–2. See also, NAI, CSO 26/2, 09488, 'Calabar Province, Annual Report, 1922'.

63 *Report of the Commission of Inquiry Appointed to Inquire into the Disturbances in the Calabar and Owerri Provinces*, para. 326.

64 NAE, Aba Dist 1/26/322, Divisional Officer, Aba Division to Resident, 28 April 1937.

65 NAE, Aba Dist 1/28/8, 'Comments on the working of the Native courts in the Ibo country' by the Divisional Officer, Aba, October 1919.

66 NAI, Kwale Dist 1, III, 'Annual Report, Aboh Division, 1935'.

67 NAI, CSO 26/3, 31225, 'Intelligence Report on the Ekpoma Village Group of the Ishan Division, Benin Province'; NAE, On Prof 1/9/23; On Prof 1/10/20; NAE, War Prof W. P. 36, I; NAE, Ow Dist, 2/1/149; NAE, Aba Dist 1/26/322; NAE, Og Prof 2/1/1971; NAI, CSO 26/2, 11679, 'Onitsha Province, Annual Report, 1939'.

68 NAE, On Prof 1/9/270.

69 NAI, Ben Prof 9/3/11, 'Native Court Review Book, 1937–1947', entry for 14 April 1937.

70 NAE, On Prof 1/9/1, a case of recovery of debt.

71 NAE, Ishan Div 1, I.D. 215/1, a case of alleged larceny of goods reviewed on 21 October 1936.

72 NAI, Ben Prof 9/3, 11, another case of recovery of debt reviewed on 1 June 1938.

73 NAI, CSO 26/2, 11679, XVI, 'Onitsha Province Annual Report, 1939'.

74 NAE, On Prof 1/9/1.

75 NAI, Ben Prof 9/3, 11, Case reviewed on 9 February 1937.

76 NAE, Ishan Div 1, I.D. 21511; NAE, Ishan Div 1, I.D. 218A; NAE, On Prof 1/9/23, 1/10/20; NAI, Ben Prof 9/3, 11.

77 NAE, Kwale Dist 1, 85, 'Minutes of D.O.'s meeting held at Warri, October 21, 1932'.
78 NAE, Og Prof 2/1/1971, 'Comments by Divisional Officer, Abakaliki Division', dated 10 July 1937.
79 Adebesin Folarin, *The Demise of the Independence of Egbaland*, pts 1 and 2, Lagos, 1916 and 1919.
80 J. A. Atanda, 'The Iseyin-Okeho Rising of 1916: An Example of Socio-Political Conflict in Colonial Nigeria', *Journal of the Historical Society of Nigeria*, IV, 4 June 1969.
81 B. A. Agiri, 'Development of Local Government in Ogbomosho, 1850–1950', Unpublished MA thesis, University of Ibadan, 1966, pp. 102–9.
82 O. Ikime, 'The Anti-Tax Riots in Warri Province, 1927–1928', *Journal of the Historical Society of Nigeria*, iii, 3 December 1966.
83 A. E. Afigbo, 'Revolution and Reaction in Eastern Nigeria'.
84 *Report of the Commission of Inquiry Appointed to Inquire into the Disturbances in the Calabar and Owerri Provinces, December 1929.*
85 *Ibid.*
86 *Nigerian Pioneer*, 18 May 1917; J. A. Atanda, 'The Iseyin-Okeho Rising . . .', pp. 502–9.
87 *Report of the Commission of Inquiry . . . Calabar and Owerri Provinces*, Illustration at the end of the *Report*.
88 Native Courts Ordinances, No. 6, 1914, sec. 21.
89 NAI, CSO 26/2, 09488, 'Calabar Province, Annual Report, 1922'.
90 Obafemi Awolowo, *Path to Nigerian Freedom*, London, 1947, p. 98.
91 *Proceedings Before the Commission of Inquiry into the Disturbances in the Calabar and Owerri Provinces*, Lagos, 1930, p. 792.
92 NAI, CSO 26/2, 12723, II, 'Oyo Province, Annual Report, 1924'.
93 NAI, OyoProf 3/OY 247/143.
94 *Ibid.*
95 NAE, Ishan Div. 1, I.D. 209/2, II.
96 NAI, Min Jus (W) 1/1, 1688, Akinpelu, N.A. police officc, Ibadan to divisional officer, 8 July 1952.
97 *Ibid.*, Evans to divisional officer, 1 December 1940.
98 *Ibid.*
99 *Ibid.*, Akinpelu to divisional officer, Ibadan, 8 July 1952.
100 NAI, CSO 26/2, 12723, II, 'Oyo Province, Annual Report, 1924'.
101 Interview with J. A. Oke-Owo, letter-writer, Mapo, Ibadan, 25 August 1966.
102 *Daily Times*, Lagos, 13 November 1940.
103 Illiterates' Protection Ordinance, No. 7, 1896.
104 Illiterates' Protection Ordinance, No. 4, 1900; No. 14, 1905; No. 5, 1910; No. 24, 1915; No. 3, 1920.
105 Illiterates' Protection Ordinance, No. 5, 1910, sec. 6.
106 *Ibid.*, secs 4, 7.
107 NAI, CSO 20/3, HC 41/15, 'Illiterates' Protection Ordinance'.
108 *Ibid.* See also NAI, Iba Div 1/1, 392, IV.
109 NAI, War Prof 3/12, 22/1930.

110 NAI, Oyo Prof 3/OY 247/113; NAI, IbaDiv 1/1, 392, IV; NAI, Oyo Prof 3/115, 1215–1217.
111 NAI, Ije Prof 1, 669, I.
112 NAE, On Prof 1/9/21; NAE, AbaDist 1/7/9.
113 NAE, On Prof 9/9/6.
114 NAI, War Prof 1, WP 36/D; NAI, War Prof 1, WP 36/A, I, II; NAI, War Prof 1, WP 36, II; NAI, Ishan Div 1, I.D. 204A, II.
115 J. A. Oke-Owo, Interview, 25 August 1966.
116 *Daily Times*, 22 June 1934.
117 NAI, Iba Div 1/1, 392, IV.
118 NAI, Ije Prof 6/15, J82/932, II.
119 *Ibid.*
120 NAI, CSO 26/3, 23610 S.158, 'Illiterates' Protection Ordinance'.
121 Interviews with A. A. Babalola and J. A. Oke-Owo, letter-writers, Ibadan, 25 August 1966.
122 NAI, CSO 26/3, 25166, 'Public Letter-writers, Western Provinces'.
123 For petitions written in this vein, see NAI, OyoProf 3/OY 247/113, OyoProf 3/115 and WarProf 1/WP 36, I.
124 *Lagos Weekly Record*, 18 October 1913.
125 Compare the petitions in NAI, WarProf 1, WP 36, II.
126 NAI, Oyo Prof 3/115/1218.
127 NAI, War Prof 3/12, 22/1930.
128 He once petitioned the Secretary of State for the Colonies over the Crown lease at Forcados, 23 December 1936. NAI, CSO 1/32, 135.
129 NAI, War Prof 1, WP 245, I, Arubi to Senior Resident, Warri, 30 August 1945.
130 Compare *Obodo v. Dolor* (1946), NAE, WarProf 1, WP 36A I, *Stephen Gbodobri v. Keruke and Menetie* (1947), *Ekaeghoro and Megbajino v. Chief Ibobi* (1947), NAE, War Prof 1, WP 36/D.
131 NAI, CSO 26/3, 23610/S. 514, 'Petition of Edema Arubi Against the Resident, Warri Province'.
132 Compare the letter-head of the Olurombi Advocating Secretariat, 1932, NAI, IjeProf 4, J.273, II.
133 'Messrs Adekoya, Bamiloshin & Co', NAI, IbaDiv 1/1, 392, IV.
134 J. A. Oke-Owo, Ibadan, Interview, 25 August 1966.
135 NAI, Ije Prof 1, 3382.
136 NAI, Ije Prof 4, J.273, VI, Suit No. 413/33, Ijebu-Ode native court.
137 NAE, On Prof 1/9/292.
138 NAE, War Prof 1, WP 37, I.
139 Compare the petition over *Ighodaro v. Osayi* (1935), NAI, BenProf 9/5, 3.
140 J. A. Oke-Owo, Ibadan, Interview, 25 August 1966.
141 O. Awolowo, *Path to Nigerian Freedom*, p. 93.
142 NAI, CSO 26/2, 09209, 'Annual Report, Warri Province, 1922'.
143 NAI, CSO 20/3, NC 41/15, Minutes by Lugard to A. G. Boyle on the Illiterates' Protection Ordinance.
144 Complaints against letter-writers were regular topics for discussion in the Egba Native Council between 1932 and 1941. See the minutes

of the council's meetings at the Ake Divisional Record Office, Abeokuta.

145 NAI, Iba Div 1/1, 392, IV, Ojo Onilado and 13 other chiefs to divisional officer, Ibadan, 25 January 1939.
146 *Lagos Daily News*, 3 May 1929.
147 A. D. A. MacGregor, Minute on the operation of letter-writers in the Eastern Provinces, NAI, CSO 20/3, NC 41/15.
148 NAI, CSO 26/3, 09488, 'Calabar Province, Annual Report, 1922'.
149 *Report on the Eastern Provinces by the Secretary for Native Affairs*, Lagos, 1922, p. 15.
150 *Record of Proceedings of a Conference on Administrative Subjects Held November 1929*, Lagos, 1929, pp. 19–20.
151 NAI, CSO 1/32, 110, Cameron to Colonial Office, 23 December 1931, enclosure.
152 NAI, CSO 26/2, 11857, V, 'Warri Province, Annual Report, 1927'; NAI, CSO 26/2, 11679, IV, 'Onitsha Province, Annual Report, 1930'.
153 NAI, CSO 26/3, 50125, 'Land Cases: Functions of Native and Provincial courts', comments by E. B. Dawson.
154 NAI, CSO 21/169, 485, 'Annual Report, Ogoja Province, 1920–1921'.
155 *Report of the Commission of Inquiry . . . Calabar and Owerri Provinces*, para. 324; *Proceedings Before the Commission*, p. 524: evidence of K. A. B. Cochrane; A. E. Afigbo, *The Warrant Chiefs*, p. 286.
156 'The Fatted Interpreters', *Nigerian Daily Telegraph*, 10 February 1931, editorial.
157 CO 657/6–CO 657/27, 'Report on the Supreme Court of Nigeria', 1920–30.
158 NAI, CSO 26/3, 21496, I, F. B. Adams commenting on the jurisdiction of the Supreme Court.
159 CO 583/118, Clifford to Devonshire, 27 March 1923.
160 NAI, CSO 26/3, 21496, I, F. B. Adams commenting on the jurisdiction of the Supreme Court.
161 NAE, Owdist 1/16/48, 1/16/52, 1/10/19; NAE, OnProf 1/9/344, 1/9/266; NAE, CalProf 5/8/491; NAE, DegDist 2/1/2.
162 NAE, OwDist 1/16/48.
163 NAI, CSO 26/2, 11967, IV, 'Ogoja Provincial Annual Report, 1929'.
164 J. C. Anene, *Southern Nigeria in Transition*, pp. 250–79; Afigbo, *The Warrant Chiefs*, pp. 81–112. O. Ikime, *Niger Delta Rivalry*, pp. 168–78.
165 NAE, CSE 1/86/194, 'Structure of Native Institutions in Southern Provinces'.
166 NAI, CSO 26/2, 09723, 'Oyo Province, Annual Report, 1922'; CSO 26/2, 03996, 'Ondo Provincial Annual Report, 1924'; CSO 26/1, 09488, 'Calabar Province: Annual Report, 1922', CSO 26/2, 11930, VI, 'Owerri Province, Annual Report, 1928'; NAI, CSO 26/2, 03316, 'Onitsha Province: Annual Report, 1921'.
167 Almost every annual Provincial report indicated the uses to which local revenues, including those from the courts, were put.

168 NAI, Ije Prof 8/2, Provincial Court, Ijebu-Ode, 'Criminal Record Book, 1906–1908'; NAI, Oyo Prof 8/2/5, 'Criminal Cases: Provincial Court Proceedings, Oyo, 1914–1926'; Oyo Prof 8/2/3, 'Civil and Criminal Cases, Oyo Native Courts, 1904–1918'; NAI, Kuku Div 11/3, 'Criminal Record Book', 1932–1937; NAI, Ughel Dist 11/1, 'Criminal Record Book', 1930–2 and 1947–51.

169 Compare Regulations Made Under the Agriculture Ordinance, No. 4, 1926, NAI, MJ (W) 8/7.

170 NAI, MJ (W) 8/7, 'Ibadan Land Rules'.

171 NAI, Abe Prof 1, ABP 445.

172 Circular letter from secretary, Western Provinces, to all Residents dated 4 January 1951, NAI, KwaleDist 1, 812/1.

173 P. C. Lloyd, *Yoruba Land Law*, London, repr. 1964, pp. 115–276; 308–53; NAI, Ondo Div 7/1, 'Civil Record Book, 1911–1913'; Ije Prof 8/1, 'Criminal Record Book, 1921–1923', Ije Prof 8/2, 'Civil Record Book, 1934–1945'; Oyo Prof 1/1, 1368; Oyo Prof 1/1, 502; Ile Div. 4/1, 'D.O.'s Appeal Court Record Book'.

174 David L. Sills, ed., *International Encyclopaedia of Social Sciences*, New York, n.d., p. 366.

175 On John Austin's view of Law, see Edgar Bodenheimer, *Jurisprudence*, Cambridge, Mass., 1962, pp. 89–102.

176 Native Courts Proclamation, No. 9, 1900, sec. 6; Native Courts Ordinance, No. 3, 1914, sec. 8; Native Courts Ordinance, No. 44, 1933, sec. 10.

177 Native Courts Proclamation, No. 9, 1900, sec. 6; T. O. Elias, *The Nigerian Legal System*, p. 97.

178 NAI, CSO 26/2, 11857, IV, 'Warri Province, Annual Report, 1926'; NAE, CSO 26/3, 27002, 'Report on the Ngbo and Ezengbo Clan, Abakaliki Division, Ogoja Province'; NAI, CSO 26/3, 31216, 'Intelligence Report on the Ijebu Remo District, Ijebu Province'.

179 NAE, CSO 26/3, 27002, 'Report on the Ngbo and Ezengbo Clan'.

180 NAI, CSO 26/3, 29806, 'Intelligence Report on Iwawa and Ndekpo Clans of the Uyo District'.

181 For the role of mission houses in this regard, see J. F. A. Ajayi, *Christian Missions in Nigeria, 1841–91*, London, 1965, pp. 11–114.

182 Afigbo, 'The Warrant Chief System . . .', quoted on p. 350.

183 Afigbo, 'Revolution and Reaction in Eastern Nigeria', pp. 541–2.

184 E. A. Ayandele, *The Missionary Impact on Modern Nigeria, 1842–1914*, London, 1966, p. 334.

185 J. A. Atanda, 'The Iseyin-Okeiho Rising of 1916 . . .', p. 502.

186 NAE, Cal Prof 4/10/16.

187 NAE, On Prof 1/14/243, 'Ibo Law', by C. K. Meek.

188 NAI, CSO 19, XVI, 'The Laws and Customs of the Yoruba Country'.

189 Compare NAI CSO 26/2, 11874, V, 'Ondo Province, Annual Report, 1926'.

190 NAI, CSO 26/2, 11929, XVII, 'Annual Report on the Calabar Province, 1946'.

191 NAI, CSO 26/2, 11930, III, 'Owerri Province, Annual Report for 1925'.

192 N. A. Fadipe, *The Sociology of the Yoruba*, Ibadan, 1970, p. 92.
193 *Ibid.*
194 NAI, Ondo Div 7/3, 'Native Court Judgment Book, 1924'.
195 NAE, Cal Prof 5/11/777.
196 Atanda, 'The Iseyin-Okeiho Rising', p. 502.
197 NAI, CSO 26/2, 12723, VII, 'Annual Report, Oyo Province, 1929'.
198 Compare NAI, BenProf 7/2/10, 'Benin Province, Annual Report, 1924'; NAI, CSO 26/3, 30957, 'Intelligence Report on the Abavo Clan of the Agbor District'.
199 NAE, CSO 1/13, XXVI, 'Annual Report for 1902'.
200 NAE, CSO 1/13, XXVI, Moor to Colonial Office, 22 August 1902; 'Annual Report on the Central Province for the Year 1908' in Lagos, *Annual Reports of the Colony of Southern Nigeria for the Year 1908*, 1909, pp. 407–13; NAI, 'Annual Report on the Eastern Province for the Year Ended 31st December 1911', in *Annual Reports of the Colony of Southern Nigeria for the Year 1911*.
201 NAE, Cal Prof 10/3, III, 'Report on Ordeal of Usere' by W. E. B. Copland-Crawford.
202 The Ordeal, Witchcraft and Juju Ordinance, No. 13, 1905, *Laws of the Colony of Southern Nigeria*, I, pp. 350–2.
203 Compare NAI, CSO 26/1, 06003, 'Annual Report, Ogoja Province, 1921'.
204 Lagos, *Annual Reports for the Year 1899*, pp. 81–3.
205 NAE, Cal Prof 5/6/181; Cal Prof 5/6/290; Cal Prof 5/6/392; Cal Prof 5/8/475; NAI, CSO 26/2, 11967, 'Annual Report, Ogoja Province, 1930'; NAI, Ben Prof 9/3, 11, 'Native Court Review Book, 1937–1947'.
206 NAI, CSO 26/2, 11967, IX, 'Annual Report, Ogoja Province, 1930'.
207 F. A. Ajayi, 'Judicial Approach to Customary Law in Southern Nigeria', Unpublished PhD thesis, London University, 1958, p. 558.
208 *Ibid.*
209 Frederick Pollock, *The Expansion of the Common Law*, London, 1904, p. 133.
210 NAE, Cal Prof 5/9/239, Divisional Officer, Ikot-Ekpene to Resident, Calabar, 1 May 1919.
211 *Nigerian Law Report*, 11, 1932, p. 47.
212 NAI, Ije Prof 1, 669, I, Circular letter from secretary, Southern Provinces, dated 17 February 1938.
213 *In re The Estate of Agboruja* (1949), 19 *Nigerian Law Report* 38; *Aileru and others v. Aribi* (1952), 20 *Nigerian Law Report* 46.
214 T. O. Elias, ed., *Law and Social Change*, Lagos, 1972, p. 266.
215 Akinola Aguda, *Select Law Lectures and Papers*, Ibadan, 1971, p. 85; G. C. Okojie, *Ishan Native Laws and Customs*, Lagos, 1960, pp. 101–2.
216 Okojie, *Ishan Native Laws and Customs*, p. 107.
217 R. O. Ekundare, *Marriage and Divorce Under Yoruba Customary Law*, Ile-Ife, 1969, p. 14; NAE, Ishan Div. 1, I.D. 218A containing the following unreported cases reviewed at Ubiaja Native court: *Elujele v. Iyamu, alias, Enigiminie* (1936); *Unuale v. Obagan* (1936), *Owobu*

v. Ugberase (1936); *Unerikpen v. Asore* (1936); *Ugbeni v. Udiase* (1937).

218 Compare NAE, Cal Prof 5/11/777, Circular letter from Resident, Calabar Province, to all divisional officers in the province, dated 12 July 1929.

219 A. B. Kasunmu and J. W. Salacuse, *Nigerian Family Law*, London, 1966, p. 176.

220 Cited in R. O. Ekundare, *Marriage and Divorce Under Yoruba Customary Law*, p. 14.

221 F. A. Ajayi, 'The Judicial Development of Customary Law in Nigeria', Paper read at the Conference on Integration of Customary and Modern Legal Systems, Ibadan, 24–29 August 1964. See also NAE, Cal Prof 5/14/179, 'Report on the Native Courts, Calabar Province, 1924'.

222 NAE, CalProf 5/11/1777, Minutes by Sir H. Moorhouse on 'Native Law of Marriage'.

223 E. A. Keay and S. S. Richardson, *The Native and Customary Courts of Nigeria*, Lagos and London, 1966, p. 35.

224 *Ibid.*

225 'Fugar Native Council Rules, No. 1, 1908', *Southern Nigeria Gazette*, August 1908; NAI, KwaleDist 1/812/1; NAI, Abe Prof 1, ABP 445; NAI, Ben Prof 7/2/9, 'Benin Province Annual Report, 1923'.

226 NAE, Cal Prof 9/1, V, F. S. James to High Commissioner, 8 September 1902; NAE, CSO 1/13, 27, Fosberry to Colonial Office, 30 December 1903; NAI, CSO 26/2, 11929, 'Calabar Province, Annual Report, 1924'; NAI, Ben Prof 8/1, 3, 'Benin City: Oba's Council: Minutes of Meetings, Vol. IV, 1926–1933'.

7 Judicial reforms, 1933-54

Pretence has been a feature of the administration in Nigeria during the last few years, and is a dangerous thing; in this case, a dishonourable thing.

Sir Donald Cameron[1]

Somewhere in West Africa . . . a new African state will be born. It will be strong. Its voice will be listened for. . . . It will have a vital need for counsellors, its own counsellors. Now is the time, and the time is already late, to train them for their work.

The Elliot Commission (1945)[2]

I

Throughout the 1920s the colonial administration did not cease to be concerned about the Nigerian judicial system. The subject of judicial administration bulked large in the correspondence among administrative officers and between the colonial regime in Nigeria on the one hand and the Colonial Office in London on the other.[3] It was also the theme of many official discussions at Residents' conferences in Nigeria and among officials at the Colonial Office. Two official visits were sponsored to Nigeria by the Colonial Office partly or mainly to examine the working of the judicial system in the territory – that of the Hon. W. G. A. Ormsby-Gore in 1926,[4] and later, in 1932, that of H. Grattan Bushe, the assistant legal adviser at the Colonial Office.[5]

A number of proposals for reforms, the details of which we have earlier examined,[6] were also made. Sir Hugh Clifford proposed in 1923 to give the provincial courts 'exclusive and final jurisdiction' in land matters. It was also suggested that the 'native' courts be 'so fostered and developed' that they would be able to handle practically all 'native' cases. In 1931, as we saw, the administration came up with the proposal to establish a Protectorate Court to augment the working of the provincial courts and as a sort of appeal court for the whole protectorate.

The lengthy discussions on the judicial system and the few modifications carried out in the system up to 1931 did not effect any radical change in the mode of administering justice. Colonial officials still thought the provincial court system suitable for the bulk of the Nigerian population and still believed it would be inherently dangerous to give the Supreme Court full rein. Anxious to preserve all that was believed to be best in the indigenous communities and to promote their gradual development under their own guidance along modern lines, in correspondence and at conferences they rehashed with great vigour the old arguments against the Supreme Court system of administering justice: its supposed disintegrating influence; its 'obstructionist' role in local administration; the exploitative activities of lawyers and so forth. Such was the predominant mode of thinking in official circles until Sir Donald Cameron arrived on the Nigerian scene as Governor early in 1931.

II

Sir Donald Cameron brought fresh thinking into the whole question of what should be the relations between the judiciary and the executive in colonial Nigeria, the basic question at the bottom of all efforts at erecting a judicial system for the territory. He was well acquainted with the existing judicial system and the storm of protest that it had engendered. He had earlier spent about ten years, from 1914 to 1924, in the Nigerian Colonial Service. For the first seven of those years, he was the chief secretary to the government. From 1925 to 1931 he served as Governor of Tanganyika, East Africa. There, he said, he worked 'under a freer judicial system'.[7] Somewhere in his career he had developed a philosophy of colonial development – if it may be so called – which ran counter to the Lugardian concept of developing indigenous institutions of a colonial territory without exposing them to 'inimical' external influences.

An ardent believer in the principles of Indirect Rule before he left Nigeria in 1925 for Tanganyika, he surprised the Colonial Office on his arrival in Nigeria in 1931 by embarking on a judicial reform that was considered 'a complete reversal of the principles hitherto governing the administration of justice in Nigeria'.[8] This surprise was all the greater since Cameron in his administration in

Tanganyika deliberately introduced the principles of Indirect Rule or 'Native Administration', as he himself preferred to call it, in the erstwhile German territory. He had also written a series of memoranda on the subject which, long after he left Tanganyika, remained 'the District Officers' Bibles'.[9]

Actually Cameron's stand on the judicial system in Nigeria should not have occasioned any surprise at the Colonial Office if his work as the Governor of Tanganyika had been sufficiently appreciated at the time. A close examination of his administration in Tanganyika reveals the man's personality and his views on colonial development.[10] He was one of those rare colonial administrators who construed their task as preparing for a future political objective. Nowhere did Cameron state explicitly that that objective was political independence; but he recognised the fact of colonial 'political evolution' and, by the same token, the duty of a colonial administration consciously to do all it could to foster it.[11] His devotion to the principles of native administration was not to make a fetish of native administrations as ends in themselves; native administrations were to Cameron temporary measures or, as he put, 'stepping stones' in the effort to train the people to stand by themselves.[12] Native administrations were therefore growing institutions which must be progressively adapted to the needs and the political development of the people. It was typical of Cameron that he initiated in Tanganyika, as no other governor did in British colonial Africa, a Federation of Native Administrations.[13]

It is easy to wax lyrical about the boldness of Cameron's ideas regarding colonial development and the tremendous energy with which he put some of them into operation in Tanganyika. He gave the territory a legislative council which, although dominated by non-Africans, played an active role in the running of its affairs. He established a labour policy in the country that was unparalleled in the other British African colonies.[14] Under him the education of Africans became a top priority in the scheme of development.[15] One of the criticisms levelled against him was that he put an 'undue emphasis upon the rapid development of the African population at the expense of the more profitable development' of the country's resources through the agency of non-Africans.[16] Altogether Cameron gave to Tanganyika's development an impetus which had far-reaching effects.

There is no space here to examine Cameron's activities in Nigeria in other spheres than the administration of justice. The

impact of his energy and of his innovating spirit was felt in economic, administrative and legislative matters. Perhaps it may be true
to say, as Sir Alan Burns claimed, that among colonial administrators, 'no abler official has ever served Nigeria'.[17]

Cameron returned from Tanganyika to Nigeria in 1931 with a
concept of colonial development that one could describe as dynamic. He made it plain to the Colonial Office that he was more
concerned with the future evolution of Nigeria than with maintaining past administrative distinctions.[18] While no 'comprehensive
forecast' of the political evolution of the territory could be made,
he said on one occasion, it was reasonable to surmise that no part or
parts of it would develop into separate, self-contained political and
economic units. Hence 'wisdom lies in the policy of treating the
country as a whole, openly and without any mental reservations'.[19]

The way the concept of native administration was being put
into practice in Nigeria received Cameron's censure. A great
amount of anxiety had been displayed in the past, he said, to save
the 'prestige' of the native administrations. There was the danger
of attaching greater importance to the machinery than to the people
it was devised to serve. There was also the danger of erecting the
native administrations into feudal oligarchies, 'prepared to be
benevolent and paternal to the native so long as he will stay put and
not raise envious eyes toward a full share in all that western
civilization can give'.[20] The products of the government and the
mission schools, because they were becoming enlightened, would
not, of course, be faithful to a native administration that was
reactionary and repressive. The inevitable result would be that
native administrations, the whole political edifice administrative
officers were keen on maintaining, would 'crumble to the ground'.

Cameron's views on African customary law and the 'native'
courts were in keeping with his general belief in progressive
colonial administration. He did not believe that customary law was
capable of developing 'of its own inherent qualities' a code of law
that would serve the purpose of the various communities as they
became progressively enlightened. There would be a tendency for
customary law to borrow more and more from statutory or English
common law. This tendency, in his view, should not be impeded
by attaching greater importance to the customary than to the
statutory law of the country.

As to the 'native' courts that administered the customary law,
'they must be modernised to suit the requirements of a more

enlightened community' – if they were to be saved. Cameron went so far as to suggest that more and more the 'native' courts 'must swing to the system of justice administered in the European courts'.[21] To the question whether such a development might not destroy 'tribal institutions', his answer was unequivocal: 'If tribal institutions cease to be acceptable to an enlightened community, they must be destroyed and it were better that they should be destroyed.'[22]

The provincial court system Cameron denounced in no uncertain terms.[23] First, the system was 'too Executive ridden'. He ridiculed the idea, which was the basis of the provincial court system, that the administrative officer, because he was presumed to be acquainted with native law and custom, was better fitted to administer justice among the 'natives' than the trained judges of the English-style courts. Justice administered in this executive fashion, according to Cameron, was not justice, but a sort of 'parental correction'.[24] Second, the twenty-two provincial courts in Nigeria were not coordinated, except in so far as they submitted periodical judicial returns to the Supreme Court. Each one was 'a law unto itself'. There was thus a centrifugal tendency inherent in the provincial court system that was out of keeping with Cameron's desired policy of developing the country as one political entity. His third and fourth objections to the provincial courts were that there was no right of appeal from them and lawyers were barred from them. Not least important: 'The broad line which should be drawn between the administrative and the judicial capacities of Administrative Officers is in some instances becoming obscure.' Above the 'native' courts Cameron wanted in the protectorate 'a system of justice as completely divorced from the Executive as the Supreme Court is divorced from the Executive'.

Such was Cameron the man, and such the moving spirit behind the judicial reform of 1933. One is struck by his sense of realism even if – as we shall see presently – his actual achievements in judicial reform belied his progressive views. More than some of his predecessors, he realised that attempts at keeping the indigenous societies uncontaminated by 'foreign' influences, under the guise of Indirect Rule, were certain to fail as they were pretentious. The wishful thinking that indigenous societies could be preserved in their pristine form underlay much of the reasoning behind the institution of the provincial courts and, of course, the policy of keeping out lawyers from the protectorate. It was because Cameron could rise above all this that he took educated Africans into his confidence to a degree never before demonstrated by any chief executive. To him educated Africans were partners in the colonial enterprise.[25] The concept of the future development of Nigeria as one entity, which was the hallmark of Cameron's administration, served as a useful tonic in the country's political advancement.

As if to belittle the importance of Cameron's role in the judicial reform of 1933, a Lagos newspaper implied that the reform was inevitable at the time it was undertaken.[26] True, there was talk of judicial reforms in some other parts of British colonial Africa in the early 1930s. The Colonial Office in the late 1920s and early 1930s seemed to show concern about the state of administration of justice in some African territories. In January 1933, six ordinances were passed on the Gold Coast (Ghana) to reform the colony's legal and judicial systems.[27] One feature of the reform was that Ashanti and the Northern Territories were open to lawyers at last. Grattan Bushe, the assistant legal adviser at the Colonial Office, headed a full commission inquiring into the administration of justice in the British territories in East Africa.[28] There is no evidence, however, to suggest that these developments had any direct bearing on the judicial reforms in Nigeria. In fact, the tendency at the Colonial Office, supposedly the coordinating centre of all overseas administration, was, in practice, to treat each colony as if it had to follow its own distinctive line of development without much regard for the events in other areas.

As a variant of the same argument about the inevitability of the political reform, a Nigerian legal scholar has suggested that by 1931, the judiciary had broken down both in Nigeria and on the Gold Coast (Ghana), and, consequently, the Colonial Office had no alternative but to remove in the direction of reforms.[29] To the Colonial Office, so runs the argument, the West African courts had demonstrated their inefficiency, and the incompetence of most of the judges had been established. Witness the reversals which the Supreme Court of Nigeria suffered at the hand of the Privy Council in London in such cases as the *Amodu Tijani* case (1915–21) and the *Eshugbayi Eleko* case (1925–31).[30] One instance of the alleged incompetence of the Supreme Court of the Gold Coast was *Dr Knowles* case (1928).[31] These factors of the breakdown of the judiciary and of the incompetence of the judges, we are told, 'provided the main stimulus for the 1931–1934 administrative and judicial reforms'.[32]

How far had the judiciary in Nigeria broken down by 1931? There is no indication of a breakdown in the judiciary if what is being suggested is that the judicial machine failed to function. Throughout the discussion on the judicial reform among officials both in Nigeria and at the Colonial Office, there was never a hint that the judicial machine was working under any strain. Nor was incompetence of the judges ever offered as an argument in favour of reform. Admittedly, the judges in Nigeria, especially those of the provincial courts, did show evidence of incompetence. But the fact of their incompetence attracted no attention at the Colonial Office. Nor was it regarded necessarily as a mark of incompetence that some of the judgments of the Nigeria Supreme Court were reversed by the Privy Council. Up till the time of Cameron's arrival on the Nigerian scene, official discussion regarding judicial reform centred, not on the breakdown of the existing judicial machine, but on what little improvements to make in it *while its component parts were to be retained.* As late as 1932 top-ranking officials at the Colonial Office shared the same view.

It is difficult to escape the conclusion that the basis of the judicial reform of 1933 was ideological, representing a shift of focus away from a paternalistic, almost static, view of government to one embodying a developmental concept. It is not true that Cameron undertook the reform in a bid to win the confidence of the lawyers in Nigeria who, by 1931, were said to have become 'so bruised and embittered by more than a decade of fruitless pressure for judicial changes and reforms, and had, in the process become so disillusioned and desperate that something simply had to give'.[33] One only needs to put into perspective his whole governorship in Nigeria and the ideas that motivated his actions to appreciate that the reform was not born of expediency.

The moving spirit behind the reform of 1933 was, undoubtedly, Cameron. Significantly, he had been influencing policy at the Colonial Office even before his appointment as Governor of Nigeria.[34] He was fortunate to have found, after some initial difficulties, an atmosphere at the Colonial Office that was conducive to the propagation of reformist ideas.

III

Cameron's judicial reform proposals provoked strong reactions. The essence of the reform was to abolish the provincial courts and give a freer scope for the legal profession than hitherto in the judicial system. His immediate subordinates, the Lieutenant-Governors for the Northern and the Southern Provinces, thought that the reform proposals were too radical for Nigeria's needs. They rehashed some of the old arguments against the supreme court and the lawyers, demonstrating an almost implacable hostility towards any judicial reform that would take administration of justice from the purview of the executive arm of government.[35]

The Lieutenant-Governors had their sympathisers at the Colonial Office. An official there, G. Hazlerigg, drew up a memorandum in which he raised five objections to Cameron's proposals. Among these objections were the extra expenditure that the reform would entail, 'the disintegrating effect of the proposed reform upon the present native political and social organizations in the North', and the effect upon 'the authority and influence of the Administrative Service'.[36] The Permanent Under-Secretary of State for the Colonies, Sir Samuel Wilson, while giving some support to Cameron's judicial proposals, advised caution. There were other considerations besides the mere desire for reforms: the cost of effecting the reforms and 'the possible consequences of increased litigation'.[37] Lord Passfield, the Secretary of State for the Colonies, was himself concerned about the possible effects of Cameron's judicial reform on the administrative arm of the colonial government in Nigeria. He was 'definitely of the opinion' that district officers should 'continue to exercise powers of summary jurisdiction in minor cases'.[38] He had misgivings about divesting political officers of judicial powers.

The only ardent supporter of Cameron's reform proposals at the Colonial Office was Grattan Bushe, who had visited Nigeria officially in January 1932. 'I do not think anyone can seriously suggest that the present condition of affairs can continue, and if we do not alter it today, we shall be forced to alter it tomorrow', Bushe wrote in support of his proposals in May 1932.[39] Until the Colonial Office finally sanctioned the judicial reform proposals in November 1932, Bushe continued to give unreserved support, defending the proposals at every opportunity.

It would appear that the opinions of those who stood in opposition to Cameron's reform inside and outside the Colonial Office had their impact on the final form the judicial reform took. At the end of the two meetings held at the Colonial Office in October 1932 on the judicial reform proposals, what emerged was a work of compromise.[40] Apparently as a concession to those who opposed the reform on financial grounds, Cameron was made to agree that no additional fully qualified judges would be appointed to the judiciary in Nigeria. From this concession it followed that administrative officers would be appointed judges of the new magistrates' courts which Cameron proposed to establish in place of the provincial courts. Another concession to political considerations was that the vast majority of the 'native' courts were not to be linked with the higher English-style courts by way of appeals. Although Cameron won his point on the question of the appearance of legal practitioners before the latter category of courts, this was perhaps because he explained that the concession to lawyers did not amount to much.[41] As will be shown presently, the scope given to the practice of the legal profession, though greater than before 1933, was not unlimited.

The following was the final form the judicial reform took.[42] In place of the provincial courts in the protectorate were established magistrates' courts and a High Court. The High Court, at the top of the hierarchy of courts in the protectorate, consisted of a chief judge, judges and assistant judges. The High Court did not exercise jurisdiction in certain matters: probate, divorce and matrimonial causes. The court also had no original jurisdiction in land disputes, although it had appellate jurisdiction in such disputes if they were transferred to it from the 'native' courts.

The magistrates' courts established throughout the protectorate were courts of summary jurisdiction. Any fit and proper person could be appointed a magistrate and legal qualification was not deemed essential. Like the High Court the magistrates' courts had no original jurisdiction in land matters. They entertained appeals from certain categories of 'native' courts and could also transfer cases from such courts either to themselves or to other 'native' courts.

The 'native' courts remained at the bottom of the judiciary in the protectorate. Over the majority of these courts administrative officers continued to exercise their control and it was in the 'native' courts that original jurisdiction in land matters was vested. There was no appeal against the decision of a 'native' court in a land dispute unless the value of the land in question was over ₦400.[43] In the few places where appeals were allowed from the 'native' courts to a higher court in criminal cases, the administrative officer was permitted to appear before the higher court to show cause why the appeal should or should not be allowed.[44]

A significant feature of the 1933 judicial reform was a somewhat cautious extension of the jurisdiction of the Supreme Court in to the protectorate.[45] The original jurisdiction of the court in the protectorate was limited to a few categories of cases, including cases arising from some fourteen special ordinances. The court, however, exercised appellate jurisdiction in all cases tried before the inferior courts, including the 'native' courts in some areas.[46]

The Supreme Court was, in turn, now linked with the West African Court of Appeal.[47] This court had a rather chequered history. Since the Commonwealth West African countries were under the same influence of the English common law, an attempt was made to establish a common court of appeal for all. The West African Court of Appeal, established in 1867, was such a court and functioned only for some time. It was formally disestablished in 1874, but revived again in 1928 with its jurisdiction limited to Gambia, Sierra Leone and the Gold Coast (Ghana).[48] On 1 April 1934, Nigeria formally came under the court's jurisdiction and remained linked with it until 1954. She withdrew her membership of the court, thus signalling its gradual disintegration. On gaining her political independence in 1957, Ghana also severed her connections with the court.

Although legal practitioners were permitted to appear before all the courts in Nigeria except the 'native' courts, they were still limited in the practice of their profession. So real was the theoretical limitation on the practice of their profession that Cameron himself expected considerable opposition to his reforms from the lawyers.[49] The old fears about lawyers 'bleeding the ignorant masses to death' in legal fees continued to govern official thinking.

It should be noted that the magistrates' courts and the High Court were not given original jurisdiction in land cases which were believed to give lawyers their 'chief profits'. Lawyers were to be involved in land cases only in so far as such cases came to the magistrates' courts or the high court on appeal from the 'native' courts. Even then they would appear only under certain conditions.

As if to ensure that not many land cases went from the 'native' courts to the higher courts on appeal, a new political machinery was established which, it was hoped, would deal with most, if not all, land disputes. The Inter-Tribal Boundaries Settlement Ordinance, No. 49, 1933, empowered any district officer to inquire into and decide any dispute between two or more communities arising over the boundaries between them. The officer could sit with assessors. Provision was made for official registration of the settlement arrived at by the district officer in a boundary dispute. No decision arrived at by the district officer in a boundary dispute was subject to review by a judicial body. In this way the administration, hopefully, took away a big proportion of land disputes from the purview of the Supreme Court and from the lawyers. Cameron himself confidently believed that 'there would be no work available for advocates on land question arising between natives, and, although, in theory, they would be allowed to appear in civil and criminal cases in the Magistrates' courts and in the High Court of the Protectorate . . . there would, in fact, be little occupation for them in purely native cases'.[50] As we shall see, things did not work out as Cameron anticipated.

Instead of totally prohibiting lawyers from practising in the protectorate, the wiser step was taken of regularising their professional activities. The Legal Practitioners' Ordinance, No. 57, 1933, set up a committee, known as the Legal Practitioners' Committee, for this purpose. The committee consisted of two officials, the Attorney-General and the Solicitor-General. There were three unofficial members – legal practitioners of at least ten years' experience in Nigeria – nominated by the unofficial Bar. Each unofficial member was to hold office for one year.

The committee was essentially a disciplinary body, empowered to examine complaints of professional misconduct brought against legal practitioners. After hearing both the complainant and the accused legal practitioner, the committee prepared a report for the consideration of the Supreme Court. At the consideration of the report by the court, both the accused legal practitioner and the complainant could be represented by counsel.

As if to say that the committee process might prove cumbersome the ineffective, the Supreme Court was empowered to admonish any legal practitioner, suspend him from practising, or even strike his name off the roll of barristers – without any previous inquiry by or reference to the Legal Practitioners' Committee. Any single judge of the Supreme Court was similarly empowered to suspend a practising lawyer pending reference to and confirmation by the Supreme Court.[51]

Like most works of compromise, the judicial reform of 1933 tried to be all things to all men. The proponents of the provincial court system could take consolation from the fact that a large proportion of the magistrates' courts in the protectorate would be manned by administrative officers and that the vast majority of the 'native' courts – the nerve-centres of 'Native Administrations' – were still under executive control, insulated from the central judiciary. Even in outward appearance the new magistrates' courts would be similar to the provincial courts. Cameron took pains to emphasise that the new courts 'should have a much simpler form of procedure than the Supreme Court' to reflect the humble environments in which they were to operate.[52]

George Graham Paul, speaking as the commercial member for Calabar in the Legislative Council during the debate on the judicial reform in 1933, expressed disappointment at the scant substance of the judicial reform. The reform, he said, only brought a proliferation of courts into the protectorate that would serve little useful purpose in the administration of justice.[53]

To most educated Africans Cameron's judicial reform, however, represented a real improvement in the administration of justice. On the occasion when Graham Paul condemned the reform as offering very little, Eric Olawolu Moore, the second African unofficial member for Lagos in the Legislative Council, welcomed it as making 'a distinct advance in the judicial administration of this country'.[54] The avenue the reform opened to the practising lawyers in Nigeria, in the opinion of a Lagos newspaper, 'is a boon to the country'.[55] Another newspaper that was very critical of Cameron's economic and other policies, praised the judicial reform as standing much to his credit. The reform, in the view of the newspaper, represented 'undoubtedly a great advance on the system in the past'.[56]

IV

Cameron left Nigeria finally on Saturday, 15 June 1935 – too early to see how his judicial reform worked out in practice. The various ordinances effecting it did not come into force until 1 April 1934.

Cameron himself thought of the judicial reform in modest terms. 'It may not be possible to go all the way at once', he declared in February 1932, 'but it will be possible, I ardently hope, to go some of the way.'[57] The judicial reform, no doubt, went some way but probably not as far as the Governor's bold views on colonial development would lead one to expect.

As late as 1940 there were only thirteen professionally qualified magistrates in Nigeria to man the magistrates' courts. It had been found necessary to empower one hundred and ten administrative officers to act as magistrates to deal with cases arising among the estimated twenty million people of the protectorate.[58] Cameron's successor, Sir Bernard H. Boudillon, noted that for the foreseeable future, the bulk of the minor cases tried before the magistrates' courts would be tried by administrative officers holding judicial positions. Given Cameron's avowed distaste for administrative officers holding judicial positions, the swamping of the magistrates' courts with administrative officers was an ironic development. Even the High Court Bench was occasionally filled from the ranks of administrative officers.[59]

To argue that the reason for this development was financial[60] is only half the truth. The appointment of administrative officers to fill the new judicial posts seems to have been a matter of policy which started with Cameron himself. In July 1933 he wrote the Colonial Office that it would be highly desirable to appoint as judges of the High Court 'officers of wide administrative experience who have the necessary legal qualifications'.[61]

One is prompted to ask why Cameron put such a premium on administrative experience as being a desirable qualification for a judge serving in the protectorate. The emphasis on administrative experience is particularly remarkable because it was the same Cameron who, on an earlier occasion, played down the importance of administrative experience in a judge. The essential thing in a judicial officer, he wrote, was that he should 'have the training and the capacity to arrive at a conclusion on a judicial question on the evidence which is placed before the Court and on that evidence alone'.[62] The conclusion seems inescapable that in spite of his reforming zeal, Cameron really did not, or could not, break with the past.

At the same time it would be wrong to argue that the new courts, because administrative officers presided over them, were the old provincial courts in a new garb.[63] Such an argument misses the essential point about the reform of 1933. Lawyers were allowed to appear before the magistrates' courts and the high court, and there was a channel of appeal that went even beyond the supreme court. Administrative officers, for political and financial reasons, might continue to preside over the new courts; but that fact little mattered as long as litigants and accused persons could be represented by counsel and could appeal against a magistrate's or a judge's decision if they were not satisfied. A political officer sitting as a judge in, say, a magistrates' court, was not the same all-powerful judge that he had been under the provincial court system. The presence of lawyers and the possibility of appeal: these were real constraining factors. The ideal judicial situation would, of course, have been a complete break between the judicial and the administrative arms of the government, but the magistrates' courts and the High Court between them minimised the chances of miscarriages of justice. There is no question that they were a real improvement on the provincial court system in spite of their limitations.

The 'native' courts were the most unsatisfactory aspect of the judicial reform of 1933. The view was once expressed by a top-ranking official of the government that nothing could be more effective in checking irregularities on the part of a 'native' court than 'the knowledge that the persons who come before it are aware that they have a right of appeal to a competent and honest court of appeal'.[64] But the right to appeal to a higher court simply did not exist in the vast majority of the 'native' courts. Of the 1,143 'native' courts in Nigeria by 1937, only in thirteen of them, all in the Southern Provinces, could appeal lie in all cases to the magistrates' courts. In 268 others appeal in land cases went to the magistrates' courts if the value of the land in question was above ₦400. In all other categories of cases, appeal in such courts went to the administrative officers. The remaining 'native' courts may be grouped together. Appeals from them went either to the administrative officer or to the 'native' court of appeal, established at some administrative headquarters like Ibadan, Benin, Abeokuta and Ijebu-Ode.[65]

It was no easy task to divide up the 'native' courts in this fashion; for no one criterion was consistently followed.[66] This complexity of the courts is another reflection of Cameron's or the Colonial Office's cautious attitude to judicial reform. A measure of reform was thought desirable, and yet, apparently, Cameron did not want to go so far as to disturb the existing concentration of political power in the hands of political officers. For political reasons most of the 'native' courts still remained firmly under the control of administrative officers. So firm was the executive control over the courts that S. B. Rhodes, a Nigerian lawyer representing the Rivers Division in the Legislative Council, called for a reconsideration of the Native Courts Ordinance in November 1937. Many provisions of the ordinance, he said, 'are not consistent with the spirit of the Ordinance' or, one might add, with the spirit of the 1933 judicial reform.[67] Although Cameron might, in theory, argue against the political self-sufficiency of the native administrations in Nigeria, he was, in practice, very much averse to interfering with them.

The desire to strike a delicate balance between a measure of reform of the 'native' courts and the maintenance of the political officers' influence in native administrations resulted in the Native Courts Ordinance (1933) being perhaps the most clumsy document ever to find its way into the Nigerian statute book. It was once described as 'a most complicated Ordinance in which it is easy to tie oneself up in knots'.[68] Within three years of its coming into force, *mirabile dictu*, it went through sixteen amendments.[69]

A word about lawyers, hitherto always an important consideration in any judicial reform. It would appear that in spite of Cameron's qualified gesture of liberalism in allowing lawyers to appear before the magistrates' courts and the High Court in the protectorate, and administration's aversion to lawyers remained unabated. W. E. Hunt, then Acting Lieutenant-Governor for the Southern Provinces, put the case for the administration when he declared in the Legislative Council in 1933: 'In the present state of these embryonic native administrations and native courts, especially in the Eastern Provinces, they should be free as far as possible from legal onsets, legal trammels, legal pitfalls, if they are not to lose their own soul.'[70]

An amendment was made in 1938 to the Inter-Tribal Boundaries Settlement Ordinance (1933) which illustrates the continued distrust of lawyers *qua* lawyers by the administration. Between 1934 and 1938 the practice had developed of lawyers appearing before tribunals presided over by administrative officers adjudicating boundary disputes in accordance with the provisions of the Inter-Tribal Boundaries Settlement Ordinance (1933). The 1938 amendment to the ordinance was designed to 'extinguish' (*sic*) all right of lawyers to appear before boundary tribunals.[71] A lawyer could only appear before a boundary tribunal if he had a personal interest in the land in dispute and provided he did not appear on a professional basis.

From the point of view of the administration, the limitations placed on the practice of the legal profession under the judicial reform of 1933 however, would not appear to have been effective. Although appeals from the 'native' courts to the higher courts were restricted in the vast majority of the 'native' courts, it is worth mentioning, when considering the avenues open to lawyers, that there were some urban areas, mostly in the Eastern Provinces, where such appeals were unrestricted, even in land cases.[72] The loopholes in some of the key provisions of the 1933 judicial reform also rendered meaningless the restrictions said to be placed on the practice of the law.[73] There was, in particular, the imprecision of the language of the Native Courts Ordinance, 1933, which often provided cover for lawyers' involvement in matters coming before the courts.

Lawyers not only 'interfered' in the administration of justice in the 'native' courts after 1933, they did so boldly. In areas where appeals from the 'native' courts were restricted and particularly in the Eastern Provinces, lawyers were taking 'native' court cases to the higher courts under one ambiguously phrased provision of the Native Courts Ordinance or another. In view of the fact that the ordinance itself was a complex document, administrative officers often found themselves helpless in the face of the demands made by lawyers for transfer of cases from the 'native' courts to the higher courts. As the magistrate for Port Harcourt magisterial area reported in 1938, most district officers he had met 'have frankly admitted that the Ordinance is of the nature of a nightmare to them'.[74] Administrative officers were also reported in other places to be putting 'peculiar constructions' on the provisions of the ordinance.

The restriction placed on the appearance of legal practitioners before the higher courts was, in the opinion of George Graham Paul, now a judge of the High Court (1933–9), 'completely ridiculous'. In the big towns like Abeokuta, Ibadan, and Ijebu-Ode in the Western Provinces, he said, lawyers were being retained 'in practically every Native court Appeal'.[75] Lawyers prepared elaborate petitions of appeal, raising technical points of the law. They then went to the magistrates' court and sat there silently to watch the determining of the appeal. The only thing they did not do was to put forward the cases for their clients in oral arguments. As always, those who suffered the penalty of the theoretical restriction placed on the legal profession were not the lawyers but their clients. For as Graham Paul noted, the lawyers were being paid as fully for their services as if such services included actually arguing their cases in court. The ease with which they engaged in 'native' court appeal cases in the higher courts made the whole notion of restricting them, in Graham Paul's words, 'a rather childish farce'.

Where there was no direct channel from a 'native' court to a magistrates' court or the High Court, the influence of lawyers on the administration of justice in the 'native' courts was not for that reason any less real. In the Southern Provinces and especially in the East, litigants whose only channel of appeal was through the political officers, increasingly employed lawyers as solicitors to address petitions to those officers.[76] Whether such petitions were welcomed as ordinary petitions written by letter-writers or, as it was suggested, discountenanced as 'illegal' appeals from lawyers' chambers was, from the lawyer's financial point of view, an entirely irrelevant issue. The lawyer, by submitting a petition or a brief to the administrative officer, rendered a professional service and received his fees; the outcome of the petition or the brief was a matter for the administrative officer.

It would also appear that under the vague provisions of the Native Courts Ordinance (1933), lawyers were able to challenge the decisions of the administrative officers when these officers 'reviewed' cases in the 'native' courts. Before 1933 'reviews' of cases by administrative officers were not open to challenge by lawyers in the higher courts. At least until 1942 when an amendment was made in the Native Courts Ordinance (1933)[77] to close the loophole in the court procedure, lawyers challenged the decisions of 'reviews' in the higher courts.

The influence of the lawyer, in fact, seemed all-pervading in spite of the restrictions still placed on the profession. The Resident for Abeokuta Province observed in 1940 that it was not unusual for people normally subject to the jurisdiction of the 'native' courts to take legal advice *before* instituting proceedings in the 'native' courts. Nor was it unusual for parties to walk out of a 'native' court in the middle of a land case and proceed to Lagos to consult lawyers.[78]

What the colonial administration failed to realise was the extent to which people were increasingly aware of the role of lawyers in the politico-judicial setting of colonial Nigeria. Things were no longer as they used to be or administrative officers would want them to be: simple, non-literate people settling their affairs in accordance with time-honoured customary laws, without legal technicalities and with minimum rancour. Any attempt to erect a rigid barrier between the 'native' courts and the higher, English-style courts was bound to fail. Those who were under the 'native' courts' jurisdiction were likely to see the higher courts as superior versions of their own 'native' courts and as places where 'better' justice could be obtained.

The developments discussed above bear witness to the point made earlier that Cameron's reform did not go far enough. Cameron fought shy of the conclusions drawn from his own admirable analysis of the Nigerian colonial situation. A man with notably progressive views on colonial matters, he stopped short of putting his bold conceptions fully into operation. Contrary to what has been suggested,[79] his judicial reform did not end the era of 'executive' justice, for political officers continued to exercise their influence in judicial matters. It can be said in his favour, however, that he devised a judicial system which set a trend of liberalism in judicial matters that became irreversible.

V

Dissatisfaction with the operation of the 'native' courts under the Native Courts Ordinance (1933) necessitated further reforms. Discussions began in official circles concerning the need for them about November 1937.

Apart from the fact that lawyers did not find any difficulty in 'interfering' with the administration of justice in the 'native' courts, it was evident that the 'native' court system itself contained many anomalies. The point was made earlier that administrative officers found the Native Courts Ordinance (1933) rather unwieldy to apply. The chief source of difficulty, especially in the Eastern Provinces, where a large number of 'native' courts were linked with the higher courts by way of appeal, was 'the network of avenues of appeal and review' provided by the Native Courts Ordinance in the administration of justice in the courts.

In the 'native' court system a distinction was made between review and appeal. While an appeal lay to a magistrates' court or to a High Court, the review process was a sort of informal appeal heard by the administrative officer. The appeal process had one advantage over the review. While a further appeal could be made after the first had taken place, the review represented the only and last chance for a dissatisfied litigant who chose this alternative. Anyone who chose the review process was usually not permitted to make an appeal over the same dispute. The reason for this last provision was to discourage protracted litigation; but the provision, as it turned out in practice, added to the complexity of the Native Courts Ordinance (1933).

Among litigants before the 'native' courts, reviews were more popular than appeals. For example, in 1936, from the 239,367 'native' court cases tried in the various provinces of Southern Nigeria, there were only about 600 appeals. The popularity of reviews is not necessarily due to their efficacy, as it was sometimes suggested by administrative officers.[80] Reviews were popular for two different reasons. Since the introduction of the 'native' court institutions into Southern Nigeria the system of review had been about the only means of appealing against the decisions of the courts. Few people considered it advisable, for fear of the consequences, to go behind the back of the administrative officer in seeking justice. Secondly, and perhaps more important, reviews were cheap. In the 1920s the minimum 'search' fee of about twenty kobo was all that was required for a review. After 1933 reviews were free.

The popularity of reviews among litigants, however, brought some difficulties in its train. In most places applications for reviews made to administrative officers became almost automatic. A dissatisfied litigant did not feel he had explored all avenues in his pursuit of justice until he had taken his case to the administrative officer, no matter how sound the decision of the 'native' court had been. The fact that reviews were free seemed to have led to an enormous increase in what administrative officers were wont to call 'frivolous reviews'.[81] Thus the centre of judicial power within the 'native' court system shifted more and more to the administrative officer's table. By the same token, the 'native' courts, contrary to the hopes and expectations of the administrative officers themselves, were losing their authority and their capacity to finalise disputes.

There was a second difficulty created by the appeal-review process. The litigant who found that the review process brought him to a blind alley in his quest for justice, found a way of dressing his grievances in a new garb before the higher courts where he would probably employ a legal practitioner. If he did succeed, his opponent could start the whole process of litigation again by initiating another action at the 'native' court. Thus within the 'native' court system litigation could easily become intractable.

Educated Africans were also dissatisfied with the operation of the 'native' courts. The restriction placed on lawyers' appearance at the hearing of appeals from the 'native' courts to the magistrates' courts or the High Court left the majority of the 'native' courts, institutionally, as powerful as they were before 1933. The result was far from satisfactory. To liberal, educated Africans it was galling, for instance, that as late as 1938, an accused person could be tried for a capital charge under the 'native' court system without the right to employ counsel even when his case reached the magistrates' court.[82] Active in the demand for further reforms were the educated Africans in the Legislative Council – lawyers and non-lawyers alike. By means of questions they brought to the attention of the administration the inadequacies of Cameron's judicial reform in respect of the 'native' courts.[83]

Legal and judicial officers of the colonial regime also commented on the need for further judicial reforms. In the main their view was that their experience of the operation of the judicial reform of 1933 did not justify the placing of any restrictions on the appearance of lawyers in the higher courts. Scott, the magistrate for Port Harcourt magisterial area, made the important point that in view of the increasing number of lawyers in Nigeria, extension of the scope for their activities rather than its restriction, was more likely to lead to honest and legitimate professional dealings.[84]

On their part, officers in the administrative wing of the colonial service maintained their old stand against any judicial reforms that might favour the legal profession. The Eastern Chief Commissioner emphasised a point which illuminates the paternalistic attitude underlying much of the administrative officers' thinking on the whole question of lawyers within the colonial framework. 'As trustees for the people', he wrote, 'Administrative Officers feel strongly that they will need protection against their own litigious obstinacy which so often involved them, even entire communities, in financial ruin.'[85]

Interestingly, the administration sought to sound out public opinion on what judicial reforms might be required. The Executive Council on 6 December 1939 directed the Chief Commissioners for the Eastern, Western and Northern Provinces to obtain the views of the people in their respective areas specifically on the question whether they wanted lawyers to appear in all 'native' court cases going on appeal before the higher courts or only in certain categories of cases.

It would have been surprising if the chief commissioners reported anything much contrary to the views they themselves had expressed on the subject. The chief commissioner for the Western Provinces reported in July 1940 that at a previous conference he held with some important Yoruba *obas* and chiefs concern was expressed by the traditional rulers about the rising cost of litigation in land cases allegedly resulting from the involvement of lawyers.[86] The general opinion in the Eastern Provinces regarding the appearance of counsel in appeal cases, reported the Eastern chief commissioner in October 1940, was that it was undesirable. There were a few places, he said, where the 'sophisticated minority' would welcome a departure from the existing system.[87] It is worthy of note that when, at last, in December 1941 the Executive Council did decide to allow lawyers to appear in appeals brought to the higher courts from the 'native' courts, the concession was qualified by the proviso that the higher courts should be empowered to impose financial penalties on lawyers who brought 'frivolous appeals' to the courts.[88] The misgivings about lawyers apparently lay deep.

The proposals for a second judicial reform in Nigeria were passed to the Colonial Office. The reform proposals were sanctioned and were embodied in five ordinances enacted in 1943.[89] The detailed discussions at the Colonial Office on proposals are not known, but it was most unlikely any strong objections would have been raised against them. For one thing, the proposals came at a time when Britain was deeply involved in a world war. For another – and the more important reason – a change of attitude seemed to be prevailing in official circles in Britain during and after the Second World War which tended to favour liberal concessions to colonial territories. The whole question of the relations between colonial rulers and dependent peoples was being re-examined. The war itself had aroused liberal sentiments towards the 'backward nations' of the world, and opinions were being expressed in favour of accelerating their development. There was even talk of these erstwhile dependent peoples at some time in the future exercising 'self-government' and, by implication, of the need to prepare them for this eventuality. Informed public opinion in Britain was in favour of a 'a dynamic programme of social and economic development' for the colonies. Indeed grants of money for such development were being made,[90] partly on humanitarian grounds and partly to serve Britain's own long-term economic interests. It was no accident that in the same year that judicial reform in Nigeria was sanctioned, the British Government took steps to quicken the pace of higher education in Commonwealth West Africa by setting up a commission 'to report on the organisation and facilities of the existing centres of higher education in British West Africa, and to make recommendations regarding future university development in that area'.[91]

The essence of the judicial reform of 1943 was to carry to its logical conclusions Cameron's judicial reform of 1933. For the first time in the legal history of Nigeria, the Supreme Court was given an unlimited civil and criminal jurisdiction throughout the country – subject to the jurisdiction of the 'native' courts in land disputes, family relationships and other matters where customary law largely applied.[92] The High Court of the Protectorate was abolished and below the Supreme Court were new magistrates' courts, established throughout the country and classified into three grades according to their powers and jurisdiction.[93] A remarkable feature of the magistrates' courts was the fact that civil or criminal action could now be taken against any magistrate in another court[94] – a safeguard, as it were, against judicial indiscretion. Below the magistrates' courts were the 'native' courts. Modifications were made here and there, but on the whole, there were no major changes in the 'native' court system. In the Eastern Provinces the 'native' court areas were reorganised and the size of the panels of chiefs comprising them was also reduced. The civil jurisdiction of the courts throughout Southern Nigeria became somewhat more limited than in the past, and their power of punishment was correspondingly reduced.

The reform of 1943 provided for a fuller scope for appeals than hitherto from the 'native' courts to the Supreme Court and even beyond to the West African Court of Appeal. The 'native' courts were linked with the higher courts more than ever before. The limitations placed on appeals from the 'native' courts to the magistrates' courts were largely swept away. The scope for appeals to the magistrates' courts in civil and criminal cases was further widened by the Magistrates' Courts (Appeals) Ordinance, No. 41, 1945.[95] That ordinance came into force on 1 June 1945, on which date also the judicial reform of 1943 went into operation.

Although the judicial reform of 1943 did not directly touch on the legal profession, its effect on the profession was far-reaching.

It could be said that in 1943 the profession secured its full freedom. True, lawyers were forbidden to practise in the 'native' courts, as they still are in certain categories of their modern counterparts, the customary courts. But with the linking of the 'native' courts to the higher courts and with the removal of limitations on appeals throughout the whole judicial system, the lawyer could appear in practically any dispute where his services might be required. The question was no longer whether or not the lawyer should 'interfere', but at what stage in the hierarchy of courts he should intervene.

In a real sense the judicial reform of 1943 laid the foundation of the modern machinery of justice in Nigeria. This is true not because of the system of courts which it refurbished, but because it established in Nigeria for the first time two important principles which, in the best common law tradition, would appear to be essential to the efficient working of a judicial system. They are a fair amount of freedom for appeals within a hierarchy of courts and, no less important, freedom for litigants to receive legal assistance formally in the pursuance of any cause. The subsequent changes that took place in the judicial system did not detract from these two principles.

VI

The judicial changes of 1954 were prompted by the country's pattern of constitutional development. Since 1951, Nigeria had been evolving a federal type of constitution.[96] Between July 1953 and February 1954 a constitutional conference was held both in London and in Lagos to resolve various issues arising from the allocation of powers between the central government and the regional governments made in 1951. A committee of the constitutional conference, while it sat in London, was charged with examining the existing judicial system in relation to the emerging federal structure of government. The committee met about the middle of August 1953 and prepared a report[97] which was discussed at the resumed constitutional conference in Lagos early in 1954.

In essence the committee recommended, and the constitutional conference approved, the regionalisation of the judicial system.[98] There was to be a Supreme Court for the whole federation consisting of a Chief Justice and puisne judges. The judges of the Supreme Court, including the Chief Justice, were to be appointed by the Governor-General on the instructions of the British Crown, and would hold office during the pleasure of the Crown. The Supreme Court was to have original jurisdiction in inter-regional disputes, and in all disputes arising between the central government and a regional government. The court would also hear and determine appeals from the decisions of the regional High Courts (discussed below) either in their original or appellate jurisdictions.

Over each of the Western, Northern and Eastern regions and Lagos (now constituted a federal territory) was to be set up a High Court, which was to exercise such jurisdiction as might be vested in it by the regional legislature. It is noteworthy that a judge of the High Court, excepting that of the Lagos High Court, was to be appointed by the Governor of the region, and not by the Governor-General. The most senior judge was to be designated 'Chief Justice'. It is equally noteworthy that a judge of the High Court 'shall receive such salary and allowances as may be prescribed by law of the Regional Legislature or, in the case of Lagos, the Federal Legislature. . . .'[99]

As from 1954 the West African Court of Appeal ceased to exercise appellate jurisdiction over Nigerian courts. Appeals lay directly to the Privy Council in London.

A word about the 'native' courts in the new scheme of things. Broadly, the regionalisation policy also affected the courts in that matters relating to them were now to be regulated by the regional legislatures. But it should be noted that long before the constitutional changes of the 1950s, more specifically since about 1939, reform of the courts had been a matter for official discussions.[100] The rather lengthy discussions culminated in the appointment in 1949 of four commissions of inquiry for each of the Northern, Eastern and Western Provinces and for the Lagos Colony, each commission headed by Neville J. Brooke, a puisne judge of the Supreme Court.[101] The terms of reference were similar: a general appraisal of the 'native' court system with particular emphasis on the constitution of the courts, the laws administered in them and the links between them and the higher courts.[102]

The important recommendations of the Brooke commissions regarding the 'native' courts were implemented in amended form by the various regional legislatures only after 1954. Broadly, for Southern Nigeria, the commissions recommended that there should be no extension of the jurisdictions of the courts, which were now to be known as customary courts.[103] There were to be four grades of them, the last two serving as 'ordinary courts of first instance'. Grade 'B' customary courts were to serve as courts of first instance in certain areas, and to exercise appellate jurisdiction over grades 'C' and 'D' courts in other areas. At the top of the hierarchy of customary courts in a division was to be a divisional court, a grade 'A' customary court. It was to be an appeal court, presided over by an administrative officer or other suitable person as judge with a panel of assessors. Customary courts generally were to be the 'natural tribunals for land cases involving customary tenures'. To ensure the proper working of the courts, there should be appointed in each region a native courts' adviser who, among other duties, would 'make a survey of the law being administered in the Native courts and arrange for the preparation of handbooks of customary law'.

The regionalisation of the judicial system provoked strong reactions. The Nigerian Bar Association submitted a memorandum to the resumed constitutional conference meeting in Lagos in which the Association strenuously opposed the regionalisation scheme. The Association felt that regionalisation of the judiciary 'would be the greatest disservice to the country'.[104] Fear was also expressed in other quarters that a system whereby regional Governors appointed High Court judges might lead to judges becoming 'mere tools in the hands of politicians'.[105] Again, the system was said to be 'sailing perilously close to the control of the judiciary by the Executive'. The provision that salaries of the High Court judges were to be determined by the regional legislatures was considered likely to introduce elements of instability into the country's judicial system. There was the possibility of the legislature 'playing politics with judges' salaries'. The regions might also compete among themselves for the best judges, each region displaying 'such petty regional arrogance [which] will ultimately make our judicial system nationally unstable'.[106]

The most formidable opponent of the regionalisation scheme was Sir John Verity, Chief Justice of Nigeria, 1946–54. He submitted a long memorandum to the resumed Lagos constitutional conference in which he discussed his objections and made his own proposals.[107] He stressed the need to remove any form of political influence on the courts or the system of administering justice. For this reason judges of the High Courts should enjoy freedom 'from all regional relations'. In a developing country, he said, there was a need to maintain a single standard of learning and professional competence in the judiciary. His own proposals were not much different from the existing judicial structure – one Supreme Court with its divisional courts and magistrates' courts exercising jurisdiction over the whole country, all the judges and other staff of the courts being under the control of the Chief Justice. 'Native' courts would be 'allowed to preserve their independence and jurisdiction', their decisions not being open to question by the Supreme Court.[108]

Under the colonial regime, Nigeria did not experience what could have turned out to be the worst aspects of the regionslisation of the judicial system. Up to the achievement of political independence in 1960, there was no indication of any unhealthy rivalry among the regions to bid for judges by offering competitive salaries and allowances. Again, up to the end of the colonial era, political considerations would not seem to have been a decisive factor in the appointment of regional High Court judges. It may be mentioned in passing that the Nigeria Independence Constitution (1960) would seem to have taken care of most of the fears expressed over regionalisation of the judiciary by the establishment of a Judicial Service Commission for the whole federation.

It is, however, too early as yet to measure the impact of a regionalised judicial system on Nigeria's development. Has a regionalised judicial system hindered or promoted the political unity of the country? To what extent have conflicts of law and of jurisdiction within a regionalised judicial system been amenable to the evolution of a Nigerian common law? In the light of conflicts of law and diversity of jurisdictions, what has been the effect, if any, of a regionalised judicial system on internal trade, internal social mobility or even external commercial relations? To answer these questions intelligibly would require a long-term perspective.

VII

One development, noticeable from the 1930s on, is worth mentioning here. It cannot be strictly considered part of the judicial reforms although it signifies the spirit of reform. I refer to the appointment of Nigerian lawyers to judicial and legal positions in the Civil Service.

The question of appointment of Nigerian legal practitioners to judicial and legal positions was one which agitated the minds of educated Africans for a long time. Kitoyi Ajasa's *Nigerian Pioneer* complained in 1919 that no single Nigerian barrister was then serving in the legal department of the Civil Service. 'They are not in the Government simply because they are not wanted', the paper acidly commented.[109] As national consciousness grew during the 1920s and 1930s and many political offences were committed, the absence of Africans in the Nigerian judiciary looked oppressive to many. An educated African, commenting in 1921 on the unwillingness of the administration to appoint Nigerian lawyers as judges, wondered when 'Jacob [that is, the African] will be saved from the power of his enemies'.[110] The absence of Africans from the judicial Bench in the country's higher courts tended to engender a feeling of helplessness in nationalist-minded Nigerians.

The unwillingness of the administration to employ African legal practitioners was simply a reflection of its general policy of closing the higher ranks of the Civil Service to well-educated Africans – a policy that had built up considerable frustration among the educated elite.

There seemed to have been a change of official attitude about 1931, when, on 13 February, Olumuyiwa Jibowu was appointed a police magistrate in Lagos. Though Jibowu's appointment was hailed with great enthusiasm, it was not until seven years later that other appointments were made, in spite of the continual demands of educated Africans for more African magistrates.[111] Then, on 1 April 1938, R. A. Doherty was appointed the first Nigerian Crown counsel. The appointment of more magistrates followed: Adebiyi Desalu, on 1 November 1938, Adetokunbo Ademola (later chief justice of the Federation of Nigeria) on 1 April 1939 and F. E. O. Euba on 1 August 1940. Shortage of staff during the Second World War led to the appointment of fourteen more African magistrates between 1941 and 1945.[112] By the end of the war, in 1945, two Nigerian lawyers had reached the high judicial posts of puisne judges of the Supreme Court. Olumuyiwa Jibowu was promoted to that post on 1 September 1944. Steven Bankole Rhodes was appointed to the post on 8 November 1945 – the first Nigerian lawyer to be appointed to the Supreme Court Bench straight from the Bar.

On the whole, up to the end of the period of this study, about seventy-five Nigerians had served or were serving in judicial capacities: seven as puisne judges of the Supreme Court, and the remaining as magistrates of various grades.[113] There was a parallel development in the legal department where, up to 1954, at least eleven Nigerians had served or were serving as Crown counsel and senior Crown counsel.[114]

Impressive as this list is of Nigerians holding legal and judicial positions in the period of this study, it is not easy to see from the records of the courts in what ways they have brought a distinctively Nigerian flavour to the quality of justice administered in the courts. This is not necessarily an indictment against the Nigerian judges and legal officers. It is an indication of their relatively small number, and perhaps of the uniformity of the mentality behind the law that they and the colonial judges had to administer, and of the common outlook it tended to breed. The situation may also be a reflection of the difficulty of making a peculiarly Nigerian contribution to judicial decisions in a judicial system that seemed to have already accepted, to a large measure, the need to adapt English common law to the Nigerian soil.

Nonetheless, with Nigerians gradually taking their rightful positions on the judicial Bench and in the legal department of civil administration, the way seemed fairly well prepared for the eventual assumption of responsibility by Nigerians in running their own affairs in judicial matters.

Notes

1 CO 583/177, Cameron to Cunliffe-Lister, 10 December 1931.
2 Colonial Office, *Report of the Commission on Higher Education in West Africa*, Cmd 6655, 1945, p. 18.
3 NAI, CSO 26/3, 26359, I, II, III, 'The Supreme Court and Its Relation to Native Policy'. The 'CO 583' series of records at the Public Records Office, London, contains much of the correspondence on judicial reforms between Lagos and London.
4 See *Report by the Hon. W. G. A. Ormsby-Gore on his Visit to West Africa during the Year 1926*, 1926, Cmd 2744.
5 CO 583/183, 'Report by H. G. Bushe on his Visit to Nigeria'.
6 *Infra*, pp. 161–4.
7 CO 657/34, 'Address to the Legislative Council, 8 February 1932' by Sir Donald Cameron.

8 CO 583/183, 'Judicial System in the Protectorate of Nigeria', Minute by A. Fiddian, 11 May 1932.
9 Donald Cameron, *My Tanganyika Service and Some Nigeria*, London, 1939, p. 283.
10 Apart from Cameron's own autobiography, see Vincent Harlow *et al*, eds, *History of East Africa*, II, Oxford, 1965, ch. X by Kenneth Ingham.
11 Donald Cameron, *Memoranda on the Principles of Native Administration and their Application*, Lagos, 1934, pp. 4–8.
12 B. T. G. Chidzero, *Tanganyika and International Trusteeship*, London, 1961, p. 57.
13 Harlow *et al*., eds, *History of East Africa*, II, pp. 576–7.
14 *Ibid*., pp. 584–5.
15 *Ibid*., pp. 585–7.
16 *Ibid*., p. 576.
17 Alan Burns, *History of Nigeria*, 6th ed., p. 246, n. 3.
18 CO 583/183, 'Judicial System in the Protectorate of Nigeria', Minute by Sir W. C. Bottomley, 12 May 1932.
19 *Address by His Excellency the Governor, Sir Donald Cameron*, Lagos, 1933, p. 6.
20 *Ibid*., p. 13.
21 NAI, CSO 1/32, 112, Cameron to Colonial Office, 17 March 1932, on the Native Courts Ordinance.
22 *Ibid*.
23 NAI, CSO 1/32, 112, Cameron to Colonial Office, 17 March 1932, on the Protectorate Courts Ordinance.
24 *Address by His Excellency the Governor, Sir Donald Cameron*, p. 25.
25 Cameron, *My Tanganyika Service*, p. 193.
26 *Nigerian Daily Telegraph*, 18 June 1935.
27 *West Africa*, 4 March 1933.
28 See *Report of the Commission of Inquiry into the Administration of Justice in Kenya, Uganda and the Tanganyika Territory in Criminal Matters, May 1933*, Cmd 4623.
29 I. M. Okonjo, *British Administration in Nigeria, 1900–1950: A Nigerian View*, New York, 1974, pp. 199, 210, 359, n. 42.
30 These cases are discussed in the next chapter.
31 *West Africa*, 22 December 1928.
32 Okonjo, *British Administration in Nigeria*, p. 199.
33 *Ibid*., p. 228.
34 *Ibid*., p. 217.
35 CO 583/184, Cameron to Cunliffe-Lister, 11 June 1932 and 19 July 1932, enclosures.
36 CO 583/183, 'Memorandum on Cameron's Proposals for Judicial Reform in the Protectorate of Nigeria'.
37 CO 583/183, 'Judicial System in the Protectorate of Nigeria', Minute by Sir S. H. Wilson, 26 May 1932.
38 CO 583/183, 'Note of a discussion regarding judicial reforms in Nigeria'.
39 CO 583/183, 'Judicial System in the Protectorate of Nigeria', Minute by H. G. Bushe, 6 May 1932.

40 CO 583/183, 'Notes of a discussion regarding reforms in Nigeria at meetings held 7 and 13 October 1932'.
41 CO 583/183, 'Minutes of Meeting held 13 October 1932'.
42 The major Ordinances that effected the reform are discussed in T. O. Elias, *The Nigerian Legal System*, pp. 140–51.
43 Protectorate Courts Ordinance, No. 45, 1933, sec. 49.
44 Protectorate Courts Ordinance, sec. 50.
45 Supreme Court (Amendment) Ordinance, No. 46, 1933.
46 Supreme Court (Amendment) Ordinance, secs. 25–7.
47 West African Court of Appeal Ordinance, No. 47, 1933.
48 Elias, *The Nigerian Legal System*, p. 52.
49 CO 583/183, 'Note of discussion regarding legal reforms in Nigeria at a meeting held 13 October 1932'.
50 *Ibid.*
51 The Legal Practitioners' Ordinance, sec. 29.
52 Cameron, *Address to the Legislative Council, 9 March 1933*, Lagos, 1933, p. 25.
53 *Legislative Council Debates*, 11th session, 1933, p. 100.
54 *Ibid.*, p 104.
55 *Akede Eko*, 29 June 1935.
56 *Nigerian Daily Telegraph*, 18 June 1935.
57 Cameron, *Address to the Legislative Council, 8 February, 1932*, Lagos, 1932, p. 64.
58 NAI, CSO 26/3, 34651/S. 1, I, Bourdillon to Colonial Office, 19 January 1940.
59 B. O. Nwabueze, *The Machinery of Justice in Nigeria*, London, 1963, p. 65.
60 *Ibid.*
61 CO 583/192, Cameron to Colonial Office, 19 July 1933.
62 NAI, CSO 1/32, 112, Cameron to Colonial Office, 17 March 1932.
63 Nwabueze, *The Machinery of Justice*, p. 65.
64 Comments by A. C. V. Prior, Attorney-General, *Legislative Council Debates*, 11th session, p. 46.
65 NAI, CSO 26/3, 20665/S. 7, I, 'Native Courts in the Southern Provinces'.
66 *Ibid.* Minutes by C. W. W. Greednidge.
67 *Legislative Council Debates*, 15th session, p. 79.
68 NAI, CSO 26/3, 20665/S. 7, I, 'Native Courts in the Southern Provinces'.
69 *Legislative Council Debates*, 15th session, p. 80.
70 *Legislative Council Debates*, 11th session, p. 108.
71 *Legislative Council Debates*, session of 28 November 1938, p. 108.
72 Protectorate Courts Ordinance (1933), sec. 49(i)(b) and Second Schedule to the Ordinance.
73 Compare Protectorate Courts Ordinance (1933) sec. 49(i)(a) and Native Courts Ordinance (1933) sec. 25(c).
74 NAI, CSO 26/3, 20665/S. 7, II, J. N. Scott to chief registrar, Supreme Court, Lagos, 28 November 1938.

75 NAI, CSO 26/3, 35084, 'The Appearance of Lawyers in Appeals from the Native Courts', Minute by Graham Paul.
76 NAI, CSO 26/3, 20665/S. 7, II, Scott to chief registrar, supreme court, 28 November 1938.
77 *Legislative Council Debates*, session of 7 September 1942, pp. 110–11.
78 NAI, CSO 26/3, 20665/S 7, II, secretary, Western Provinces to chief secretary, Lagos, 10 November 1937.
79 I. M. Okonjo, p. 225.
80 NAI, CSO 26/3, 20665/S. 7, I, chief commissioner to chief secretary, Lagos, 10 January 1938.
81 *Ibid.*, secretary, Southern Provinces to chief secretary, Lagos, 10 January 1938.
82 Question raised by Dr C. C. Adeniyi-Jones, *Legislative Council Debates*, session of 11 July 1938.
83 Their questions were commented on by officials in NAI, CSO 26/3, 35084.
84 NAI, CSO 26/3, 20665/S. 7, II, Scott to chief registrar, Lagos, 28 November 1938.
85 NAI, CSO 26/3, 35084, secretary, Eastern Provinces to chief secretary, Lagos, 6 November 1939, enclosure.
86 NAI, CSO 26/3, 20665/S. 7, II, secretary, Western Provinces to chief secretary, Lagos, 2 July 1940, enclosure.
87 NAI, CSO 26/3, 35084, secretary, Eastern Provinces, to chief secretary, Lagos, 25 October 1940, enclosure.
88 NAI, CSO 26/3, 35084, Decision of executive meeting held 9 December 1941.
89 Elias, *The Nigerian Legal System*, pp. 152–65.
90 Lord Hailey, *The Future of Colonial Peoples*, London, 1944.
91 Colonial Office, *Report of the Commission on Higher Education in West Africa, 1945*, 1945, Cmd 6655.
92 Supreme Court Ordinance, No. 23, as amended by No. 33, 1943.
93 Magistrates' Courts Ordinance, No. 24, as amended by No. 43, 1943.
94 Magistrates' Courts Ordinance, 1943, sec. 28.
95 Magistrates' Courts (Appeals) Ordinance, 1945, secs. 3–7; 9–11.
96 For more on the constitutional development of Nigeria, see O. I. Odumosu, *The Nigerian Constitution: History and Development*, London, 1963.
97 'Report of Committee on the Administration of Justice', in Colonial Office, *Report by the Conference on the Nigerian Constitution held in London in July and August 1953*, Cmd 8934, Annex IV, pp. 17–20.
98 *Report by the Resumed Conference on the Nigerian Constitution held in Lagos in January and February 1954*, Cmd 9059, pp. 48–53.
99 *Ibid.*, p. 50.
100 NAI, MLG (W) 2, 18211, I.
101 *Ibid.*, chief secretary to secretary, Western Provinces, 25 May 1949.
102 *Report of the Native Courts (Western Provinces) Commission of Inquiry*, Lagos, 1952, p. 1.
103 For the detailed recommendations, see *Native Courts Commissions of Inquiry, 1949–1952: Summary and Recommendations*, Lagos, 1953.

On the implementation of the recommendations, see Keay and Richardson, *The Native and Customary Courts of Nigeria*, London, 1966, pp. 81–97.

104 *Daily Times*, Lagos, 25 January 1954.
105 *Ibid.*
106 Bola Adewunmi, 'Searchlight on "Report of the Committee on Judicial Administration"', *Daily Times*, 18 January 1954.
107 *Daily Times*, 27 January 1954; O. I. Odumosu, *The Nigerian Constitution*, pp. 103–6.
108 *Daily Times*, 27 January 1954.
109 *Nigerian Pioneer*, 4 April 1919.
110 *Times of Nigeria*, 14 February 1921.
111 NAI, CSO 26/3, 25005, II.
112 *Staff Lists, Nigeria, 1941–1955*, Lagos, 1941–55.
113 *Ibid.*
114 *Ibid.*

8 The Supreme Court, 1914-54

> It is the case, whatever the form behind which it has
> been concealed, that the work of English courts from
> the medieval period onwards represents a great achieve-
> ment in legislation by reference to the changing facts of
> social life as seen in the actual behaviours of associations of
> men for the time being.
>
> Julius Stone, *The Province and Function of Law*,
> Sydney, 1946, p. 167

I

Except in so far as the Supreme Court of Nigeria was limited in its
operation throughout the country, the judicial reorganisation of
1914 did not disturb the structure of the court as basically a
judicial rather than a judico-administrative entity like the provincial or the 'native' court. Nor was this structure tampered with
by the subsequent judicial reforms. In the colonial context of
Nigeria the Supreme Court purported to stand for the rule of law,
at least in theory, taking cognisance of no extraneous considerations, economic or political, outside the law. Part of the reason for
the curtailment of the jurisdiction of the court in 1914 was precisely
this notion of it as an institution which knew 'nothing of [political]
policies'. The limitations placed on the court's jurisdiction, as has
been shown in the last chapter, were removed in 1933 and 1943.
The intention now is to review the judicial activities of the court –
to see how far it lived up to the ideal of judicial independence,
what principles, if any, underlay its judgments, and what impact
it had had on the development of Southern Nigeria.

II

Popular notions among administrative officers notwithstanding,
the position of the Supreme Court in Nigeria was not quite comparable with that of the High Court in England (its rough equivalent

of the court). In this connection the positions of the judges in the two courts are revealing. Since the Act of Settlement, 1700, judges of the High Court in England hold office during good behaviour and are removable only with the consent of the British Parliament.[1] The case of *Terrel v. Secretary of State for the Colonies* (1953) is the *locus classicus* on the position of a colonial Supreme Court judge.[2] That case affirmed what had all along been felt to be the position of a colonial judge: that he held office at the pleasure of the British Crown. In effect the Act of Settlement, 1700, was held inapplicable to them. It is important to note, too, that colonial judges were members of the Colonial Legal Service (since 1957 replaced by the Overseas Civil Service), and that a judicial career under the service was 'not radically different in quality . . . from that of a Civil Servant'.[3] It is a reflection of the 'civil servant' status of colonial judges that the Governor of a territory was empowered to submit periodical reports to the Colonial Office in London on the Chief Justice who, in turn, had to send similar reports on the judges under him through the Governor.[4] The idea of a territorial Governor having to furnish reports on judges within his territory is clearly 'out of harmony with judicial independence'.

There is nothing surprising about the subordinate position held by judges in the Colonial Service. The point was made earlier that the exigencies of a colonial situation precluded putting in to practice the English ideal of judicial independence. A colonial authority, at least until 'the power of the Executive [was] strengthened', and its position seemingly 'accepted' by the colonised indigenous population, could hardly afford to have its actions challenged by any other authority within its area of jurisdiction. A colonial authority had to remain paramount; otherwise, it would be ineffective, and colonial rule might be impossible. This was, by and large, the broad framework within which a colonial judiciary had to operate.

Long before *Terrell*'s case there was ample indication of the non-independent posture of the Supreme Court in Nigeria. We saw the shabby treatment of Willoughby Osborne as Chief Justice of amalgamated Southern Nigeria Protectorate, and how the Colonial Office in 1910 adjudicated that Sir Walter Egerton, the colonial Governor, had power over the disposition of staff within the judicial department – the Chief Justice, as a matter of courtesy, enjoying only the right of consultation.[5] Judges whose judicial outlook appeared unduly robust for the colonial situation of Southern Nigeria or who seemed too conscious of the independence of action they ought to enjoy were not long in the territory's judicial service. Willoughby Osborne, once described by Lugard as 'an excellent man to work with and deservedly popular' was 'summarily retired' on the eve of the judicial reorganisation of 1914, to the great consternation of Lagosians and of informed circles in England.[6] Willoughby Osborne had always shown he had a mind of his own. On the issue of judicial reorganisation in particular, his views differed from Lugard's in some vital respects, showing that he might indeed be inclined to obstruct Lugard's plans.[7] Justice William H. Stoker, the independent-minded puisne judge of the Supreme Court who ruled against the Executive in *Davies v. Rising* (1910),[8] was compelled to resign his judicial appointment in the same year.[9] Like Osborne, he was out of sympathy with Lugard's reforms, contending with the Colonial Office that many irregularities had been perpetrated in the process of establishing a new judicial system for Nigeria.[10]

For much of the colonial period after 1914 it is significant that most judges of the Supreme Court were men who seemed to believe in judicial self-restraint and were willing to cooperate with the executive arm of the colonial government. Edwin Speed, the first Chief Justice of amalgamated Nigeria, was given his appointment in preference to Willoughby Osborne and William H. Stoker, perhaps not because he demonstrated any superior judicial ability to these two gentlemen, but because, in contrast to them, he 'has always shown himself ready to assist the Executive in every possible way by advising on legal matters'.[11] There is evidence to suggest that of the three men, Willoughby Osborne was, in fact, the most suitable for appointment to the post of Chief Justice and that Speed's 'judicial experience and reputation' were inferior to his.[12] It will be recalled that Speed was the brain behind the judicial reorganisation of 1914, and the foremost champion of the institution of provincial courts. It may be rather harsh to describe him as 'Lugard's man ready to do what he was told',[13] but he was certainly hand-in-glove with the colonial government.

Speed's successors on the Supreme Court Bench were no less sympathetic to the position of the Executive in Nigeria. In this connection it is significant that only one judge of the court, Justice Webber, expressed reservations about the provisions of the judicial reorganisation of 1914.[14] Sir Ralph Combe, Chief Justice

1919–29, fully supported the operation of the provincial court system, although he was aware of its inherent weaknesses.[15] Justice Frederick Alan van der Meulen, a puisne judge of the court, 1919–26, and several times Acting Chief Justice, once wrote that he was convinced of 'the suitability of the Provincial courts for the primitive peoples of the interior of the Nigeria Protectorate'.[16] He added what might have been an important canon of his judicial belief: '*Festina lente* must undoubtedly be the watchword when applying [British] institutions to peoples such as those in Nigeria'[17] – precisely the same viewpoint held by the colonial government up to the 1940s.

In trying to understand the personalities of the judges of the court, it is worth noting that not a few of them were products of the 'Colonial Service' and were therefore likely to be sensitive to the requirements of a colonial situation. Sir Edwin Speed joined the Colonial Service as a district commissioner on the Gold Coast (Ghana), and was Attorney-General, first of Lagos Colony, and later of Southern Nigeria between 1900 and 1908. On several occasions before 1908 he also acted as Colonial Secretary and Deputy Governor of Lagos.[18] Sir Ralph Combe began is career in the Colonial Service as Crown Advocate for the East African Protectorate (later Tanganyika) in 1905. For the four or five years before his appointment as Chief Justice, he was Nigeria's Attorney-General (1914–18), that is to say, a member of the executive arm of the colonial government.[19] Sir Ralph's successor as Chief Justice, Sir Donald Kingdon (1929–46), had even wider experience of colonial administration. He began his career in Gambia as legal assistant and inspector of schools, was a member of the colony's Legislative Council in 1912, and briefly acted as Colonial Secretary. Between 1912 and 1920 he served on the Gold Coast and in Uganda as Attorney-General, member of the Legislative Council and Acting Colonial Secretary. From 1921 until his appointment he, like his predecessor, was Nigeria's Attorney-General.[20] Sir John Verity, Chief Justice 1946–54, began his career in 1908 in British Honduras. He was later called to the English Bar, and served in legal and judicial positions in many parts of the West Indies and in Zanzibar before his appointment as chief justice of Nigeria.[21]

The puisne judges of the Supreme Court were no exceptions. Frederick van der Meulen started his career in the Colonial Service as assistant district commissioner in Sierra Leone in 1907, becoming the colony's Solicitor-General the following year.[22] Sir Mervyn

Lawrence Tew, puisne judge of the court 1923–9, rose to that position from the rank of colonial administrator. He started off as assistant district commissioner in Southern Nigeria in 1904 and, having been called to the English Bar in 1913, was Nigeria's Solicitor-General 1920–3.[23] Neville John Brooke, puisne judge 1940–8 and sometime Acting Chief Justice, was primarily an administrative officer who turned judge apparently without any formal legal education. He started his career in Nigeria in 1915, rising to the rank of a Provincial Resident in 1932.[24] It was for this reason not surprising that in his investigations of the 'native' courts in Southern Nigeria between 1949 and 1952, he came up with reports reiterating the same misgivings about the Supreme Court as were held by administrative officers and commending what he believed to be the virtues of the provincial court.[25] Some other notable puisne judges – Sir Philip Bertie Petrides (1926–30),[26] Charles T. Abbott (1944–50),[27] Percival Cyril Hubbard (1949–1955),[28] – held legal or administrative positions in the Colonial Service in Nigeria or other colonies before their judicial appointments in Nigeria. Indeed in the period of this study, it was rare to find a British judge of the Supreme Court who had not risen from the ranks of the Colonial Service. To the best of the writer's knowledge, the only exception would seem to be Sir George Graham Paul, puisne judge of the Supreme Court, 1933–9, who for about twenty years before his appointment was in private legal practice at Calabar in south-eastern Nigeria.[29]

The point being made is not that the judges of the Supreme Court were mere tools of the colonial government, but that most of them were likely to possess an outlook on colonial questions not radically different from that of their contemporaries in the purely administrative wing of the Colonial Service. It was an outlook bred of common experience of the problems of colonial administration. In matters of policy colonial judges were apt to be willing collaborators of the executive rather than its critics. It would be over-stating a case to call colonial judges latter-day versions of 'lions under the throne', but in Southern Nigeria, they tended to show a high degree of sympathy for the position of the executive on vital issues of administration and government.

The collaboration of the members of the judiciary with the Executive in devising the provincial court system or in openly defending it provides one indication of this tendency. One is also tempted to believe that the court could be sensitive to the economic and political interests of the colonial regime. In a series of land cases in Lagos at the beginning of this century,[30] there is no evidence that the court was directly influenced by the Executive or that it was doing anything other than interpreting the law according to its best lights. But the general attitude of the court was capable of being interpreted as serving the economic interests of the colonial power in Southern Nigeria. The central issue in all the cases revolved around the meaning of the Treaty of Cession 1861, by which King Dosunmu was said to have ceded Lagos to the British Crown,[31] and the title of the indigenous population to their land. The operative portion of the treaty in these cases is part of Article 1 which reads:

> I, Docemo, do, with the consent and advice of my Council, give, transfer and by these presents, grant and confirm unto the Queen of Great Britain, her heirs and successors for ever, the Port and Island of Lagos, with all the rights, profits, territories and appurtenances thereunto belonging, and as well the profits and revenue as the direct, full and absolute dominion and sovereignty of the said port, island and premises with all the royalties thereof, freely, fully, entirely and absolutely. . . .[32]

In the famous foreshore case, *Attorney-General v. John Holt & Co. and others* (1910), and *Attorney-General v. W. B. McIver & Co. and others* (1910), the full court (that is, the Supreme Court in its appellate jurisdiction with at least three judges on the Bench), held that the title to the land of Lagos, including the foreshore, was vested in the British Crown, and that the Treaty of 1861 was 'a cession of territory'.[33] Under the treaty, according to the Chief Justice, Ralph Combe, 'the foreshore round the island of Lagos became vested in the Crown, subject, however, to the then existing rights of riparian occupiers to use it for the purpose of access to the water, and for landing and embarking and mooring, and hauling up canoes'.[34] In short, the interest of the local inhabitants in the foreshore of Lagos was no more than a licence to use it. Again, in February 1912, the full court reversed the decision earlier given by the Supreme Court in *The Commissioner of Lands v. The Oniru*,[35] declaring the latter a trustee entitled to the land whereupon stood a group of villages near Lagos. The basis of the full court's action in reversing the decision was that the defendant, Chief Oniru, did not possess the land in question before 1861, and that in view of the Treaty of Cession, 'possession of the land subsequent to this date gave the possessor no legal title or interest in the land'.[36]

In what now appears as a judicial flash in the pan, the higher courts in Nigeria in *Oduntan Onisiwo v. Attorney-General* (1912) held that the Treaty of 1861 notwithstanding, 'the ownership rights of private landowners, including the families of the [land-owning chiefs of Lagos] were left entirely unimpaired, and as freely exercisable after the cession as before'.[37]

But the test case for this interpretation of the treaty came in 1915 in *Amodu Tijani v. The Secretary, Southern Provinces*,[38] and the honour fell on Chief Justice Edwin Speed to destroy its authority. The facts of the *Tijani* case were simple. The Government of Southern Nigeria, under the Public Lands Ordinance, 1903,[39] had in November 1913 acquired a certain area of land at Apapa for public use. Amodu Tijani, *alias* Chief Oluwa, one of the white-cap, land-owning chiefs of Lagos, claimed that the acquired land was his own and his family's. He therefore demanded full compensation, first as absolute owner, then (on appeal) in a representative capacity, in accordance with the provisions of the Public Lands Ordinance. Once again, the Treaty of Cession was prominently in issue, for the Apapa land was part of the territory supposedly ceded to the British Crown in 1861. The Supreme Court in 1915, and, three years later, the full court, held that Chief Oluwa was entitled to some compensation, but this was not to be assessed on the basis of absolute ownership which he claimed over the land. In the phraseology of Chief Justice Speed, Chief Oluwa's interest in the Apapa land was 'merely a seigneurial right, giving the holder the ordinary rights of control and management of the land in accordance with the well-known principles of native law and custom'.[40] The invocation of 'native law and custom' was of no practical value, for, clearly, this decision gave to Chief Oluwa no more than merely administrative rights over the land in question The authority of *Oduntan Onisiwo v. Attorney-General* was set aside, both the Supreme Court and the full court implying that the judgment in that case was given *per incuriam*.[41]

It required the intervention of the Privy Council in London to reverse the decision of the courts in Nigeria in the *Tijani* case and to clarify once and for all the position of the British Crown in relation to Nigerian land. On 11 July 1921, Lord Viscount Haldane delivered the judgment of the judicial committee of the Privy Council.[42] In essence the decision of the Nigerian courts was reversed because it failed 'to recognize the real character of the title to land occupied by a native community'. Chief Oluwa in his representative capacity was to be compensated for the Apapa land acquired by the Southern Nigeria Government 'on the footing that he [was] transferring to the Governor the land in full ownership . . . along with his own title to receive rent or tribute'. On the Treaty of Cession, Lord Haldane declared:

> No doubt there was a cession to the British Crown along with the sovereignty of the radical or ultimate title to the land in the new Colony; but this cession appears to have been made on the footing that the rights of property of the inhabitants were to be fully respected. This principle is a usual one under British policy and law when such occupations take place. . . . A mere change in sovereignty is not to be presumed as meant to disturb rights of private owners, and the general terms of a cession are *prima facie* to be construed accordingly.[43]

It has been suggested that the decision of the Privy Council in the *Tijani* case was, at bottom, grounded not on construction of the Treaty of Cession, but on policy.[44] The rights of Nigerians to land in Lagos were unaffected, not because the treaty bore a construction making absolute grant to the British Crown impossible, but because the British Government had, by its profession in Parliament in 1862, and by its conduct subsequently, indicated its willingness to leave undisturbed the beneficial interests of Lagosians in their own land.[45]

But if the Privy Council decision in the *Tijani* case was more of policy than of law, the trend of judicial thinking leading up to that decision was not unknown to the courts in Nigeria. In the leading case of *Cook v. Sprigg* (1899),[46] involving a treaty ceding Pondoland in South Africa to the British Crown, the Privy Council had declared that a change of sovereignty by cession 'ought not to affect private property', even though no court 'could enforce such an obligation'. A corollary of this doctrine was that unless the Crown indicated expressly or by conduct a clear intention to alienate the proprietary interests of a subject people, such interests should be presumed to continue to exist. The effects of *Cook v. Sprigg* had echoed through the Nigerian courts. Its basic doctrine and its corollary seem to have been followed by Chief Justice Osborne in *Oduntan Onisiwo v. The Attorney-General* (1912), declaring inalienable the private interests of Lagosians in their land.

Reference was made to the *Onisiwo* case and to *Cook v. Sprigg* in the *Tijani* case, but the doctrine was conveniently ignored.

On the political scene, opinions would perhaps continue to differ on the extent to which the Supreme Court exercised its independence of judgment in *Eshugbayi Eleko v. The Officer Administering the Government of Nigeria and another* (1925–31) – a highly politically charged constitutional case which journeyed twice to the Privy Council.[47] Although Chief Justice Ralph Combe took pains in *Rex v. Thomas Horatius Jackson* (1925) to affirm the independence of the court over the case, the impression of the intelligentsia in Lagos was that in the *Eshugbayi Eleko* case, as in the *Tijani* case, the court was under the influence of the executive arm of the colonial government.

The story of the turbulent power tussle between the colonial government and Eshugbayi *Eleko*, traditional ruler of Lagos, has been related elsewhere.[48] The antipathy between the *Eleko* and the government began in 1915 when he refused to cooperate with the government over the water-rate agitation.[49] In 1919. he appointed some Muslim headmen, without notifying the Governor and was consequently suspended. In 1920, Herbert Macaulay, a staunch supporter of the *Eleko* and the foremost nationalist leader of his time, held a press conference in London in which he was very critical of the cavalier attitude of the Nigeria government to the *Eleko*. Macaulay was in London in connection with the *Tijani* land case, then on appeal to the Privy Council. In the eyes of the colonial authorities in Lagos, it was a veritable indication of the conspiratorial link between him and the *Eleko* that he held the latter's staff of office while he was in London. Back in Nigeria, *Eleko* Eshugbayi was asked to repudiate Macaulay's 'irresponsible vapourings'. On his refusal to denounce his chief supporter, the Governor published a notice 'ceasing to recognize' him as the *Eleko*.

Although two successors were recognised by the government, one after another, Lagos metropolis enjoyed no peace. Eshugbayi's support increased in strength, and he became a focal point of opposition and intrigues. In the circumstances, the colonial government, somewhat naively believing that the removal of Eshugbayi's person from the scene would end all political intrigues, decided to deport him to Oyo. That decision was effected by an order signed on 8 August 1925 under the Deposed Chief Removal Ordinance, 1917, as amended in 1925.

The deportation order touched off one of the most hard-fought battles in Nigerian legal history.[50] The central issue was whether a detained person could apply successively for a writ of *habeas corpus* to one judge after another regardless of how many times it was refused him. Application for a writ of *habeas corpus* was filed on behalf of Eshugbayi at the Supreme Court in Lagos on 18 September 1925. The application was heard by Justice Webber as acting chief justice. After hearing arguments of counsel he refused to issue the writ. On 4 December 1925 another application for a writ, essentially the same as the first, was filed at the divisional court (of the same Supreme Court) before Justice M. L. Tew. In his judgment, delivered on 14 December, Tew held he had no jurisdiction to entertain an application which had already been refused by the Supreme Court.[51] The full court to which Eshugbayi appealed in March 1926 also met his application with a *non possumus*, declaring that the successive applications to Webber and Tew 'were made to the same Court – namely to the Supreme Court of Nigeria'. Only that court had jurisdiction to entertain application for a writ of *habeas corpus*, and once Eshugbayi's application had been determined by a judge exercising the jurisdiction of that court, no other judge could reopen the issue. It is a reflection of the lowly posture which the Supreme Court apparently ascribed to itself in Nigeria that in the view of the Chief Justice, Sir Ralph Combe, judges of the Supreme Court did not possess common law powers to issue the writ of *habeas corpus*. 'The Judges of the Supreme Court', he declared, 'deserve their jurisdiction in relation to writs of *habeas corpus* from the Ordinances of the Colony and Protectorate, and not otherwise. . . .'[52] Again, as if to underline its policy of judicial self-restraint, the full court accepted the argument, which was put forward by the government at the Supreme Court, that the exercise of the powers under the Deposed Chiefs Removal Ordinance by the Governor was 'beyond question'.

The first appeal in the *Eleko* case to the judicial committee of the Privy Council was in 1928. Their lordships of the Privy Council, in a judgment delivered in London on 19 June, overturned the decisions of both the Supreme Court and the full court. They declared that successive applications for a writ of *habeas corpus* could be made to different judges of the same court, and that it was up to each one to consider the application on its own merit.[53] In contrast to the unquestioned acceptance by the courts in Nigeria of the view that the orders made by the Governor deposing and deporting Eshugbayi in 1925 could not be subject to judicial investigation, their lordships declared that the powers of the Governor under the Deposed Chiefs Removal Ordinance 'were purely executive' and that it was the duty of the court in Nigeria 'to investigate the questions raised by the appellant's [Eshugbayi's] contentions and to come to a judicial decision thereon'.[54]

It was on the basis of this finding that the Privy Council remitted the case to the Supreme Court in Lagos. Successive rehearings of the case at the Supreme Court and at the full court (on appeal) went on between 15 January 1929 and 3 March 1930. Ultimately Eshugbayi *Eleko* was refused the writ of *habeas corpus*, and a second appeal to the Privy Council was made in 1931.[55] The Supreme Court and the full court in Nigeria seemed most unwilling to question the legality of the action of the executive in deposing and deporting Eshugbayi *Eleko*. At the Supreme Court, Justice Tew held that the court was not competent to decide the two issues raised by Eshugbayi in his application: whether or not Eshugbayi was a 'chief' under the Deposed Chiefs Removal Ordinance, and whether or not by customary law he was deposed or removed from office. One learned judge even suggested that the deposition and deportation of Eshugbayi constituted 'an act of state' not subject to questioning by the courts.[56]

The judicial committee of the Privy Council in its judgment delivered by Lord Atkin on 24 March 1931, shattered many of the judicial views held by the Supreme Court and the full court in Nigeria. It was an erroneous view, the board declared, that the courts in Nigeria were incompetent to investigate the legality of an order of the Executive deposing or deporting an indigenous chief. The colonial Governor acting under the Deposed Chiefs Removal Ordinance, in the view of their lordships, was acting 'solely under executive powers' and could be called into question by the courts. As the chief executive, the Governor could 'only act in pursuance of the powers given by law'. The board also rejected the notion that the deportation of Eshugbayi *Eleko* was 'an act of state':

. . . As applied to acts of the executive directed to subjects within the territorial jurisdiction, [that phrase] has no special meaning, and can give no immunity from the jurisdiction of the Court to inquire into the legality of the act [of deposition and deportation].[57]

In a memorable passage which certainly did not reflect well on the role of the Nigerian courts in the unhappy history of the *Eleko* case, Lord Atkin declared:

> In accordance with British jurisprudence no member of the executive can interfere with the liberty or property of a British subject except on condition that he can support the legality of his action before a court of justice. And it is the tradition of British justice that judges should not shrink from deciding such issues in the face of the executive.[58]

The Privy Council threw the case back to the Supreme Court in Nigeria to be heard *de novo*. It was at this juncture that Sir Donald Cameron, as the new Governor of Nigeria, brought political wisdom in to the tussle between Eshugbayi and the colonial government. He allowed Eshugbayi to return to Lagos as the *Eleko*, having arranged that the reigning government-backed *Eleko*, Sanusi, should retire with his stipend of ₦800 per annum guaranteed for life.[59]

How far, if at all, the Supreme Court in Lagos was under the influence of the Executive in the *Eshugbayi Eleko* case is probably impossible now to determine. Up to the first Privy Council appeal, the question of law involved in the case, as Lord Hailsham indicated, was 'one of grave constitutional importance to His Majesty's subjects' in the United Kingdom and overseas; namely, whether successive applications for a writ of *habeas corpus* could be made to different judges exercising concurrent jurisdiction. In deciding the issue against Eshugbayi *Eleko* the courts in Nigeria were most probably interpreting the law in their best lights without any interference from the Executive. It is instructive in this connection that the Privy Council decision in the case favouring Eshugbayi *Eleko*, is probably no longer good law. *Re Hastings* (1958–9)[60] seems to establish or affirm what the Supreme Court and the full court in Lagos upheld in the *Eleko* case: that at common law a detained person has no right to make successive applications for a writ of *habeas corpus*.

But the proceedings in the *Eleko* case after the first Privy Council appeal leave room for doubts in one's mind as to the independence of the Nigerian judiciary in the case. One has the impression of a judiciary that was unwilling to pry into the legality of an executive action perhaps out of deference to the Executive, or simply out of excessive judicial self-restraint.

It is only fair in assessing the position of the Supreme Court *vis-à-vis* the Executive in Nigeria to point out that in cases of lesser political colouring than the *Eleko* case the court demonstrated an unmistakable independence of outlook. Reference was made in the previous chapter to a number of cases decided by political officers at the provincial courts and reversed by the Supreme Court. Quite a substantial number of such cases involved the liberty of the individual citizen. In resolving them in favour of the convicted prisoners the court showed its readiness, in a way that Lord Atkin would have approved, to champion the cause of personal liberty against the arbitrariness of political officers.

A case in point which finds its way into the official *Law Reports* is *Onowu of Onitsha v. B. E. Nzekwu*.[61] Ben Nzekwu was in December 1927 charged before the 'native' court with contravening 'native law and custom' by inciting persons to ignore the rights of the chief and elders of Onitsha in certain ceremonies known as the second burial. He was convicted of an entirely different offence: refusing to make peace with certain persons at Onitsha. He was later sentenced to one year's imprisonment with hard labour.

Much more was involved in the charge and conviction than meets the eye. Nzekwu was a letter-writer, 'an educated intelligent man'. By virtue of his education and profession, he was 'the natural spokesman' of a family in Onitsha local politics, presumably the family who were by tradition entitled to rule, but who now found themselves out of power under the colonial regime. In the process of espousing the cause of this family, Nzekwu became 'troublesome to the constituted native authority'.[62] The curious charge brought against him and the even more curious one for which he was convicted were a direct result of the fractional political struggle then prevailing at Onitsha. As one would expect, the white officials in Onitsha district were on the side of the local authorities. Nzekwu applied for a writ of *habeas corpus* to the station magistrate at Onitsha. Apparently for political reasons, not only did the magistrate refuse to issue the writ, he also refused to grant leave to appeal to the Supreme Court against his decision.

It was in these circumstances that the Supreme Court asserted its power to intervene in the case. After 1914 there was no direct link between the Supreme Court and the 'native' court. For this reason the government maintained in this case that the Supreme Court had no power to inquire into a matter which had been determined by a 'native' court. But the Supreme Court would not accept such a curb on its power. It ordered Nzekwu to be discharged from prison immediately, maintaining that where a 'native' court acted illegally, it had power, at any rate where the cause of action fell within its area of jurisdiction, to right a wrong 'in the interests of justice'.[63] The court observed 'an unpleasant savour of persecution about [the] proceedings' in the case at the Onitsha 'native' court and, in effect, castigated the station magistrate for supporting the 'extremely harsh sentence' passed on the man by the 'native' court.

III

Whatever may be said about the position of the Supreme Court in relation to the executive arm of the colonial regime in Southern Nigeria, there can be no doubt about the imprint left by the court on the territory's social and economic development. Much of what was said about the provincial and the 'native' courts in their impact on Southern Nigeria is applicable to the Supreme Court. The court did not touch the lives of the masses as directly as the 'native' courts did; yet the latter category of courts derived much of their 'judicial' orientation from it, as they tended to copy its judicial methods and procedure.

In terms of social development, the protection which the Supreme Court gave to individual rights to property within the family and in the wider society could not have failed to enhance the growth of individualism. It was laid down in *Thomas v. Thomas* (1932)[64] and *Bajulaiye v. Akapo* (1938)[65] that every member of the family has a right to live and continue to live in the family house, including the right to enter and live at will. A related principle tending to the same result was upheld in *Chief Archibong and others v. Etubom Archibong and others* (1947);[66] namely, that the head of a family or 'house' was a kind of trustee in relation to the other members of the 'house', and that his actions 'must be capable of reasonable explanation at any time to the reasonable satisfaction of any of the members of his "house"'. On a slightly different level, yet upholding the principle of individual rights to property, the court in *Agwu v. Nezianya* (1949)[67] ruled that a self-acquired property does not belong to the owner's family and is freely disposable by him.

An aspect of the spur given by the court to the growth of individualism was the affirmation of equality between the sexes, particularly in respect of disposition of family property. In 1897, Johnson in his *History of the Yorubas* wrote as follows regarding the rights of women under Yoruba customary law:

> When a man dies his farm is inherited by his children and so from father to son in perpetuity and like the house, it is not subject to sale. If his children are females they will pass on to the male relatives.[68]

Similar rules existed in most other communities of Southern Nigeria. But hand in hand with the other factors of change discussed in Chapter 6, the Supreme Court by its judicial policy tended to upturn the servile position in which customary law put women in matters of rights to property. In a string of cases the court recognised the equality of right to father's property as between males and females, contrary to strict customary law.[69] In *Manana Lopez and others v. Domingo Lopez and others* (1924), the full court in Lagos was prepared to order the partition of a family property if that would be 'the only effective means of ensuring that a female and her issue shall live on her father's lands without being disturbed by other members of the family'.[70] By the 1930s the idea of equality of sex in relation to the distribution of family property had become established,[71] and may now be regarded as a cardinal principle of Nigerian common law[72] and a fact of Southern Nigerian social life.

Colonial law certainly did not achieve 'a radical social transformation of indigenous African society',[73] but it has gone some way to bring about some modifications in the cultures of African peoples. In this development, as far as Southern Nigeria was concerned, the Supreme Court has contributed in no small measure.

In importing modifications into the indigenous cultures of Southern Nigeria, the potent tool in the hands of the Supreme Court, as in those of the provincial and the 'native' courts, has been the 'Repugnancy' doctrine, applied in the administration of indigenous customary laws. It has been suggested that the doctrine 'was a device to escape from English law, not to call it in'.[74] But even if they tried to 'escape from English law', the Supreme Court judges, just as administrative officers at the provincial and the 'native' courts did, inevitably brought their English cultural and legal background into play.[75]

The Supreme Court has applied the 'Repugnancy' doctrine on numerous occasions. The overall result has been that many customary legal rules 'have either been judicially abolished altogether or have had their asperity in operation mollified'.[76] The court, for instance, did in *Chawere v. Aihenu and Johnson* (1935)[77] reject the customary rule that an adulteress *ipso facto* of the adultery becomes the wife of the adulterer. The court in *Ekpenyong Edet v. Nyon Essien* (1932)[78] affirmed the decision of the provincial court at Calabar rejecting the customary rule that if a man's wife leaves him without the 'dowry' on the wife being repaid, he has a claim to all the children she may have by a subsequent union with any other man.

On the same principle of repugnancy, any claim to property smacking of slavery has not found favour with the court. Thus in *Abassi Okon Akpan v. Chief Elijah Henshaw and Ita* (1930),[79] it was held that the personal property of an emancipated slave was his own, and not subject to the control of the head of his 'house'. The same note was struck in *Victoria Fanny Martin v. Johnson and Henshaw* (1935)[80] in which the defendants' claim to the property of a deceased member of a 'house' on the strength that the deceased's father was a slave of the 'house' was held untenable.

The impression should not be given that the Supreme Court has in all its judicial activities represented a dynamic and progressive force in society. Indeed the court exhibited a marked tendency to be cautious about overturning traditional practices where they did not seem to be particularly offensive to British notions of justice or civilisation. Thus, as was mentioned in Chapter 6, the traditional practice of levirate has been upheld. Some traditional constitutional arrangements, which might seem offensive to modern egalitarian sentiments, have similarly been upheld by the Court.[81] The customary rule awarding the guardianship of an illegitimate child to the family to which his mother was married rather than to the mother's family by birth has been left undisturbed in *Oruboroma Charlie Amachree v. Inko Taria alias Goodhead* (1923).[82] In the economic sphere the court continued to recognise the principles of group ownership of land and of its inalienability by individual members.[83]

It can therefore be seen that in its impact on the socio-cultural development of Southern Nigeria, the Supreme Court, like the provincial and the 'native' courts, has tended to play a dual role. While the court has through its judicial policies leaned against some undesirable aspects of the indigenous customary practices, thus stimulating 'social regeneration, enlightenment and progress', it has in its conservative vein assisted in strengthening the cultural fibres of the society making for social stability.

In certain spheres of the socio-cultural life of Southern Nigeria, particularly in marital relations, the court's role can be seen as that of laying down lines of possible development. In what seems like an attempt at fostering English 'moral and social thinking' in Nigeria, the colonial regime promulgated a Marriage Ordinance in 1863, followed by a similar subsequent ordinance in 1884, and a Marriage Act.[84] The Marriage Ordinance, 1863, the essence of which was embodied in the Ordinance of 1884 and the later Marriage Act, was a direct importation of the English Matrimonial Causes Act 1857.[85] Marriage under the Act is monogamous – a 'voluntary union of one man and one woman to the exclusion of all others'. Incidents of marriage under the Act (as under the 1863 Ordinance in Southern Nigeria) follow the English law. For instance the property of the man would pass exclusively to the wife and her children if he died intestate.

It is of interest to note that marriage under the ordinance was deliberately placed 'on a higher pedestal' than the other forms of marriage in Nigeria.[86] For instance under the Marriage Ordinance of the later Marriage Act, customary marriage may be converted to monogamous marriage, but not *vice versa*.[87] The reason for the discrimination is obvious. The British colonial rulers were imposing on Nigerians what they considered a superior moral and social order. The same reason would explain why criminal sanctions were attached to violations of certain provisions of the Marriage Ordinance or the Marriage Act. It was made an offence for any person to 'mix' customary marriage with marriage under the ordinance.[88] Besides, the Criminal Code, 1916, created a felony, punishable by seven years' imprisonment, which consisted in a man or a woman married under the ordinance purporting to marry again while his or her spouse was alive.[89]

There is much doubt about the success of the criminal sanctions attached to the marriage statutes in effecting any change in the marriage practices of Nigerians. The provisions of the marriage statutes have been honoured more in the breach than in the observance, and reported cases of bigamy and other related offences under the statutes and the criminal code have been very few.

But although the law and the courts might have failed to 'alter the temperament of the people'[90] in respect of marriage practices, the Supreme Court has insisted on the observance of the lines of development laid down in the marriage statutes. A string of cases since *Cole v. Cole* (1898) has established the principle that when two parties contract a Christian monogamous marriage or marriage under the marriage law, the marriage contract and its incidents should be governed by English, and not customary, law. It is instructive that the Supreme Court and the higher courts in Nigeria still insist on the observance of the incidents (in accordance with the received English law) of monogamous Christian marriage or marriage under the marriage law whenever it appears to be the intention of the parties to contract such a marriage. In *Olubunmi Cole and another v. Akinyele* (1960),[91] the federal Supreme Court decided that children 'born out of wedlock' in a monogamous union cannot inherit. To some extent, then, the principle established by the Supreme Court in *Cole v. Cole* may continue to influence Nigeria's cultural development.

IV

The same ambivalence noticeable in the role of the Supreme Court in the socio-cultural development of Southern Nigeria is also observable in the role of the court in the economic sphere, although, on the whole, the court would seem to have exerted a greater influence in this sphere than in the socio-cultural sphere.

In its 'progressive' vein and with the repugnancy doctrine as its main tool of operation, the Supreme Court in a series of cases would seem to have championed the cause of economic freedom and economic progress. Thus, for instance, in *Amachree Charles King Amachree v. Daniel Kalio and others* (1914)[92] a customary claim to monopolistic fishing rights on the New Calabar River, 'a great water highway', was held to be repugnant to natural justice and, one may add, to the principles of free enterprise. Under its equitable jurisdiction, the full court in modifying a customary rule of land tenure, allowed the defendants in *Chief Uwani v. Nwosu Akom and others* (1928)[93] to retain for themselves and four hundred others a large piece of land they had occupied for a considerable length of time at Ukpom in the Bende District of Owerri Province on condition they paid an annual rent. In a similar vein, the court regarding itself as 'the keeper of the conscience of native communities in regard to the absolute enforcement of alleged native customs', held in *Chief Mojolagbe Ashogbon v. Saidu Oduntan*

(1935)[94] that there must be a strong, irrefragable evidence of 'misconduct' on the part of a customary tenant before he can lose his rights under customary law. Similarly in *Bashua v. Oduntan and Ilubanto* (1940)[95] the court refused to apply a customary law whereby a landlord could eject his tenant for denying his owner-ship of the premises, to a case where the tenant paid monthly rents for his tenancy. On the basis of equity and natural justice, the defendants in *Ogbakumanwu and others v. Chiabolo and others* (1950)[96] were held entitled to continue to enjoy occupational rights as customary tenants over a piece of land in Enugu District, against the claim of the plaintiffs that they were the true owners of the land.

Of great economic significance was the readiness of the court to uphold sale or partition of family property where such a course of action was deemed equitable. An illustration of this attitude of the court is found in *Aganran v. Olushi and others* (1907).[97] A piece of family land in the Badagry District of Lagos Colony was sold in March 1902 to the defendants by the head of the family, but without consulting the plaintiff, Aganran, whose approval was necessary to any valid sale. A family meeting was later held at which Aganran was present. He then consented to the sale, receiving ten naira as his share of the purchase money. He later returned the money and withdrew his earlier consent. In the meantime the defendants, who were the purchasers of the property, had entered into posses-sion and erected houses on it. In April 1905 Aganran took steps to set aside the sale and recover possession of the land. The Supreme Court, and later the full court, on appeal, dismissed his claim, holding that his unexplained delay in asserting his right under customary law to oppose the sale of the land in question was 'deemed to amount to an expression of intention or promise on his part not to exercise that right'.

Other decisions of the Supreme Court in the direction of enhanc-ing individual rights to property within the group are worthy of note. It was held in *Bassey Egbo Bassey v. Archibong Boco Cobham and others* (1924)[98] that the position of a head of a family in relation to communal land was analogous to that of a trustee, and that any member of the family might claim his rights in respect of such communal land if the head neglects or refuses to assert such rights. In *Nimota Sule v. M. A. Ajisegiri* (1937)[99] the court put male and female children 'on a footing of equality without discrimin-ation on account of sex' in the disposition of family property.

The full court did not hesitate in *Manana Lopez*'s case to order the partition of a family property when partition was deemed the only equitable course of action. In the same vein, it was held in *Ajibabi v. Jura and others* (1948)[100] that a family property no longer serving its traditional and main purpose of providing residence for family members could be sold, the members of the family sharing the proceeds of the sale. The West African Court of Appeal seems to have confirmed the 'progressive' judicial leaning of the Supreme Court in matters of family property when it decided in *Balogun v. Balogun* (1943),[101] a Nigerian case, that family property could be partitioned among the members of a family to terminate their joint ownership of it and vest in each member the absolute ownership of his share.

As if to facilitate the process of sale or easy transfer of property, the Supreme Court laid down in *The Secretary, Lagos Town Council v. N. B. Soule and Elo Aiyedun, Chief Aromire* (1939),[102] that where a family held out one of its members (who was not necessarily the head) as having authority to act on its behalf in the sale of a family property, the family would be bound by such sale. The principle established by the court in *Kasumu Aralawon v. Yesufu Aromire and another* (1940)[103] should be seen in the same light of the court striving to promote easy transfer of property. In that case it was held that the head of a family, acting on behalf of the family in an emergency to effect a sale of property, could bind the family to the purchaser without the usual customary consultation with and approval by the family as a whole.

So much for the 'progressive' aspect of the Supreme Court's judicial activities in relation to economic development. In its conservative vein, the same court handed down judgments which would seem to run counter to the prevailing economic circumstances. In its concern to safeguard the integrity of family property, the court, in a series of cases, has underscored the principle of group ownership of land, and, by the same token, has emphasised its inalienability by the individual.[104] In the celebrated *Amodu Tijani* case Lord Haldane, quoting Chief Justice Rayner of Lagos, affirmed at the Privy Council: 'Land belongs to the community, the village or the family, never to the individual'.[105] This was the high water-mark in the perpetration of a judicial notion which continued to cloud the vision of the courts in giving a realistic interpretation to Nigerian customary land tenure system, one that would be consonant with the needs for rapid economic and social development. 'One consequence of the emphatic assertion of the universality of communal ownership [of land]', A. E. W. Park has written, 'was for some time to inhibit judges from recognizing readily a natural evolution of customary law so as to incorporate individual ownership and free alienability of land.'[106] But should judges, as judges, consciously promote economic and social development? It is a truism that judges do not operate in a vacuum. In matters of broad judicial policies, it is not too much to expect judges of developing nations to be sensitive to the overall yearning of their people for rapid economic and social progress. Colonial judges did not always exhibit this kind of sensitivity.

A case in point is *Bassey Egbo Bassey v. Archibong Boco Cobham and others* (1924)[107] in which it was held that the act of reclaiming a piece of swamp land 'does not confer any special property in the land reclaimed on the individual who reclaims it, as against the communal title of the family'. Some judges would apparently not even recognise the possibility of absolute ownership in the land tenure system of Southern Nigeria. It was Justice Kingdon who declared in *Brimah Balogun v. Saka, Chief Oshodi* (1931):[108]

> Under native customary tenure an individual cannot alienate the land he occupies, consequently the rights of his descendants are safeguarded and cannot be realised by him. But once the tenure becomes fee simple [that is, absolute], the rights of generations yet unborn can be sold and the proceeds squandered by the present generation. This alone should, in my opinion, make the Court slow to implement, in the exercise of its equitable jurisdiction, the actions of persons who have selfishly sold or purported to sell the fee simple of land previously held under native customary tenure.[109]

There is much that is admirable in preserving the integrity of land for the benefits of 'generations yet unborn'. Yet, in terms of economic development, as the history of English land law amply demonstrates,[110] there is danger in overdoing it. The land itself might lack physical development precisely because, as in *Bassey Egbo Bassey*'s case, individual efforts at improving it might be frustrated by the claims of others harping on the 'communal' nature of the ownership of the land. Again, land might not be rendered easily transferable, a state of affairs which would necessarily impede the rate of economic development.

In spite of the conservative outlook of the Supreme Court in some of its decisions pertaining to the disposition of land, the court on the whole, has been a most potent force in the economic development of Southern Nigeria. I have in mind commercial development in particular, and one only needs to realise the inadequacy of Nigerian customary law to meet the exigencies of modern commerce to appreciate the cardinal role of the court in this sphere. The inadequacy of customary law stems partly from the novelty of modern commercial transactions in Southern Nigeria and partly from the fact of the colonial situation opening the territory to the wider commercial world. Almost from the beginning of its establishment, the Supreme Court administering English common law, has, to a great extent, supplied what is lacking in the indigenous customary rules of law, thus helping to lay the foundations for easy commercial relations at the domestic and international levels. The other English-style courts like the provincial courts, the protectorate and the high courts, to some extent, played a role similar to that of the Supreme Court in the commercial field. But because it was the highest territorial court, it was the Supreme Court which ultimately formulated the principles of law that became operative in many fields of commercial transactions.

It would be pertinent, first of all, to illustrate the usefulness of the Supreme Court in resolving disputes arising from commercial activities – disputes which were by their nature somewhat novel in their circumstances and which the rules of customary law in Southern Nigeria were inadequate to meet. The plaintiffs in *Najib Nabham and others v. Edem Davies* (1926)[111] were claiming a sum of ₦124 as value of the goods which were entrusted to the defendant, a Nigerian, to be carried by him for reward in his motor lorry from Lagos to Ibadan, but which were burnt and lost in transit. Given the obviously non-customary nature of the transaction between the parties, the court applied the English law on common carriers and gave judgment for the defendant.

In *Emmanuel Ladipo Francis v. Oseni Ibitoye* (1936),[112] the plaintiff was claiming ₦240 as cost of a building he erected on defendant's land at Ebute Metta, Lagos, without the latter's knowledge. The land in question had been the subject of a previous litigation between the parties, and had been declared to be the defendant's. Justice Graham Paul refused to accede to the request of the plaintiff, declaring that the house was a fixture within the context of English law, and that the maxim *quicquid plantatur solo, solo cedit* applied 'without qualification'.

As in *Abudu Kadiri v. Adamo Akeju* (1937),[113] whenever a contract of sale was purported to have been made, the court seems to have been inclined to apply English law, removing the transaction from the purview of customary law. In that case the plaintiff sought to recover the price of land allegedly purchased by him from the defendant. There was no memorandum of agreement (as required by the English Statute of Frauds, 1677) indicative of the sale of the land. No receipt for the money paid was produced; nor was there any act of part performance which, under the rules of equity, the court might have construed in favour of the plaintiff. In the circumstances, the court held that the English Statute of Frauds applied and that the alleged contract of sale was 'clearly unenforceable'. Money paid under such a contract could not be recovered.

One factor seems to underlie these cases. They were instances where the Supreme Court has called in the aid of the English law, either to meet the inadequacies of customary rules of law or to decide an issue which the court felt lay outside the pale of customary law. In invoking the assistance of English law in these circumstances the court helped to strengthen the framework of commercial relations in Nigeria.

English law was not always imported wholesale. The Supreme Court, administering the English common law in the furtherance of commercial development, sought to adapt it to suit Nigerian conditions. Take for instance the question of 'passing off' in commercial transactions. 'Passing off' is a common occurrence in the commercial world and it consists in deliberately acting to induce the belief in the general public that one's goods are those of another 'so as to take illicit and unfair advantage of the reputation of that other'.[114] Realising that the likelihood of deception of consumers will vary with the intelligence and education of consumers, the Supreme Court in Nigeria often took into consideration the factor of illiteracy among the masses of the population. It was on account of this factor that the court evolved the principle that when a trade mark has become known under some general appellation such as 'Anchor', 'Horseman', 'Cask' and so on, or their equivalents in the local language, it will be protected against another mark to which the same general appellation might apply.[115] Thus the following pairs of pictorial representations have been held to be capable of being confused: two lions in different positions (the *Ibadan* case);[116] a guinea fowl and a turkey (*C.F.A.O. v. Miller*

Brothers (1912));[117] two anchors emerging from a crown and a single anchor (the *Houtman* case (1912));[118] a figure with a bow and arrow standing on a horse and a man on horseback going in the opposite direction and attacking a leopard with a spear (*G. B. Ollivant & Co. Ltd. v. John Christian* (1925));[119] a parrot and a toucan (*Voorheen Van Berckel & Co. v. Netherlands Distilleries* (1928));[120] a cask in an upright position being coopered by three men and a cask being rolled along the ground by one man (*W. B. McIver & Co. v. C.F.A.O.* (1917));[121] a white man in the uniform of a bandmaster and a white man in the robe of a barrister (*The United Kingdom Tobacco Co. Ltd. v. Carreras Limited* (1931)).[122]

There were, no doubt, sufficient differences in each pair of representations and some of the decisions in the cases cited 'may seem a little startling' to a literate mind. But underlying them was the principle that in the commercial world of Southern Nigeria where the bulk of the population was non-literate, trade marks must be so different that they were not liable to be confused by the ordinary man. In evolving the principle the court took into account the local conditions of the territory, using a standard of similarity and comparison vastly different from what it was in Europe. The rationale behind the stand of the court in matters of trade marks has long been stated by Chief Justice Osborne in the *Houtman* case. It was that the law must be administered 'with a view to protecting not only a vast illiterate population little acquainted with pictorial representations, but also the pioneers of trade who have earned a reputation' for their products.[123]

Contracts are of the essence of commercial relations. The Supreme Court has, since its establishment, expounded different aspects of the English law of contract to suit the Nigerian soil, admittedly, not always consciously to aid commerce, but with undoubted benefit to its cause. Set in the commercial environment of Lagos, the court seemed destined to play a crucial role not only in the resolution of disputes arising from commercial relations, but also in the formulation of legal principles that would serve Nigeria's commercial needs. For as early as 1913, 'the greatest number of cases [tried at the court] are of a mercantile nature, such as actions brought by European firms for goods sold and delivered, for shortages in stock, and so forth'.[124]

The legal significance of printed conditions or exemption clauses often attached to contracts of carriage of goods was examined in the context of West Africa with a large non-literate population in *Animotu Otegbeye v. Little* (1907) and *Adam Lemomu v. Little* (1907)[125] – two cases which were said to be 'of considerable importance both to the traders and to the shipping firms in West Africa'. The plaintiffs in both cases were traders in Lagos. In February 1907 they were transporting bags of kola nuts from the Gold Coast (Ghana) through their servants in the steamship belonging to the defendant's shipping company. In transhipping the kola nuts at the Lagos harbour from the steamship to a surf boat belonging to the same shipping company, the surf boat capsized in what was alleged to be a bad weather and the kola nuts were lost. To counter the claim of the plaintiffs for damages, the defendant harped on the exemption clause at the foot of the receipt given to the plaintiffs' servants: 'The company will not be responsible for any damage however caused on kola shipments or loss in transhipment.' In rejecting this plea and giving judgment for the plaintiffs, the full court said that in a country where '90 per cent of the people' were illiterate, the defendants ought to have done 'all that they could reasonably be expected to do' to bring the exemption clause to the notice of the plaintiffs' servants. Moreover, exemption clauses, the court implied, must be reasonable. They should not be 'of such an extraordinary and special nature that no ordinary man of business would believe them to be there'.

It was in these two cases that the full court also considered the concept of 'act of God' as a legal defence – for that was the second limb of the defendant's plea; namely, that the loss of the kola nuts was due to the prevailing rough weather on the sea. The court's full exposition of the plea of 'act of God' need not detain us; it is sufficient to state that for the plea to succeed, the intervening act absolving the defendant from liability must be a *vis major*, and the defendant himself must have acted reasonably in the circumstances in which he finds himself.[126] This judicial view, like the numerous other decisions of the court, amounted to setting up a standard of behaviour in commercial relations.

There are many other areas of contractual relations which have been examined by the court: effect of customary practice on written contractual terms (*African Association Ltd. v. Elder Dempster & Co. Ltd.* (1921));[127] duration of the liability of a shipping company (*F. G. Osborne v. Elder Dempster & Co.* (1922));[128] the circumstances giving rise to impossibility of performance of contract (*Mann Poole & Co. v. Salami Agbaje* (1922));[129] false representation in inducing contracts (*Sule v. Aromire* (1951);[130]

goods ordered but not accepted and the measure of damages that may be claimed (*Roche and Henshilwood Ltd. v. Adeniran and another* (1951));[131] Master and servant relations (*Okunoren v. United Africa Co. Ltd.* (1951),[132] and (*Taiwo v. Kingsway Stores Ltd.* (1950));[133] effectiveness of oral agreement rescinding a clause in a written contract (*United Africa Co. Ltd. v. A. U. John Argo* (1938)).[134]

The principles of law enunciated in these and other cases have served (and some of them would continue to serve) as guide-posts for commercial interactions in Nigeria.

Notes

1 E. C. S. Wade and G. G. Phillips, *Constitutional Law*, London, 7th ed., 1965, pp. 323–4.
2 T. O. Elias, *British Colonial Law*, London, 1962, pp. 64–9.
3 K. Roberts-Wray, *Commonwealth and Colonial Law*, London, 1966, p. 476.
4 *Ibid.*, pp. 482–3.
5 *Infra*, pp. 91–93.
6 'New Justice in Nigeria: Natives and the Supreme Court', *Pall Mall Magazine*, 11 April 1914; I. F. Nicholson, *The Administration of Nigeria, 1900–1960*, Oxford, 1969, pp. 202–3.
7 NAI, CSO 20/2 NC 198/14, A. W. Osborne to Lugard, 17 December 1912; NAI, CSO 1/21, XII, Lugard to Colonial Office, 21 May 1913, enclosure 6 containing Osborne's views on proposed judicial reforms.
8 *Infra*, pp. 114–5.
9 NAI, CSO 20/2, NC 175/14, 'Memorial by Justice Stoker'.
10 *Ibid.*
11 NAI, CSO 1/21, 13, Lugard to Colonial Office, 21 July 1914.
12 I. F. Nicholson, *The Administration of Nigeria*, p. 203, n. 2.
13 *Ibid.*, p. 201.
14 NAE, Cal Prof 4/3/23, Minutes by A. Webber, 5 May 1915.
15 CO 657/9, *Nigeria Administration Reports*, 'Reports on the Supreme Court of Nigeria, 1923–1924'.
16 *The Times*, London, 9 September 1932, Letter to the Editor by F. A. Van der Meulen.
17 *Ibid.*
18 *Who Was Who*, IV, *1941–1950*, London, 1952, p. 1085.
19 *Ibid.*, p. 241.
20 *Who Was Who*, VI, *1961–1970*, London, 1972, p. 634.

21 *Who's Who*, London, 1969, p. 3170.
22 *Who Was Who, III, 1929–1940*, London, repr. 1947, p. 1382.
23 *Who Was Who, VI, 1961–1970*, London, 1972, p. 1109.
24 *Ibid.*, pp. 139–40.
25 *Reports of the Native Courts (Western Provinces) Commission of Inquiry*, Lagos, 1952, pp. 6–8; *Report of the Native Courts (Eastern Provinces) Commission of Inquiry*, Lagos, 1953, pp. 4–6.
26 *Who Was Who, V, 1951–1960*, London, 1961, pp. 868–9.
27 *Ibid.*, p. 1.
28 *Who Was Who, VI, 1961–1970*, London, 1972, p. 559.
29 CO 583/187, Cameron to Cunliffe-Lister, 20 July 1933.
30 *Attorney-General v. John Holt and others* (1910), *Attorney-General v. W. B. McIver and Co.* (1910), 2 N.L.R. 1; *Oduntan Onisiwo v. Attorney-General* (1912), 2 N.L.R. 79; *The Commissioner of Lands v. The Oniru* (1912), 2 N.L.R. 72; *Amodu Tijani v. The Secretary, Southern Provinces*, (1915–21), 3 N.L.R. 24.
31 J. F. A. Ajayi, 'The British Occupation of Lagos, 1851–1861'. *Nigeria Magazine*, No. 69, August 1961.
32 2 N.L.R. at pp. 8–9.
33 3 N.L.R. at p. 10.
34 *Ibid.*, pp. 10–11.
35 3 N.L.R. 72.
36 *Ibid.*, p. 74.
37 3 N.L.R. 79, 86.
38 3 N.L.R. 24.
39 Public Lands (Acquisition) Ordinance, No. 5, 1903, *Laws of the Colony of Southern Nigeria*, II, pp. 1196–1201.
40 3 N.L.R. 24, 31.
41 *Ibid.*, pp. 30, 38.
42 *Ibid.*, at p. 56.
43 *Ibid.*, p. 62.
44 A. E. W. Park, 'The Cession of Territory and Private Land Rights: A Reconsideration of the Tijani Case', *The Nigerian Law Journal*, i 1, 1964, p. 45.
45 3 N.L.R. 24, 61.
46 Cited by A. E. Park, *The Nigerian Law Journal*, i, 1, 1964, p. 45.
47 6 N.L.R. 73; 8 N.L.R. 1.
48 R. L. Buell, *The Native Problem in Africa*, London, repr. 1965, I, pp. 662–7; Margery Perham, *Native Administration in Nigeria*, London, repr. 1962, pp. 264–70.
49 On the water-rate agitation, see James Coleman, *Nigeria: Background to Nationalism*, Berkeley and Los Angeles, repr. 1971, pp. 25–32.
50 6 N.L.R. 73; 8 N.L.R. 1; A.C. (1931), 662.
51 6 N.L.R. 73, 82.
52 *Ibid.*, at p. 84.
53 8 N.L.R. 1.
54 A.C. (1931), 662.
55 *Ibid.*

56 *Ibid.*, at p. 671.
57 *Ibid.*, at p. 670.
58 *Ibid.*
59 Margery Perham, *Native Administration in Nigeria*, pp. 266–7.
60 Cited by A. E. W. Park, *The Sources of Nigerian Law*, London, 1963, p. 64.
61 (1928), 9 N.L.R. 65.
62 *Ibid.*, at p. 71.
63 *Ibid.*, at p. 68.
64 (1932) 16 N.L.R. 5.
65 (1938) 14 N.L.R. 10.
66 (1947) 18 N.L.R. 117.
67 (1949) 12 W.A.C.A. 450.
68 Samuel Johnson, *History of the Yorubas*, London, 1897, p. 96.
69 Compare *Thomasia Ricardo v. John Abal* (1926) 7 N.L.R. 58; *Joao Salako Andre v. Adeniyi, Agbebi and Johnson* (1931) 10 N.L.R. 79; *Nimota Sule and others v. M. A. Ajisegiri* (1937), 13 N.L.R. 146.
70 (1924) 5 N.L.R. 50, 55.
71 Compare the judgment of Butler Lloyd, J, in *Nimota Sule and others v. M. A. Ajisegiri*, (1937), 13 N.L.R. 146, 147.
72 Compare *Ramotu Salami v. Saibu Salami* (1957), *Western Region of Nigeria Law Reports 10*, 538.
73 Antony Allott, 'Law in the New Africa', *Insight*, April 1968, p. 13.
74 J. N. D. Anderson, (ed.), *Changing Law in Developing Countries*, London, 1963, p. 151.
75 F. A. Ajayi, 'Judicial Approach to Customary Law in Southern Nigeria', Unpublished PhD thesis, London University, 1958, p. 564.
76 *Ibid.*, p. 569.
77 (1935) 12 N.L.R. 4.
78 (1932) 11 N.L.R. 47.
79 (1930) 10 N.L.R. 65.
80 (1935) 12 N.L.R. 46.
81 *Akinwande Thomas and others v. Oba Alaiyeluwa Ademola II and others* (1945), 18 N.L.R. 12; *Chief Eyo Archibong and others v. Etubom Ededem Archibong and others* (1947), 18 N.L.R. 117.
82 (1923) 4 N.L.R. 101.
83 *D. W. Lewis and others v. Bankole and others* (1908), 1 N.L.R. 81; *Oduntan Onisiwo v. The Attorney-General* (1912), 2 N.L.R. 79; *Amodu Tijani v. Secretary, Southern Provinces* (1915–21), 3 N.L.R. 24; *Sakariyawo Oshodi v. Moriamo Dakolo and others* (1928), 9 N.L.R. 13.
84 Marriage Ordinance, No. 10, 1863 and No. 14, 1884; Marriage Act, Cap. 115 of Laws of the Federation of Nigeria, 1958.
85 Akinola Aguda, *Select Law Lectures and Papers*, Ibadan, 1971, pp. 94–5.
86 *Ibid.*, p. 85.
87 Marriage Act, Cap. 115, Law of the Federation of Nigeria 1958, sec. 35.
88 Marriage Act, Cap. 115, secs. 47, 48.

89 Criminal Code Ordinance, No. 15, 1916, sec. 370.
90 Aguda, *Select Law Lectures*, p. 82.
91 (1960) 5 Federal Supreme Court 84.
92 (1914) 2 N.L.R. 108.
93 (1928) 8 N.L.R. 19.
94 (1935) 12 N.L.R. 7.
95 (1940) 15 N.L.R. 107.
96 (1950) 19 N.L.R. 107.
97 (1907) 1 N.L.R. 66.
98 (1924) 5 N.L.R. 92.
99 (1937) 13 N.L.R. 146.
100 (1948) 19 N.L.R. 27.
101 (1943) 9 W.A.C.A. 73.
102 (1939) 15 N.L.R. 72.
103 (1940) 15 N.L.R. 90.
104 *Lewis and others v. Bankole* (1908), 1 N.L.R. 81; *Amodu Tijani v. Secretary, Southern Provinces* (1915–21), 3 N.L.R. 24; *Oduntan Onisiwo v. Attorney-General* (1912), 2 N.L.R. 79; *Miller Brothers v. Abudu Ayeni* (1924), 5 N.L.R. 42; *Bassey Egbo Bassey v. Archibong Boco Cobham,* (1924), 5 N.L.R. 92; *Sakariyawo Oshodi v. Moriamo Dakolo and others* (1928), 9 N.L.R. 13.
105 3 N.L.R. at p. 59.
106 A. E. W. Park, 'The Cession of Territory . . .', p. 46.
107 (1924) 5 N.L.R. 92.
108 (1931) 10 N.L.R. 36.
109 *Ibid.*, at p. 58.
110 E. H. Burn, *Cheshires's Modern Law of Property*, London, 11th ed., 1972, pp. 73–7.
111 (1926) 7 N.L.R. 38.
112 (1936) 13 N.L.R. 11.
113 (1937) 13 N.L.R. 186.
114 J. G. M. Tyas, *Law of Torts*, London, 1968, p. 156.
115 *United Kingdom Tobacco Co. Ltd. v. Carreras Limited* (1931), 16 N.L.R. 1.
116 Cited in 3 N.L.R. 18, at p. 20.
117 Cited in 16 N.L.R. 1, at p. 2.
118 *Ibid.*
119 (1925) 6 N.L.R. 102.
120 (1928) 8 N.L.R. 48.
121 (1917) 3 N.L.R. 18.
122 (1931) 16 N.L.R. 1.
123 Quoted in *W. B. McIver & Co. v. C.F.A.O.* (1917), 3 N.L.R. L'18, at p. 19.
124 CO 520/128, Lugard to Harcourt, 26 November 1913, enclosure.
125 (1907) 1 N.L.R. 70.
126 *Ibid.*, at p. 72.
127 (1921) 3 N.L.R. 94.
128 (1922) 4 N.L.R. 39.

129 (1922) 4 N.L.R. 8.
130 (1951) 20 N.L.R. 20.
131 (1951) 20 N.L.R. 29.
132 (1951) 20 N.L.R. 25.
133 (1950) 19 N.L.R. 122.
134 (1938) 14 N.L.R. 105.

9 Conclusion

> The struggle for law is an everlasting one, for 'public power', whether in the hands of the individual or of the community, is never at any time or in any place ready to acknowledge any limits.
>
> Rudolf von Jhering[1]

I

A country's laws and its judicial system are invariably a reflection of its historical development. An attempt has been made in the previous chapters to go behind the judicial institutions of Southern Nigeria and show how they are essentially a product of the territory's historical development. They reflect the influence of colonial conquest, the importation of law as an instrument of administration and control, the fashioning of a judicial system to meet the exigencies of a colonial situation.

There is more that can be gathered about a colonial situation from this study. Henry Bretton has aptly described the British colonial establishment in Nigeria as 'a mixture of authoritarian and nominally democratic rule'.[2] The 'democratic' aspect of British rule in Nigeria consists, first, in the fact that, in comparison with say, the Belgian or the Portuguese colonial authority in Africa, allowance was made for the political evolution of the country. Over the years changes were made in Nigeria's Constitution, even though they usually lagged behind the country's political development. Secondly, in the realm of judicial administration, there was a measure of respect for the rule of law, especially after 1914. True, there was much that was politically motivated in the establishment of the judicial system that operated in Nigeria during the greater part of the colonial era. Yet it was under the same colonial regime that the judicial decisions of political officers were sometimes reversed by the Supreme Court. It was under the same regime that *Amodu Tijani v. Secretary, Southern Provinces* (1915–21), and *Eshugbayi Eleko v. Officer Administering the Government of Nigeria* (1925–31) were taken as far as the Privy Council in London and resolved in favour of Nigerians and against the interests of the colonial establishment.

At the same time the judicial system in Southern Nigeria in the period covered by this study reflects a somewhat authoritarian aspect of British rule. The circumscription of the Supreme Court system during the greater part of the period; the administration's distrust of lawyers and its predilection for 'executive' justice, or justice as administered by political officers; the role of political officers, up to 1943, as the final arbiter of cases in the 'native' courts – these were elements of authoritarianism.

Paternalism is of the essence of a colonial situation. In Southern Nigeria, this was indicated also in the judicial system that was in operation for much of the period of this study. When one talks of paternalism in colonial administration on the African continent, one invariably thinks of the Belgian regime in the Congo (Zaire) up to 1960.[3] The point is not often made that *every* colonial establishment was paternalistic to some extent. A parent-offspring relationship was inescapable in a colonial situation. We saw how administrative officers in Southern Nigeria consciously strove to keep the Supreme Court and the lawyers out of the protectorate because of their belief that lawyers were preying on the ignorance of their non-literate countrymen and bleeding them to death through exorbitant legal fees. No less paternalistic was the feeling, particularly pronounced from the 1920s on, that both the lawyers and the Supreme Court represented foreign influences, harmful to the development of indigenous institutions. Until the arrival of Sir Donald Cameron on the Nigerian scene as Governor it was the fashionable theory that the indigenous institutions should, as much as possible, be shielded from foreign influences so that they could develop along lines that were not necessarily European.

The antagonism shown by the administration towards the Supreme Court and the lawyers was understandable in the context of colonial Southern Nigeria. The Supreme Court system of administering justice, in the best common law tradition, is an impartial machinery, often typified by the figure of a blindfolded maiden holding evenly balanced the scales of justice, ready to wield her sword in the pursuit of what is right in accordance with the law. At its best, it is the bulwark of a citizen's rights against any acts of oppression by individuals within the state or by the state itself. For obvious reasons, this ideal of the Supreme Court could not operate or be allowed to operate fully in a dependency – at any rate until the colonial authority was firmly established. The judicial arm of the colonial administration could not be allowed frequently to challenge the actions of its executive arm lest governmental authority be undermined. Moreover, the full operation of the Supreme Court could prove a serious impediment to the political organisation of a colony or to the building up of its infrastructure to facilitate economic development. We saw how the Supreme Court and the lawyers were considered obstacles to the political 'pacification' of the Eastern and Central Provinces of Southern Nigeria in the first decade of this century. The exaction of forced labour in most colonial situations is another illustration of the point. Forced labour may be wrong in the eyes of the law, but it may be expedient to exact it in order to construct a railway line, make a new road, or, more mundanely, to remove an officer's belongings, if not the officer himself physically, from one place to another.[4]

Related to the need to preserve the authority of the colonial establishment in Southern Nigeria as elsewhere on the continent was the question of the prestige of the colonial rulers themselves. Intangible as it was, consideration of prestige had some bearing on the nature of the judicial system that was devised for Southern Nigeria. As Secretary of State for the Colonies, Joseph Chamberlain declared in the British House of Commons on 22 July 1904:

> We hold our position [overseas] by being the dominant race and, if we admit equality with the inferior races, we shall lose the power which gives us our predominance.[5]

Although this Darwinian concept of racial superiority became progressively outmoded, consideration for the prestige of the colonial ruler remained a real force in colonial administration on the African continent. As late as the 1920s, a number of administrative officers admitted that the full operation of the Supreme Court posed a serious threat to the prestige of the political officer in Southern Nigeria. The same consideration lurked behind much of the antagonism towards the African lawyer. It will be recalled that one argument against the admission of lawyers before the provincial courts was that lawyers would tend to bully administrative officers presiding over the courts on technical points of the law. At bottom was fear for the prestige of the administrative officer who, in official thinking, should remain supreme within his area of jurisdiction if he was to be effective. 'Power in the courts', reasoned H. L. Ward-Price, an administrative officer and a lawyer, 'leads to power outside the courts.'[6]

It is worth noting that the restrictions placed on the Supreme Court system in Nigeria and in British colonial Africa generally, and the quasi-subordinate position of the judiciary in these areas, were by no means unique phenomena in African colonial history. For the same reasons that the British authorities in Nigeria could not allow the fully-fledged functioning of the type of judicial system operating in Britain, the judicial system in the French African colonies was not the same as in France.[7] The French policy with regard to African lawyers and the administration of justice was, in fact, worse than the British. While Britain restricted the operation of the Supreme Court and sought to curb the professional activities of lawyers, it never set a limit on the number of Africans who could qualify to practise. In the French territories it was a matter of policy to keep the number of African lawyers to the barest minimum. An increasing number of lawyers, in French official thinking, would tend to create 'an intellectual proletariat in a new country where questions of race and religion would be raised unknown in France'.[8] In 1920, 1921 and 1923 the Colonial Council in Senegal passed a number of resolutions calling for a 'free Bar'. But as late as 1927 there were only 'one or two native barristers' among the handful of French barristers practising in French West Africa.[9]

The Belgian authorities in the Congo (Zaire Republic), in theory, separated the judicial from the executive arm of the colonial administration. In practice, proper legal procedure often gave way to political expediency.[10] By 1923, even the theoretical dichotomy between the executive and the judicial powers in the administration was becoming very much blurred.[11] As for the development of the unofficial Bar, the Belgians were the worst offenders. While Nigeria had about 540 African lawyers at the time of political independence in 1960,[12] the Congo had none.[13] Since the accent in the educational policy of the Belgian authorities was on the technical, it was virtually impossible for a Congolese to enter the Lovanium Law School in Belgium which insisted on a knowledge of Ancient Greek as a prerequisite for admission.[14]

On the surface the policy adopted by the colonial administration in Nigeria of restricting the operation of the Supreme Court and of limiting the scope for the practice of the legal profession in the protectorate appears commendable. Some of the arguments in support of curtailing the jurisdiction of the Supreme Court and establishing the provincial courts are noble indeed. Who would not agree that the few educated Africans, or more specifically, the lawyers, should not take advantage of the illiteracy of the masses of their countrymen? At a time when the African feels the need to project the 'African Personality' in the comity of nations, who would argue against the desirability of African culture evolving in a pattern all its own without baneful external influences?

In considering the whole question of colonial rule and the foreign influences it brought with it, however, one must be realistic. It was this element of realism which was lacking in much of the official thinking about the judicial system that operated in Southern Nigeria for the greater part of the period covered by this study. It was not realised, or not realised sufficiently acutely, that Western colonialism 'shook all the societies in the world loose from their old moorings'.[15] The old order of life was slowly receding into the background and things were falling apart.[16] It was not realised that a social revolution had been brought about by colonialism that would have permanent results. The accoutrements of the colonial establishment – schools, churches, white-collar jobs, and the like – were imbuing the younger generations of Africans with new values. Surely, in the judicial sphere, the traditional machinery of justice could not deal with all the complications arising from these novel developments, particularly since its religious and metaphysical props were being seriously eroded by the new values. In retrospect, wisdom lay in recognising the reality of the social revolution taking place in Nigeria and attempting to direct its course rather than in combating it. It was futile to embark upon a policy aimed at simply 'preserving' the traditional.

The judicial system in operation in Southern Nigeria for much of the colonial period was a failure from the point of view of its political objectives. The judicial system did not effectively prevent lawyers from 'interfering' in land cases. The uneducated litigants in the protectorate, whom the judicial system was designed to protect, rarely enjoyed the full benefits of protection. In the British colonies, as Buell found in the French, when the uneducated litigant sought justice in the European or European-established courts, 'he almost inevitably becomes the prey of intermediaries of all sorts who exploit him'.[17] We saw in this connection the activities of the letter-writers, the champions-at-law and the money-lenders in Southern Nigeria.

Not only was the policy of restriction ineffective but it also appeared to have had some adverse effects on the development of

Nigerian law. The obsessional fear of lawyers on the part of British officials which characterised much of the colonial period, and the emphasis on preserving the traditional, tended to hamper the evolution of what may be called the Nigerian common law: a system of law, that is to say, based on the bedrock of the English common law, but different in its adaptations to the Nigerian soil.[18] Whether or not English common law itself is good for Nigeria is beside the point. The social revolution referred to earlier has swept Nigeria irreversibly into the common law world, and it is from that viewpoint that one must argue. The part Nigerian lawyers and Nigerian judges could have played in the development of a Nigerian common law becomes evident the moment it is realised that English common law grew imperceptibly out of the customs and usages of English people and decisions of English law courts. The agents in the process of its evolution were English lawyers and English judges.[19]

It is true that the English-style courts in Southern Nigeria, even within their limitations, influenced to some degree the development of the Nigerian customary laws. But it is debatable whether or not a Nigerian common law system has yet emerged. There are those who hold the view that the English common law has not been sufficiently adapted to Nigerian conditions.[20] It may be that one reason for this state of affairs, as L. C. B. Gower has suggested, was a sort of ritualistic mentality on the part of most of the lawyers, a tendency on their part to regard English law as 'the perfection of human reason'.[21] But the restriction placed on the appearance of lawyers in the territory's higher courts up to the 1930s, and the general distrust in which African lawyers were held for a long time by the colonial administration certainly did not provide an atmosphere conducive to the development of Nigerian law. If Nigerian lawyers had been given a freer scope for their professional activities and had been allowed to participate more in the administration of justice, the development of a Nigerian common law could have been fostered.

A Yoruba ruler, the *Alake* of Abeokuta, Sir Oladapo Ademola II, pointed the way the administration could have followed. In 1929, the Alake appointed a lawyer, Adebesin Folarin, as president of the Ake grade 'A' 'native' court – a post which he held until 1941. The decision to appoint a lawyer to preside over the Ake grade 'A' court was taken as early as 1923. When the question of the appointment was being debated, the Alake explained to his council that a lawyer on the Bench of the Ake court would enhance the prestige and efficiency of the court. He added, significantly, that the lawyer 'will be useful to us not only in the court work but [also] in the work of the codification of the Egba laws'.[22] How much 'codification' of the Egba laws Folarin did is not known; but the position of the Alake regarding the role lawyers could play in the development of Nigerian customary laws is evident enough.

Since the late 1950s, the former Western Region of Nigeria has led the way in appointing lawyers to preside over grade 'A', and certain categories of grade 'B', customary courts.[23] The result of their appointments, in terms of the evolution of the Nigerian common law, will be interesting to watch. But it is clear that when judges fully qualified in English law administer Nigerian customary laws, they will inevitably bring their knowledge of the English law to bear on their application of the customary laws and, to that extent, influence their development.

The case of Adebesin Folarin presiding over the Ake grade 'A' court leads one to suspect that the tone of justice administered in the 'native' courts would have improved considerably if the lawyers had been taken in to the confidence of the colonial administration. In 1931, F. B. Adams, the Senior Resident for Abeokuta Province, reported on the Abeokuta 'native' courts two years after Folarin's appointment. He noted that 'an increase of efficiency in this [Ake grade "A" court] and all other courts has been the result, and the general public has real confidence in the most important court of Egbaland'.[24] Generally speaking, the Egba courts had a high reputation in official circles in the 1920s and 1930s. Perhaps much was due to Folarin's personal efficiency and the incorruptibility for which he was noted. But it is arguable that when the highest court in the 'native' court system is presided over by a person qualified in law, the chances of irregularities in the lower 'native' courts are minimised. A lower 'native' court would be aware that a litigant before it could ultimately appeal to a court presided over by a person qualified in law, thus putting to the test the integrity of the lower court.

II

In spite of the restrictions inherent in the judicial system operating in Southern Nigeria for the greater part of the colonial period, the impact of English law and the English-established courts on the society has been considerable. It was suggested earlier that it would be impossible as well as historically unrealistic to attempt to define the limits of this impact. As Under Secretary for State for the Colonies, W. G. A. Ormsby-Gore summed up the position of the judicial and legal systems imposed on Southern Nigeria when he wrote in 1926: 'Nothing tends to undermine native traditions, society and organization more than the substitution of European for native legal forms.'[25]

An attempt was made to show how English law and the new judicial system in Southern Nigeria have reinforced the influence of economic, educational, missionary and other factors making for an increase in the sense of personal freedom, consciousness of personal rights and the growth of individualism. The higher courts not only modified indigenous customary practices under the impact of the repugnancy doctrine; they also attempted to lay down, in the sphere of marital relations, possible lines of development. What was true of the Supreme Court and the provincial courts in all these respects was also true of the High Court or the magistrates' courts that were established after 1933. Like the Supreme Court or the provincial courts, they too administered the English common law, importing a set of values that were not quite in consonance with the indigenous traditional values.

The impact of English law and the judicial system in Southern Nigeria has perhaps been particularly remarkable in the economic and criminal spheres. In laying the foundations for modern commerce in Nigeria, certainly the courts and English law have been a crucial factor, meeting the inadequacies of customary law and customary practices at several points. In spite of occasional conservative judicial decisions on the nature of customary land tenure in Southern Nigeria, the British notions of individual land ownership gained ground, partly through acquaintance with the English land tenure system, and partly through the orders of the courts, not least the 'native' courts. There has been a considerable relaxation in the customary land tenure system in Southern Nigeria, and by declaring land alienable, at least in certain circumstances, the courts may be said to have directly fostered economic development.

In the criminal sphere, the English common law and the courts in Nigeria, have, by importing categories of offences unknown in the pre-colonial society, met the inadequacies of the indigenous customary laws in terms of regulating modes of behaviour in a modern society.

English law and the operation of the colonial judicial system in Southern Nigeria also had political repercussions. It may be suggested, first, that they influenced the development of political awareness among the indigenes of the territory. The growth of individualism and the increase in the sense of personal freedom, noted as a consequence of the operation of the courts and the law in interpersonal relations, had political implications. The same mentality that prompted the assertion of individual rights in the courts inevitably led to a questioning of the *raison d'être* of foreign rule. Secondly, because British colonial rule was not completely authoritarian, the cases in which the administration was a party provided occasions when educated Nigerians, through the instrumentality of Nigerian lawyers, called its actions into question. The fact that the lawyers were working for fees was irrelevant. The important thing was the visual impression created in the minds of the masses: that Africans could stand up to their white overlords.

The celebrated *Amodu Tijani* and *Eshugbayi Eleko* cases illustrate the point about African political awareness being enhanced in the judicial process. The fact that the colonial regime in Nigeria suffered serious reverses at the Privy Council in the two cases rendered it contemptible in the eyes of many. When the Privy Council handed down its decision in favour of Amodu Tijani in July 1921, an educated African proclaimed: 'Today, the dictum that "white men and Governments make no mistake" has been exploded and proved to be erroneous and untrue.'[26] The result of the *Tijani* case was occasion for over two weeks of popular rejoicings in Lagos.[27] It was estimated that between thirty and forty thousand people welcomed the victorious plaintiff in the case when he arrived on the Lagos shores from London on 25 August 1921. The enthusiasm displayed by the Lagos population over the success of Amodu Tijani was, no doubt, 'proof positive of the far reaching effects of the Privy Council decision and the consciousness of that fact on the part of the community'.[28]

The reverses suffered by the administration in the *Eshugbayi Eleko* case were even more pointedly political in their implication than those suffered in the Amodu *Tijani* case. When the news reached Lagos on 19 June 1928 of the *Eleko*'s success in his appeal in the *habeas corpus* case at the Privy Council, thousands went about the streets singing and merry-making.[29] The demonstrations were no mere indication of popular support for *Eshugbayi Eleko*'s cause. Underlying them was a feeling of triumph – triumph over the policy of a colonial government 'which takes little or no account of the people's interests . . . and conspires constantly to keep down the aboriginal inhabitants'.[30] Whatever measure of confidence the indigenous population of Lagos might have gained over the Privy Council decision in the *Eleko* case in 1928 must have been heightened in 1931 when the administration suffered a second reverse over the same case. Confidence led to contempt for the colonial regime and such contempt, or the realisation that the power of the regime was not absolute, was surely an important ingredient in the development of political consciousness among the intelligentsia, particularly in Lagos.

Thirdly, the existence of a unitary judicial system between 1914 and 1954 – with all its imperfections – could not have failed to serve as a unifying force in Nigeria. Much of the period covered by this study was a time when, in the graphic phraseology of T. O. Elias, one writ ran throughout the country.[31] There was one Supreme Court with its several divisions, one Attorney-General and one Solicitor-General. All judicial officers and all lawyers 'enjoyed great mobility throughout a united legal system'. Almost all the local statutes, the criminal code, the laws of non-customary marriage, public lands acquisition, customs offences, weights and measures and so on were of country-wide application within the unified legal system, and have even survived the regionalisation of the judiciary that came in 1954 in the universality of their application.[32] On the whole, the operation of English law and of the British-imposed judicial system have left a legacy in many parts of Nigeria of a common pattern in legal development which it is fair to regard as one of the cementing factors in the making of the Nigerian nation.

In the face of the impact of English law and the colonial judicial system on Southern Nigeria's social, economic and even political development, the attitude of the British administration towards the operation of English law and the Supreme Court in the territory reminds one of the woman in Aesop's fable who was told by the fortune-tellers that her little boy would be killed by a crow. To forestall the fulfilment of this prophecy, she made a great perforated chest in which she shut up the boy, taking him out only occasionally to nourish him. No crow ever flew near him, but he was killed nonetheless by some mishap inside the very chest in which he was caged. There was some air of inevitability about the march of Western civilisation on the African continent as a consequence of colonialism. The best that colonial rulers could have done would have been to guide its course in a positive fashion. The obvious line of action in the legal and judicial spheres, as in others, would have been the adaptation of Western civilisation, the colonial heritage, to African conditions. True adaptation is never easy; it would require, on the part of Africans themselves, a considerable amount of effort and much creative thinking.

To talk of the need for adaptation in the legal and judicial spheres is not to deny the reality of the legacy left by the British in those spheres. Apart from the common law, the greatest legacy is perhaps the concept of the rule of law. 'One of the greatest blessings brought to this country by the British Administration', wrote Sir Ralph Combe, Chief Justice, in *Rex v. Thomas H. Jackson* (1925),

> is the establishment of an absolutely impartial Judiciary, and I have every reason to believe that the inhabitants of this Colony and Protectorate have complete confidence in the British courts which have been established, and rejoice in having courts to which they can come with certain knowledge that justice will be administered without fear and without favour.[33]

The existence of 'an absolutely impartial Judiciary', justice administered 'without fear and without favour' – these are two major connotations of the concept of the rule of law. The notable English jurist, A. V. Dicey, has defined it to mean 'the absolute supremacy or predominance of regular law, as opposed to the influence of arbitrary power, of prerogative or even of wide discretionary authority on the part of the Government'.[34] To him the concept also connotes 'the equal subjection of all classes to the ordinary law of the land administered by the ordinary law courts'. A similar idea was expressed recently by a Nigerian judge in a famous case involving the liberty of the citizen: 'The meaning of the rule of law in practical terms is that no person is beyond the law while those concerned with the law should act with the fear of God.'[35]

In the light of what has been said about the position of the judiciary in a colonial context, and of what we know about the practical working of the judicial system in Southern Nigeria for much of the colonial period, Sir Ralph's claim stands out as a piece of overstatement. Colonial judges could not be as independent as their counterparts in England. Not only were they apt to share the same type of outlook on matters of colonial policy and administration as the officers in the administrative wing of the colonial service, as was shown earlier, they also occupied a subordinate position in the scheme of things in the colonies. The judges of the provincial courts were political officers first and judges second. Their type of 'executive' justice was not often devoid of political considerations.

But there is no doubt that the concept of the rule of law was an ideal that came in the train of the imported British legal and judicial systems. It is part of the English legal culture, harking back to the struggle for law between King James I and Sir Edward Coke, Lord Chief Justice of England, 1606–1616.[36] Even though not to the extent that Sir Ralph Combe would want us to believe, the colonial regime in Nigeria did, in some areas, operate by the concept. There were instances, as we saw, when, to its own financial or political detriment, the regime bowed to the dictates of its own courts of law or of the higher court in England in the resolution of conflicts arising between it and its subjects. In this connection, it is also instructive that at a time when the regime could have used force to consolidate its position or to gain certain ends, it sought at least the appearance of legality. The relatively free atmosphere in which the Nigerian press could be critical of actions taken by the regime from time to time almost throughout the colonial era in Nigeria[37] was in keeping with the spirit of the rule of law.

The concept of the rule of law is probably not so much a legalistic notion as simply the acceptance of certain fundamental human values in the structure of government and the operation of the legal system. Such values include the right to life, the right to liberty and privacy, freedom of expression and of peaceful association, freedom of movement and so on – all of them hinging on the dignity of man.

It is because the dignity of man is at the heart of the concept of the rule of law that certain features of its operation are often emphasised. The first is that law should prevail, not the wishes and caprices of an individual or group of individuals. From this follows the second feature: those in political power must be subject to rules laid down in advance and enforced by an organ of government, the judiciary, not dependent on them. A third feature – now generally considered the dynamic aspect of the rule of law – is the result of the efforts of the International Commission of Jurists. It is that the concept should be used not only to protect the individual from arbitrary power by the government, but also 'to establish social, economic, educational and cultural conditions under which the individual's legitimate aspirations and dignity may be realized'.[38]

These three features of the rule of law make it a heritage worth preserving. For many developing nations today, the crucial question is whether they can achieve social and economic progress without turning to the path of force. I believe that the rule of law offers a viable alternative to force, and is, indeed, superior to it. The climate of legality and the freedom of expression implied in the concept are not only a potent stimulus to economic and social progress, but are also conducive to the attainment of personal growth and development by the individual. Any form of imposed leadership is often a factor of stagnation and obscurantism. Socio-economic development is not, by itself, enough. It must be achieved in an atmosphere of freedom of thought and expression, facilitating a free circulation of ideas and the enjoyment of a rich and meaning-ful life by the individual.

Although recent developments in Nigeria are encouraging,[39] the rule of law, as a politico-legal ideal, is not easy to establish. The forces standing in the way of its operation are numerous, a good proportion of them stemming from the absence of any strong tradition of legality. The present legal order in the country and the philosophy behind it have yet to take firm root. The colonial regime did little consciously to entrench the rule of law. Tradition-ally, judicial administration was the preserve of the ruling elite, an adjunct of power. Law was rarely regarded as an independent entity for the benefit of the ruled. As one can gather from the opening chapter of this book, people had recourse, not to law as such, but to the wisdom of their rulers and elders in the resolution of interpersonal conflicts.

One basic task, then, in establishing the rule of law, is to bring the law much closer to the heart of the common man than it is at present as a tangible factor in his life. For this purpose a coura-geous, honest and independent judiciary, capable of holding the scales of justice evenly between the demands of the state and the rights of the individual citizens, is a necessity. These are no times for the judge who 'quavers or retreats before an impending crisis of the day', or one who 'surrenders his own conviction for a passing expediency'.[40] The supremacy of law must be established.

The point cannot be over-emphasised that judicial independence is not a matter merely of the structural arrangement of the judiciary within the framework of government. In the final analysis, it is a question of outlook, an attribute of the mind of the individual judge, a matter of conscience. Only the judges themselves, by their official actions, can safeguard it and pass it on as a living tradition.

Notes

1 Quoted by Hans Klecatsky, in 'Reflections on the Rule of Law and in particular on the Principle of the Legality of Administrative Action', *Journal of the International Commission of Jurists*, IV, No. 2, 1963, p. 205.
2 Henry L. Bretton, *Power and Stability in Nigeria: The Politics of Decolonization*, New York, 1962, p. 15.
3 For a short account of the Belgian administration of the Congo, see Colin Legum, *Congo Disaster*, Baltimore, 1961.
4 T. N. Tamuno, *The Evolution of the Nigerian State*, London, 1972, pp. 45–6, 55, 109.
5 Quoted by A. E. M. Gibson, 'Constitutional Method in Nigeria', *Times of Nigeria*, 7 April 1914.
6 NAI, CSO 26/3, 21496, I, Memorandum by H. L. Ward-Price on the supreme court and its relation to native policy.
7 R. L. Buell, *The Native Problem in Africa*, London, 2nd impr. 1965, I, pp. 1002–1005.
8 Quoted by R. L. Buell, I, p. 1004.
9 Buell, I, p. 1005.
10 Ruth Slade, *King Leopold's Congo*, London, 1962, p. 173.
11 Buell, II, p. 472.
12 *Nigerian Bar Journal*, VI, pp. 14–34.
13 Colin Legum, ed., *Africa: A Handbook to the Continent*, New York, 2nd ed., 1967, p. 159.
14 *Ibid.*, 1st edition, 1962, p. 195.
15 Barbara Ward, *The Rich Nations and the Poor Nations*, New York, 1962, p. 54.
16 Chinua Achebe's novel, *Things Fall Apart*, London, 1959, depicts the beginning of the breakdown of the traditional order under the impact of Christianity, new commercial enterprises and the colonial establishment itself.
17 R. L. Buell, I, p. 1009.
18 A. N. Allott, 'The Common Law of Nigeria', in *Nigerian Law: Some Recent Developments*, Commonwealth Law Series, III, London, 1964, p. 43.
19 Master Jacques Abady, *The Inns of Court and Civilization*, London, 1954, pp. 1–14.

20 Compare L. C. B. Gower, *Independent Africa: The Challenge to the Legal Profession*, Cambridge, Mass., 1967, pp. 90–6.
21 *Ibid.*, p. 91.
22 NAI, Abe Prof 6/4/6/24B, 'Minutes of Egba Council held 26 February 1923'.
23 E. A. Keay and S. S. Richardson, *The Native and Customary Courts of Nigeria*, London, 1966, pp. 97–8; 193–4.
24 NAI, CSO 26/2, 11875, VIII, 'Abeokuta Province: Annual Report, 1931'.
25 Colonial Office, *Report by the Hon. W. G. A. Ormsby-Gore on his Visit to West Africa*, 1926, Cmd 2744, p. 16.
26 *Daily Telegraph*, 1 August 1921.
27 *Lagos Weekly Record*, 10 September 1921. This edition of the news-paper was 'Chief Oluwa's Edition'.
28 *Daily Telegraph*, 1 August 1921.
29 *The Nigerian Spectator*, 23 June 1928.
30 *Ibid.*
31 T. O. Elias, *The Impact of English Law on Nigerian Customary Law*, Lagos, 1958, p. 30.
32 T. O. Elias, *Law in a Developing Society*, Lagos, 1969, pp. 24–5.
33 (1925) 6 N.L.R. 49, at p. 53.
34 A. V. Dicey, *Introduction to the Study of the Constitution*, London, 10th ed., 1959, p. 202.
35 Mr Justice Ambrose Allagoa in the *Amakiri* case (1974), *Daily Times*, Lagos, 23 March 1974.
36 A. K. R. Kiralfy, *Potter's Historical Introduction to English Law*, London, 1958, pp. 287–8.
37 Fred. I. A. Omu, 'The Nigerian Newspaper Press . . .', pp. 181–310.
38 International Commission of Jurists, *The Dynamic Aspects of the Rule of Law in the Modern Age*, Geneva, 1965, p. 15.
39 Compare the following recent cases in which Nigerian courts have demonstrated their independence: *Mandilas Ltd. v. Board of Customs and Excise* (1972), a case of official high-handedness, *Selected Judgments of the High Court of Lagos State*, September 1972, pp. 35–45; *Dr Sehindemi* case (1974), in which a medical practitioner was acquitted of the criminal charge of attempting to procure abortion, the sensation aroused by the case notwithstanding, *Sunday Times*, Lagos, 20 January 1974; *Dr Olunloyo* case (1974), in which the former Rector of the Ibadan Polytechnic was awarded ₦12,850 damages (pending an appeal in the case) against the Western State Government by the High Court of Ibadan for alleged wrongful dismissal from office, *Daily Times*, Lagos, 9 March 1974, 9 April 1974; *Amakiri* case (1974), in which the plaintiff, a journalist, was awarded ₦10,750 damages against one Iwowari, the aide-de-camp of the governor of the Rivers State, for alleged false imprisonment, assault and battery, *Daily Times*, 23 March 1974, and *Sunday Times*, 31 March 1974.
40 William O. Douglas, 'In Defense of Dissent', in Alan F. Westin, ed., *The Supreme Court: Views from Inside*, New York, 1961, p. 55.

Appendix A

Judicial and legal appointments: Africans[1] 1931-54

JUDICIAL DEPARTMENT

Olumuyiwa Jibowu
Police magistrate, 13 Feb. 1931; assistant protectorate judge, 22
May 1942; puisne judge, Supreme Court, 1 Sept. 1944.

Adebiyi Desalu
Magistrate, 1 Nov. 1938; police magistrate, 1 Nov. 1938.

Adetokunbo Ademola
Magistrate, 1 April 1939; puisne judge, Supreme Court, 22 April
1949.

F. E. O. Euba
Magistrate, 1 Aug. 1940.

G. F. Dove-Edwin
Acting magistrate, 30 Nov. 1940; magistrate, 13 Dec. 1941;
puisne judge, Supreme Court, 12 Feb. 1951.

F. O. Lucas
Magistrate, 1 March 1941.

S. P. J. Q. Thomas
Temporary magistrate, 1 April 1941; magistrate, 1 April 1943;
puisne judge, Supreme Court, 17 June 1953.

E. A. Franklin
Magistrate, 1 April 1942.

S. H. A. Baptist
Acting magistrate, 13 April 1942.

[1] Source: *Staff Lists, Nigeria: 1941–55*, Lagos, 1941–55.

J. T. Nelson Cole
Temporary magistrate, 4 June 1942.

Ayodele Williams
Temporary magistrate, 8 June 1942; magistrate, 1 April 1943.

Stella J. Thomas (Miss)
Temporary magistrate, 28 April 1942.

I. K. Roberts
Temporary magistrate, 17 Aug. 1942.

Asifo Egbe
Temporary magistrate, 1 Sept. 1942.

W. W. Awunor-Renner
Temporary magistrate, 12 Nov. 1942; temporary assistant judge,
1 January 1945.

Adeleke Adedoyin
Temporary magistrate, 1 April 1943.

A. S. E. Brown
Temporary magistrate, 18 May 1943; magistrate, 1 April 1944.

A. O. Abayomi
Temporary magistrate, 1 Feb. 1945; magistrate, 1 Feb. 1947.

P. W. Holm
Magistrate, 1 August 1945.

S. B. Rhodes
Puisne judge, Supreme Court, 8 Nov. 1945.

E. C. Pyne
Temporary magistrate, 1 Feb. 1945.

B. J. Ferreira
Temporary magistrate, 9 June 1947.

H. O. Lucas
Temporary magistrate, 20 Oct. 1947.

A. Kudehinbu
Temporary magistrate, 20 Oct. 1947.

A. A. Adesigbin
Temporary magistrate, 2 Jan. 1948.

R. E. Lardner
Temporary magistrate, 28 May 1948.

W. O. Egbuna
Temporary magistrate, 25 May 1948.

W. A. Savage
Temporary magistrate, 5 June 1948.

J. A. A. Kester
Temporary magistrate, 1 July 1948.

N. O. A. Morgan
Temporary magistrate, 1 July 1948.

E. A. Caxton-Martins
Temporary magistrate, 1 July 1948.

J. J. Marinho
Temporary magistrate, 16 Aug. 1948.

L. O. Fadipe
Temporary magistrate, 1 Sept. 1948.

J. O. Kassim
Temporary magistrate, 15 Oct. 1948.

I. S. John
Magistrate, 23 Dec. 1948.

E. O. A. Morgan
Temporary magistrate, 1 Nov. 1949.

M. O. Oyemade
Temporary magistrate, 7 Nov. 1949.

S. A. Thomas
Temporary magistrate, 20 Feb. 1950.

C. O. Alakija
Temporary magistrate, 20 Feb. 1950.

W. J. Palmer
Magistrate, 22 May 1950.

R. W. Rhodes-Vivour
Magistrate, 1 Aug. 1950.

E. Allswell-Uranta
Temporary magistrate, 27 Sept. 1950.

E. B. Craig
Magistrate, 17 Nov. 1950.

F. O. Allagoa
Magistrate, 20 Nov. 1950.

V. A. Delumo
Temporary magistrate, 23 Nov. 1950.

G. S. Sowemimo
Temporary magistrate, 22 March 1951.

J. N. Odogwu
Temporary magistrate, 1 April 1951.

H. S. Palmer
Puisne judge, Supreme Court, 2 Aug. 1951.

S. O. Lambo
Temporary magistrate, 4 Sept. 1951.

N. Uwechie
Temporary magistrate, 7 Sept. 1951.

Chief K. Sikuade
Temporary magistrate, 26 Nov. 1951.

D. O. Peters
Temporary magistrate, 1 Jan. 1952.

I. S. M. Sotire
Temporary magistrate, 1 April 1952.

T. O. Odunlami
Temporary magistrate, 28 April 1952; magistrate, 6 June 1953.

M. A. Begho
Temporary magistrate, 3 June 1952.

J. A. Eke
Temporary magistrate, 3 June 1952.

B. F. Adesola
Temporary magistrate, 12 June 1952.

L. N. Mbanefo
Puisne judge, Supreme Court, 1 Aug. 1952.

J. O. Ajomale
Temporary magistrate, 3 Aug. 1952.

C. D. Onyeama
Chief magistrate, 23 Aug. 1952.

O. R. I. George
Magistrate, 7 March 1953.

G. C. Nkemena
Magistrate, 9 Oct. 1953.

J. A. Adefarasin
Magistrate, 13 Oct. 1953.

C. A. Johnson
Magistrate, 25 Jan. 1954.

A. O. Lapite
Magistrate, 25 Jan. 1954.

J. O. Obianwu
Magistrate, 1 March 1954.

F. A. S. Ogunmuyiwa
Magistrate, 6 July 1954.

F. E. Pereira
Temporary magistrate, 3 Aug. 1954.

LEGAL DEPARTMENT

R. A. Doherty
Crown counsel, 1 April 1938; senior Crown counsel, 12 Jan. 1948.

G. K. J. Amachree
Crown counsel, 3 Feb. 1949.

C. O. Madarikan
Crown counsel, 16 Feb. 1949.

B. A. Adedipe
Crown counsel, 12 Aug. 1949.

E. N. Egbuna
Crown counsel, 1 April 1950.

F. A. Williams
Crown counsel, 2 Oct. 1950.

T. A. B. Oki
Crown counsel, 1 April 1952.

O. O. Omololu
Crown counsel, 1 April 1952.

B. O. Kazeem
Crown counsel, 1 April 1954.

S. D. Adebiyi
Crown counsel, 1 Sept. 1954.

Appendix B

Specimens of legal instruments drawn up by public letter-writers

(a) *An agreement*[1]
This agreement was made and entered into this 13th day of the month of June, 1940, between Alliu Ajagbe, a native of Ibadan, Nigeria, on behalf of himself, and the other members of his family, his heirs, assigns and successors (hereinafter called the Grantor) of the first part, and Madam Esther Latundun, a native of Ibadan, Nigeria, for herself, her heirs, assigns and successors (hereinafter called the Grantee) of the second part.

Whereas the Grantor has hereby agreed and cede (*sic*) voluntarily to the Grantee as an extension of land, a piece of parcel of land being and situate at Onireke Road, Ibadan, measuring 50′ × 0″ on the East, 54′ × 0″ on the West, and 35′ × 0″ on the North and 15′ × 0″ on the South, as an additional land to the previous one granted to the Grantee in perpetuity. Consideration 10/– (Ten Shillings).

Dated this 13th Day of June, 1940.

> Alliu Ajagbe (His mark)
> _____
> Grantor
>
> Esther Latundun (Her mark)
> _____
> Grantee
>
> Lemomu Sanni (His mark)
> _____
> Witness

The above was read over and truly explained in Yoruba language to the parties concerned.

Fee: 2/6d.   Writer: (Sgd.) A. A. Babalola

[1] Source: From the file of Mr A. A. Babalola, Letter-writer, Mapo, Ibadan.

(b) *An agreement of a loan of £40*[1]

This certifies the fact that I the undersigned Mr. Mustapha Alawusa of Gbogunjah Street, Ijebu-Ode, hereby receives a sum of £40 (Forty pounds) for Trading purposes from one Mr. N. J. Oloko of Agunshenbi Quarter, Ijebu-Ode, and we both agreed further to abide with the following agreements:

That I, the undersigned Borrower hereby faithfully and solemnly promised that whatever gain or income that the principal (£40) may bring should be divided equally into two parts between we two (both the lender and the borrower) per each respective annual Ileya Festival.

That, regard the refund of this money to the lender, he, the lender is of right and liberty to demand this money from me at any time he likes, and this document should then be cancelled.

That, in case I fail to pay this money at such a time or attempt to deny any part thereof, a legal steps (*sic*) should be taken against me in an open court of justice for the claim of the money (£40).

Dated at Ijebu-Ode this Wednesday the 9th day of July, 1930.

Declarations:

Read and interpreted.
Contained 225 words.

Fee paid: 5/–.

(Sgd.) E. A. Benjah
Public Letter Writer
"Ireti" Office
Ijebu-Ode

---

[1] Source: NAI, Ije Prof 4, J.273, I, Noshiru to Resident, 5 February 1932, enclosure.

(c) *Power of attorney*[1]
KNOW ALL MEN BY THESE PRESENTS that I, Bankole,
the present Mogaji Bola, of Bola Compound, Ibadan, Nigeria, on
behalf of myself and the entire members of Bola family, do hereby
make, constitute, and appoint Daniel Adegunle Lasoju, Contractor
of Oke-Foko, Ibadan, Nigeria, my true and lawful Attorney with
full power and authority in my name or on my behalf or otherwise
as the case may require to do all or any of the acts and things
hereinafter mentioned, that is to say:—

1. To demand, sue for, enforce payment of and receive and
give effectual receipts and discharges for all moneys, securities for
money, debts, legacies, goods chattels, and personal estate of or to
which I am now or may become due, owing, payable, or transferable to me from any person or persons or corporation.

2. To receive and give effectual receipts and discharges for all
and any moneys which shall come to the hands of the said Attorney
by virtue of the powers herein contained, which receipts whether
given in my name or in the name of the said Attorney shall
exonerate the person or persons or corporation being such moneys
from seeing to the Application thereof or being responsible for the
loss or misapplication thereof.

3. And I declare that these presents shall be for all time unless
and until the same shall be duly revoked in writing by me.

Dated at Ibadan this 14th day of November 1947.

The above was read over and
truly explained in Yoruba
language. Gratis.

(Sgd.) J. K. Adeyinka
——————————
Public Letter Writer

(Sgd.) Bankole (His right thumb)
(Sgd.) Adedeji (His right thumb)

[1] Source: NAI, Iba Div 1/1, 1338, vol. viii, p. 297.

Bibliography

MANUSCRIPT SOURCES

I. *Private papers*
(a) Alakija, Sir Adeyemo: Ake Divisional Council Record Office, Abeokuta.
(b) Anti-Slavery and Aborigines' Protection Society (London): Papers at Rhodes House, Oxford: Mss. Brit. Emp. S22/G 232–G252.
(c) Ayorinde, Chief T. A., Ibadan: Some of the papers are relevant to the local administration of Ibadan between 1914 and 1933.
(d) Coker, Chief J. K.: Catalogued papers at the Nigerian National Archives, Ibadan.
(e) Creech-Jones: Catalogued papers at Rhodes House, Oxford: Mss. Brit. Emp. S332.
(f) Doherty, Chief T. A., Lagos: Uncatalogued miscellaneous papers.
(g) Lethem, Gordon J.: Catalogued papers at Rhodes House, Oxford: Mss. Brit. Emp. S276. A great proportion of the papers deal with judicial reforms in Nigeria, 1924–33.
(h) Lugard, Sir Frederick: Catalogued papers at the Rhodes House, Oxford: Mss. Brit. Emp. S76, especially vol. 47.
(i) Macaulay, Herbert: Catalogued papers at the Ibadan University Library.
(j) Taylor, Justice J. I. C., Lagos: Uncatalogued miscellaneous papers.

II. *Public record office, London*
CO 96: Gold Coast, Original Correspondence, 1874–1886.
CO 147: Lagos, Original Correspondence, 1861–1905.

CO 151: Lagos, Blue Books, 1862–1905.
CO 444: Northern Nigeria, Original Correspondence, 1900–1913.
CO 520: Southern Nigeria, Original Correspondence, 1906–1913.
CO 583: Nigeria, Original Correspondence, 1914–1933.
CO 588: Southern Nigeria: Acts 1906–1913.
CO 592: Southern Nigeria, Gazette, 1906–1913.
CO 656: Nigeria: Ordinance, 1914–1945.
CO 657: Nigeria: Administration Reports, 1914–1933.
CO 879: Africa: Printed Documents, 1874–1919.

III. *Nigerian National Archives, Ibadan and Enugu*
CSO 1/3–CSO 1/36: Original correspondence to the Colonial Office, London, 1900–1940.
CSO 26: Original internal correspondence, 1900–1940.
CSO 26/2: Annual and Quarterly Reports, Southern Nigeria Provinces, 1920–1940.
CSO 26/3: Intelligence Reports, Southern Nigeria Provinces, 1933–1937.
CSE Series.
Divisional and District Papers.

IV. *Supreme Court Archives, Lagos*
Roll of Barristers, 2 vols.

V. *High Court Archives, Lagos*
Uncatalogued records of civil and criminal cases covering the period 1861–1956. There are also 'Letter Books' and other miscellaneous papers.

VI. *Ake Divisional Council Records Office, Abeokuta*
Catalogued papers and manuscripts pertaining to Egba Council affairs mostly for the period 1900–1956.

VII. *Ibadan Divisional Council Records Office, Ibadan*
Uncatalogued materials consisting mainly of native court records for the period 1925–47 and two volumes of the Minute Book of the Ibadan Council, 1904–1914.

OFFICIAL PUBLICATIONS

I. *Great Britain*
    Great Britain. *Parliamentary Debates*, 5th Series, Commons, vols. LIX–CCCCXI.
    Great Britain, Colonial Office. *Report by Sir F. D. Lugard on the Amalgamation of Northern and Southern Nigeria and Administration, 1912–1919*. Cmd 468.
    Great Britain. Colonial Office. *Report by the Hon. W. G. A. Ormsby-Gore on his Visit to West Africa During the Year 1926*, 1926. Cmd 2744.
    Great Britain. Colonial Office. *Report of Commission of Inquiry into the Administration of Justice in Kenya, Uganda and the Tanganyika Territory in Criminal Matters, May 1933*. Cmd 4623.
    Great Britain. *Report of the Committee on Legal Education for African Students, 1961*. Cmd 1255.

II. *Nigeria*
    Burns, A. C. (Compiler), *The Nigeria Handbook*, Lagos, 1917.
    Burns, A. C., *The Nigeria Handbook*, Lagos, 1929.
    Cameron, D. C., *Address by His Excellency, the Governor, Sir Donald Cameron*, Lagos, 1933.
    Cameron, D. C., *The Principles of Native Administration and Their Application*, Lagos, 1934.
    Governors' Addresses and Council Debates, 1920–1925, Lagos, 1920–5.
    Laws of the Colony of Southern Nigeria, 2 vols., London, 1909.
    Legislative Council Debates, 1923–1951, Lagos, 1923–51.
    Lugard, F. D., *Native Courts in the Southern Provinces: Memorandum to Political Officers*, Lagos, 1914.
    Lugard, F. D., *Memorandum No. 3; Judicial and Legal*, Lagos, 191. 8
    Nigeria: Government Gazette, 1900–1954, Lagos, 1900–54.
    Nigeria: Staff List, 1941–1955, Lagos, 1941–55.
    Nigerian Council Meetings, 1914–1918, Lagos, 1914–18.
    Ordinances &c of the Colony of Lagos, December 1893, London, 1894.
    Report of Commission of Inquiry into Land Tenure in Ibadan by E. A. Speed, 1916, Lagos, 1916.

Report on the Eastern Provinces by the Secretary for Native Affairs, Lagos, 1922.
Report on a Tour in the Eastern Provinces by the Assistant Secretary for Native Affairs, Lagos, 1923.
Report of the Proceedings of a Conference of Residents held November 1929, Lagos, 1930.
Report of the Commission of Inquiry Appointed to Enquire into the Disturbances in the Calabar and Owerri Provinces, December 1929, Lagos, 1930.
Proceedings Before the Commission of Inquiry into the Disturbances in the Calabar and Owerri Provinces, Lagos, 1930.
Report on the Social and Economic Progress of the People of Nigeria, 1931, Lagos, 1932.
Report on the Southern Provinces of Nigeria, 1932, Lagos, 1933.
Report of the Position, Status, and Influence of Chiefs and Natural Rulers in Eastern Region of Nigeria, Enugu, n.d.
Report of the Native Courts (Eastern Region) Commission of Inquiry, Lagos, 1953.
Report of the Native Courts (Lagos Colony) Commission of Inquiry, Lagos, 1954.
Report of the Native Courts (Western Region) Commission of Inquiry, Lagos, 1954.

JOURNALS AND NEWSPAPERS

Gold Coast Assize, Cape Coast, 1883–4.
Nigerian Bar Journal, vols. I–VIII.
Nigerian Law Journal, vols. I–VI.
African Mail, London, 1908–15.
African Times, London, 1866–88.
Akede-Eko, Lagos, 1932–9.
Anglo-African, Lagos, 1863–5.
Daily Service, Lagos, 1938–45.
Daily Times, Lagos, 1926–54.
Eagle and Lagos Critic, Lagos, 1883–8.
Eleti-Ofe, Lagos, 1923–9.
Lagos Daily News, Lagos, 1925–38.
Lagos Observer, Lagos, 1882–8.
Lagos Standard, Lagos, 1893–8.
Lagos Times and Gold Coast Advertiser, Lagos, 1880–3.

Lagos Weekly Record, Lagos, 1891–1930.
Nigerian Advocate, Lagos, 1923–30.
Nigerian Chronicle, Lagos, 1908–1920.
Nigerian Eastern Mail, Calabar, 1935–43.
Nigerian Pioneer, Lagos, 1914–32.
Nigerian Spectator, Lagos, 1923–30.
The Times, London, 1913–14; 1925; 1932–3.
Times of Nigeria, Lagos, 1921–30.
West Africa, London, 1917–54.
West African Nationhood, Lagos, 1932–5.
West African Pilot, Lagos, 1938–54.
West African Review, London, 1925–40.

THESES AND DISSERTATIONS

Afigbo, A. E., 'The Warrant Chief System in Eastern Nigeria, 1900–1929', PhD thesis, University of Ibadan, 1964.
Agiri, B. A., 'Development of Local Government in Ogbomosho, 1850–1950', Master's dissertation, University of Ibadan, 1966.
Ajayi, F. A., 'Judicial Approach to Customary Law in Southern Nigeria', PhD thesis, University of London, 1958.
Akintoye, S. A., 'The Ekiti-Parapo and the Kiriji War', PhD thesis, University of Ibadan, 1966.
Atanda, J. A., 'The New Oyo Empire: A Study of British Indirect Rule in Oyo Province, 1894–1934', PhD thesis, University of Ibadan, 1967.
Fadipe, N. A., 'The Sociology of the Yoruba', PhD thesis, University of London, 1940.
Gordon, J., 'The Development of the Legal System in the Colony of Lagos, 1862–1905', PhD thesis, University of London, 1967.
Hopkins, A. G., 'An Economic History of Lagos, 1880–1914', PhD thesis, University of London, 1964.
Igbafe, P. A., 'Benin Under British Administration, 1897–1938', PhD thesis, University of Ibadan, 1967.
Mbaeyi, P. M., 'Military and Naval Factors in British West African History, 1823–1874', DPhil thesis, Oxford University, 1965.
Nwabara, S. N., 'Ibo Land: A Study in British Penetration and the Problem of Administration, 1860–1930', PhD thesis, Northwestern University, 1965.

Nworah, K. D., 'Humanitarian Pressure Groups and British Attitudes to West Africa, 1895–1915', PhD thesis, University of London, 1966.

Omu, F. I. A., 'The Nigerian Newspaper Press, 1859–1937: A Study in Origins, Growth and Influence', PhD thesis, University of Ibadan, 1965.

Onipede, F. O., 'Nigerian Plural Society: Political and Constitutional Development, 1870–1954', PhD thesis, Columbia University, 1956.

Onwuka, U., 'The Development of the Teaching Profession in Nigeria, 1926–1964', BLitt thesis, Oxford University, 1966.

Smith, S. R., 'The Ibo People: A Study of the Religion and Customs of a Tribe in the Southern Provinces of Nigeria', 2 vols. PhD thesis, Cambridge University, 1929.

Tamuno, S. M. (later T. N.), 'The Development of British Administrative Control of Southern Nigeria, 1900–1912: A Study in the Administrations of Sir Ralph Moor, Sir William MacGregor and Sir Walter Egerton', PhD thesis, University of London, 1962.

Udoma, E. U., 'Law and British Administration in South-Eastern Nigeria: An Analytical Study', PhD thesis, Trinity College, Dublin, 1944.

SELECTED ARTICLES AND PAPERS

Adewoye, O., 'Self-taught Attorneys in Lagos, 1865–1913', *Journal of the Historical Society of Nigeria*, v, 1, 1969.

Adewoye, O., 'The Judicial Agreements in Yorubaland, 1904–1908', *Journal of African History*, xii, 4, 1971.

Adjaye, N. A., 'The Judicial System in West Africa: We Ask for Reforms', *Elders Review of West African Affairs*, x, 40, 1931.

Afigbo, A. E., 'Revolution and Reaction in Eastern Nigeria, 1900–1929', *Journal of the Historical Society of Nigeria*, iii, 3, 1966.

Ajayi, F. A., 'The Future of Customary Law in Nigeria', *The Future of Customary Law in Africa: Symposium Organized by the Afrika Instituut, Amsterdam*, Leiden, 1956.

Ajayi, F. A., 'The Judicial Development of Customary Law in Nigeria', Paper read at the Conference on Integration of Customary and Modern Legal Systems, held 24–29 August 1964 at Ibadan.

Ajayi, J. F. A., 'Henry Venn and the Policy of Development', *Journal of the Historical Society of Nigeria*, i, 4, 1959.

Allott, A. N., 'The Common Law of Nigeria', *Nigerian Law: Some Recent Developments*, British Institute of International and Comparative Law, Commonwealth Law Series, iii.

Anderson, J. N. D., 'Law and Custom in Muslim Areas in Africa: Recent Developments in Nigeria', *Civilizations*, vii, 1, 1957.

Anfam, J. A., 'The Judicial Embargo in Ashanti', *The West African Review*, ii, 49, October 1931.

Atanda, J. A., 'The Iseyin-Okeiho Rising of 1916: An Example of Socio-Political Conflict in Colonial Nigeria', *Journal of the Historical Society of Nigeria*, iv, 4, 1969.

Driberg, J. H., 'The African Conception of Law', *Journal of the African Society*, xxxiv, Supplement, July 1935.

Geary, W. N. M., 'Some West African Personalities I have Known', *Elders West African Review*, x, 43, April 1931.

Geary, W. N. M., 'More West African Personalities I have Known', *Elders West African Review*, xi, 47, August 1931.

Geary, W. N. M., 'Justice and Colour Bar', *West African Review*, xi, 51, 1932.

Gwam, L. C., 'The Honourable Christopher Sapara Williams', *Sunday Times*, Lagos, 25 October 1964.

Gwam, L. C., 'The Honourable John August Otonba Payne', *Sunday Times*, Lagos, 29 November 1964.

Howell, D. R., 'The Status of Teachers in Nigeria', *Overseas Education*, xxx, 3, October 1958.

Igbafe, P. A., 'British Rule in Benin to 1920: Direct or Indirect?', *Journal of the Historical Society of Nigeria*, iii, 4, 1967.

Ikime, O., 'Reconsidering Indirect Rule: The Nigerian Example', *Journal of the Historical Society of Nigeria*, iv, 3, 1968.

Larbi, O., 'The Ashanti Judiciary', *Elders' Review of West African Affairs*, x, 42, March 1931.

Mair, L. P., 'Modern Developments in African Land Tenure: An Aspect of Culture Change', *Africa*, xxi, 1951.

Matson, J. N., 'The Supreme Court and the Customary Judicial Process in the Gold Coast', *The International Comparative Law Quarterly*, ii, pt 1, January 1953.

Park, A. E. W., 'The Cession of Territory and Private Land Rights: A Reconsideration of the Tijani Case', *The Nigerian Law Journal*, i, 1, 1964.

Smith, M. R., 'Nigeria's Legal System', *West Africa*, 2 September 1933.

Solanke, Ladipo, 'Yoruba (or Aku) Constitutional Law and its Historical Developments', *WASU* Magazine, London, ii, 1, 1927.

Sutcliffe, R. B., 'A Note on the Use of Local Courts in the Northern Province of Tanganyika, with special reference to the Masai', Raymond Apthorpe, ed., *From Tribal Rule to Modern Government*, Lusaka, 1959.

Tamuno, T. N., 'Before British Police in Nigeria', *Nigeria Magazine*, no. 89, 1966.

Wood, A. H. St. John, 'Nigeria: Fifty Years of Political Development Among the Ibos', Raymond Apthorpe, ed., *From Tribal Rule to Modern Government*, Lusaka, 1959.

SELECTED BOOKS

Abady, M. J., *The Inns of Court and Civilization*, London, 1954.

Afigbo, A. E., *The Warrant Chiefs*, London, 1972.

Aguda, A., *Select Law Lectures and Papers*, Ibadan, 1971.

Ajayi, J. F. A., *Christian Missions in Nigeria, 1841–1891: The Making of a New Elite*, London, 1965.

Ajisafe, A. K., *The Laws and Customs of the Yoruba People*, London, 1924.

Allott, A. N., *Essays in African Law*, London, 1960.

Allott, A. N., *New Essays in African Law*, London, 1970.

Anene, J. C., *Southern Nigeria in Transition, 1885–1906*, Cambridge, 1966.

Anyiam, F. U., *Men and Matters in Nigerian Politics, 1934–1958*, Yaba, Lagos, n.d.

Awolowo, O., *Path to Nigerian Freedom*, London, 1947.

Ayandele, E. A., *The Missionary Impact on Modern Nigeria, 1842–1914: A Political and Social Analysis*, London, 1966.

Bodenheimer, E., *Jurisprudence*, Cambridge, Mass., 1962.

Bretton, H. L., *Power and Stability in Nigeria: The Politics of Decolonization*, New York, 1962.

Buell, R. L., *The Native Problem in Africa*, 2 vols., London, 2nd impr., 1965.

Burns, Alan, *History of Nigeria*, London, 6th ed., 1963.

Cameron, D. C., *My Tanganyika Service and Some Nigeria*, London, 1939.

Cardozo, B. N., *The Nature of the Judicial Process*, New Haven, 24th printing, 1965.

Coker, G. B. A., *Family Property Among the Yorubas*, London, 2nd ed., 1966.

Coleman, J. S., *Nigcria: Background to Nationalism*, Berkeley and Los Angeles, 1965.

Cook, A. N., *British Enterprise in Nigeria*, London, 2nd impr., 1964.

Crocker, W. R., *Nigeria: A Critique of British Colonial Administration*, London, 1936.

Daniels, W. C. E., *The Common Law in West Africa*, London, 1964.

Dike, K. O., *Trade and Politics in the Niger Delta, 1830–1885*, Oxford, 1956.

Elgee, Captain C. H., *The Evolution of Ibadan*, Lagos, 1914.

Elias, T. O., *The Nature of African Customary Law*, Manchester, 1956.

Elias, T. O., *Makers of Nigerian Law*, London, 1957.

Elias, T. O., *The Impact of English Law on Nigerian Customary Law*, Lagos, 1958.

Elias, T. O., *The Nigerian Legal System*, London, 2nd ed., 1963.

Elias, T. O., *Law in a Developing Society*, Lagos, 1969.

Elias, T. O., ed., *Law and Social Change in Nigeria*, Lagos, 1972.

Flint, J. E., *Sir George Goldie and the Making of Nigeria*, London, 1960.

Folarin, A., *The Demise of the Independence of Egbaland*, Lagos, 1916.

Friedman, W., *Law in a Changing Society*, Baltimore, 1964.

Fyfe, C., *A History of Sierra Leone*, London, 1962.

Geary, W. N. M., *Nigeria Under British Rule*, London, new impr., 1965.

Gluckman, M., ed., *Ideas and Procedures in African Customary Law*, London, 1969.

Gower, L. C. B., *Independent Africa: The Challenge to the Legal Profession*, Cambridge, Mass., 1967.

Green, M. M., *Igbo Village Affairs*, London, 2nd ed., 1964.

Harlow, V. *et al*, eds, *History of East Africa*, vol. ii, Oxford, 1965.

Hunter, G., *New Societies of Tropical Africa*, New York, 1964.

Ikime, O., *Merchant Prince of the Niger Delta*, London, 1968.

Ikime, O., *Niger Delta Rivalry: Itsekiri-Urhobo Relations and the European Presence, 1884–1936*, London, 1969.

Irving, R. F., *A Collection of the Principal Enactments and Cases Relating to Titles to Land in Nigeria*, London, 1916.

Jones, G. I., *The Trading State of the Oil Rivers*, London, 1963.

Kasunmu, A. B. and Salacuse, J. W., *Nigerian Family Law*, London 1966.

Keay, E. A. and Richardson, S. S., *The Native and Customary Courts of Nigeria*, London, 1966.

Kimble, D., *A Political History of Ghana, 1851–1928*, Oxford, 1963.

Kingsley, M., *West African Studies*, London, 3rd ed., 1964.

Kopytoff, J. H., *Preface to Modern Nigeria: The Sierra Leonians in Yoruba, 1830–1890*, Maddison, 1965.

Legum, C., *Congo Disaster*, Baltimore, 1961.

Legum, C., *Africa: A Handbook to the Continent*, New York, 2nd ed., 1967.

Lloyd, D., *The Idea of Law*, London, 1964.

Lloyd, P. C., *Yoruba Land Law*, London, 1962.

Losi, J. B., *History of Lagos*, Lagos, 1914.

Lugard, F. D., *The Dual Mandate in British Tropical Africa*, London, 1922.

Lugard, F. D., *Political Memoranda, 1913–1918*, London, 1919.

Macaulay, H., *Justitia Fiat: The Moral Obligation of the British Government to the House of Docemo of Lagos*, London, 1921.

Macmillan, A., *The Red Book of West Africa*, London, 1920.

McPhee, A., *The Economic Revolution in British West Africa*, London, 1926

Mair, L., *Native Policies in Africa*, London, 1936.

Malinowski, B., *The Dynamics of Culture Change*, New Haven, 1945.

Mannoni, O., *Prospero and Caliban: The Psychology of Colonization*, New York, 1964.

Meek, C. K., *Law and Authority in a Nigerian Tribe*, London, 2nd impr., 1950.

Morel, E. D., *Affairs of West Africa*, London, 1902.

Morris, H. F. and Read, J. S., *Indirect Rule and the Search for Justice*, London, 1972.

Nicholson, I. F., *The Administration of Nigeria, 1900–1960*, London, 1969.

Nwabueze, B. O., *The Machinery of Justice in Nigeria*, London, 1963.

Obi, S. N., *The Ibo Law of Property*, London, 1963.

Okojie, C. C., *Ishan Native Laws and Customs*, Lagos, 1960.

Okonjo, I. M., *British Administration in Nigeria, 1900–1950 – A Nigerian View*, New York, 1974.

Park, A. E. W., *The Sources of Nigerian Law*, Lagos, 1963.

Payne, J. A. O., *Payne's Lagos and West African Almanack and Diary for 1887*, London, 1887.

Payne, J. A. O., *Table of Principal Events in Yoruba History*, Lagos, 1893.

Payne, J. A. O., *Payne's Lagos and West African Almanack and Diary for 1894*, London, 1894.

Perham, M., *Native Administration in Nigeria*, London, 1937.

Perham, M., *Lugard: The Years of Authority, 1898–1945*, London, 1960.

Pollock, F., *The Expansion of the Common Law*, London, 1904.

Pound, R., *The Spirit of the Common Law*, Boston, 2nd printing, 1966.

Renner, P. A., *Cases in the Court of the Gold Coast and Nigeria, 1861–1905*, London, 1915.

Slade, R., *King Leopold's Congo*, London, 1962.

Talbot, P. A., *The Peoples of Southern Nigeria*, 4 vols, London, 1926.

Tamuno, T. N., *The Police in Modern Nigeria*, Ibadan, 1970.

Tamuno, T. N., *The Evolution of the Nigerian State: The Southern Phase, 1898–1914*, London, 1972.

Temple, C. L., *Native Races and their Rulers*, Cape Town, 1918.

Thompson, F. W. B., *The First Generation of Sierra Leoneans*, Freetown, 1952.

Ward, B., *The Rich Nations and the Poor Nations*, New York, 1962.

Ward-Price, H. L., *Land Tenure in the Yoruba Provinces*, Lagos, 1933.

Wheare, J., *The Nigerian Legislative Council*, London, 1949.

OTHER SOURCES

I. *Registers of admissions, the English Inns of Court*
    Register of Admissions to the Honourable Society of the Middle Temple, vols. II, III.
    Inner Temple Admissions, 2 vols.
    The Records of the Society of Lincoln's Inn, vols. II, III.
    Gray's Inn: Call List, 2 vols.

II. *Interviews*

Part of the material for this study was the information gathered from personal interviews conducted in Nigeria between 1966 and 1967 on various aspects of the actual operation of the Nigerian judicial system. The interviews were limited mainly, though not exclusively, to people who had been connected with the administration of justice. Altogether thirty-two persons were interviewed, including Sir Adetokunbo Ademola, the first Chief Justice of Independent Nigeria, and other former or contemporary judicial officers like the late Chief Adebiyi Desalu, the late Chief Ayodele Williams, P. W. Holm, F. O. Lucas, the late Mr Justice J. I. C. Taylor, Mr Justice Kayode Esho, Mr Justice Olu Ayoola, Mr Justice Akinola Aguda. Among others were such veteran legal practitioners as E. A. Franklin, C. H. Obafemi, Chief T. A. Doherty, O. O. Alakija, the late L. B. Agusto, the late Chief Adegunle Soetan, the late Oladipo Moore, Chief Obafemi Awolowo and Chief F. R. A. Williams. Two letter-writers were interviewed: Messrs A. A. Babalola and J. A. Oke-owo, both at Ibadan.

Index

Index

Apapa, 259–60

appeal, right of, 42, 48, 49, 50, 51, 59, 139–40, 148, 154, 163, 182, 193, 199, 221, 225, 229, 230, 233–234, 236–7, 238–43, 244, 245, 262, 265, 288, 289; *see also* review, power of

arson, 37, 54

Arubi, Edema, 170, 190, 191–2, 193, 196

Asaba, 15, 121–2, 131, 183, 184; supreme court, 38, 70, 72

Ashanti, Gold Coast, 148, 226

assault, 37, 73, 125, 191

assessors, 72, 73, 77, 80, 81, 162, 163, 174, 181, 231, 245

assizes, 73, 76, 126, 127, 145

Atkin, Lord, 263–4, 265

Attorney-General v. John Holt and Co. and others, 1910, 258

Attorney-General v. W. B. McIver and others, 1910, 258

Attorneys-General (*previously* Queen's Advocates), 76, 124, 137, 231, 256, 259, 292

attorneys *see* solicitors

Austin, John, 1–2, 112, 202

Awkuzu, 193

Awolowo, Obafemi, 194–5

Ayisa tu v. Niwo, 1933, 193

babaogun (patrons), 11, 185–8

Badagry District, 271

Bajulaiye v. Akapo, 1928, 266

Bakana, 162

Baker, Isaac, 79

Balogun v. Balogun, 1943, 272

banishment, 37, 177, 191; *see also* deportation

Banjoko v. Tiwo, 1877, 51

bankruptcy, 49

barristers, 71, 109, 110, 112, 113, 118, 141, 154, 159, 190, 247, 286, 302

Bashua v. Oduntan and Ilubanto, 1940, 271

Bassey Egbo Bassey v. Archibong Boco Cobham and others, 1924, 271, 273

Beecroft, John, 17, 38

Belgian colonialism, 283, 284, 286

Bende District, 270

Benin, 32, 33, 82, 83, 84, 85–9, 138, 140, 183, 187, 197, 234; *Oba* of, 85–7, 88, 89

Benin River, 37, 95

Bewa, 176

Biafra, Bight of, 34

bigamy, 269

Bindloss, Harold, 43–4

Bonny, xi, 9, 17, 32, 33, 36, 37, 38, 40, 90, 138, 177

Boudillon, *Sir* Bernard H., 233

boycott, 35

Brass, 17, 32, 33, 35, 36, 37, 38, 39, 131

Brass River, 35

Brazil, immigrants from, 46, 108

breach of contract, 21

breach of promise, 48

breach of the peace, 83, 176

Bretton, Henry, 283

Bright, Jacob Galba, 117

Brimah Balogum v. Saka, Chief Oshodi, 1931, 273

British colonialism, 31–63, 69–70, 72, 78–91, 96–101, 107, 108, 109, 115–17, 119, 120, 123–33, 137–165, 176–9, 196, 200–2, 210–11, 221–48, 253–66, 283–95

British Cotton Growing Association, 144

British Guiana (Guyana), 118

Brooke, Neville John, 244–5, 257

Buchanan-Smith, W., 164

Buell, R. L., 287

Buguma, 40, 162

burglary, 174

Burns, *Sir* Alan, 35, 224

Burutu, 138

'bush lawyers' *see* letter-writers

Bushe, H. Grattan, 221, 226, 228

C.F.A.O. v. Miller Brothers, 1912, 275–6

Calabar, 11, 13, 32–6, 38, 40, 44, 77, 108, 110, 117, 119, 122–3, 131, 138, 146, 147, 151, 153, 154,

Index

Index

MacGregor, *Sir* William, 15, 20–1, 22, 53, 55–6, 59, 115, 141–2

McIntosh, Captain, 82

McIver, Allan, 114

Macleod, *Justice* Hector W., 80–1, 114–15

McNaughton rules (on insanity), 174

magistrates, 55, 75, 109, 233, 234, 236, 247–8, 265–6, 298–302; *see also* chief magistrates

magistrates' courts, 229–39, 242, 246, 290; *see also* Lagos, Chief Magistrate court

Magistrates' Courts (Appeals) Ordinance, 1945, 242

Manana Lopez and others v. Domingo Lopez and others, 1924, 267, 272

Mann Poole and Co. v. Salami Agbaje, 1922, 277

manslaughter, 5, 55, 173

marriage, 25, 206, 208, 209–11, 229, 269–70, 290; *see also* divorce *and* levirate, practice of

Marriage Act, 269

Marriage Ordinance, 1863, 269

Marriage Ordinance, 1884, 269

Marshall, Justice (Gold Coast), 32

Marshall, *Sir* James, 70, 73, 74–5, 76, 92–4, 98

Maxwell, J. W., 117

Mayne, R. D., 76

Mbiam oath, 8

Melton, W., 92

Menendez, M. R., 70

Mgbeke v. Okolie, 1937, 184

Middle Temple, London, 110–11

Minike Eyo Asibon v. Edet Edem and two others, 1903, 89–90

'minor courts', 40, 42, 62, 76, 95

missionaries, 14, 16, 20, 90, 138, 144, 147, 202, 203–4, 210, 224, 290

mixed court, Egba, 55

Moloney, *Sir* Alfred, 15

money-lenders, 180, 196, 198, 287

Moor, *Sir* Ralph, 31, 38, 40, 41, 43, 82–4, 86–9, 94–5

Moore, Eric Olawolu, 232

Moore, H. M. M., 159

Moss, George Ernest, 114

murder, 5–6, 54, 55, 76, 87, 173–4, 175, 178

Najib Nabham and others v. Edem Davies, 1926, 274

Nana, *Olomu of Itsekiriland*, 15, 37, 82–5

National African Company (*later* Royal Niger Company), 36, 38

National Congress of British West Africa, Accra, 1920, 148

'Native Administrations', 223–5, 232, 235; *see also* Indirect Rule

native authorities, 140, 201, 265; *see also* native courts

'native' councils, 3, 42–3, 58–9, 62, 76, 90, 94, 95, 129, 158

Native Councils Ordinance, 1901, 58

'native' courts (*later* customary courts), 10, 32, 40–5, 61–3, 70, 72, 76–8, 88, 95, 115, 118–19, 123, 133, 137, 138, 140, 142–3, 148–54, 162, 163, 170–2, 179–211, 221, 224–5, 229–46, 253, 257, 265–8, 284, 288–90

native courts' advisers, 245

Native Courts Commissions of Inquiry, 1949–52 (Brooke Commissions), 244–5

'native' courts of appeal, 234

Native Courts Ordinance, 1914, 185, 208, 235

Native Courts (Amendment) Ordinance, 1920, 162

Native Courts Ordinance, 1933, 235, 236, 237, 238–40

Native Courts Proclamation, 1900, 41, 42, 58

Native Courts Proclamation, 1906, 61–2

native law and custom, 1–11, 20–1, 24–6, 44, 46, 50–2, 54, 57–8, 87, 90, 111–14, 118, 126, 139, 140, 143, 156, 157, 159, 160, 182, 186, 191, 193–4, 202–3, 207–10, 221, 224–5, 237, 242, 245, 259, 262, 265–75, 288–93

Index